I0877054

Teaching Modernist Women's Writing in English

Teaching Modernist Women's Writing in English

Edited by

Janine Utell

The Modern Language Association of America
New York 2021

© 2021 by The Modern Language Association of America
All rights reserved
Printed in the United States of America

MLA and the MODERN LANGUAGE ASSOCIATION are trademarks owned by the Modern Language Association of America. For information about obtaining permission to reprint material from MLA book publications, send your request by mail (see address below) or e-mail (permissions@mla.org).

Library of Congress Cataloging-in-Publication Data

Names: Utell, Janine, 1975- editor.
Title: Teaching modernist women's writing in English / edited by Janine Utell.
Description: New York : The Modern Language Association of America, 2021.
Series: Options for teaching, 10792562 ; vol 51 | Includes bibliographical references. | Summary: "Offers pedagogical techniques for teaching anglophone modernist writing by Virginia Woolf, Gertrude Stein, Dorothy Richardson, Jean Rhys, Nella Larsen, and others. Gives syllabus suggestions for undergraduate and graduate courses in literature and writing. Covers topics such as feminism, gender identity, canon formation, politics, activism, and war. Suggests many digital humanities approaches"—Provided by publisher.
Identifiers: LCCN 2020052174 (print) | LCCN 2020052175 (ebook) | ISBN 9781603294850 (hardcover) | ISBN 9781603294867 (paperback) | ISBN 9781603294874 (EPUB) | ISBN 9781603294881 (Kindle edition)
Subjects: LCSH: American literature—Women authors—Study and teaching (Higher) | American literature—20th century—Study and teaching (Higher) | English literature—Women authors—Study and teaching (Higher) | English literature—20th century—Study and teaching (Higher) | Modernism (Literature)—Study and teaching (Higher)
Classification: LCC PS41 .T4255 2021 (print) | LCC PS41 (ebook) | DDC 810.9/92870711—dc23
LC record available at https://lccn.loc.gov/2020052174
LC ebook record available at https://lccn.loc.gov/2020052175

Options for Teaching 51
ISSN 1079-2562

Published by The Modern Language Association of America
85 Broad Street, Suite 500, New York, New York 10004-2434
www.mla.org

Contents

Part V: Modernist Cultures

Part VI: Radical Women

Part VII: Digital Humanities

Acknowledgments

Thanks are due first and foremost to the authors who made this volume possible. I could not have asked for better collaborators. I have learned so much from them, have found their work exciting and their commitment to their students inspiring, and have been awed by their alacrity and collegiality in responding to feedback and requests (so many requests!). I am deeply grateful for the privilege of getting to work with them all and thrilled others will have the opportunity to learn from them as well.

I am also deeply grateful to the Modern Language Association's office of scholarly communication and its editorial team. Margit Longbrake, Katherine Kim, and James Hatch all contributed to the development of this project. Jaime Cleland led us through the publication process with unwavering support and patience, and to her go infinite thanks. Susan Doose vastly improved the manuscript during the copyediting process. Nicky Agate was instrumental in formulating the digital component of the volume featured on *MLA Commons* and brought an exciting new dimension to our work that we believe readers will find valuable. Many thanks are due to the Publications Committee of the Modern Language Association for their enthusiastic support of this project and for their constructive feedback. Thank you also to the anonymous external peer reviewers who provided invaluable support and feedback.

As part of our development of this volume, we had the pleasure of sharing reflections on and approaches to teaching modernist women's writing at roundtables held at the annual meetings of the Modernist Studies Association (2016) and the Modern Language Association (2017). Thank you to the Program Committees of these associations, to our very receptive audiences, and to those contributors who participated. Deep appreciation goes to participants in "Thinking Back through Our Mothers: Feminist Revolutions in Modernism," a seminar held at the 2015 Modernist Studies Association conference; an early version of my introduction was shared there, and the conversations led by the organizers Linda Camarasana and J. Ashley Foster (Foster is also a contributor to the present volume) reverberate throughout these pages, as does the influence of Jane Marcus, whom I was lucky to know during my PhD studies at the Graduate Center, City University of New York. Thank you to Megan Quigley and Claire Buck for providing new and urgently needed spaces for thinking about teaching modernist literature in the twenty-first century and for inviting me to participate in those spaces.

I would like to thank my colleagues—the faculty members, staff members, and administrators at Widener University in the English and Creative Writing Department; in the gender, women's, and sexuality studies program; and beyond—for their ongoing support and always enlivening conversations about teaching and learning. I would also like to express my gratitude to my students. Finally, as always, thank you to my family, with love: John and Linda Utell, Tracy and Glen Farber, and John-Paul Spiro. As always, and with love, this book is dedicated to my niece, Abigail Lindh Farber.

Janine Utell

Introduction

This volume is intended to provide novice and seasoned instructors with conceptual models and useful tools for teaching modernist women's writing in English and modernist literary cultures through the women who shaped them. Thirty-three institutions are represented here: among them, regional, broad-access, comprehensive universities; community colleges; research universities; large public institutions; small liberal arts colleges; STEM-oriented programs; and a college that focuses almost entirely on business and entrepreneurial studies. Contributors are at a variety of stages in their careers and address an array of teaching situations: surveys of British, American, and global literatures; first-year writing and composition courses; courses for English majors; courses in general education; upper-level seminars; capstone experiences; and graduate-level courses.[1] Contributors provide suggestions for adapting approaches to different settings, needs, and objectives: how to design a syllabus unit on a particular writer, text, or genre; how to apply a new technique or tool to a familiar author; how to incorporate into existing courses new developments and materials from the field of modernist studies. Points of dialogue and dispute among the essays are highlighted. Different aspects of what it means to be modernist exist in temporal, geographic, cultural, political, formal, and institutional relation to one another. Throughout this volume, connections, themes, and methods are often prioritized over individual authors, and contributors offer strategies for managing the task of selection, recognizing the challenges of teaching the wide variety of genres, modes, and textualities in which modernist women writers worked: not only short fiction and novels, poetry, and plays but also manifestos, reportage, essays, letters and diaries, and periodicals.

Conceptual Framing

In *Modernism: Evolution of an Idea*, Sean Latham and Gayle Rogers define modernism as "the widely distributed networks of writers, artists, and institutions" that strove to articulate the changes that constitute a "modern body of experience" in terms of "a characteristic form" (16).[2] The nature of the modernist form is open to debate, and the attempt to define modernism as a set of cultural and aesthetic responses to the experience of modernity raises its own questions: Whose modernity, in terms of race, class, gender, sexuality, and education? When and where does modernity occur? (Latham and Rogers 137–38). Many of the contributors to this volume position themselves within the generative spaces created by the new modernist studies, even as the texts, themes, and methodologies they elucidate through that lens reveal certain tensions in the field.[3] Some of their chosen texts, authors, genres, modes, and registers may indeed prompt readers to ask the following: How is this modernist? Do I revise my existing course or praxis to accommodate these competing understandings within the field? Do I reexamine my own definition of modernism? Such questions are productive, particularly in the light of the field's examination of itself, as captured in those interrogations posed above by Latham and Rogers.

The contributors to this volume evince both similar and dissimilar viewpoints. Some envision reading and writing practices shaped by difficult experimental texts assumed to be integral to aesthetic definitions of modernism, especially high modernism, and even look to reimagine them through a feminist lens. Others present a capacious understanding of modernism that includes the middlebrow, the sentimental, the regional, and the noir as "prisms" for apprehending modernity (Latham and Rogers 18). Still others assume a modernism founded in representations and experiences of women in modernity that may be progressive, even liberating—a modernism that also harbors a deep ambivalence toward changing attitudes about gender and sexuality. As Urmila Seshagiri writes, "*Any* account of modernism is also an account of women's art and women's lives." For many contributors, race is also essential to an understanding of modernism, and specifically to ways of presenting it formally, materially, thematically, affectively, and politically. Some emphasize the shift to what Susan Stanford Friedman has termed "planetary modernism"—"multiple modernities that have unfolded in a global framework" (Sim)—or a global modernism that extends the national or geographic boundaries of the field. These contributors detail the work of an intersectional feminism with an awareness of the diasporic while grappling with assumptions that underlie a modernist-colonial perspective or potentially problematic cosmopolitan transnationalism.

All contributors present compelling claims for the inclusion of their chosen texts, authors, and methods in the modernist studies classroom—for many, the feminist-modernist studies classroom. Their essays reflect a recognition of institutional and disciplinary constraints and opportunities, as well as a spirit of questioning with respect to the mechanisms of canonicity, even as they sometimes argue for expanding the canon rather than dismantling it (see the conclusion of Emily Kopley's essay in particular). As these contributions show, the work of feminist-modernist studies, including its landscape-altering recovery efforts, is ongoing and incomplete.

Certain aesthetic and formal qualities are often conventionally associated with modernism, and with its purported difficulty. Erin K. Penner offers that this difficulty includes experimentation with narrative and the representation of subjectivity, perception, and interior life; temporal innovations that warp the experience of linear time; and a subversion of the conventional uses of language and form; further, and particularly for students, modernist difficulty presents an "interpretive burden" (1–2). Many contributors premise their understanding of modernism on the "newness" Latham and Rogers see as central to the very idea of modernism, looking to Ezra Pound's exhortation to "make it new" as foundational (Latham and Rogers 9).[4] At the same time, they also take up the idea of newness, unsettling it as a criterion and extending the idea of what it means to be difficult, both affectively and aesthetically. Strategies are suggested for teaching the high modernist narrative, poem, and drama, with a focus on both formal innovation and the representation of radical ideas and social change. Such considerations show, however, that women's participation in such newness was not and is not uncomplicated.

Contributors further define and debate modernism through various lenses: the dynamics that exist among high, middlebrow, and mass cultures; the proliferation of emerging media; and a questioning of traditions and institutions.[5] These lenses reveal the significant influence of feminism, feminist theory, and feminist recovery on modernist studies in general, and on our volume authors in particular. Jennifer P. Nesbitt directs attention to Sylvia Townsend Warner, a figure recuperated by feminist scholars who does not always fit neatly within conventional definitions of modernism. The recovery of many such women writers brings with it the challenge of redefining the field, only to see these women excluded and conventional definitions of modernism and the canons dependent on and manifesting them reified. Such troublesome women writers appear throughout this volume, raising important issues concerning the study of modernism through the lens of feminism. They also challenge the notion that modernism is the only category we have for understanding the literary culture of the twentieth century, including and especially that produced by women. Thus, their writing provides a valuable portal into teaching the discipline.

In her essay, Nesbitt cites T. S. Eliot's assertion that "the canon changes only for 'the new' (the really new) work of art" (Eliot, "Tradition" 38). Naomi Milthorpe and Robbie Moore also reassess Eliot, specifically with respect to the notion of difficulty. In Eliot, we find the privileging of "newness" that renders a figure like Warner troublesome for modernists (she is "insufficiently innovative," as Nesbitt writes), which results in the perpetuation of entrenched definitions of modernism. One way in which figures such as Warner have been accommodated is through the concept of *intermodernism* formulated by Kristin Bluemel and Phyllis Lassner, among others (Bluemel; Bluemel and Lassner). At the same time, politically engaged writers, as well as more recent women writers and indeed the scholars and teachers who contributed to this volume, wrestle with the boundaries of modernism while looking for ways to claim a modernist-feminist newness for themselves and their students.

Contributions that propose an understanding of modernist forms and genres through other media and cultural objects, or through the middlebrow or the popular, serve not so much as an imperative to incorporate these objects or modes into definitions of modernism but rather as a means of facilitating understanding and, where necessary, revisions of those definitions. High and late modernisms, urban and regional modernisms, mass and popular cultures—these circle around one another, settling into points of contact and friction or coalescing into divergent, new configurations.

Collectively, the instructors participating in this volume make the persuasive argument that women's writing and the teaching of it enable these revisions and reconfigurations.

The study of modernism has thus expanded across a plethora of vectors: vertical, temporal, planetary or global, and by way of interdisciplinarity and media (Mao and Walkowitz). Yet as Seshagiri argues, the expansion of the categories of modernism resulting from the new modernist studies makes new demands on feminist scholarship, reading, and teaching that threaten to "overwhelm" its efforts. For some, therefore, feminist pedagogy and the teaching of feminist-modernist studies are rendered all the more urgent. Women's lives were transformed as part of the experience of modernity, and those transformations are understood as constitutive of modernism. Feminist movements surrounding suffrage, the struggle for reproductive rights, pacifism, and increased educational opportunities were—and in some cases continue to be—monumental, and perhaps call on us to envision and practice a feminist pedagogy. Women shaped modernism through formal experimentation and their participation in publishing networks. Feminist recovery work has irrevocably reshaped the terrain of twentieth-century literature.

Still, the relation of feminism to the practices, canons, and institutions of modernist studies remains fraught. This volume offers ways to teach those practices, canons, and institutions through women's writing—not to reconcile feminism to them but to demonstrate how feminism and women's writing have changed and continue to change the study of modernism, inviting us to look at it yet again—yes—anew.

How to Use This Book

The challenges of teaching modernist literature—the formal difficulties of the texts; the logic of selection; the need to address the transnational and the global; students' limited knowledge of historical, cultural, social, and artistic contexts; the work of defining the lineaments of the field—are addressed in the eight sections of this volume: "Reading, Writing, Revising," "Modernist Difficulty," "Genres," "Places and Races," "Modernist Cultures," "Radical Women," "Digital Humanities," and "Transformational Pedagogy." Many essays direct readers to our companion website on *MLA Commons* (modwomen.mla.hcommons.org). Essays that include digital resources contain notes within the body of the text directing readers to the website. Resources are organized by contributor/chapter and by type (syllabi, multimedia, recommended readings, websites, digital collections and archives, and professional organizations).

Opening the volume, Beth C. Rosenberg's essay provides an overview of the teaching of literary modernism, the new modernist studies, and feminist-modernist studies, offering ideas for course design and a helpful scholarly orientation. Emily Kopley and Bronwen Tate share strategies for teaching the foundations of a modernist writing practice through genetic criticism and creative writing, respectively. Their essays also provide introductions to important authors.

In the second section of this volume, Milthorpe and Moore provide an introduction to—and interrogation of—modernist difficulty as well as practical suggestions for engaging students at all levels. Another approach to difficulty is presented by Lois Cucullu, who suggests teaching modernist form through the narrative experimentation of Dorothy Richardson's *Pilgrimage*, particularly its use of stream of consciousness. The focus on form and genre continues in the third section, in which contributors offer ways of teaching genres that found new forms in modernism, including less commonly taught genres like the diary-novel and drama. Instructors looking for introductions to modernist reformulations of genre should consider Steven Ambrose's and Sarah Cornish's essays on the novel, Robert Reginio's essay on poetry, and Beth Wynstra's on drama. In particular, Wynstra situates formal and political shifts in American drama within the scope of transnational aesthetics and cultural modernism while also suggesting hands-on ways to engage students through dramaturgy. Melissa Dinsman turns our attention to the potential of transmedial genres in offering strategies for teaching melodrama and film of the Second World War alongside adaptation theory while also raising questions about late modernism and the middlebrow. Other contributions that address the teaching of war include the essay by Laura Heffernan, Aislinn Kelly, and Deanna McMichael on the First World War and J. Ashley Foster's essay on the Spanish Civil War. Other essays on genre are Celia Marshik's on the middlebrow novel, Nancy Berke's on poetry of protest, and Carey Snyder's on the drama of the suffrage movement. Each approaches the teaching of form while also considering how those forms and their content exist at variance with conventional definitions and categories of modernist writing.

The next three sections focus on the expansion of modernist studies. The fourth section engages the global, transnational, and planetary: the four essays that make up this section—those by Tamara Slankard, Emily

Hinnov, Amanda Golden, and Bridget Chalk—should be read together in order to appreciate the complexity of transnational modernism and its emphasis on intersectional identity and place in relation to regionalism, cosmopolitanism, imperialism, colonialism, diaspora, migration, and racism. For additional insight into global modernism, instructors might consult Louise Kane's essay, which invites an investigation of transnational networks of modernist periodicals, particularly in the Caribbean. In the following section, Marshik, Sarah Fedirka, and Vicki Tromanhauser engage a variety of modernist cultures. Marshik's essay situates modernist texts alongside their middlebrow counterparts, illuminating their respective qualities by focusing on the artist as an exemplary figure of modernist aesthetics. Fedirka examines modernism and its mainstream appropriations through the lens of consumer culture and advertising, while Tromanhauser formulates the concept of a "gastronomical modernism" through the teaching of food writing. Together with Dinsman's essay, those by Fedirka and Tromanhauser engage the "everyday turn" in modernist studies (Olson; Davis). This cluster concludes with a section on women's radical politics, emphasizing the political charge inherent to the social upheaval of the twentieth century. Foster's essay on feminist activism could be read alongside this section as well.

The last two sections focus on pedagogical innovations and opportunities for institutional critique, including writing and pedagogy that critically reexamine the very idea of modernism. Readers looking for an introduction to the place of digital humanities in modernist studies should begin with Elizabeth Willson Gordon and Helen Southworth's essay, and with Kane's for an introduction to modernist periodical studies; Lisa Mendelman introduces quantitative methods within broader disciplinary conversations about the future of literary criticism and its methods. Heffernan, Kelly, and McMichael's essay suggests that the modernist classroom and its literary histories can be broadened by means of digital archives and the positioning of students as researchers; Foster suggests that it can be opened further through collaborative work and feminist pedagogy, focused in this context on transnational responses to the Spanish Civil War. Other essays that address digital humanities methodologies and tools, and which might be read together with those in this section, are those by Kopley, Jennifer Sorensen, Dinsman, and Golden. This opening of the classroom to radical potential is the argument of two of our closing essays: Julia Bloch's on teaching Gwendolyn Brooks's poetry and Brooks's own radical pedagogy, and that by Megan Hicks, Emma Slotterback,

Katie Starliper, and Julie Vandivere, which calls on readers to think of the study of modernist women's writing as forming a community of scholars. The essays in this last section encourage instructors to use modernist women's writing to rethink the nature of our pedagogical praxis.

In *Art Objects*, Jeanette Winterson pays homage to the modernist women writers who have shaped her aesthetic, asserting that their work can and should open up the world. We hope these essays support instructors seeking to bring such texts into the classroom. Teaching the texts and tensions of modernism fosters a critical stance toward modernity, and teaching modernist women's writing in particular offers an invaluable perspective on that necessary project.

Notes

1. All student work referred to throughout this volume is used with permission.

2. Part of Bloomsbury's New Modernisms series, this book is a helpful resource for instructors. It traces the emergence of the concept of modernism as a critical term, highlighting the ways it has been debated and challenged within various institutional and theoretical contexts. It also provides a glossary and a collection of critical bibliographies covering modernism as a concept, gender and sexuality, race, global context, print cultures, mass media, law, war and violence, science and technology, and environments.

3. Cited throughout this volume, the new modernist studies, as described by Douglas Mao and Rebecca L. Walkowitz, is understood as an expansion of the definition of modernism to accommodate broader periodization and geographic boundaries, a wider range of cultural registers and identities, and greater attention to media, materiality, and the archive. This work has been very influential, including for those contributing to this volume, while also prompting disagreement concerning the discipline and its parameters (see Seaber and Shallcross for an overview). Important challenges come from those working in feminist-modernist studies, precisely because the expanding conceptualization of modernism continues to displace and exclude women writers and feminist methodologies. The fruits of this ongoing intervention may be found in special issues of *Modern Fiction Studies* (edited by Fernald) and *Literature Compass* (edited by Young and Wallace), a cluster in *Modernism/Modernity* (edited by Seshagiri), and the inaugural issue of the journal *Feminist Modernist Studies* in 2018 (edited by Laity).

4. Michael North points out that Pound appropriated the phrase from his reading of thirteenth-century Confucian thought and that it does not appear in Pound's own writing until 1928. North writes, "Make It New was not itself new, nor was it ever meant to be."

5. This list was inspired by my reading of Latham and Rogers; here I paraphrase the authors' discussion of the lenses through which we consider modernism (14).

Works Cited

Bluemel, Kristin. "Introduction: What Is Intermodernism?" *Intermodernism: Literary Culture in Mid-Twentieth Century Britain*, edited by Bluemel, Edinburgh UP, 2011, pp. 1–18.

Bluemel, Kristin, and Phyllis Lassner. "Feminist Inter/Modernist Studies." Laity, pp. 22–35.

Davis, Thomas S. *The Extinct Scene: Late Modernism and Everyday Life*. Columbia UP, 2016.

Eliot, T. S. "Tradition and the Individual Talent." *Selected Prose of T. S. Eliot*, edited by Frank Kermode, Farrar, Straus and Giroux, 1975, pp. 37–44.

Fernald, Anne E., editor. *Women's Fiction, New Modernist Studies, and Feminism*. Special issue of *Modern Fiction Studies*, vol. 59, no. 2, 2013.

Friedman, Susan Stanford. *Planetary Modernisms: Provocations on Modernity across Time*. Columbia UP, 2015.

Laity, Cassandra, editor. *Feminist Modernist Studies*, vol. 1, nos. 1–2, 2018.

Latham, Sean, and Gayle Rogers. *Modernism: Evolution of an Idea*. Bloomsbury Academic, 2015.

Mao, Douglas, and Rebecca L. Walkowitz. "The New Modernist Studies." *PMLA*, vol. 123, no. 3, May 2008, pp. 737–48.

North, Michael. "The Making of 'Make It New.'" *Guernica*, 15 Aug. 2013, www.guernicamag.com/the-making-of-making-it-new/.

Olson, Liesl. "Everyday Life Studies: A Review." *Modernism/Modernity*, vol. 18, no. 1, 2011, pp. 175–80.

Penner, Erin K. "Making No Apologies for Difficulty: Putting Modernist Form at the Center of Classroom Discussions." *Journal of Modern Literature*, vol. 37, no. 2, 2014, pp. 1–19.

Seaber, Luke, and Michael Shallcross. "The Trouble with Modernism: A Dialogue." *The Modernist Review*, 10 June 2019, modernistreviewcouk.wordpress.com/2019/06/28/the-trouble-with-modernism/.

Seshagiri, Urmila, editor. *Mind the Gap! Modernism and Feminist Praxis*. Cluster of *Modernism/Modernity* Print Plus, vol. 2, cycle 2, 7 Aug. 2017, doi.org/10.26597/mod.0022.

Sim, Lorraine. Review of *Planetary Modernisms*, by Susan Stanford Friedman. *Affirmations*, vol. 4, no. 1, 2016, affirmationsmodern.com/articles/45/.

Winterson, Jeanette. *Art Objects*. Alfred A. Knopf, 1996.

Young, Tory, and Jeff Wallace, editors. *The Future of Women in Modernism*. Special issue of *Literature Compass*, vol. 10, no. 1, 2013.

Part I

Reading, Writing, Revising

Beth C. Rosenberg

A Curriculum of Our Own: Teaching Modernist Women's Literature

This essay is more theoretical than practical; its purpose is to offer options, not only for students but also for their teachers. Here I propose a planetary model of modernist literary history that is not tethered to chronology, and I explain why I see modernist women's writing as a plurality of canons. Instead of focusing on one thread or lineage of women's literary history, my courses prioritize an interrogation of the processes of canon formation. This allows students to make their own connections and to relate modernists in new and innovative ways.

I have taught modernist women's literature at the University of Nevada, Las Vegas (UNLV), for over twenty years. UNLV is one of only two state universities in Nevada, both of which share the mission of educating in-state students. Students at these institutions come from working- or middle-class families and are often the first in their families to attend college. Undergraduate English courses tend to focus on critical writing and reading skills. Graduate seminars in modernist studies—in addition to providing historical and aesthetic contexts—encourage original and publishable research. How does a teacher of modernist women's literature reconcile the goals of making modernism relevant and engaging to students who lack a background in history and aesthetics while simultaneously strengthening their critical reading, writing, and research skills? My courses are guided by this question as students are given the flexibility to investigate and articulate the diversity of women's literature they study.

I teach an undergraduate course called Gender and Modern Literature and a graduate course called Modernist Women Writers. Among my objectives in these courses is to expose students to the significant issues that define modernist fiction and poetry: the idea of experimentation, the importance of the First and Second World Wars, changes in women's writing after 1920 as women entered the public sphere and the workforce in greater numbers, and a concept of modernism that transcends the Anglo-American tradition. Works are situated within three broad networks: global, early, and interwar (or late) modernisms, each of which constitutes one of the course's three modules. I don't expect students to master all three modules. I do, however, encourage them to see the canon of modernist women writers as dynamic, fluid, and permeable rather than static or entrenched. Students discover genres and writers that resonate with their interests, and they are challenged to articulate the formal and thematic issues that connect the writers and their works.

Where so much is expected of one course, I've found that a feminist pedagogy—that is, a pedagogy that decenters the authority and expertise of the instructor—is most effective.[1] I use group work, in the classroom and in online discussion boards, to encourage collaboration and dialogue. Students post 250 words per week on the class's online discussion board; each week, they also write a one-hundred-word response to a classmate's post. These low-stakes assignments move the conversation outside the classroom and give me the opportunity to provide weekly feedback on students' writing. Students also lead one class discussion (or, as an alternative, give a presentation introducing one of the authors); this, in conjunction with the discussion board, leads to dynamic interactions inside the classroom. I don't abdicate my authority, but rather use it to guide the class, to articulate and fill in the connections among ideas and concepts that arise in conversations and writing. My biggest surprise is always how much background material students bring to the classroom after conducting their own research and how seldom I have to reinforce their acquired knowledge. My approach also assumes that writing is thinking and that through the process of writing and discussion students come to understand difficult texts. My courses consider the heterogeneous mix of narrative styles, themes, and sociohistorical contexts that are impossible to reconcile as part of a cohesive canon, allowing me to cover a range of texts without feeling compelled to articulate them as part of a monolithic modernist project.

In Gender and Modern Literature, I spend time on close reading as students become acquainted with modernist cultures; student-led discussions, the community created in the online forums, and writing workshops help us piece together the apparently divergent and difficult styles and ideas of modernist women's writing. From the first day of class, I introduce the idea of a literary canon and consider how the modernist canon has been taught, at least early on, as a predominantly white, male, European phenomenon. As I move through the modules, from global modernism to early-twentieth-century modernism to interwar and late modernisms, I express regret that I cannot give students a definitive canon of modernist women writers who fall neatly within a lineage of influence. However, after their initial frustration with my inability to communicate to them a unified narrative of modernist women's literature, students begin to feel more liberated and creative.

The graduate course, Modernist Women Writers, explicitly addresses and furthers arguments introduced and alluded to in the undergraduate course. I begin with the introduction to Malcolm Bradbury and James McFarlane's anthology *Modernism: A Guide to European Literature*, which outlines previous understandings of modernism as a primarily Eurocentric movement. Bradbury and McFarlane identify New York, Chicago, London, Paris, Berlin, and Vienna as centers of modernist production, and traditional movements such as impressionism, symbolism, and futurism as exemplifying modernist aesthetics. The authors also define what they see as the dominant modernist genres—the long lyric poem, the stream-of-consciousness novel, and drama.

I offer as a point of comparison with Bradbury and McFarlane's conception of modernism Susan Stanford Friedman's *Planetary Modernisms*. Friedman argues against identifying the modernist period as specifically American and European movements that took place between 1890 and 1930. Instead, she posits the idea of an "aesthetic dimension of any given modernity" (x) that can be found wherever or whenever "transformational rupture and rapid change" occur (ix). Planetary modernisms transgress the boundaries of national modernisms and histories and allow for multiple and simultaneous networks of women writers. The concept of planetary modernisms doesn't negate Bradbury and McFarlane's paradigm; rather, it allows for multiple modernisms that do not always adhere to a linear construction of influence and tradition. It points, moreover, to modernisms outside Europe and America—to India, Africa, China, and other places—making modernism global. The transformational ruptures Friedman describes are historical moments of epistemological change that may occur far earlier than those captured by conventionally defined twentieth-century modernism—such as the pre-1500 modernities of Tang Dynasty China—and that may also transcend the conventional time frame. In defining a feminist modernism, the ruptures and rapid changes inherent to modernism become moments when women enter the economic, social, and political spheres. As Friedman explains and as I seek to illustrate through my modules, each of these moments brings with it unique aesthetic dimensions.

In my introduction to the module on global modernist women writers through the lens of planetary modernism, I begin with Jean Rhys's *Voyage in the Dark*, which presents the notion of intersectional identity through representations of race, colonialism, and social class.[2] Rhys's novel expands the notion of transnational modernism in its representation of the migrant experience. After a discussion of the challenges of placing Rhys's work within an exclusively Anglo-American modernist context, other works outside this context are considered as additions to the canon of modernist women's literature reveal themselves. For example, I teach works such as Nawal El Saadawi's *Woman at Point Zero*, Tsitsi Dangarembga's *Nervous Conditions*, Anita Desai's *Clear Light of Day*, and Marguerite Duras's *The Lover*—which stem from cultures as different as Egypt, Zimbabwe, India, and France—within the context of planetary modernism. In these works, we find themes of socioeconomic oppression, educational limitations, and sexual abuse, in addition to stylized narratives representing women's subjectivity. I pair these texts with Gayatri Spivak's "Diasporas Old and New: Women in the Transnational World" to emphasize the economic and political conditions experienced by women of color and colonial origins. We then begin to think more deeply about canon formation and how these narratives address women's rejection of patriarchal conventions in periods of rapid social change. The module on global modernism ends with Gertrude Stein's "Melanctha" from *Three Lives*. Stein's experimental style addresses the construction of race, gender, and class and illuminates the transnational relationship between the American Stein and other global women writers. "Melanctha" also provides a transition to works of early-twentieth-century Anglo-American modernists.

The second module on early modernism draws on conventional framings and chronologies that have defined modernist literature. However, as a result of the first module, students are able to identify moments of cultural rupture focusing on experimentation, the avant-garde, and regional modernisms, all of which constitute distinct narratives. The second module also allows me to introduce New Criticism and its privileging of modernist difficulty. Our focus on close reading throughout the semester enables us to uncover complexity in texts beyond those privileged by conventional definitions of high modernism.

Both the undergraduate course and the graduate course address Virginia Woolf's *A Room of One's Own*, allowing the class to theorize experimental modernism—from its use of nonlinear narration to its mixing of literary genres to its highly allusive language. The idea of a women-only literary canon is interrogated through Woolf's text as we read her vision of the tragic circumstances of women writers, such as those experienced in her story of a hypothetical Shakespeare's sister, and the anxiety provoked by the spectral influence of male writers, embodied in her conjuring of "Milton's bogey," a reference to the poet John Milton (*Room* 112). Common themes of modernist women writers and the idea of intersectionality are also introduced; Woolf uniquely outlines the value of income, the limitations of patriarchy, and the necessity of anonymity. Regional modernisms are introduced as literary-historical moments when the position of women delineated by Woolf intersects with particular social and political conditions.

After this, we turn our attention to the Harlem Renaissance, recognizing its own planetary qualities. We read Zora Neale Hurston's *Their Eyes Were Watching God* and Nella Larsen's *Passing*, which allude to boundaries of race, gender, and class. I pair these works with Alice Walker's *In Search of Our Mothers' Gardens*, where Walker argues for a canon composed of Black women writers. In this section, we also investigate the role Black women played during the Harlem Renaissance as well as in the broader context of a global modernism.

The use of modules makes possible the juxtaposition of different modernist aesthetics. The experimental modernism of Woolf's *To the Lighthouse* and H.D.'s epic poem *Helen in Egypt* situate them alongside texts conventionally considered part of high modernism.[3] Woolf's *To the Lighthouse* introduces techniques such as stream of consciousness; it also focuses on the construction of gender roles, the significance of relationships between women, the masculine desire to control knowledge, and the centrality of the First World War. *Helen of Egypt*, H.D.'s long poem, is distinctly modernist and can be read along the lines of Ezra Pound's *Cantos* or Jean Toomer's *Cane.* It is, as Friedman suggests in "When a 'Long' Poem Is a 'Big' Poem," a women's epic, full of myth and allusion describing women's experiences by appropriating Homer. Planetary modernism lets us read these experimental texts as performing a kind of cultural rupture with respect to conventional forms.

The graduate seminar also emphasizes the theoretical and critical work of new modernist studies, creating connections with the writers examined in the second module. We read Anne Fernald's introduction to her special issue of *Modern Fiction Studies* on modernist women's writing, which provides an overview of criticism and contextualizes feminism within the wider framework of modernist studies.[4] We also read the 2013 special issue of *Literature Compass* on women in modernism, edited by Tory Young and Jeff Wallace, concentrating on the contributions by Jane Garrity, Sonita Sarker, and Barbara Green. These articles comment on the history and future of modernist women's writing and criticism, the origins of the feminist ideal of the New Woman, and the social contexts surrounding working women, single women, women of color, and women in the literary and periodical marketplace.

The third module focuses on interwar and late modernisms and brings to the discussion of modernist women writers changes in genre and style.[5] As Anglo-American modernism enters the 1930s and 40s, writing shifts in some respects to a more realist style (though not always a realist subject), contrasting with experimental modernism. I choose writers of mid-century British modernism as examples: Nancy Mitford writes a merciless satire of the rise of Fascism in *Wigs on the Green*; Sylvia Townsend Warner's *Lolly Willowes* is a satirical comedy of manners that incorporates elements of fantasy to critically examine society's views on single or unmarried women;[6] Muriel Spark's *Girls of Slender Means* addresses the lives of working girls in Kensington immediately after the Second World War. I couple these novels with critical works by Michelle Tusan, Sally Alexander, Robin Hackett and Gay Wachman, and Liz Conor, all of which outline the social and economic positions of women in the inter- and postwar periods, giving the approach of planetary modernism, in this module and others, the power to develop context for each reading.

Rather than feel compelled to present students with a consistent, unified canon of women writers, rather than present ourselves as arbiters through processes of inclusion and exclusion, teachers can use writing and research as dynamic and enterprising means of canon recombination and interrogation, helping students create various networks of reading based on their own experiences. Planetary modernism allows readers to draw connections among a range of writers and aesthetics occurring in different historical moments under different social conditions. Global modernism allows us to view women's literature as untethered from nation, while still connected to early and late Anglo-American modernist innovations with regard to content, theme, style, and technique. By the end of the semester, students have become aware of the critical issues surrounding modernist women writers by devising their own trajectories for research and the acquisition of knowledge. They come to understand, as Woolf cautions, that no one canon is sacred, and that through reading and writing, they have the power to create their own.

Notes

1. For more on feminist pedagogy, see Foster's and Goodspeed-Chadwick's essays in this volume.

2. See Mattis's and Goodspeed-Chadwick's essays in this volume for intersectional approaches to teaching modernist women's writing; see also Chalk on teaching Rhys in the context of colonialism.

3. For the teaching of high modernist poetry, see Reginio in this volume.

4. In "Mind the Gap! Modernism and Feminist Praxis," Urmila Seshagiri introduces a *Modernism/Modernity* Print Plus cluster on feminism and the modernist canon that represents an explicit intervention into modernist canon formation. The journal *Feminist Modernist Studies* offers another way into framing modernist women's literature and history. It brings a gendered perspective to new modernist studies readings of transnationalism, culture, and interdisciplinarity. The inaugural volume, edited by Cassandra Laity, is organized in three sections: intermodernist women writers of the Second World War; African American feminism; and issues of female and transgender embodiment. These three sections could be used as an alternative framework for organizing a course.

5. For interwar and late modernisms, see in this volume Nesbitt; Cornish; Dinsman; Slankard; and Tromanhauser.

6. Lolly Willowes is a witch with evil powers; see Nesbitt in this volume.

Works Cited

Alexander, Sally. *"Becoming a Woman" and Other Essays in Nineteenth- and Twentieth-Century Feminist History.* New York UP, 1995.

Bradbury, Malcolm, and James McFarlane, editors. *Modernism: A Guide to European Literature, 1890–1930.* Penguin Books, 1978.

Conor, Liz. *The Spectacular Modern Woman: Feminine Visibility in the 1920s.* Indiana UP, 2004.

Dangarembga, Tsitsi. *Nervous Conditions.* Seal Press, 1988.

Desai, Anita. *Clear Light of Day.* Houghton Mifflin, 2000.

Duras, Marguerite. *The Lover.* Pantheon Books, 1997.
Fernald, Anne E. Introduction. *Women's Fiction, New Modernist Studies, and Feminism*, special issue of *Modern Fiction Studies*, edited by Fernald, vol. 59, no. 2, 2013, pp. 229–40.
Friedman, Susan Stanford. *Planetary Modernisms: Provocations on Modernity across Time.* Columbia UP, 2015.
———. "When a 'Long' Poem Is a 'Big' Poem: Self-Authorizing Strategies in Women's Twentieth Century 'Long Poems.'" *Literature Interpretation Theory*, vol. 2, no. 1, 1990, pp. 9–25.
Garrity, Jane. "Modernist Women's Writing: Beyond the Threshold of Obsolescence." Young and Wallace, pp. 15–29.
Green, Barbara. "Recovering Feminist Criticism: Modern Women Writers and Feminist Periodical Studies." Young and Wallace, pp. 53–60.
Hackett, Robin, and Gay Wachman. "Making the Private Public: Women Writers, Modernism, and Empire." *At Home and Abroad in the Empire: British Women Writers in the 1930s*, edited by Hackett et al., U of Delaware P, 2009, pp. 13–30.
H.D. *Helen in Egypt.* Grove Press, 1961.
Hurston, Zora Neale. *Their Eyes Were Watching God.* 1937. HarperCollins Publishers, 2000.
Laity, Cassandra, editor. *Feminist Modernist Studies*, vol. 1, nos. 1–2, 2018.
Larsen, Nella. *Passing.* Penguin Books, 1997.
Mitford, Nancy. *Wigs on the Green.* Thornton Butterworth, 1935.
Rhys, Jean. *Voyage in the Dark.* 1934. W. W. Norton, 1982.
Saadawi, Nawal El. *Woman at Point Zero.* Zed Books, 1998.
Sarker, Sonita. "On Remaining Minor in Modernisms: The Future of Women's Literature." Young and Wallace, pp. 8–14.
Seshagiri, Urmila. "Mind the Gap! Modernism and Feminist Praxis." *Mind the Gap! Modernism and Feminist Praxis*, cluster of *Modernism/Modernity* Print Plus, edited by Seshagiri, vol. 2, cycle 2, 7 Aug. 2017, doi.org/10.26597/mod.0022.
Spark, Muriel. *The Girls of Slender Means.* Alfred A. Knopf, 1963.
Spivak, Gayatri Chakravorty. "Diasporas Old and New: Women in the Transnational World." *Textual Practice*, vol. 10, no. 2, pp. 245–69.
Stein, Gertrude. "Melanctha." *Three Lives*, by Stein. 1909. Vintage Books, 1936, pp. 83–235.
Tusan, Michelle. "Inventing the New Woman: Print Culture and Identity Politics during the Fin-de-Siècle." *Victorian Periodicals Review*, vol. 3, no. 2, pp. 169–82.
Walker, Alice. *In Search of Our Mothers' Gardens: Womanist Prose.* Harcourt Brace Jovanovich, 1983.
Warner, Sylvia Townsend. *Lolly Willowes.* Chatto and Windus, 1926.
Woolf, Virginia. *A Room of One's Own.* Annotated and introduced by Susan Gubar, Harcourt, 2005.
———. *To the Lighthouse.* Hogarth Press, 1927.
Young, Tory, and Jeff Wallace, editors. *The Future of Women in Modernism.* Special issue of *Literature Compass*, vol. 10, no. 1, 2013.

Emily Kopley

Teaching the Revisions of Virginia Woolf and Others

Exposing students to the analysis of textual revision—that is, to genetic criticism—has at least three pedagogical virtues. First, students practice paying close attention to language and form. Second, they become more alert to their own processes of revision. Third, they learn how material culture, such as a writer's manuscripts or the mechanics of typesetting, informs aesthetics and contemporary critical practice. Here I describe strategies for teaching Virginia Woolf's revisions as well as those of other modernist women writers. I have taught Woolf's revisions in the composition classroom, an upper-level undergraduate seminar on Woolf, and a master's seminar on modernism, and students have been fascinated and happily challenged every time. The topic is eminently adaptable; instructors must judiciously choose passages and define terms, building on the preparedness of their students.

When teaching Woolf, I use the Harcourt series published under the general editorship of Mark Hussey because these books are the most affordable annotated editions available in the United States and Canada and because they supply instructive apparatuses. This series takes as its copy-text the first American edition of each Woolf title, consistent with American copyright law (Briggs, "Editing" 68) and Harcourt's history as Woolf's first American publisher. If one teaches in the United Kingdom, the Penguin series overseen by Julia Briggs in the early 1990s is a good choice; it uses the first British edition of each Woolf title as copy-text. An advantage of emphasizing the revision and publication process is that students learn the value of reading a particular edition and become less likely to buy or borrow whichever edition is readiest at hand or to consult texts online.

I begin teaching Woolf's practice of revision by citing the following passage from *A Room of One's Own*.[1] The autobiographical speaker, strolling near what is implicitly Trinity College, Cambridge, where the manuscript of Milton's *Lycidas* is held, recalls, "Lamb wrote how it shocked him to think it possible that any word in *Lycidas* could have been different from what it is" (7). She continues, "This led me to remember what I could of *Lycidas* and to amuse myself with guessing which word it could have been that Milton had altered, and why" (7). With guessing she must be content, because, as a woman, she is barred from entering the college's library. Charles Lamb might have wished *he* had been barred. He professes in his 1820 "Oxford at the Vacation" that he lacks the "curiosity to disturb the elder repose of MSS," for, he writes, those manuscripts would "disturb and unsettle my faith." To this last phrase he appends a note that begins as follows:

> There is something to me repugnant, at any time, in written hand. The text never seems determinate. Print settles it. I had thought of the Lycidas as of a full-grown beauty—as springing up with all its parts absolute—till, in evil hour, I was shown the original written copy of it, together with the other minor poems of its author, in the Library of Trinity, kept like some treasure to be proud of. I wish they had thrown them in the Cam, or sent them, after the latter cantos of Spenser, into the Irish Channel. How it staggered me to see the fine things in their ore!

Whereas witnessing Milton's changes to the *Lycidas* manuscript "shocked" Lamb (Woolf's word) or "staggered" him (his own word), speculating about these changes "amuse[s]" Woolf's narrator. These contrasting reactions point to the difference between the Romantic and the modern conception of artistic genius. Perhaps too they point to the difference between imagining what an author might have changed—which allows one to assume the role of author—and seeing what the author did indeed change—which forces one to accept unthought-of textual possibilities.

Students then discuss Lamb's and Woolf's views on revision and their own. Do they share Lamb's "repugnan[ce]" at the evidence of revision or

Woolf's interest in it? Do they think that art is the product of inspired genius or of strenuous reworking, or that the process varies from one writer to another? Does genre affect the revision process? Do writers' approaches to revision differ across time periods or change with the advent of new technologies such as computer composition? Do we read works differently when we know how much they were revised, and how? After considering these issues, if time allows and students are keen on further discussion, I might offer a definition and brief history of genetic criticism, drawing on Graham Falconer's "Genetic Criticism" and the first chapter of Hannah Sullivan's *The Work of Revision*. I might also hand out a list of pertinent vocabulary (e.g., *holograph*, *autograph*, *manuscript*, *proof*, *edition*, *impression*, *copy-text*, *eclectic edition*, etc.) informed by Michael F. Suarez and H. R. Woudhuysen's *Oxford Companion to the Book*.

In this or a subsequent class, I lecture on Woolf's particular revision process and a few interpretations of her revisions, interpretations made possible by Woolf's vast surviving archive, much of which is accessible through published manuscript drafts and online repositories. Briggs offers an excellent account of Woolf's revision habits, especially her postpublication ones, in "Between the Texts: Virginia Woolf's Acts of Revision." And Brenda Silver's "Textual Criticism as Feminist Practice" addresses how our image of Woolf has changed with the study of her draft materials. These essays could be assigned in a course for graduate students or upper-level undergraduates.

After this lecture, I lead a discussion focused on some brief examples of Woolf's revisions. *A Room of One's Own* presents an intriguing passage that Woolf reworked. The proof copy reads: "I often like women. I often find them very interesting. I like their unconventionality. I like their subtlety" (qtd. in Gewirtz 76). Woolf excised the second sentence before publication, such that the first American and British editions read as follows: "I often like women. I like their unconventionality. I like their subtlety" (*Room* [Bradshaw and Clarke] 80; *Room* [Gubar] 109–10). In the second British impression Woolf revised this to "I often like women. I like their unconventionality. I like their completeness" (qtd. in Briggs, "Between the Texts" 208). Women are described as "unconventional," "interesting," and "subtle"; later only as "unconventional" and "subtle"; and finally, as "unconventional" and "complete." What has been lost, or gained, in the process of revision? Looking at the holograph of *Mrs. Dalloway*, we might discuss the titles that Woolf discarded for the work, such as "The Hours" (*"Hours"* 2–3), "At Home," and "The Party" (411). The holograph also reveals that Clarissa Dalloway's epiphany at the novel's end was initially set at midnight (398–99), while in the published version this timing can only be inferred. Why, I ask, might Woolf have made this change? Similarly, why might she have excised specific dates from *Orlando*, including that of Orlando's sex change (Orlando*: The Holograph Draft* 106)?[2] We might also examine the opening page of the second holograph draft of *The Waves*, where Woolf replaces simile—"like a grey cloth," "grey like a cloth"—with a sort of simile-aiming-at-metaphor—"as if a cloth had wrinkles in it" (Waves: *The Two Holograph Drafts* 401). This analysis could prompt a discussion of the differing effects of simile and metaphor in this passage and throughout the novel.

A short passage from one of Woolf's texts can also serve as the topic of a writing assignment of 200–300 words in which students make an argument about the effect of Woolf's revisions. For instance, one could assign a passage from *To the Lighthouse* that differs between the American and British first editions, such as the conclusion to the novel's "The Window" section, the bracketed phrase informing us of Mrs. Ramsay's death, or the passage about Mr. Ramsay's finding an earwig in his milk.[3] And with any novel, one could ask students to compare the extant versions of the first or last few sentences.

I have found that students react in opposing ways to Woolf's pre- and postpublication revisions. They expect and welcome many drafts but only one published product. They tend to be delighted to see how Woolf revised a draft into a published version, but they are dismayed to learn that there are multiple published versions. The published text should be a "sanctuary," said one student. It represents a "contract" with the reader, said another. Issuing multiple versions, whether at once or over time, reflects "a self-doubting temperament," and thus diminishes the reader's trust in the author, said one young woman. Textual teleology and unity satisfy my students more than simultaneity and multiplicity. An example of the problem is evident in the holograph draft of *To the Lighthouse*, where we read of Mrs. Ramsay at her dinner party: "here tonight was the heaven for such as her" (172). Our Harcourt edition trades this phrase, with its tortured syntax, for another: "Of such moments, she thought, the thing is made that endures" (107). My students agree that this is an improvement—and more than that, beautiful and memorable. But they are annoyed with Woolf when they find that in the British edition the passage reads, "the thing is made that remains for ever after. This would remain" (qtd. in Lavin 205). If only Woolf's published words were as immutable as "the thing" that "is made"! In an attempt to turn students' annoyance into appreciation, I suggest that the differences between Woolf's American and British first editions, together with her postpublication revisions, reflect her tireless care for the work of art. She kept revising on whichever proof sheets (or indeed, published pages) were last to leave her hands. For Woolf, the work of art was always perfectible.

In my upper-level undergraduate seminar on Woolf, the unit on revision culminated with an essay assignment of four to six pages in which students chose to write on one of four pairs of passages, each pair comprising selected manuscript or typescript pages and their published versions. My assignment asks students to evaluate what Woolf cut, added, or rearranged. I encourage them to think about genre, literary innovation, audience, public versus private meanings, and the relation between form and content; I might provide some passage-specific guidance. As with the short assignment described earlier, the beginning and end of books are good choices, as are especially dramatic or unusual moments in the text. For instance, comparing Septimus's noonday confrontation with Dr. Bradshaw in *Mrs. Dalloway* (91–96) and the same passage in "The Hours" (124–42) works well. Another provocative pairing is "Time Passes" as published in *To the Lighthouse* and the version that Woolf sent to Charles Mauron for French translation.[4] There is also much for students to seize on in reading chapter 5 ("Chloe Liked Olivia") of *Women and Fiction: The Manuscript Version of* A Room of One's Own (110–22) alongside the same in the book's first edition (*Room* [Gubar] 78–93). Another possibility is to contrast the long passage about the library in the first typescript of *Pointz Hall* (48–54) with the single paragraph on the library in *Between the Acts* (14), or, directly following these, the respective descriptions of Isa reading in the newspaper about a rape.[5] For all pairings, I suggest choosing only a few pages within the ranges given here.

Students find the draft versions of *Jacob's Room*, *To the Lighthouse*, and *The Waves* most manageable because these are facsimile transcriptions of Woolf's manuscripts, which visually approximate her actual page. Facsimile transcription typographically reproduces Woolf's manuscripts, page for page and line for line, including her strikeouts, replacements, marginalia, etc., exactly as they appeared to Woolf. It is not the same as a facsimile, an exact copy of a manuscript or published text. The draft versions of *Orlando*, *A Room of One's Own* (*Women and Fiction*), and *Mrs. Dalloway* (*"Hours"*) incorporate elements of facsimile transcription, such as reproducing Woolf's line and page breaks. Whichever draft one assigns,

I recommend spending class time explaining how the draft has been reproduced and guiding students in interpreting editorial symbols.[6]

I have had particular success assigning the passage in *Jacob's Room* in which Jacob and Sandra climb to the Acropolis (166–70 of the Harcourt edition, compared with 258–69 of the holograph draft). Woolf's revisions invite a consideration of gender, the role of the narrator, and whether we can know others—and if so, how. My students offered attentive readings, as suggested by the thesis of one student, Chelsea Latremouille:

> In comparing these passages, I will study Woolf's diminishment of character and suggest that this diminishment serves an artistic purpose. Woolf's revisions are mainly cases of excision, and this sheer textual removal testifies to her diminishment of character. Looking at the way Woolf removes particularizing details reduces Sandra's interiority, makes the narrator appropriate Sandra and Jacob's thoughts, and shows how Woolf reveals her concerns with the limits of knowing.

In anonymous course evaluations at the end of the term, several students mentioned this essay assignment appreciatively. One wrote, "I thought the [essay on Woolf's revision] was so neat and want to do more exercises in it!"

Among modernist women writers, Woolf is ideal for teaching genetic criticism because of the tremendous amount of primary material available, in print and online.[7] Why is this material available? One reason is that wise library curators thought to acquire Woolf's manuscripts even during the thirty-year ebb in her reputation following her death. Another reason is that the scholars who helped revive her reputation were interested in editing these draft materials. A third reason is that, at least in the 1970s, the "golden age of facsimile reproduction for modernist authors" (Sullivan 55), both university and commercial publishers welcomed the lavish, technically elaborate volumes. Donald Reiman has observed that the market allowing publication of draft materials "seems to arise whenever teachers and critics demonstrate enough intellectual curiosity to wish to analyze different versions of a major author's works—a desire usually produced by exposure to the primary evidence for one of them" (171).

For Woolf's fellow modernist women writers, "enough intellectual curiosity" to motivate "versioning," in Reiman's words (169), has been slow to come. In recent years, Americans in particular, especially poets, have benefited from such curiosity. Cheryl J. Plumb's 1995 edition of Djuna Barnes's *Nightwood* includes draft pages in facsimile and reveals how

T. S. Eliot toned down the text's sexual and religious references. Gertrude Stein's revisions to *Stanzas in Meditation* were detailed in Susannah Hollister and Emily Setina's 2012 edition of the poem. In 2002 Robin Schulze published *Becoming Marianne Moore*, a facsimile edition of Moore's first American book, *Observations* (1924), that also contains facsimile pages of the first publication of each of the *Observations* poems, along with variorum tables charting other versions of each poem. Moore's revision practice justifies Schulze's massive undertaking: "The bulk of her poems appear in numerous, at times vastly different, published versions that occur over a period of some fifty years. For Moore, no text was ever stable or finished; each opportunity to publish offered an opportunity to revise" (Schulze 2). Moore considered texts "processes rather than finished products" (11). *Becoming Marianne Moore* provides students and scholars with a sharper sense of Moore's changing intentions over the course of her career. The volume allows one to teach, for instance, many versions of Moore's famously unfixed "Poetry," the poem beginning "I too, dislike it" (205).[8] Heather Cass White has built on Schulze's work in her facsimile-and-variorum editions of *The Pangolin and Other Verse* (1936; republished in Moore, *A-Quiver with Significance*) and *What Are Years* (1941; republished in Moore, *Adversity and Grace*).

The many and shifting intentions of Elizabeth Bishop and Sylvia Plath, daughters of modernism, are now likewise published. In *Edgar Allan Poe and the Jukebox*, a 2006 collection of Bishop's previously unpublished work, edited by Alice Quinn, draft versions appear in notes, and an appendix includes sixteen drafts of the most celebrated poem Bishop published in her lifetime, the villanelle "One Art." The 2004 subtitles of Plath's last completed poetry manuscript imply the recovery of the poet's will: Ariel*: The Restored Edition: A Facsimile of Plath's Manuscript, Reinstating Her Original Selection and Arrangement.*

Draft materials by H.D., such as those of early poems and *Notes on Thought and Vision*, are available through the digital collections of Yale University's Beinecke Rare Book and Manuscript Library. Available there too are Zora Neale Hurston's holograph manuscripts of *Their Eyes Were Watching God* and *Dust Tracks on a Road*, as well as the corrected mimeographs of *Mule Bone*, the play Hurston wrote with Langston Hughes. On the cover of the holograph manuscript of *Dust Tracks*, her autobiography, Hurston wrote, "Parts of this manuscript were not used in the final composition of the book for publisher's reasons" (*Dust Tracks* [Yale]). These "parts"—politically sensitive, sexually frank, or libelous—were restored in the Library of America's 1995 edition, which also includes four chapters that Hurston herself chose to discard. For material available only digitally or without critical commentary, one might ask students, "Does this merit print publication?" and "What information or apparatuses would facilitate the reader's experience?"

In Woolf's case, published draft material generally preceded critical editions. This is also the case for Katherine Mansfield. The notes to the new Edinburgh edition *The Poetry and Critical Writings of Katherine Mansfield* point readers to draft material published (or sometimes only analyzed or mentioned) elsewhere. For example, the editors Gerri Kimber and Angela Smith acknowledge that Mansfield tried out some poems as prose vignettes and refer readers to these versions as published in *The Katherine Mansfield Notebooks*. Relying on these two books, then, one could invite students to assess the difference between "Pic-Nic" and "Malade" when they are divided into lines (*Poetry* 119–20) and when they are not (*Katherine Mansfield Notebooks* 127–29). No critical edition exists for the work of Sylvia Townsend Warner, but the original ending of *Lolly Willowes* (1926) was published in 2001 ("Original Ending").[9] The work of Jean Rhys also lacks a critical edition. Andrew Thacker imagines an edition of *Wide Sargasso Sea* (1966) that "would trace the [novel's] complex versions and revisions" (513), and an edition of *Voyage in the Dark* (1934) that would include the ending both as published and as Rhys initially wrote it, with Anna Morgan dying of an abortion gone awry (517–18).

A more usual sequence is that the critical edition precedes the publication of draft material or the critical edition contains draft material. The notes to Allan Hepburn's 2008 editions of previously uncollected Elizabeth Bowen material trace changes the author made to versions of a given piece, when the material evidence exists (Bowen, *"Bazaar"* and *People*). And sometimes the Bowen pieces themselves are drafts of better-known works: for instance, *People, Places, Things* includes the essay "Britain in Autumn," which later became "London, 1940." But most of Bowen's drafts were destroyed by the Blitz or her own hand. Bernard Schweizer and Charles Thorne's 2010 edition of Rebecca West's *The Return of the Soldier* (1918) is the first to detail the significant differences between the American and British editions; according to Schweizer and Thorne, the British edition more accurately reflects West's intentions. No manuscript is extant for this novel, but many of West's other manuscripts and drafts remain. In 2006 Ann V. Norton published a chapter that West's editors saw fit to exclude from the posthumously published *This Real Night*

(1984).[10] A critical edition of Dorothy Richardson's writing, to be published with Oxford University Press, is underway ("About the Richardson Editions Project"); the research team includes George H. Thomson, who in 2001 published, with Dorothy F. Thomson, an extensive study of variants across *Pilgrimage* editions.

Genetic criticism, relying as it usually does on published draft materials, privileges canonical writers, and the modernist canon itself closely reflects how extensively authors revised—witness, for instance, T. S. Eliot, Ernest Hemingway, Henry James, James Joyce, and Woolf herself. Few modernist women writers are considered canonical, even today, but by publishing and studying draft materials, we can expand the canon by emphasizing a woman writer's effort and artistry. And while some feminist instructors might reject the notion of a canon, they may yet embrace genetic criticism for its appreciation of change. After all, teaching revision means teaching that things—words, plots, archives, hierarchies—can be otherwise.

Notes

1. Unless otherwise noted, I cite Gubar's edition of *A Room of One's Own*.

2. See Hoffmann's analysis in "Fact and Fantasy" 437–39.

3. Lavin's article neatly lists, side by side, all differences between the American and British first editions.

4. The typescript that Woolf sent to Mauron can be found in Haule's article, and, with slightly different transcription, in Dick's 1992 edition of the novel.

5. In crafting the assignment, instructors might look at Whittier-Ferguson's consideration of the library scene.

6. Another classroom approach, described by Karen Levenback, is to teach from the holographs themselves, some images of which are available digitally; see, for instance, *Woolf Online*, the link to which is available on the companion website to this volume (modwomen.mla.hcommons.org). Jane Lilienfeld outlines an assignment in which students confront a passage of Woolf's published work from which all punctuation and capitalization have been removed. Students supply these themselves, and then compare their own version with the passage as Woolf wrote it. For more on teaching Woolf, see the collections edited by Barrett and Cramer, Barrett and Saxton, and Daugherty and Pringle, as well as Daugherty's "Teaching Woolf / Woolf Teaching."

7. For additional resources on teaching Woolf's revisions, see this volume's companion website.

8. I recommend Kappel as a source that can helpfully inform or accompany one's teaching of "Poetry."

9. Nesbitt in this volume describes the work of students creating a critical edition of *Lolly Willowes*.

10. See also appendix 1 ("Cordelia Chapter" [Schweizer 261–309]) for the full text of West's chapter and appendix 2 ("Notes on Editing the 'Cordelia Chapter'" [310–12]), which provides crucial scaffolding and an interpretation of the unpublished chapter.

Works Cited

"About the Richardson Editions Project." *Dorothy Richardson*, 2017, dorothyrichardson.org/drsep/aboutdrsep.htm.

Barnes, Djuna. Nightwood*: The Original Version and Related Drafts.* 1936. Edited by Cheryl J. Plumb, Dalkey Archive Press, 1995.

Barrett, Eileen, and Patricia Cramer, editors. *Re: Reading, Re: Writing, Re: Teaching Virginia Woolf: Selected Papers from the Fourth Annual Conference on Virginia Woolf.* Pace UP, 1995.

Barrett, Eileen, and Ruth O. Saxton, editors. *Approaches to Teaching Woolf's* Mrs. Dalloway. Modern Language Association, 2009.

Bishop, Elizabeth. *Edgar Allan Poe and the Jukebox: Uncollected Poems, Drafts, and Fragments.* Edited by Alice Quinn, Farrar, Straus and Giroux, 2006.

Bowen, Elizabeth. *"The Bazaar" and Other Stories.* Edited by Allan Hepburn, Edinburgh UP, 2008.

———. *People, Places, Things.* Edited by Allan Hepburn, Edinburgh UP, 2008.

Briggs, Julia. "Between the Texts: Virginia Woolf's Acts of Revision." *Reading Virginia Woolf*, Edinburgh UP, 2006, pp. 208–30.

———. "Editing Woolf for the Nineties." *South Carolina Review*, vol. 29, no. 1, 1996, pp. 66–77.

Daugherty, Beth Rigel. "Teaching Woolf / Woolf Teaching." *Virginia Woolf and Literary History: Part II*, special issue of *Woolf Studies Annual*, vol. 10, 2004, pp. 275–307.

Daugherty, Beth Rigel, and Mary Beth Pringle, editors. *Approaches to Teaching Woolf's* To the Lighthouse. Modern Language Association, 2001.

Falconer, Graham. "Genetic Criticism." *Comparative Literature*, vol. 45, no. 1, 1993, pp. 1–21.

Gewirtz, Isaac. "'With Anger and Emphasis': The Proof Copy of *A Room of One's Own*." *Woolf Studies Annual*, vol. 17, 2011, pp. 1–76.

Haule, James M. "'Le Temps Passe' and the Original Typescript: An Early Version of the 'Time Passes' Section of *To the Lighthouse*." Translated by Charles Mauron. *Twentieth Century Literature*, vol. 29, no. 3, 1983, pp. 267–311.

Hoffmann, Charles G. "Fact and Fantasy in *Orlando*: Virginia Woolf's Manuscript Revisions." *Texas Studies in Literature and Language*, vol. 10, no. 3, 1968, pp. 435–44.

Hurston, Zora Neale. *Dust Tracks on a Road.* 1942. *Folklore, Memoirs, and Other Writings*, edited by Cheryl A. Wall, Library of America / Literary Classics of the United States, 1995, pp. 557–808.

———. *Dust Tracks on a Road.* Zora Neale Hurston Collection, Yale Collection of American Literature, Beinecke Rare Book and Manuscript Library, Yale

University, JWJ MSS 9. *Beinecke Rare Book and Manuscript Library*, brbl-dl.library.yale.edu/vufind/Record/3520846.

Kappel, Andrew J. "Complete with Omissions: The Text of Marianne Moore's Complete Poems." *Representing Modernist Texts: Editing as Interpretation*, edited by George Bornstein, U of Michigan P, 1991, pp. 125–56.

Lamb, Charles. "Oxford at the Vacation." *London Magazine*, vol. 2, Oct. 1820, pp. 365–69. *English Poetry, 1579–1830: Spenser and the Tradition*, spenserians.cath.vt.edu/TextRecord.php?textsid=36313.

Lavin, J. A. "The First Editions of Virginia Woolf's *To the Lighthouse*." *Proof: The Yearbook of American Bibliographical and Textual Studies*, edited by Joseph Katz, vol. 2, U of South Carolina P, 1972, pp. 185–211.

Levenback, Karen. "Wielding One's Own Pen: Virginia Woolf's Holographs in the Classroom." *Woolf Editing / Editing Woolf: Selected Papers from the Eighteenth Annual Conference on Virginia Woolf*, edited by Eleanor McNees and Sara Veglahn, Clemson UP, 2018, pp. 123–28.

Lilienfeld, Jane. "Versioning, Audience, and Performative Editing: Woolf, Composition Theory, and Freshman Composition." *Woolf and Pedagogy*, special issue of *Virginia Woolf Miscellany*, edited by Madelyn Detloff, vol. 73, 2008, pp. 19–21.

Mansfield, Katherine. *The Katherine Mansfield Notebooks: Complete Edition*. Edited by Margaret Scott, U of Minnesota P, 2002.

———. *The Poetry and Critical Writings of Katherine Mansfield*. Edited by Gerri Kimber and Angela Smith, Edinburgh UP, 2014.

Moore, Marianne. *Adversity and Grace: Marianne Moore, 1936–1941*. Edited by Heather Cass White, ELS Editions / Dept. of English, U of Victoria, 2012.

———. *A-Quiver with Significance: Marianne Moore, 1932–1936*. Edited by Heather Cass White, ELS Editions / Dept. of English, U of Victoria, 2008.

———. *Becoming Marianne Moore: The Early Poems, 1907–1924*. Edited by Robin Schulze, U of California P, 2002.

Norton, Ann V. "Cordelia and Mrs. Crosthwaite: An Unpublished Chapter of *This Real Night*." Schweizer, pp. 112–24.

Plath, Sylvia. Ariel*: The Restored Edition: A Facsimile of Plath's Manuscript, Reinstating Her Original Selection and Arrangement*. Foreword by Frieda Hughes, HarperCollins Publishers, 2004.

Reiman, Donald. *Romantic Texts and Contexts*. U of Missouri P, 1987.

Schulze, Robin. Introduction. Moore, *Becoming*, pp. 1–17.

Schweizer, Bernard, editor. *Rebecca West Today: Contemporary Critical Approaches*. U of Delaware P, 2006.

Silver, Brenda. "Textual Criticism as Feminist Practice; or, Who's Afraid of Virginia Woolf Part II." *Representing Modernist Texts: Editing as Interpretation*, edited by George Bornstein, U Michigan P, 1991, pp. 193–222.

Stein, Gertrude. Stanzas in Meditation*: The Corrected Edition*. 1932. Edited by Susannah Hollister and Emily Setina, Yale UP, 2012.

Suarez, Michael F., SJ, and H. R. Woudhuysen, editors. *The Oxford Companion to the Book*. Oxford UP, 2010. 2 vols.

Sullivan, Hannah. "Textual Criticism, the History of Revision, and Genetic Reading." *The Work of Revision*, by Sullivan, Harvard UP, 2013, pp. 13–61.

Thacker, Andrew. "Texts and Editions of Jean Rhys: Another Voyage in the Dark?" *Women: A Cultural Review*, vol. 23, no. 4, 2012, pp. 510–24.

Thomson, George H., with Dorothy F. Thomson. *The Editions of Dorothy Richardson's* Pilgrimage*: A Comparison of Texts.* ELT Press, 2001. *ELT Press*, www.eltpress.org/richardson/pdf/ch1bk1intro.pdf.

Warner, Sylvia Townsend. "The Original Ending of *Lolly Willowes*." *The Journal of the Sylvia Townsend Warner Society*, 2001, pp. 32–34.

West, Rebecca. *The Return of the Soldier.* 1918. Edited by Bernard Schweizer and Charles Thorne, Broadview, 2010.

Whittier-Ferguson, John. "The Burden of Drafts: Woolf's Revisions of *Between the Acts*." *Text: An Interdisciplinary Journal of Textual Studies*, vol. 10, 1997, pp. 297–319.

Woolf, Virginia. *Between the Acts.* 1941. Annotated and introduced by Melba Cuddy-Keane, Harcourt, 2008.

———. *"The Hours": The British Museum Manuscript of* Mrs. Dalloway. Edited by Helen Wussow, Pace UP, 1996.

———. *Jacob's Room.* 1922. Annotated and introduced by Vara Neverow, Harcourt, 2008.

———. Jacob's Room*: The Holograph Draft.* Edited by Edward Bishop, Pace UP, 1998.

———. *Mrs. Dalloway.* 1925. Annotated and introduced by Bonnie Kime Scott, Harcourt, 2005.

———. Orlando*: The Holograph Draft.* Edited by Stuart N. Clarke, S. N. Clarke, 1993.

———. Pointz Hall*: The Earlier and Later Typescripts of* Between the Acts. Edited by Mitchell A. Leaska, University Publications, 1983.

———. *A Room of One's Own.* 1929. Annotated and introduced by Susan Gubar, Harcourt, 2005.

———. *A Room of One's Own.* 1929. Edited by David Bradshaw and Stuart N. Clarke, Blackwell Publishing / Shakespeare Head, 2015.

———. *To the Lighthouse.* 1927. Edited by Susan Dick, Blackwell Publishing / Shakespeare Head, 1992.

———. *To the Lighthouse.* 1927. Annotated and introduced by Mark Hussey, Harcourt, 2005.

———. To the Lighthouse*: The Original Holograph Draft.* Edited by Susan Dick, U of Toronto P, 1982.

———. The Waves*: The Two Holograph Drafts.* Edited by J. W. Graham, U of Toronto P, 1976.

———. *Women and Fiction: The Manuscript Version of* A Room of One's Own. Edited by S. P. Rosenbaum, Blackwell Publishing / Shakespeare Head, 1992.

Jennifer P. Nesbitt

Creating a Critical Edition of *Lolly Willowes*: Feminist Teaching, Canonicity, and Institutional Labor

As the prospectus for the 2012 conference Re-visiting Sylvia Townsend Warner announced, "Despite attempts to recover Warner's work for a wide readership, she is rarely found on university syllabi in the UK or abroad" ("Re-visiting"). This lack of pedagogical attention prevails despite the now substantial critical literature on Warner's works—particularly on her novels, and especially on *Lolly Willowes* (1926)—and despite Warner's good fortune in having a journal and a society dedicated to her.[1] Although disheartening, this disregard presents an opportunity for instructors. *Lolly Willowes*, which chronicles a single, older woman's escape from the confines of domestic life in London to freedom and independence in the countryside, introduces many themes and topics central to modernist women's writing: feminism, political action, sexuality, the First World War, and work. Warner's life and career echo these themes: the link between Warner's biography and her work allows students to wrestle with the material conditions enabling and constraining modernist women writers then and now.

The critical fortunes of *Lolly* allow students to apply theories of canon formation and literary authority to a real-world example. Together we construct a critical edition that confronts students with the politics of the form.[2] I use *Lolly Willowes* for this purpose, but works by any number of modernist women writers—among lesser-known English prose writers, Bryher (Annie Winifred Ellerman), Mary Butts, Dorothy Edwards, Winifred Holtby, Rose Macauley, Dorothy Sayers, and Elizabeth von Arnim—could provide material for this assignment. Analyzing the critical edition as a genre and then emulating its constituent forms in what I call a "Norton *Lolly*," students study the power dynamics of critical reception and academic forms that create canonicity as a type of "cultural capital" (Guillory viii). While this essay outlines a multistage group assignment in an introduction to critical approaches course, the assignment can be segmented, condensed, extended, or reframed according to time constraints, student level, and resources.

Pedagogical critical editions engage the politics of canonicity as literary anthologies do. Anthologies validate canonicity by selection.[3] Similarly, inclusion in a series like the Norton Critical Editions series indicates that a text is worth creating a critical edition for, stamping the text as canonical and artistically significant. Whether the editors wish to or not, these selections shape syllabi and text selection in powerful ways. In the headnote to a 2003 *College English* symposium, "Editing a Norton Anthology," the authors state, "They [anthologies] concretize the canon—Norton anthologies are both widely used for their serviceable reproduction of the canon and decried for the same reason" (Leitch et al.). William L. Andrews reports that his efforts to interrogate canonicity as he edited *The Literature of the American South* (1997) went largely unnoticed; critics perceived the tome as hegemonic (111)—a perception that was paradoxically validated by Andrews's expertise. In much the same way, pedagogical critical editions curate material related to the primary text in one accessible place for instructor and student, and the material included is deemed more significant than what is left out. Expert editors guarantee the intellectual legitimacy of the materials included. In general, the texts transformed into critical editions are classics, and the volumes contain a set of materials that implicitly validate certain types of authority and interpretation.[4] Critical editions—again as with anthologies—present organized, comprehensive exteriors that occlude a myriad of procedures and judgments that determine content.

Inclusivity, it turns out, is expensive. Laurie Finke, an editor of *The Norton Anthology of Theory and Criticism*, cites women writers as one group often disadvantaged when an outward criterion for inclusion in critical editions is "genius" because that criterion masks "the collective work—

the institutions, practices, and discourses that create, preserve, and circulate 'works of art'" (194). Writers from marginalized groups benefit less from the "collective work" of literary institutions than do traditional (i.e., white male) authors, who have had long-standing access to the powers and connections provided by networks of reviewers, editors, publishers, and colleges. For the students in my course, the workload is part of the lesson. It is one thing to recover a woman writer from obscurity, another to maintain her visibility by keeping her work in print (paper or electronic) and academically relevant in conference presentations, journals, and books. Sharon Marcus demonstrates the failure of male authors to cite feminist work (1724–25); Jane Garrity reiterates this claim and shows that women writers receive short shrift in guides to modernist authors ("Modernist Women's Writing" 16–17). The task of citing and furthering the work of women scholars falls disproportionately to women, and it is well that Marcus warns all scholars to "monitor this unconscious tendency" to replicate implicit biases that favor the citation of men as authorities (1725). Scholarly literature examining institutional barriers for marginalized groups emphasizes the Sisyphean labor required by such groups to remain visible. In a retrospective review of Paul Lauter's *Canons and Context*, Michael Bérubé marvels that Lauter mentions Francis E. W. Harper and Charles W. Chesnutt so frequently—"almost 20 times apiece"—"as if Lauter had to throw down the gauntlet again and again and yet again, calling his colleagues to come to terms . . . with the limits of their own discipline-sanctioned ignorance" (461). Women writers also expend energy on tasks that distract from actual writing, like creating alternative publication venues that accept and value work by women or demanding equitable representation on prize panels. Julie R. Enszer contends that some women poets had to choose: "Devote time to creative production or devote time to address institutional inequality" (725). Elizabeth Savage charts the ways "women's writing could disappear without being missed, even when those writers . . . were right in front of them [younger women poets]" (244). Because literary institutions, including publishers concerned about sales and costs, capitalize on existing investments instead of ensuring the presence of women writers, women have to do extra work to remedy this oversight.

This combination of factors means that new women writers may have difficulty following the path blazed by their female forebears, and the business of literary production is hard enough without having your breadcrumbs eaten minutes after they land on the forest floor. Making a critical edition for a modernist woman writer teaches students not only about the writer but also about the role economics plays in literary reputation, and thus in the presence—or absence—of diverse authorial voices in classrooms and libraries. Students learn that canonicity is constructed, a process that relies on consistent reinvestment to guarantee presence; they may sense the invidious marginalization of women writers that results from institutional reproduction of patriarchal cultural capital. T. S. Eliot's claim, in "Tradition and the Individual Talent," that the canon changes only for "the new (the really new) work of art" (38) tacitly judges Warner insufficiently innovative, but the critical edition assignment investigates the labor and the material relations that enable Eliot's assured definition of greatness.

The first insight I offer students is therefore less about individual genius than consistent institutional practice: the standard contents of critical editions are my starting point. I ask each student to bring in a critical edition—from a previous class, a friend's collection, or the library—and to complete a worksheet tallying common elements. Comparing a variety of critical editions, students deduce that critical editions share a form—front matter, a primary text with annotations, and back matter—and present similar contents. Typical front matter includes an introduction by an editor, an expert on the author and the author's oeuvre who summarizes the text's claims to greatness, places it in a historical and literary context, and reviews the rigorous selection process for inclusion in the series. Where textual variants exist, the introduction is sometimes followed by a note on the text: the note justifies the choices made in creating an authoritative version, while also recording the painstaking work of an artist to create, and an expert to verify, the version presented.

The primary text that follows the front matter includes substantial annotations noting textual variations, defining unfamiliar or obsolete words, explaining allusions, and providing historical context. Annotations demonstrate complexity and craftsmanship, furnishing the work with intellectual and aesthetic credentials. Diverse references to other fields, such as science, mythology, philosophy, literature, and art, also implicitly confirm the credentials of the editor(s), just as the sometimes arcane and always varied knowledge establishes a broad claim to editorial expertise. Critical editions thus enact Eliot's claim that the artist's "complete meaning" lies in "the appreciation of his relation to the dead poets and artists" (38) while also confirming the role of expert editors as guarantors of canonicity. Some annotations also refer students to critical and biographical material at the back of the volume, creating a circularity that supports the organic sufficiency of the volume.

In critical editions, ancillary contextual material guides students as they learn to interpret texts. This material, situated after the primary text, continues the authorizing process by balancing selectivity and volume. The section often begins with responses (reviews, etc.) to the text at the time of publication and additional works by or about the author; it may also contain relevant historical documents, such as maps, artwork, and photographs. After the primary documents, Norton editions provide excerpts from scholarly articles representing key approaches or foregrounding debates about the work. The juxtaposition of these documents with a vast bibliography, located at the end of the volume, acknowledges the wealth of material available. The implication is this: a text about which so much has been written, over a long period of time, by so many, cannot be insignificant. In other words, neither the practice of excerpting nor the presence of the bibliography undermines the selection process; rather, this arrangement attests to the acuity and effort of the experts involved in selecting representative works for pedagogical purposes. The editors of critical editions offer what Matthew Arnold calls "the best that has been thought and said" (x) about what they believe to be the best that has been thought and said.

Once students understand the components of a critical edition, we begin phase two of the assignment: the construction of "the best that has been thought and said" in the form of a *Lolly Willowes* critical edition. While I function as editor—we discuss my credentials—with the final authority on materials that the edition will include, students eventually locate materials for the edition that go beyond my suggestions, using what they know about critical editions and the novel to justify including what they find. The assignment takes place in three stages: shared readings to establish parameters of relevant material, a search for editor-approved materials to bolster these parameters, and, finally, independent research. These components reinforce ideas that emerge in our discussions of readings assigned from Jeffrey Nealon and Susan Searls Giroux's *The Theory Toolbox*, which approaches critical discourse through key terms. Our first critical term, *author*, with its attendant term, *authority*, introduces the idea that experts (in this case, editors) justify specific interpretations of the text by using statements from the author that appear to address intended meaning. Although Nealon and Giroux problematize the idea of authorial intent, they do not underestimate the power, echoed in critical editions, of the commonsense assumption that the author is an authority on a text's meaning: "If the author were here, he or she could tell us what the text means" (17). Thus, we begin with materials that seem to point to Warner's intent. Sections of Warner's correspondence with David Garnett indicate that Warner agreed with Garnett's comparison of *Lolly*'s protagonist, Laura Willowes, to "the Beauty in the wood" (*Sylvia* 26). How much credence should be given to Warner's assent? In a later letter to Garnett, Warner describes the response of Margaret Alice Murray, author of *The Witch-Cult in Modern Europe*, to *Lolly Willowes*: Murray "liked my witch, though she was doubtful about my devil" (29). This reference suggests possible connections between Warner's novel and Murray's treatise, and indeed students frequently include sections of Murray's work in the critical edition.[5]

Warner's texts also place her within the context of early-twentieth-century debates about women's rights and women's writing, thus tacitly validating feminist approaches to *Lolly Willowes.* We read Warner's lecture "Women as Writers" because it deliberately echoes and rebuts Virginia Woolf's influential feminist treatise, *A Room of One's Own.* How are Warner's ideas about women's roles reflected in the character of Laura Willowes? What do we make of Laura's declaration that "[n]othing is impracticable for a single, middle-aged woman with an income of her own" (95), which predates Woolf's thesis that "[a] woman must have money and a room of her own if she is to write fiction" (*Room* 4)? Students have advocated for including in their critical edition of *Lolly Willowes* selections from *A Room* to demonstrate Warner's contribution to feminist debates of the time and to encourage connections between these two texts and their authors.

Students also consider how they can use textual annotations, a characteristic feature of critical editions, to identify references and allusions that enhance the feminist critique in the novel. My typical example is Laura's distaste for her nephew Titus's obsession with "Fuseli the man, Fuseli the sign of his times, etc." (145) and her subsequent comparison of her situation to that of John Milton's daughters. Students may know who John Milton is, but they do not know who Henry Fuseli is, meaning that the implications of the reference remain obscure. An annotation might read, "Henry Fuseli, English-Swiss painter (1741–1825) of *The Nightmare* (1781)," leaving students, and possibly most readers, none the wiser. However, when students read a sketch of Fuseli from Allan Cunningham's *The Lives of the Most Eminent British Painters*, the account of Fuseli's obstreperous personality (in a book Warner could plausibly have found on a family bookshelf) clarifies Laura's reaction to Titus's admiration of this artist. The connection to Milton becomes evident in Barbara Lewalski's description of Milton's daughters' unhappiness in being made to act as amanuenses when blindness incapacitated their father (407–09). The bitter comparison Laura makes between Milton's daughters, *Paradise Lost*, and her own conscription as amanuensis for Titus's intended biography of Fuseli underlines Warner's critique of the expectation that women will sacrifice their desires to masculine priorities, and authenticates her capacious range of cultural reference.

This section of the assignment concludes with a discussion of two critical articles relevant to a central debate surrounding the novel—Warner's depiction of Laura's sexuality. Warner lived openly with her lover, the poet Valentine Ackland, for thirty-nine years, and scholarly interest in Warner surged when women's studies entered the academy and again when gay and lesbian studies did. The positioning of sexuality in Warner's work continues to fascinate critics and—in keeping with standard critical edition practice—I choose articles that bear on this debate. Garrity considers how sexuality and gender both are and are not made legible in the text ("Encoding"), and Alison Oram places Warner in conversation with other women writing about spinsterhood during this period. There are more recent articles that complicate the feminist politics of the novel—Jacqueline Shin's or June E. Dunn's, for example—and instructors may vary their choices according to the particular debates surrounding a specific author or work. It is vital to choose readings that students can grasp. Working with sophomores and juniors, I choose readings that do not require extensive theoretical knowledge because complex terminology adds an extra hurdle to an already challenging project.

Working through this set of materials establishes parameters for the types of information and materials usually considered relevant for critical editions. From this shared frame of reference, I—in my capacity as editor—then ask each student to locate a text that provides important and relevant context for the novel. The types of texts I assign are all typical of critical editions, and I vary those I assign based on interest and discussion. I always assign a nineteenth-century edition of the Russian fairy tale "The Baba Yaga" (from William Ralston's *Russian Folk-tales*) that illuminates Laura's ruminations on "Russian witches" (134). Other choices extend themes we have discussed in class, show Warner's connections to and influence on other writers, or develop her critical history. Since Laura's escape from domestic bondage may hinge on her experiences during the First

World War, Warner's unsigned article about her wartime work, "Behind the Firing Line: Some Experiences in a Munition Factory," links *Lolly Willowes* to both Warner's biography and the text's historical context. Questions of textual variation and of intent arise from the original ending of *Lolly Willowes*, in which the protagonist dies ("Original Ending"). This momentous change creates additional links with Woolf's work; Woolf had planned to kill off Clarissa Dalloway at the end of *Mrs. Dalloway* (Woolf, "Introduction" 11). I have also assigned critical reflections on Warner's life and work from a special issue of *PN Review* (Harman), additional short stories and poems by Warner, John Updike's appreciation "The Mastery of Miss Warner," book reviews, and scholarly articles. These texts build on prior knowledge, and I test student comprehension when asking them to explain the criteria for relevance in terms of disciplinary practice.

We complete our critical edition with texts students locate independently, allowing students to demonstrate conceptual knowledge of the critical edition genre. Students can seek out additional works by Warner, critical articles, biographies, or book reviews; compose an annotation ("mugwort" is always popular because students are fascinated by Laura's interest in folk medicine [Warner, *Lolly Willowes* 30]); or look for images or source texts for the novel. Students have surprised me with the range of relevant materials they find. There have also been productive arguments: I have defended limitations on the number of book reviews or critical articles given the scope of the assignment; we have also debated whether a student selection is too far afield and whether to include excerpts of scholarship about other works by Warner. These discussions allow the class to reflect on "the sovereignty . . . of the professional 'expert'—another mechanism for managing the proliferation of discourse, for authorizing who can speak to what issues" (Nealon and Giroux 19). Students are forced to reflect on their authority: students routinely excerpt larger sections from secondary sources than a critical edition generally includes. Pages, after all, are money. Being cast in the role of an expert who selects material for others to read triggers feelings of discomfort similar to those voiced by anthology editors about the politics, often unseen in the final product, of choosing or cutting.

In poring over a variety of sources, students find more than enough material to construct the edition: creating a critical edition of *Lolly Willowes* is possible because—just like the works more typically available in critical editions—the novel demonstrates a wealth of intertextual reference, resonates with its historical context, and has acquired a substantial body of literary-critical work supporting it. Laura Willowes voices arguments like those made in Woolf's *A Room of One's Own*, just as Jean Rhys and Katherine Mansfield share with Woolf the stylistic pyrotechnics of experimental modernism, yet Woolf dominates research and syllabi. We are decades out from the first edition of Bonnie Kime Scott's *The Gender of Modernism* and Margaret Crosland's survey *Beyond the Lighthouse*. Each book catalogs the richness and sheer number of modernist women writers, yet the undergraduate curriculum is slow to change, and Woolf remains a spoiler. How does the purported necessity of teaching Woolf justify the occlusion of other modernist women writers? The scholarship on other writers that has blossomed as a result of surveys and anthologies such as those of Scott and Crosland has not generated similar shifts in undergraduate classrooms, a situation partly attributable to a lack of accessible and available editions, critical or otherwise. Indeed, scholarly volubility regarding the merits of *Lolly Willowes* appears to reify Warner's secondary status. She is part of a list of writers that proves the richness and variety of the work produced under the aegis of modernism—so much richness and variety that a legitimate survey is now impossible. Syllabi often retain traditional materials in order to avoid the issue of selection.

From a student's perspective, the effect of a critical edition is tautological and often invisible: the text is on the syllabus so it must be important, and the wealth of critical materials contained in the edition guarantees that the syllabus is appropriately constructed of important literary works. But as Gordon McMullan, an editor of the third edition of the *Norton Shakespeare*, states, "Our editing is pedagogical: we continue our work as teachers through our work as editors" of texts assigned to students (77). Instructors and scholars must take responsibility for what we reproduce. Critical editions remain part of a pedagogical system that "distributes cultural capital *unequally*" (Graff ix), and there is no historical guarantee that investments in alternative forms of capital pay off: that which has been found can be lost or simply ignored. Without continued attention in the form of critical editions, bibliographies, articles, books, reviews, and classroom presence, modernist women writers—like other marginalized groups of writers—will languish. This assignment demonstrates the effort involved in keeping women's texts alive and teaches students at all levels to be wary of the ways canonicity reproduces itself in undergraduate classrooms through various means, including critical editions.

Notes

Originally developed for the 2012 Sylvia Townsend Warner conference, a version of this essay first appeared in *The Journal of the Sylvia Townsend Warner Society* in 2014. That essay was substantially revised for this volume.

1. Jane Garrity makes this point in her 2013 survey of scholarship on modernist women writers ("Modernist Women's Writing" 22).

2. For the purposes of this essay, I focus on Norton, Bedford, and Broadview critical editions; I use Norton editions because I have a collection of them. As teaching tools, such volumes differ in aim from traditional (i.e., nonpedagogical) critical editions—the type moderated by the MLA's Committee on Scholarly Editions (MLA Committee)—although they share authorizing modes.

3. On processes of canon formation, see also Goodspeed-Chadwick in this volume.

4. Norton now includes a much broader range of material relevant to literary analysis, and some recent titles demonstrate that curricular priorities have shifted and copyrights (an issue that stymies critical editions of some twentieth-century texts) have been negotiated. The expiration of extended copyrights, which began in 2019, may reduce costs for critical editions of important works (Fleishman).

5. Mimi Winick provides useful confirmation of the ways scholars develop such evidence into full-throated readings.

Works Cited

Andrews, William L. "Postmodern Southern Literature: Confessions of a Norton Anthologist." *Studies in the Literary Imagination*, vol. 35, no. 1, 2002, pp. 105–12.

Arnold, Matthew. Preface. 1869. *Culture and Anarchy: An Essay in Political and Social Criticism*, Smith, Elder, 1882, pp. i–xlix. *Wikisource*, en.wikisource.org/wiki/Culture_and_Anarchy/Preface.

Bérubé, Michael. "*Canons and Contexts* in Context." *American Literary History*, vol. 20, no. 3, 2008, pp. 457–64.

Crosland, Margaret. *Beyond the Lighthouse.* Constable, 1981.

Cunningham, Allan. "Henry Fuseli." *The Lives of the Most Eminent British Painters*, by Cunningham, rev. ed., vol. 2, Bell and Sons, 1879, pp. 40–101.

Dunn, June E. "Tracking Sylvia Townsend Warner's Red Footsteps." *The Journal of the Sylvia Townsend Warner Society*, 2012, pp. 1–20.

Eliot, T. S. "Tradition and the Individual Talent." *Selected Prose of T. S. Eliot*, edited by Frank Kermode, Farrar, Straus and Giroux, 1975, pp. 37–44.

Enszer, Julie R. "'She Who Shouts Gets Heard!' Counting and Accounting for Women Writers in Literary Grants and Norton Anthologies." *Feminist Studies*, vol. 42, no. 3, 2016, pp. 720–37.

Finke, Laurie. "The Hidden Curriculum." *College English*, vol. 66, no. 2, 2003, pp. 189–96.

Fleishman, Glenn. "A Landslide of Classic Art Is about to Enter the Public Domain." *The Atlantic*, 8 Apr. 2018, www.theatlantic.com/technology/archive/2018/04/copywritten-so-dont-copy-me/557420/.

Garrity, Jane. "Encoding Bi-Location: Sylvia Townsend Warner and the Erotics of Dissimulation." *Lesbian Erotics*, edited by Karla Jay, New York UP, 1995, pp. 241–68.

———. "Modernist Women's Writing: Beyond the Threshold of Obsolescence." *The Future of Women in Modernism*, special issue of *Literature Compass*, edited by Tory Young and Jeff Wallace, vol. 10, no. 1, 2013, pp. 15–29.

Graff, Gerald. *Beyond the Culture Wars: How Teaching the Conflicts Can Revitalize American Education*. W. W. Norton, 1992.

Guillory, John. *Cultural Capital: The Problem of Literary Canon Formation*. U of Chicago P, 1993.

Harman, Claire, editor. "Sylvia Townsend Warner, 1893–1978: A Celebration." *PN Review*, vol. 8, no. 3, 1981, pp. 30–61.

Leitch, Vincent B., et al. Headnote to "Editing a Norton Anthology." *College English*, vol. 66, no. 2, Nov. 2003, p. 172.

Lewalski, Barbara. *The Life of John Milton*. Blackwell Publishing, 2000.

Marcus, Sharon. "Feminist Criticism: A Tale of Two Bodies." *PMLA*, vol. 121, no. 5, Oct. 2006, pp. 1722–28. *JSTOR*, www.jstor.org/stable/25501653?seq=1.

McMullan, Gordon. "Reflections on the Politics of Editing a Complete Works of Shakespeare." *The Politics, Processes, and Practices of Editing*, special issue of *Contemporary Theatre Review*, edited by Maria M. Delgado and Joanne Tompkins, vol. 25, no. 1, 2015, pp. 76–79.

MLA Committee on Scholarly Editions. "The Committee on Scholarly Editions: Aims and Policies." *PMLA*, vol. 103, no. 4, Sept. 1988, pp. 414–16.

Nealon, Jeffrey, and Susan Searls Giroux. *The Theory Toolbox*. 2nd ed., Rowan and Littlefield, 2012.

Oram, Alison. "Repressed and Thwarted, or Bearer of the New World: The Spinster in Interwar Feminist Discourses." *Women's History Review*, vol. 1, no. 3, 1992, pp. 413–34.

Ralston, William Ralston Shedden. "The Baba Yaga." *Russian Folk-tales*, by Ralston, Smith, Elder, 1873, pp. 139–49. *HathiTrust*, babel.hathitrust.org/cgi/pt?id=pst.000001065633&view=1up&seq=13.

"Re-visiting Sylvia Townsend Warner (1893–1978)." *University of Exeter*, humanities.exeter.ac.uk/english/research/conferences/townsendwarner/. Conference prospectus.

Savage, Elizabeth. "Token Women, Male Movements, and Literary History's Feminist Shadow." *A History of Twentieth-Century American Women's Poetry*, edited by Linda Kinnehan, Cambridge UP, 2016, pp. 241–57.

Scott, Bonnie Kime, editor. *The Gender of Modernism: A Critical Anthology*. Indiana UP, 1990.

Shin, Jacqueline. "*Lolly Willowes* and the Arts of Dispossession." *Modernism/Modernity*, vol. 16, no. 4, 2009, pp. 709–25.

Updike, John. "The Mastery of Miss Warner." Review of Sylvia Townsend Warner's *Swans on the Autumn River*. *The New Republic*, 5 Mar. 1966, pp. 23–25.

Warner, Sylvia Townsend. "Behind the Firing Line: Some Experiences in a Munition Factory." *Blackwoods Magazine*, Feb. 1916, pp. 191–207.

———. *Lolly Willowes*. 1926. New York Review Books, 1999.

———. "The Original Ending of *Lolly Willowes*." *The Journal of the Sylvia Townsend Warner Society*, 2001, pp. 32–34.

———. *Sylvia and David: The Townsend Warner/Garnett Letters*. Sinclair-Stevenson, 1994.

———. "Women as Writers." *Collected Poems*, edited by Claire Harman, Carcanet, 1982, pp. 265–74.

Winick, Mimi. "Modernist Feminist Witchcraft: Margaret Murray's Fantastic Scholarship and Sylvia Townsend Warner's Realistic Fantasy." *Modernism/Modernity*, vol. 22, no. 3, 2015, pp. 565–92.

Woolf, Virginia. "An Introduction to *Mrs. Dalloway*." *The Mrs. Dalloway Reader*, edited by Francine Prose, Harcourt, 2003, pp. 10–12. *Google Books*, books.google.com/books?id=NBvFfI7g5y8C&pg=PA10#v=onepage&q=clarissa%20dalloway%20dies&f=false.

———. *A Room of One's Own*. 1929. Annotated and introduced by Susan Gubar, Harcourt, 2005.

Jennifer Sorensen

Bookish Embodiment: Teaching Modernist Women's Writing Materially through Print Cultures

Virginia Woolf famously documented her intensively material encounters with print production, particularly in her work as an owner and operator of the Hogarth Press. In a letter to the artist Barbara Bagenal about the labor of publishing *The Waste Land*, Woolf links print production with the female body: "I assure you the Press is worse than 6 children at breast simultaneously . . . I have just finished setting up the whole of Mr Eliots poem with my own hands: You see how my hand trembles" (*Letters* 55–56). Yet the bodily strain of working at the press was offset by the intellectual and creative freedom it enabled, as Woolf emphasized in a September 1925 diary entry:

> How my writing goes downhill! Another sacrifice to the Hogarth Press. Yet what I owe the Hogarth Press is barely paid for by the whole of my handwriting. Haven't I just written . . . refusing to do a book for the Home University Series on Post Victoria—knowing that I can write a book, a better book, a book off my own bat, for the Press if I wish! To think of being battened down in the hold of those University dons fairly makes my blood run cold. Yet I'm the only woman in England free to write what I like. (*Diary* 3: 42–43)

Woolf begins by describing her bodily sacrifice to the intensive labor of the press, but concludes by relating a profoundly physical escape from "being battened down in the hold" of those "dons," even the thought of which "makes [her] blood run cold." Woolf stresses her uniqueness as a self-publishing woman and hints at the stifling power dynamics facing most women writers of her day.

While Woolf could perhaps justly claim to be the "only woman in England" who was "free to write" what she liked, modernist women writers negotiated the print marketplace from their own positions. In this essay, I advocate for teaching modernist women writers through their original print contexts by analyzing what I call the "bookish embodiments" of these writers and their texts; I use the phrase to underscore how the modernist print marketplace often entangled the real and imagined bodies of women authors with the material forms of their texts. I incorporate print culture and textual scholarship approaches to make the historical conditions of the circulation of modernist women authors visible and tangible. By teaching modernist women writers through print culture and its materials—dust jackets, correspondence with publishers and editors, early reviews, and advertisements—instructors can create exciting ways to help students access modernist literary history and understand how women navigated and shaped a complex print marketplace.

In upper-division courses focused on the intersections of modernism and print culture, students examine how modernist texts first appeared in journals, newspapers, and first editions and read critical literature that trains them in materially attentive methodologies, such as those developed in the work of Patrick Collier, Ann Ardis, Jayne E. Marek, Robin Schulze, Jerome McGann, and George Bornstein.[1] In my Women Writing Modernism: Modernism "When Women Are Alone" course,[2] we draw from a modernist print archive, housed on our course website, of scans of the first circulating versions of modernist women's writing obtained from my visits to archives over the years as well as from online resources like the *Modernist Journals Project*;[3] in addition, students engage with dust jackets, advertisements, and early reviews to consider how texts by modernist women were initially marketed and received. When teaching Djuna Barnes's *A Book*, I ask students to consider the puzzling first-edition jacket and the series of advertisements developed by Boni and Liveright to market Barnes's experimental mixed-genre work.[4] We analyze how the jacket text develops a physical link between Barnes's iconic body and her writing—for instance, the text of the jacket advertises the book as "things written down and drawn by a woman who acknowledges the charm of unnecessary evil." Framed by the image of Barnes's photographed profile, the jacket subtly constructs Barnes's unique and mysterious presence as entwined with both the material book and the writerly body that produced it. The jacket text concludes by suggesting that the form of *A Book* itself comes to embody the material evidence of Barnes's injured body: "It is evident that she has been shot once too often. But what a gallant wound! What a devastating convalescence." This remarkable dust jacket allows students to analyze an example of a broader trend in the marketing and packaging of modernism that often positions the modernist woman writer as simultaneously mythical and manifest, concrete and spectral, material and abstract.[5] Students examine a range of archival materials documenting the pervasive embodiment of women modernists: these include a *Gentlemen Prefer Blondes* dust jacket iconizing Anita Loos by means of a snapshot and a description of her as a girlish prodigy "in pigtails and sailor suit"[6] and an advertisement for Katherine Mansfield's *"Bliss" and Other Stories* featuring a large photographic portrait of Mansfield with no room to describe the text.[7] Advertising women modernists using their pictures and strange jackets that mystify their bodies continued into the 1960s when the Alfred A. Knopf editor Judith Jones admitted to Sylvia Plath, when Jones requested a photograph for the jacket of *The Colossus*, that "the American public seems to have a sort of prurient need to know what a lady poet looks like" (Jones).

Reading women modernists through the materials of print culture generates questions about the print marketplace and the gendered coding of popularity. Woolf anticipated and dreaded the "popular success" of *Flush*, writing in her diary that critics would say "its 'charming,' delicate, ladylike"; Woolf resisted this reception, asserting, "I must not let myself believe that I'm simply a ladylike prattler: for one thing its not true" (*Diary* 4: 181). Woolf's diary articulates her fear of being derided with faint praise tainted by belittling gendered qualifications. She fears that critics who praise her work as "ladylike" will also reduce her to "simply" a "popular" "prattler." Woolf's diary speaks to her internalization and anticipation of sexist critiques of her writing. In the next section I show one example of how modernist women writers faced censorship that altered their work before it could even reach the public. I then show examples of how modernist women's writing circulated in journals and books and how these texts and their authors were marketed on dust jackets. These examples illuminate how teaching modernist women writers in and through print culture allows students to examine issues of gender and power as contextualized within tangible material histories.

Censoring Women

When teaching Jean Rhys's *Voyage in the Dark*, I incorporate the novel's original uncensored ending and Rhys's letter responding to her publisher's demands and articulating her fears that her ending will have to be "mutilated" (*Jean Rhys* 25). In our final class session on Rhys's novel, students analyze the differences between the two endings—the original, uncensored ending is included in Bonnie Kime Scott's *The Gender of Modernism* (381–89)—and discuss Rhys's response to a resistant print marketplace. Rhys's novel follows the protagonist Anna Morgan from her early uncomfortable days navigating her transplantation from the West Indies to life as a London chorus girl through a series of unsatisfying sexual relationships with men. The novel culminates with Anna hemorrhaging from a back-street abortion. In a letter to the novelist Evelyn Scott, Rhys laments the novel's rough "voyage" on its way to publication: "I'd been feeling as down as hell. The book is having decidedly stormy weather" (*Jean Rhys* 24). Rhys then describes the manuscript's multiple rejections and her anxiety about the changes proposed by Michael Sadleir, her editor at Constable:

> Cape had written and told me how grey I was, without light or shade, how much people would dislike it, that he couldn't hope to sell it even as well as Mackenzie etc and so on, then Hamish Hamilton wanted it cut so much that it would become meaningless.[8]
>
> . . . My dear I really began to feel as if I were crazy or wrong headed or something. . . .
>
> Sadleir of Constable likes it and has written very kindly about it but he also wants it cut. Not of course his own taste he explains but to please prospective readers.
>
> Evelyn I don't know what to do. I suppose I shall have to give in and cut the book and I'm afraid it will make it meaningless. The worst is that it is precisely the last part which I am most certain will have to be mutilated.
>
> My dear it is so mad—really it is not a disgusting book—or even a very grey book. And I *know* the ending is the only possible ending.

> I know if I tinker around with it I'll spoil it, without helping myself a bit, from the being popular point of view. (25)

Critics have been divided over the novel's two endings—Rhys's original draft concludes with Anna's death from hemorrhaging, while the revised version ends with Anna echoing the doctor's trite language about "starting all over again" (*Voyage* 188). My interest lies in Rhys's description of Sadleir's required "cut" as a "mutilat[ion]" and her insistence that her original version is "the only possible ending." Rhys's language here seems to echo Anna's repeated attempts throughout the novel to claim agency through small acts of violence. I ask my students to think about how the original ending enacts violence on Anna (through the botched abortion) while also featuring one last burst of violence from her that is erased in the "mutilated" ending demanded by her publisher.

In the ending that Rhys was forced to "mutilate," a final act of bracketed, remembered violence emerges, a few paragraphs before Anna fades away, as "everything is blotted out and the blackness comes. . . ." (qtd. in Scott 389). In this ending, Anna remembers her father's blue lips and then narrates a fragmented scene of rebellion filtered through the response of others to her remembered act of revolt against the man proclaiming her father's coming death:

> (your father's going to die your father's got heart disease his lips are blue *it's not true he isn't going to die* yes he is you look at him you look at his lips his lips are blue he's going to die I wasn't saying a thing she just flew at me she just flew at him and scratched him like that she's a dreadful girl what's going to become of that girl I wonder but there you are what can you expect). (qtd. in Scott 383; emphasis added)

Unlike earlier moments when Anna's attempts at violence allow for narrative progression within clear syntactical structures, this passage is marked by elisions and gaps in the page layout and fragmented, alien perspectives as Anna's voice is overpowered by the man asserting her father's impending death. Here the violence is bracketed in parentheses and further distanced from Anna's voice as her revolt—which takes the form of flying and scratching—is conveyed in the voice of the man she attacks and then in the unsympathetic retelling of her cruel stepmother, Hester. Students discuss how, as part of the larger "cut" Sadleir demanded, Rhys "mutilated" her ending by eliminating this final moment of aggression and instead foregrounded Anna's passivity in the published ending. Reading Rhys's correspondence about having to change her ending because of the demands of male publishers and comparing the two endings helps students understand the barriers women faced and the compromises they were often forced to make when publishing their work.[9]

Circulation in Periodicals and Books

Many of the most frequently taught works by modernist women writers were circulated in multiple print contexts. As instructors, we enhance our readings of modernist literary experimentation when we resituate these texts in relation to their original engagements with print cultures. Texts by modernist women can be productively reread in print contexts ranging from coterie publications like little magazines or handprinted small editions to widely circulated venues like popular illustrated magazines and newspapers as well as a broad range of book formats. For example, our experience of Willa Cather's *The Professor's House* shifts when we read the novel in its initial serial run in *Collier's Weekly* (printed in nine installments running from 6 June through 1 August 1925) as opposed to scholarly editions, or even the initial book publication by Knopf in 1925.[10] Cather's novel was encountered by millions in serial format—the novel was copiously illustrated by Frank Street during its *Collier's* run and was embedded within other contents (e.g., advertisements) of the weekly magazine. The *Collier's* version makes certain themes of Cather's story more visible; the illustrations often focus on the domestic dramas of the St. Peter household, picturing Professor Godfrey St. Peter's interactions with his living family members and the servant Augusta, while tending to deemphasize his nostalgic connection to the absent figure of Tom Outland. The cover of the issue containing the novel's first installment features the swimming-capped visage of the professor surrounded by his two daughters, who fill the sides of the picture plane and partially obscure the looming faces of their husbands. In contrast, readers encountering the novel as framed by the jacket image of the 1925 Knopf edition are encouraged to view the mystical landscape of Tom's blue mesa as if through Tom's perspective. The book's cover design foregrounds Tom and evokes his discovery of the almost magically preserved relics of the American past signaled by the decorated pottery in the right-hand corner.[11]

I project each cover side by side at the beginning and end of discussions of Cather's novel. Before reading the novel, students discuss their expectations based on each image and then, after reading it, they consider how each image does and does not align with their readings of the novel as a whole. Students often remark that the *Collier's* cover glorifies the human drama and are surprised to see the professor in his unacademic swimming garb, while noting that the Knopf cover emphasizes the novel's meditation on American history, offering an idyllic window on the past and the landscape of the Southwest, omitting the novel's human agents in favor of the landscape and Tom's discoveries. While the Knopf cover resonates with the novel's nostalgia for an idealized past—embodied by Tom Outland and figured in his mesa—the context in which the *Collier's* version is embedded—surrounded by the advertisements and news of the day—situates the story firmly within the historical present of 1925. The material form of the *Collier's* version offers a contrast to the professor's desire to cling to the past, resist change, and cordon himself off from the vulgar world of money and the women who surround him. While Cather herself may have had more control over the design of the book version, the *Collier's* version offers access to the hypermediated format through which most early readers of Cather would have first encountered the novel and shows us how this initial print context would have resonated with and challenged certain themes of Cather's text. I provide scans of the serial version for students to examine, allowing them to contextualize the novel through advertisements and other features like articles, photo spreads, and other literary contents; students write weekly blog posts recording how the material context of *Collier's* shifts their understandings of the novel.[12] Students also develop original research projects using accessible resources like the *Modernist Journals Project* to situate modernist women writers in hypermediated print contexts.

Marketing Women of Color

While many modernist women writers had to contend with marketing campaigns that leveraged their bodies to sell their texts, African American women writers were even more aggressively marketed as embodiments of authentic Black experience. When I teach Zora Neale Hurston's *Their Eyes Were Watching God*, students notice that among the editions we compare almost all packagings of the novel include some version of the author's photographic portrait. Students analyze how these editions seem to market Hurston as an authentic Black voice by featuring images of her body. We also read M. Genevieve West, who has demonstrated how the marketing and packaging of Hurston's texts by the publisher J. B. Lippincott has had long-lasting effects on the author's literary reputation and reception. West includes an advertisement for *Jonah's Gourd Vine* that praises Hurston's literary expertise—"Negro folk-lore interpreted at its authentic best in fiction form of a high order"—while also flaunting her racial "authentic[ity]" in the headline, which promises "A Book No White Person *Could Write*!" (65). Students read Richard Wright's scathing review of *Their Eyes Were Watching God* and discuss how Lippincott's dust jackets and advertisements contributed to the negative responses of Black intellectuals like Wright who criticized Hurston for capitalizing on the desire of white audiences for stereotyped portrayals of Black life.[13]

Claims to authentic Blackness were common in advertisements and on dust jackets, and students come to understand this prevalence when they analyze materials like the dust jacket for the edition of Jessie Redmon Fauset's *There Is Confusion* published by Boni and Liveright in 1924, which repeatedly positions Fauset as a spokeswoman for her race. The back of the jacket features an extended blurb by Zona Gale asserting that Fauset is one of a mass of "long-silent folk" who are finally able to "speak in art." This claim to racial authenticity is echoed in a bookstore advertisement for Fauset's novel (appearing alongside Waldo Frank's *Holiday* and Jean Toomer's *Cane*) that cites a *New York Post* review claiming that "in it the educated Negro becomes articulate" ("There Is Confusion").

When teaching the first edition of Gwendolyn Brooks's *A Street in Bronzeville* published by Harper and Brothers in 1945, I have students examine the dust jacket and archival correspondence about the production of Brooks's first poetic volume.[14] While the front cover of the jacket depicts a partially visible brick wall and a blurb describing "Negro life in a great American City," the back cover foregrounds the wartime production context of the volume by including an intriguing appeal for readers to "BUY WAR BONDS!" and a large reproduction of Brooks's signature at the bottom. Like several of the soldier sonnets from inside the volume, the text on the back of the jacket cites a letter from a soldier. Here Brooks moves between her own position as an author on the home front and her voicing of the soldier's warning and visions:

> "Remember, when you read laudatory accounts of us in the newspapers, that killing Japs wins hill 250—not victory necessarily." That is the unhappy warning we have from an infantryman in New Guinea. A soldier who, like others and others and others, has not found it pleasant to watch men he laughed with fall about him, abruptly crumpled dreams; or to watch many men "buried by bulldozers, rumbling, able and indifferent." No, the war is not yet won, nor should we dare breathe

> deeply till every active hostility has come to an end. But meanwhile we need not be ineffective. We can buy—and hold onto—extra war bonds, and take pride in thus contributing the more to that international health and quiet sure, one day, to come. "None of us can object to speeding the end of the war and guaranteeing future personal advantages as well!"

Brooks's use of the soldier's letter, her construction of the image of "abruptly crumpled dreams," and her citation of the "rumbling" indifference of the burying bulldozers link the back cover to the volume's final sonnet sequence and its exploration of the irresolvable tension between hoping for a better future and despairing in the midst of a seemingly inescapable war. Students are fascinated by the hybridity of the volume design: the front cover shows the urban bricks to which the soldiers hope to return, while the back cover reinscribes the ongoing war as "not yet won."

In each of these examples, African American modernist women writers are positioned as speaking for their race and, in the case of Brooks, for soldiers and for the cause of war. Students analyze how these materials fetishize the authorial body and racial authenticity through photographic portraits and jacket and advertising blurbs, and they question how these marketing strategies affected the reception of these writers in their own time and as part of the canon.

I offer these examples of how to bring modernist women writers' engagement with print cultures into the classroom to suggest that these publication histories enhance the study of women's literary modernism. More materials are being digitized and new teaching resources like the *Modernist Archives Publishing Project* enable original scholarly research by students studying modernism in graduate and undergraduate classrooms. Teaching women modernists using the materials of print culture allows students to engage with tangible histories of modernism, showing them how the cultural production of modernist literature was inflected by gender, race, and power.

Notes

1. Students read selections from Ardis and Collier, from Southworth, and from a recent special issue of *Modernism/Modernity* edited by Ardis. In graduate courses, students learn about critics and scholars who have used archives to recover a vision of modernism's messy connections to diverse cultural fields and markets, including Michael Anesko, Lawrence S. Rainey, Catherine Turner, Jay Satterfield, and Lise Jaillant (*Cheap Modernism* and *Modernism*).

2. The quotation in the title of my course is taken from Woolf, *A Room* 83.

3. For more on the *Modernist Journals Project*, see this volume's companion website (modwomen.mla.hcommons.org).

4. In the case of the first-edition jacket of Barnes's book and those advertisements developed by Boni and Liveright, I use archival materials from my own research (published in Sorensen, *Modernist Experiments*). In many other cases I use online resources to find images of jackets and advertisements to share with students.

5. For more examples of this phenomenon, see Sorensen, "Female Embodiment."

6. I consulted this dust jacket at the Harry Ransom Center.

7. The Mansfield advertisement was printed in *The Sphere*, 6 November 1920, and is available at the *British Newspaper Archive* (www1.britishnewspaperarchive.co.uk).

8. Rhys had first tried to sell her novel to the publisher Jonathan Cape, who rejected it on the grounds that it wouldn't be as popular as Rhys's earlier novel *After Leaving Mr. Mackenzie* (published by Cape in 1931). Rhys also explains that the British publisher Hamish Hamilton wanted to cut it too extremely.

9. Rhys's experience can be situated within the censorship of modernist writing by assigning Marshik.

10. For more details about the likely readers of each version of Cather's novel, see Johanningsmeier.

11. For reproductions of these images, see Sorensen, *Modernist Experiments* 6–7 (in color on the insert facing 146).

12. Unfortunately, the serialized version of Cather's novel isn't yet easily accessible. (I made my own scans from a copy of the serial run held at Oberlin College.) However, there are many excellent images of the illustrations to be found in Johanningsmeier's essay.

13. For examples of the dust jackets and advertisements used by Lippincott to promote Hurston's work, see West.

14. I ordered images of the first-edition jacket from the Newberry Library in Chicago (General Collection, call number: PS3503.R7244 S8 1945). While no libraries offer electronic access to the jacket, many rare books sites, such as AbeBooks, do offer images of it. Archival correspondence can be found in the Selected Records of Harper and Brothers, Manuscripts Division, Department of Special Collections, Princeton University Library, box 5, folders 26–30.

Works Cited

Anesko, Michael. *Friction with the Market: Henry James and the Profession of Authorship*. Oxford UP, 1986.

Ardis, Ann, editor. *Mediamorphosis: Print Culture and Transatlantic/Transnational Public Sphere(s)*. Special issue of *Modernism/Modernity*, vol. 19, no. 3, 2012.

Ardis, Ann, and Patrick Collier, editors. *Transatlantic Print Culture, 1880–1940: Emerging Media, Emerging Modernisms.* Palgrave Macmillan, 2008.

Barnes, Djuna. *A Book.* Boni and Liveright, 1923.

Bornstein, George. *Material Modernism: The Politics of the Page.* Cambridge UP, 2001.

Brooks, Gwendolyn. *A Street in Bronzeville.* Harper and Brothers, 1945.

Cather, Willa. *The Professor's House.* Alfred A. Knopf, 1925.

———. *The Professor's House. Collier's Weekly,* 6 June–1 Aug. 1925.

Fauset, Jessie Redmon. *There Is Confusion.* Boni and Liveright, 1924.

Jaillant, Lise. *Cheap Modernism: Expanding Markets, Publishers' Series, and the Avant-Garde.* Edinburgh UP, 2017.

———. *Modernism, Middlebrow and the Literary Canon: The Modern Library Series, 1917–1955.* Routledge, 2014.

Johanningsmeier, Charles. "Determining How Readers Responded to Cather's Fiction: The Cultural Work of *The Professor's House* in *Collier's Weekly.*" *American Periodicals: A Journal of History, Criticism, and Bibliography,* vol. 20, no. 1, 2010, pp. 68–96.

Jones, Judith. Letter to Sylvia Plath. 22 Nov. 1961. Alfred A. Knopf, Inc. Records, Harry Ransom Center, University of Texas at Austin, box 362, folder 2.

Loos, Anita. *Gentlemen Prefer Blondes.* Boni and Liveright, 1925.

Marek, Jayne E. *Women Editing Modernism: "Little Magazines" and Literary History.* UP of Kentucky, 1995.

Marshik, Celia. *British Modernism and Censorship.* Cambridge UP, 2006.

McGann, Jerome. *Black Riders: The Visible Language of Modernism.* Princeton UP, 1993.

Rainey, Lawrence S. *Institutions of Modernism: Literary Elites and Public Culture.* Yale UP, 1998.

Rhys, Jean. *Jean Rhys: Letters, 1931–1966.* Andre Deutsch, 1984.

———. *Voyage in the Dark.* 1934. W. W. Norton, 1994.

Satterfield, Jay. *The World's Best Books: Taste, Culture, and the Modern Library.* U of Massachusetts P, 2002.

Schulze, Robin, editor. *Becoming Marianne Moore: The Early Poems, 1907–1924.* U of California P, 2002.

Scott, Bonnie Kime, editor. *The Gender of Modernism: A Critical Anthology.* Indiana UP, 1990.

Sorensen, Jennifer. "Female Embodiment in the Marketing of Modernism." *Intervalla,* vol. 4, 2016, pp. 99–124, www.fus.edu/intervalla-files/vol4/4-JS.pdf.

———. *Modernist Experiments in Genre, Media, and Transatlantic Print Culture.* Routledge, 2017.

Southworth, Helen, editor. *Leonard and Virginia Woolf: The Hogarth Press and the Networks of Modernism.* Edinburgh UP, 2010.

"There Is Confusion. Holiday. Cane." 1925. Schomburg Center for Research in Black Culture, Manuscripts, Archives and Rare Books Division, The New York Public Library. *The New York Public Library Digital Collections,*

digitalcollections.nypl.org/items/510d47df-8de0-a3d9-e040-e00a18064a99.
Turner, Catherine. *Marketing Modernism between the Two World Wars.* U of Massachusetts P, 2003.
West, M. Genevieve. *Zora Neale Hurston and American Literary Culture.* UP of Florida, 2005.
Woolf, Virginia. *The Diary of Virginia Woolf.* Edited by Anne Olivier Bell, Harcourt Brace Jovanovich, 1977–85. 5 vols.
———. *The Letters of Virginia Woolf.* Vol. 3 (1923–28), edited by Nigel Nicolson and Joanne Trautman, Harcourt Brace Jovanovich, 1977.
———. *A Room of One's Own.* Annotated and introduced by Susan Gubar, Harcourt, 2005.
Wright, Richard. "Between Laughter and Tears." *New Masses*, 5 Oct. 1937, pp. 22–23.

Geneviève Brassard

Learning Feminist Reading Strategies from Virginia Woolf's *A Room of One's Own*

I teach in a department and at an institution that allows me to design upper-division courses aligned with my areas of interest and expertise, and thanks to this freedom and flexibility, the course in our catalog titled Studies in Women Writers has become a course on British women authors. My choice to begin this survey course with Virginia Woolf's *A Room of One's Own* serves multiple pedagogical functions: it foregrounds feminist theory as a key component of the course, offers a model of feminist criticism for students' interpretive work, and introduces the concept of what I call "speculative literary criticism," which informs students' final assignment of the semester. Using *A Room of One's Own* as a model of critical reading effectively moves Woolf's essay "across time," to borrow Rita Felski's phrase (154), and allows students to recognize its resonance and relevance as a feminist approach when they read more recent authors later in the semester. Felski's "postcritical" (154), comparative method, while not explicitly or overtly feminist, lends itself well to the feminist lens I encourage students to apply to the literature they read in Studies in Women Writers. As Felski notes, "History is not a box"; the "temporality" of texts is "dynamic, not fixed or frozen"; and texts "speak to, but also beyond, their own moment, anticipating future affinities and conjuring up not yet imaginable connections" (159). By the end of the term, students recognize how *A Room* anticipates such "affinities" and "connections" with modern-day women's fiction. This essay explains the theoretical underpinnings and main objective of the course design, describes the assignment prompt and summarizes students' engagement with it, and invites instructors to consider adapting the design for their own purposes in their specific institutional contexts.

As excited as I was the first time I offered the course, I covered as many authors as possible without a specific thematic focus or framework; the survey unfolded chronologically, with canonical texts ranging from Jane Austen's *Persuasion* to Zadie Smith's *On Beauty*. Although I assigned *A Room* as the first reading of the semester, I did not explicitly foreground Woolf's essay as a model of critical reading in the first iteration of the course. I did, however, ask students in a bonus question on their final exam to speculate on Woolf's views of more recent authors on our syllabus. This bonus question turned into an actual assignment the next time I taught the course; the assignment provided the capstone for the framework of a course more deliberately focused on reading comparatively and through an intentionally feminist lens inspired by Woolf's ideas about women's fiction.

Two events provoked reflection and revision in my course planning between the course's first and second iterations. First, the course was listed as an elective in my institution's newly approved women's and gender studies minor. As a result, I expected more students from outside the English major to enroll, and my syllabus therefore needed to become more diverse and inclusive. Second, in my new role as advisory board member for the minor, I helped assess our first graduate's capstone, and her reflections brought to my attention an unconscious bias in my reading selections: she noted that in general, most of her courses had overlooked queer voices and perspectives. This student's observations, combined with the inclusion of the course as part of the minor, led to changes in my reading list: I replaced Woolf's *To the Lighthouse* with *Orlando* and Smith's *On Beauty* with *NW*, and added Jeanette Winterson's *Oranges Are Not the Only Fruit*. For a short analysis paper where students read one feminist theorist of their choice (from a list provided), I also added Adrienne Rich's classic essay on compulsory heterosexuality. These changes signaled my awareness of a prevalent heteronormativity not only in many canonical texts centered on the marriage plot but also underlying canon formation as it is typically taught in survey courses. At the same time, I wanted to create a space for students to interrogate or challenge this heteronormativity within and beyond the texts assigned. These changes also allowed for the exploration of queer themes and issues in Woolf's *A Room* and in late-twentieth- and twenty-first-century novels.

I knew that beginning the course with *A Room* would be challenging for some, since Woolf's nonlinear and digressive style, to say nothing of the text's many allusions, often surprises and puzzles first-time readers. But starting with Woolf's essay served multiple purposes, and this pedagogical strategy proved fruitful. First, reading *A Room* before a series of novels foregrounded feminist criticism as an important component of a course dominated by fiction and reminded students that our class was not only a course on women writers but also a study of feminist literary criticism. As a foundational text within that critical tradition, Woolf's essay provides a grounding that serves students well when they encounter later feminist theorists like Sandra M. Gilbert and Susan Gubar or Elaine Showalter, as they do in the short essay assignment. Foregrounding Woolf's critical attention to distinctive features of canonical authors, such as Austen's development of a "perfectly natural, shapely sentence proper for her own use" (76), or Charlotte Brontë's expression of anger at women's oppression in *Jane Eyre*, provides students with nuanced ways to redefine what might constitute feminist literature. In other words, just as Woolf reminds us in some of her readings of past authors, I remind students to question the assumption that texts by women must necessarily manifest feminist agendas. I draw a key distinction between the explicitly feminist aim of a course devoted to women writers as crucial to continued efforts to redress the balance of content typically assigned in literature classrooms and the complex range of issues women writers tackle, some of which may not be feminist in intent.

Using *A Room* as a model for critical reading, students engaged in what I have termed "speculative literary criticism": I asked students to imagine how Woolf would have interpreted fiction by women of our contemporary moment. Asking students to read present-day writers through Woolf's theoretical extrapolations about future women writers encourages them to reflect on *A Room*'s sophisticated rhetorical strategies in their own right, instead of as side commentary on the primary texts on our syllabus such as *Jane Eyre*. In addition, associating less frequently studied modern-day authors with a central figure such as Woolf legitimizes some reading selections that may appear arbitrary or idiosyncratic to students primarily exposed to male authors in their literature courses. Authors such as Smith and Penelope Lively may not yet have the cultural cachet that students associate with works they understand to be classics. Thus, juxtaposing *A Room* with Smith's *NW* or Lively's *Moon Tiger* provides a sort of stamp of approval, as if Woolf vouches for these literary descendants, telling us that they are worthy of being taken as seriously as she herself considers Aphra Behn or George Eliot. Moreover, structuring a course around *A Room* as a model of critical reading foregrounds feminist literary criticism and a woman-centered literary tradition as still important, especially at a time when gender equality continues to be under attack. A classroom with women's concerns at its core provides a space for students to express ideas they might hesitate to voice publicly, and offers Woolf's example as a model that shapes how they approach women's texts.

The end-of-term essay assignment prompted students to select a more recent author from our reading list (Lively, Winterson, or Smith) and to develop a speculative interpretation of their work using statements from *A Room* as models for analyzing formal and thematic features.[1] Directives encouraged students to review key sections from Woolf's essay and to explore how their chosen author echoed, extended, or revised Woolf's ideas. The main goal was to get students to read comparatively in order to draw connections across time periods and highlight, in Felski's terms, "affinities" and "connections" among British women writers, especially because Woolf so explicitly and daringly looked to the future when she developed her claims and speculations about women and fiction.

Key sections from *A Room* proved especially resonant and suggestive, especially the "Chloe liked Olivia" passage from the fictitious Mary Carmichael's *Life's Adventures*. When the fictional narrator of Woolf's *A Room* picks up a copy of *Life's Adventures* and muses over its flaws and strengths, she does so after reviewing centuries of challenges to potential women writers and after recognizing the achievements realized in spite of those challenges, and her assessment of this novel by a young contemporary of hers includes the following reminder: "One must read it as if it were the last volume in a fairly long series. . . . For books continue each other, in spite of our habit of judging them separately" (79). This focus on continuity as opposed to tropes of literary judgment relying on "solitary genius" not only anticipates Felski's appeal to consider "affinities" and "connections" but also informs my course design and pedagogical aims, as it fosters the practice of reading openly and comparatively for points of convergence among seemingly diverse authors. This passage invites students to look for, and to acknowledge in their analyses, thematic intersections and stylistic echoes among different writers.

Other sections from Woolf's essay likewise serve as productive lenses through which to interpret the narrative strategies of Winterson, Smith, or Lively. For example, the delightfully subtle yet subversive way Woolf introduces the possibility of same-sex desire as an alternative to the marriage plot in women's fiction draws students' attention when we first read it and stays with them when we later encounter Winterson's *Oranges Are Not the Only Fruit*: "Are there no men present? . . . We are all women, you assure me? Then I may tell you that the very next words I read were these—'Chloe liked Olivia . . .' Do not start. Do not blush. Let us admit in the privacy of our own society that these things sometimes happen. Sometimes women do like women" (Woolf 80–81). This famous rhetorical move highlights a break in the women's literary tradition Woolf has traced, and one her literary descendants have extended. The "Chloe liked Olivia moment," as we referred to it throughout the semester, strikes twenty-first-century students like a breath of fresh air in a text sometimes weighed down by exhaustive erudition. The focus on a women-only audience also reinforces the communal sense women students already feel in the classroom, and the playful tone of complicity underscores their sense of participating in a feminist project of recovery and discovery, since they often lament their lack of exposure to women writers in other literature courses. And last, but certainly not least, the passage authorizes an already-existing curiosity on the part of students about plots centered on women without the obligatory (male) romantic interest and subsequent race to the altar. As Woolf notes, "[I]t struck me how immense a change was there. Chloe liked Olivia perhaps for the first time in literature" (81). Students with even a passing familiarity with texts predating Woolf's recognize how momentous Woolf's claim is in its historical context of the First World War, suffrage, and a generation of women left behind by their fallen male peers. As a rhetorical device, "Chloe liked Olivia" serves multiple purposes in *A Room*, one of which is the associations it fosters in students' minds with subsequent authors on our syllabus.

When, soon after "Chloe liked Olivia," Woolf laments Shakespeare's reductive portrayal of Cleopatra and Octavia, she also makes a plea for complex fictional portrayals still too rare in the literature of her time: "But how interesting it would have been if the relationship between the two women had been more complicated. All these relationships between women, I thought, rapidly recalling the splendid gallery of fictitious women, are too simple" (81). This passage resonates when students read Winterson and Smith later in the term: they recognize in these authors' choices of protagonists and relationships an affinity between Woolf's move to counter simplistic and reductive representations of women with complex and layered ones, and Winterson's and Smith's representations of flawed and complicated women for whom relationships with other women displace the tyranny of the heterosexual marriage plot.

Students also recognize the importance of Woolf's follow-up claim about fictional representations of women in texts written by men: "Almost without exception they are shown in their relation to men. It was strange to think that all the great women of fiction were, until Jane Austen's day, not only seen *by* the other sex, but seen *only* in relation *to* the other sex" (81; emphasis added). This passage not only provides a sweeping critique of male authors' blind spots when it comes to imagining women's lives in the absence of men but also signals a call to arms for women writers to move beyond the circumstances Woolf describes. When students read *Oranges*, *NW*, and *Moon Tiger* later in the term, they remember Woolf's claims and understand these texts as embracing Woolf's call to focus on friendships and relationships between women characters as a corrective to earlier representations focused on men in which women play marginal or supporting roles. In the flawed and at times infuriating protagonists Claudia and Natalie, for instance, students applaud the messiness of real life that Lively and Smith, respectively, seek to represent. These novelists do not idealize or demonize their characters: contrary to what male authors have often done in Woolf's assessment, Lively's and Smith's women characters do not alternate between "heavenly goodness and hellish depravity" (Woolf 81).

Woolf's "Chloe liked Olivia" meditation moves further away from the marriage plot and traditional romantic tropes when Woolf notes that Chloe and Olivia "shared a laboratory together" (82). This highlights thematic preoccupations that differ from the more traditional, primarily domestic pursuits of women depicted in texts by male authors. When Woolf imagines "how literature would suffer" if roles were reversed and men were "only represented . . . as the lovers of women, and were never the friends of men, soldiers, thinkers, dreamers" (82), she seemingly applauds modern-day women's choices to introduce work and collaboration between women as appealing fictional options, expressing hope that new fictional worlds will emerge: "For if Chloe likes Olivia and Mary Carmichael knows how to express it she will light a torch in that vast chamber where nobody has yet been" (83). Students recall this wish and argue for its realization in the works of Winterson and Smith especially, with their marginalized male characters, their exploration of same-sex desire, their focus on work and friendship, and their deep ambivalence toward motherhood. In these thematic strands they hear echoes of Woolf's expressed desire to expect more from women writers: "For I wanted to see how Mary Carmichael set to work to catch those unrecorded gestures, those unsaid or half-said words, which form themselves, no more palpably than the shadows of moths on the ceiling, where women are alone, unlit by the capricious and coloured light of the other sex" (83). Scenes of complicity and competitiveness between Leah and Natalie in *NW*, or moments of frustration and misunderstanding between mother and daughter in *Oranges*, for instance, certainly capture the complexity of relationships between women, and students celebrate the ways in which Woolf's hopes and extrapolations emerge in the fictional worlds of Winterson and Smith.

In addition to clamoring for more complex fictional representations of women's lives, Woolf implores future writers to shed light on a variety of experiences: "All these infinitely obscure lives remain to be recorded," Woolf notes, "feeling in imagination the pressure of dumbness, the accumulation of unrecorded life" (88). Woolf reminds aspiring writers of fiction of the need to explore the multiplicity of marginalized voices and visions, and of the possibility of revisiting the historical past to uncover these obscured lives, a strategy Lively deploys through historical fiction. With her fierce and feisty historian-protagonist, Lively returns to key moments from twentieth-century history from the margins and effectively recenters women's contributions to historical events that deserve to "be recorded" (Woolf 88). As one student argued in her essay, through Claudia's uncompromising consciousness, Lively responds to Woolf's call to "illumine your own soul with its profundities and its shallows, its vanities and its generosities . . ." (88). Woolf wants women writers to represent the truth of women's lives, as a corrective to centuries of male writers' distorted views of women that oscillate between glorification and degradation, and students see such truthful representations in modern-day texts.

Just as important, Woolf wants women to write about men in a way that is equally truthful, as she somewhat playfully states: "For there is a spot the size of a shilling at the back of the head which one can never see for oneself. It is one of the good offices that sex can discharge for sex—to describe that spot the size of a shilling at the back of the head" (89). This arguably feminist move—to encourage women to examine men as thoroughly as men have purported to reveal "with what humanity and brilliancy . . . to women that dark place at the back of the head!" (89)—prefigures feminist efforts in literary criticism to redress the balance between women and men by pointing out problematic representations of women in men's writing. This concept resonated with students as they examined Lively's portrayal of Claudia's lover Jasper and Smith's use of free indirect discourse to render Felix's doomed last day in *NW.* Both portrayals sensitively yet honestly imagine well-rounded characters of different genders as successfully as they create women protagonists, and students recognize this feminist strategy as an extension of Woolf's call to describe that "spot the size of a shilling" (89).

Ultimately, Woolf's hopes as expressed in *A Room* anticipate choices made by present-day writers, thematically and stylistically, and reading Woolf's essay introduces students to an open-minded and complex way of thinking about fiction akin to Felski's "postcritical" model of reading. Assigning *A Room* early in the semester provides students with a compelling model for reading modern-day fiction later. Students recognize narrative strategies intimated in *A Room* and explorations of plots and themes already at work in Woolf's extrapolations concerning the work of future writers. In the narrow context of this particular course and reading list, and potentially in other and broader contexts, Woolf has an afterlife in Lively's provocative protagonist, in Winterson's inventive wordplay and experimental storytelling, and in Smith's immersive exploration of London's interconnectedness. Woolf's hopes for women's fiction live on in these texts, and others, because they encourage and compel women writers to explore the truth of women's experiences, an inexhaustible project for Woolf's literary descendants.

Notes

For their keen insights and thoughtful engagement throughout the term, I thank the students enrolled in Studies in Women Writers at the University of Portland in spring 2016; this essay grew out of their inspiring work.

1. For approaches to teaching present-day women writers alongside modernist women writers, see in this volume Quynn; Reginio; and Chalk.

Works Cited

Felski, Rita. *The Limits of Critique*. U of Chicago P, 2015.

Gilbert, Sandra M., and Susan Gubar. *The Madwoman in the Attic: The Woman Writer and the Nineteenth-Century Imagination*. Yale UP, 1979.

Lively, Penelope. *Moon Tiger*. Grove Press, 1987.

Rich, Adrienne. "Compulsory Heterosexuality and Lesbian Existence." *Signs*, vol. 5, no. 4, 1980, pp. 631–60.
Showalter, Elaine. *A Literature of Their Own*. Princeton UP, 1977.
Smith, Zadie. *NW*. Penguin Books, 2012.
Winterson, Jeanette. *Oranges Are Not the Only Fruit*. Grove Press, 1985.
Woolf, Virginia. *A Room of One's Own*. 1929. Annotated and introduced by Susan Gubar, Harcourt, 2005.

Bronwen Tate

Guided Creative Writing Imitations as Entry into Modernist Women's Writing

Imagine a room full of students who've just read Gertrude Stein's *Tender Buttons*: "A kind in glass and a cousin, a spectacle and nothing strange a single hurt color and an arrangement in a system to pointing" (11)—"What is she even talking about?" they ask. Instead of instructing them to discuss or write about the book, what if we first invited them to write their own poems in the style of *Tender Buttons*?

When we write in the style of a poem rather than about that poem, we stand in a different psychic relationship to the poem and its author. We bring a different quality of attention to an artifact when we plan to replicate it ourselves. To illustrate, when students write metaphors in the style of Willa Cather and Djuna Barnes—reverse engineering each in order to recreate them—they think deeply about how metaphor works. In particular, they slow down. It's not enough to be able to point out the metaphor; students must figure out how each piece of the metaphor takes shape. At the same time, the pressure to analyze and interpret literature using potentially alienating jargon is deferred. Through creative imitation, students come to an analytic understanding by means of a process of recognition and replication with room for trial, error, and play. The following exercises—which encourage creative writing based on imitation—not only offer a point of entry into the work of women modernists for students who might otherwise find themselves excluded from these works but also invite students to hone their critical thinking skills and to develop aesthetic judgment.

I developed the following exercises while teaching an upper-level seminar on modernist women's writing in English. While these exercises are adaptable across levels and institutions, depending on students' previous experience, instructors may want to dedicate some class time to discussing key terms in order for the exercises to be approachable and useful. Each week, I pair one major work with a brief essay or statement of poetics by that author that illuminates either her formal choices or her approach to writing. These pieces offer an introduction to writers with whom students may be unfamiliar. Instructors interested in fostering students' research skills might consider developing these contextual materials into research projects. For example, students could work in pairs or small groups to locate several possible supporting texts and then select one or two to assign to the class. Students could then write about why they chose the texts they did and what the chosen texts add to the ongoing conversation. Participation in this process also challenges students to consider the inevitable acts of selection and exclusion involved in the creation of a syllabus.

The pairing of literary works with contextualizing documents of the same period—essays by the writer discussing literary craft, as well as related reviews, introductions, and manifestos—help situate women writers within larger movements and establish parameters for discussing what it meant to write as a woman during the modernist period. When students read Barnes's article on the force-feeding of women's suffrage activists on hunger strike, for example, they confront the constraints placed on women's self-determination that Barnes experienced ("How It Feels"). Reflecting on activism and issues of gender in their own historical moment, students may link Barnes's work with hunger strikes in California prisons or with protests of abortion bans by women dressed as characters from Margaret Atwood's *The Handmaid's Tale.* Barnes's article also prompts students to consider why Barnes chose to write an oblique novel like *Nightwood* when she was clearly capable of straightforward prose. Likewise, an essay by the detective novelist Dorothy Sayers on ambiguity in the poetry of T. S. Eliot shows how connected Sayers is to questions of modernist form even while she might initially be dismissed as a writer of genre fiction ("Poetry"). Reading Ezra Pound's praise of Mina Loy and F. T. Marinetti's futurist manifesto alongside Loy's own poems and essays, we observe Loy in deliberate dialogue with men who simultaneously championed and constrained her and other women modernists (Pound, "Marianne Moore"; Marinetti). As connections accumulate throughout the course, students develop a nuanced sense of the contexts in which these works were produced and the significance of these women's formal choices. Beyond this, as students write in the styles they observe, they become active participants in a similar negotiation of form and meaning-making. Each writing exercise below begins with close attention to a specific poem, passage, or technique; has students search a passage for particular formal elements or reflect on questions; and directs them to attempt a specific technique in their own piece of creative writing.[1]

Edith Wharton: *The House of Mirth*; "In General"; "Constructing a Novel"

In *The House of Mirth*, Edith Wharton makes use of what is known as free indirect discourse. When using this technique, Wharton writes from a third-person point of view focalized through the thoughts, impressions, and reactions of a single character.

Pay attention to how Wharton moves between omniscient or distant third-person narration and limited third-person narration and free indirect discourse. For an example of free indirect discourse, look at the shift in Lily's perception of her companions (41–45). Lily attempts to resign herself to marrying Percy Gryce; she sees the advantages of joining wealthy society and perceives everyone around her through "a rosy glow" (41). A few moments later, however, Seldon reenters the scene, and Lily, "turning her eyes from him, [finds] herself scanning her little world through his retina" (45).

How does Wharton make clear that she is conveying Lily's thoughts without repeating phrases such as "she thought," "she felt," or "it seemed to her"? What advantage does free indirect discourse have compared with first-person narration?

Write a scene involving a formal dinner using third-person narration that makes use of free indirect discourse.

Willa Cather: *O Pioneers!*; "My First Novels"; "The Novel Démeublé"

The connection between people and the land runs throughout Willa Cather's *O Pioneers!*. On numerous occasions, Cather links human emotions to the environment or uses agricultural metaphors to explain human lives. In the following passage, for instance, Emil contrasts his friend Amédée's public and exuberant celebration of his marriage with his own secret and tormented affair with a married woman. The image of two ears of corn, one thriving and one blighted, invites readers to see the difference between the two men as one of fate or nature, rather than as a result of choices each one has made:

> It was like that when Alexandra tested her seed-corn in the spring, he mused. From two ears that had grown side by side, the grains of one shot up joyfully into the light, projecting themselves into the future, and the grains from the other lay still in the earth and rotted; and nobody knew why. (71)

The next passage offers a metaphor for Alexandra's self-awareness as both present and absent. The image of the subterranean river suggests a depth and power to her "realization of herself," even when it is not detectable:

> Her personal life, her own realization of herself, was almost a subconscious existence; like an underground river that came to the surface only here and there, at intervals months apart, and then sank again to flow on under her own fields. (85)

Just before the following passage, Frank has discovered his young wife, Marie, with her lover, Emil, and has shot them both. Although Frank is clearly an aggressor, Cather's metaphor of the hare set on by dogs depicts him as vulnerable and under attack, acting out of panic:

> Frank had been wont to see himself in dramatic situations; but now, when he stood by the windmill, in the bright space between the barn and the house, facing his own black doorway, he did not see himself at all. He stood like the hare when the dogs are approaching from all sides. (109)

Observe in these passages the power of metaphor to establish or occlude agency and responsibility. If we are moved by an image of blighted corn or a frightened hare, if we accept the terms of the metaphor, we're likely to accept the metaphor's implied conclusions, even if we might otherwise disagree. If we agree, for example, to see Frank as a hare cornered by dogs, in the role of a victim, do we then stop seeing him as a perpetrator of violence?

Write a scene in which human action or emotion is metaphorically linked to a specific natural object, space, or phenomenon. Consider the implications of this link and how it works rhetorically.

Gertrude Stein: *Tender Buttons*; "Composition as Explanation"; "Portraits and Repetition"; "Poetry and Grammar"

Gertrude Stein helps us understand her techniques in *Tender Buttons* when she writes that "the words which were the words that made whatever I looked at look like itself were not the words that had in them any quality of description" (115). Is it possible to evoke something through the mood, sound, tone, or associations of words instead of, or in addition to, relying on their semantic meaning?

Read Stein's *Tender Buttons* carefully, out loud, repeatedly, and get a feel for how it works. You may start to find surprising links between the language used and the thing named.

Stein writes in "Poetry and Grammar":

> So then in *Tender Buttons* I was making poetry but and it seriously troubled me, dimly I knew that nouns made poetry but in prose I no longer needed the help of nouns and in poetry I did need the help of nouns. Was there not a way of naming things that would not invent names, but mean names without naming them.
>
> I had always been very impressed from the time that I was very young by having had it told me and then afterwards feeling it myself that Shakespeare in the forest of Arden had created a forest without mentioning the things that make a forest. You feel it all but he does not name its names.
>
> Now that was a thing that I too felt in me the need of making it be a thing that could be named without using its name After all, one had known its name anything's name for so long and so the name was not new but the thing being alive was always new.
>
> What was there to do.
>
> I commenced trying to do something in *Tender Buttons* about this thing. (141–42)

Write a brief series of object portraits in the style of Stein using words other than the name or obvious attributes of the object to make whatever you're describing "new."

H.D.: *Sea Garden*; *Notes on Thought and Vision* (Notes 17–53); Pound, "A Few Don'ts by An Imagiste"; Flint, "Imagisme"; Fletcher, "H. D.'s Vision"; Sappho Translation Folio

H.D. was influenced by her reading of Sappho's fragments and by her practice of translating ancient Greek poetry. I've chosen Sappho's *Poem of Jealousy* and have included a transcription of it into Roman characters as well as translations of it by poets throughout the centuries.[2]

Read through the translations, paying attention to the choices each translator makes in terms of word choice, rhyme, meter, and spacing.

Write your own version (a translation or an imitation) of this poem. Think about which element you want to prioritize (sound? sense? distance?).

Next, read H.D.'s poems alongside Pound's list of "Don'ts by an Imagiste." Write a poem imitating H.D. that observes some of Pound's "don'ts." For an added challenge, choose a specific poem by H.D. to mirror as closely as you wish. You may replicate the form in terms of number of lines and stanzas, number of words per line, or even parts of speech in the order H.D. employs them.

Mina Loy: *The Lost Lunar Baedeker*; Pound, "Marianne Moore and Mina Loy"; Marinetti, "Manifesto of Futurism"

Mina Loy wrote several poems about other writers and artists, sometimes about specific works (for example, "Poe," "Brancusi's Golden Bird," "Joyce's Ulysses," "Gertrude Stein"). Read these poems with particular attention to the following: When or why does Loy address her poem to the artist she invokes? When and how does she describe work that interests her?

Write a poem in the style of Loy about an artist, writer, or work of art that inspires you. "Gertrude Stein" and "Poe" offer particularly interesting formal models.

Virginia Woolf: *Orlando*; *A Room of One's Own*; "Character in Fiction"

In *Orlando*, Virginia Woolf simultaneously makes use of and satirizes the tools and conventions of both the novelist and the biographer. Woolf moves rapidly from flights of lyricism to scathing mockeries of such lyricism, blends factually relevant biographical details with utter absurdity, and invites us to question the nature of time, narrative, sex, gender, and love. Throughout *Orlando*, the anonymous yet intrusive narrator constantly steps in to regale and enlighten us, like and yet profoundly unlike the conventional Victorian biographer.

Write the introductory scene for a biography in the voice of an intrusive narrator. Pay attention to how Woolf treats typical biographical elements such as physical description, location, family history, personality, etc.

The following are examples of noteworthy techniques:

Woolf creates humor by juxtaposing the sublime and the ridiculous: "Having stumbled over a chest, Orlando naturally loved solitary places, vast views, and to feel himself for ever and ever and ever alone" (*Orlando* 14).

Woolf takes typical elements of the novel or biography and exaggerates them to the point of absurdity, as in the description of the view from the hilltop (*Orlando* 14).

Nella Larsen: *Passing*; "The Rhinelander/Jones Case"

Read the tense scene between Irene and her husband, Brian (*Passing* 60), paying attention to how we see Brian from Irene's perspective.

Write a scene describing a conflict between two intimates told using limited third-person narration. You may wish to include ambiguity as Larsen does. Read closely to see how Larsen gives us direct access to Irene's thoughts and feelings but only hints at Brian's mental state through Irene's observation of his actions, as is the case in the following passage:

> Irene cried out: "But Brian, I—" and stopped, amazed at the fierce anger that had blazed up in her.
>
> Brian's head came round with a jerk. His brows lifted in an odd surprise.
>
> Her voice, she realized, had gone queer. But she had an instinctive feeling that it hadn't been the whole cause of his attitude. And that little straightening motion of the shoulders. Hadn't it been like that of a man drawing himself up to receive a blow? Her fright was like a scarlet spear of terror leaping at her heart.
>
> Claire Kendry! So that was it! Impossible. It couldn't be. (*Passing* 60)

As part of the same scene or as a follow-up exercise, observe and imitate how Larsen creates tension between a character's internal state and external behavior. For example, Irene hosts a tea party and goes through the motions of a good hostess, even while she's clearly still reeling from the trauma of discovering (or believing she's discovered) her husband's infidelity (62).

Write a scene in which a character has received some kind of traumatic news but is nonetheless obliged to go through with a social interaction. Pay attention to how Larsen moves between action and thought, present and past, making use of stream of consciousness, description, fragmented dialogue, physical cues, etc.

Dorothy Sayers: *Gaudy Night*; "Poetry, Language, and Ambiguity"; "Are Women Human?"

In *Gaudy Night*, Harriet writes five drafts of a letter to Peter Wimsey in which she explains his nephew Gerald's accident. She condemns the first four drafts in various ways and the reader only sees the fifth and final draft (201–04).

Write one of the rejected drafts, imitating Sayers's style as closely as possible.

Next, observe the way Sayers uses action and detail to reveal character. Harriet and Miss de Vine play a game of chess as several other members of the Senior Common Room look on (428–29). Pay attention to how Sayers uses the players' actions during the game to hint at aspects of their personalities or worldviews.

Write a brief scene in which two or more people are engaged in a commonplace activity (having a meal, playing a card game, or performing a household chore, for example). Use minor actions and attitudes related to the task at hand to hint at the individuals' personality traits and life philosophies. Avoid excessive exposition as well as interior access to the characters' thoughts.

Djuna Barnes: *Nightwood*; "The Confessions of Helen Westley"; "How It Feels to Be Forcibly Fed"

In her lyrical novel *Nightwood*, Barnes composes metaphors that are either completely surprising or strange, drawn out far longer than seems natural, embedded in one another so that even her metaphors have metaphors, or slippery, so that we move from the literal to the figurative and back in ways that are hard to pin down. Here are a few examples:

> As the altar of a church would present but a barren stylization but for the uncalculated offerings of the confused and humble; as the corsage

> of a woman is made suddenly martial and sorrowful by the rose thrust among the more decorous blooms by the hand of a lover suffering the violence of the overlapping of the permission to bestow the last embrace, and its withdrawal: making a vanishing and infinitesimal bull's eye of that which had a moment before been a buoyant and showy bosom, by dragging time out of his bowels (for a lover knows two times, that which he is given, and that which he must make)—so Felix was astonished to find that the most touching flowers laid on the altar he had raised to his imagination were placed there by the people of the underworld, and that the reddest was to be the rose of the doctor. (34)
>
> Love becomes the deposit of the heart, analogous in all degrees to the "findings" in a tomb. As in one will be charted the taken place of the body, the raiment, the utensils necessary to its other life, so in the heart of the lover will be traced, as an indelible shadow, that which he loves. In Nora's heart lay the fossil of Robin, intaglio of her identity, and about it for its maintenance ran Nora's blood. Thus the body of Robin could never be unloved, corrupt, or put away. Robin was now beyond timely changes, except in the blood that animated her. (62)

Write three metaphors that make use of one or more of Barnes's approaches to metaphor. Your metaphors might be odd and jarring, extended and excessive, or embedded within other metaphors. You may also wish to adopt Barnes's use of long highly coordinated and subordinated sentences. Metaphor allows a writer to introduce images and contexts absent from the established setting of a novel. In writing your metaphors, consider what function Barnes's extravagant metaphors serve in *Nightwood*.

Zora Neale Hurston: *Their Eyes Were Watching God*; "Characteristics of Negro Expression"

At the beginning of chapter 2 of *Their Eyes Were Watching God*, Janie describes the moment she realizes that she's different from her friends the Washburns:

> "Ah was wid dem white chillun so much till Ah didn't know Ah wuzn't white till Ah was round six years old. Wouldn't have found it out then, but a man came long takin' pictures and without askin' anybody, Shelby, dat was de oldest boy, he told him to take us. Round a week later de man brought de picture for Mis' Washburn to see and pay him which she did, then give us all a good lickin'.

> "So when we looked at de picture and everybody got pointed out there wasn't nobody left except a real dark little girl with long hair standing by Eleanor. Dat's where Ah wuz s'posed to be, but Ah couldn't recognize dat dark chile as me. So Ah ast, 'where is me? Ah don't see me.'
>
> "Everybody laughed, even Mr. Washburn. Miss Nellie, de Mama of de chillun who come back home after her husband dead, she pointed to de dark one and said, 'Dat's you, Alphabet, don't you know yo'ownself?'
>
> "Dey all useter call me Alphabet 'cause so many people had done named me different names. Ah looked at de picture a long time and seen it was mah dress and mah hair so Ah said:
>
> "'Aw, aw! Ah'm colored!'
>
> "Den dey all laughed real hard. But before Ah seen de picture Ah thought Ah wuz just like de rest." (8–9)

Write a scene in which a character becomes aware of a difference separating him or her from other people, or of belonging to one group rather than another.

Asking students to write creative imitations modeled after the work they read puts them in the position of apprentice rather than critic. This vantage point offers new insights into the work of writers across genres and styles. Focusing on Wharton and free indirect discourse, for example, students confront a technique they are so accustomed to that it is almost entirely naturalized and invisible to them. After completing the Wharton exercise, they bring a new attention to narrative voice and the psychic distance between narrator and character throughout the remainder of the term. With Stein's *Tender Buttons*, in contrast, students encounter a mode they initially find impenetrable. When asked to imitate Stein's book rather than comprehend it or analyze it, however, many not only find pleasure in reading it but carry over a keener ear for sound into their future reading and writing.

The benefits of creative imitations are not limited to form. When students write metaphors that connect natural landscapes to human emotions, they inevitably consider differences between their own relationship to landscape in an age of climate change and environmental crisis and Cather's visions of fertile farmlands. They may also reflect critically on Cather's use of the word *pioneer*, a word that, as Eula Biss observes when discussing her Chicago neighborhood in *Notes from No Man's Land*, is still used to describe white people settling in an area that is already populated.

Similarly, the exercise drawing on Hurston that asks students to think about group identity and difference forms a connection between Hurston's explorations of Black womanhood and students' own experiences with identity formation. When invited to read as writers, students see connections among the writers they read and their own socially and historically embedded lives, and bring a heightened degree of personal investment to discussions of modernist difficulty, the intersections of race and gender, and the class implications of, for instance, Woolf's financial independence in contrast with Sayers's need to write for the marketplace. These creative imitations and rich conversations in turn lead to analytic papers that engage literary form with attention and precision. Modernism is often characterized by its ruptures, but it is also a site of continuities, reclaimings, and reworkings. When students write in the diverse styles of women modernists, they likewise talk back to literature. Whether they reject Stein's opacity, delight in Hurston's use of the vernacular, or join in Woolf's parody of biography, they begin to see themselves as potential contributors to literature's long history of invention, revision, and recuperation.

Notes

1. Many of the writers discussed here are also considered in Kopley's discussion of teaching revisions in this volume; the two essays might be read fruitfully together.

2. Many writers from antiquity to the present day have translated Sappho, and multiple versions of a single poem, including *Poem of Jealousy*, can easily be found for comparison.

Works Cited

Barnes, Djuna. "The Confessions of Helen Westley." Scott, pp. 40–45.

———. "How It Feels to Be Forcibly Fed." *The World Magazine*, 6 Sept. 1914. *Wikisource*, en.wikisource.org/wiki/How_It_Feels_to_Be_Forcibly_Fed.

———. *Nightwood.* 1936. New Directions Publishing, 2006.

Biss, Eula. *Notes from No Man's Land: American Essays.* Graywolf, 2018.

Cather, Willa. "My First Novels (There Were Two)." Cather, *O Pioneers!*, pp. 178–80.

———. "The Novel Démeublé." Scott, pp. 53–56.

———. *O Pioneers!* 1913. Edited by Sharon O'Brien, W. W. Norton, 2007.

Fletcher, John Gould. "H. D.'s Vision." Review of *Sea Garden*. *Poetry*, vol. 9, no. 5, 1917, pp. 266–69.

Flint, F. S. "Imagisme." *Poetry*, vol. 1, no. 6, 1913, pp. 198–200.

H.D. *Collected Poems, 1912–1944.* Edited by Louis L. Martz, New Directions Publishing, 1983.

———. Notes on Thought and Vision *and* The Wise Sappho. Edited by Albert Gelpi, City Lights, 1982.

———. *Sea Garden.* H.D., *Collected Poems*, pp. 3–42.

Hurston, Zora Neale. "Characteristics of Negro Expression." Scott, pp. 175–87.

———. *Their Eyes Were Watching God.* 1937. HarperCollins Publishers, 2000.

Larsen, Nella. *Passing.* 1929. Edited by Carla Kaplan, W. W. Norton, 2007.

———. "The Rhinelander/Jones Case." Larsen, *Passing*, pp. 129–48.

Loy, Mina. "Brancusi's Golden Bird." Loy, *Lost Lunar Baedeker*, p. 79.

———. "Gertrude Stein." Loy, *Lost Lunar Baedeker*, p. 94.

———. "Joyce's Ulysses." Loy, *Lost Lunar Baedeker*, p. 88.

———. *The Lost Lunar Baedeker: Poems of Mina Loy.* Edited by Roger L. Conover, Farrar, Straus and Giroux, 1999.

———. "Poe." Loy, *Lost Lunar Baedeker*, p. 76.

Marinetti, F. T. "Manifesto of Futurism." 1909. *The Norton Anthology of American Literature*, vol. D (1914–45), 9th ed., edited by Robert S. Levine et al., W. W. Norton, 2017, pp. 316–18.

Pound, Ezra. "A Few Don'ts by an Imagiste." *Poetry*, vol. 1, no. 6, Mar. 1913, pp. 200–06.

———. "Marianne Moore and Mina Loy." *Selected Prose, 1909–1965*, by Pound, edited by William Cookson, New Directions Publishing, 1973, pp. 424–25.

Sayers, Dorothy L. "Are Women Human? Address Given to a Women's Society, 1938." *Logos: A Journal of Catholic Thought*, vol. 8, no. 4, 2005, pp. 165–78.

———. *Gaudy Night.* 1935. Harper Torch, 1995.

———. "Poetry, Language, and Ambiguity." *The Poetry of Search and the Poetry of Statement: On Dante and Other Writers*, Wipf and Stock, 2006, pp. 263–86.

Scott, Bonnie Kime, editor. *The Gender of Modernism: A Critical Anthology.* Indiana UP, 1990.

Stein, Gertrude. "Composition as Explanation." Stein, *Look at Me*, pp. 21–30.

———. *Look at Me Now and Here I Am: Writings and Lectures, 1909–1945.* Edited by Patricia Meyerowitz, Penguin Books, 1971.

———. "Poetry and Grammar." Stein, *Look at Me*, pp. 125–47.

———. "Portraits and Repetition." Stein, *Look at Me*, pp. 99–124.

———. *Tender Buttons.* 1914. Edited by Seth Perlow, City Lights, 2014.

Wharton, Edith. "Constructing a Novel." Wharton, *Writing*, pp. 61–121.

———. *The House of Mirth.* 1905. W. W. Norton, 1990.

———. "In General." Wharton, *Writing*, pp. 3–29.

———. *The Writing of Fiction.* 1925. Octagon Books, 1966.

Woolf, Virginia. "Character in Fiction." *The Essays of Virginia Woolf*, vol. 3 (1919–24), edited by Andrew McNeillie, Hogarth Press, 1988, pp. 420–38.

———. *Orlando.* 1928. Mariner, 1973.

———. *A Room of One's Own.* 1929. Annotated and introduced by Susan Gubar, Harcourt, 2005.

Part II

Modernist Difficulty

Matthew Cheney

How to Write and Gertrude Stein and How to Read

I first stumbled on the usefulness for students of Gertrude Stein's most abstract writing when I was a high school teacher. At the beginning of one of my first years of teaching, I set on my desk a few conventional writing handbooks as well as a ragged copy of Stein's *How to Write* (bought at a yard sale). I used Stein's book primarily as a paperweight, and never thought about incorporating it into my classes. And then one day I was sitting at my desk, talking with a student about her writing, and, for whatever reason, I was struggling and failing to help her understand that her obsession with grammatical correctness was keeping her from being able to write much of anything for fear that whatever she wrote would be, somehow, wrong.

In desperation, I grabbed *How to Write.* "Gertrude Stein is a famous writer," I said. "She wrote a book called *How to Write.* On page 109 she says, 'Forget grammar and think about potatoes.'"

My student flipped through the pages. "I don't understand," she said. I told her to read something aloud. She opened to page 187: "A sentence is made when they like the sun. If they like the sun." She glared at me. "I don't understand," she said angrily.

I told her she was excused from doing any other homework until she had completed the assignment I was now giving her: she was to write two pages in the style of Stein.

It took her a week or so, but she did it, and not only that, she wrote three pages. Her writing wasn't a convincing imitation of Stein, but that didn't matter, because it was nothing like anything she had written before, and everything she wrote for my class afterward showed at least a little bit more playfulness, a little bit more freedom.

Stein's work remains on the more avant side of the avant-garde, which can make it a difficult model for a finished product. But as a model of a compositional process and of an innovative attitude toward language and play, it can provoke revelations. Hazel Smith writes that "language-based strategies encourage you to think in ways which are non-linear, and to make unconscious connections. They coax the associative modes of thinking which are pivotal to creative endeavor" (4). Encouraging student writers to be inspired by Stein not only helps them develop creative thinking skills; it may also strengthen their awareness of the possibilities of language and help them overcome the debilitating habit of thinking that there is one right way to write.

I still keep *How to Write* nearby for moments when I need to appeal to an authority that will shock students out of their assumptions about writing, but when introducing Stein in class nowadays I typically use her poems—"Susie Asado," "If I Told Him: A Completed Portrait of Picasso," or sometimes selections from *Tender Buttons.*[1] In literature courses and writing courses, my goal in using Stein is for students to imagine new ways of reading and writing. I use similar exercises across all courses I teach, because even when I'm not teaching a course for an English department, my interests are similar: analysis, research, and writing. I offer students an environment where they can experiment and play, an environment that will help them expand their imaginations. My experience as a literary scholar and a creative writer influences my feeling that the separation between literature, on the one hand, and writing courses, on the other, is artificial and sometimes, in fact, detrimental. Nonetheless, different types of courses obviously require different emphases.

Many students find comfort in formulas and templates, and in introductory courses particularly, I do provide some. But formulas and templates must be strategic and provisional. At some point in every course, I want students to move beyond their perceptions of what reading and writing should be.

How to Write

The most common assignment for which I use Stein in writing courses is a simple one: I tell students we are going to perform an experiment, and I ask for a volunteer to read aloud, carefully and seriously, the poem "Susie Asado." They inevitably struggle a bit, and sometimes a tone of disbelief or mockery enters their voice (if it's noticeable and consistent, I stop them and ask them to continue reading more seriously). When the first student is finished, I hand the poem to another student and have them read it aloud. The other students do not have the text in front of them, which is important because I don't want them to be thinking about how they would read it themselves; I want them to be listening to their peers and hearing the different tones and styles each reader uses. Depending on time and the class's patience, I sometimes pass the poem to a third reader.

After this, I give a copy of the poem to everyone in the class. Usually, students want to discuss what the poem means, because previous English classes have taught them to treat the reading of poetry like cryptography, the cracking of the poem's code yielding a succinct summary of theme or a chart of symbols. Depending on where we are in the course and my goals for that day, I will sometimes tell students that the poem was intended to be a portrait of a flamenco dancer; usually, however, I will say that the poem has no referential meaning.[2] No matter what I tell students about the poem, though, my ultimate goal is to encourage discussion of its unique features: How would students describe this poem to somebody who hasn't read it? How is this poem similar to, say, Robert Frost's "Stopping by Woods on a Snowy Evening"?

Early on in our discussion of the poem, I begin a list on the board of the poem's unique features. Then, I give students copies of "If I Told Him." Often, I play a recording of Stein herself reading the poem, which is illuminating because of the serious, fluent, and rhythmic manner in which she reads it. Students are always a little afraid that Stein's abstract writings are some sort of joke whose punchline they don't get, but hearing Stein herself read helps dispel that fear. After reading "If I Told Him," we return to our list of the unique features of Stein's writing and see if we need to add anything. If there is time, we move on to some pieces from *Tender Buttons.*

For homework, I give students a simple prompt: write at least five hundred words in the style of Stein. It's important that this assignment be of some significant length, because it will be much more frustrating that way, and, perverse as it may sound, frustration is key to the success of this assignment.

In every class, there are one or two students who have a lot of fun with the assignment and who struggle only very little, but the majority usually find the assignment nearly impossible, and some don't even complete it. The ones who do complete it usually apply a kind of surrealism or absurdism to their writing that is different from Stein's nonsensical use of language. "Your words conjure images," I often say. "If you write, 'The purple cow jumps over the wombat-dog,' that's very different from what Stein writes in 'Susie Asado': 'A lean on the shoe this means slips slips hers.'" Recognizing this difference can be revelatory for students, and they can go on to discuss what Stein's radical move away from referential meaning does to language. We can discuss shapes and sounds, rhythms, repetitions, and patterns.[3]

Texts such as "Susie Asado," "If I Told Him," and *Tender Buttons* are so far removed from what most people think writing must be and do that reading, discussing, and imitating these works helps broaden students' perspectives on writing more effectively than would a text easily shoehorned to fit students' expectations at the beginning of the semester. The radical shock of an encounter with Stein gives students permission to move away from what Peter Elbow calls defensive writing: "Defensive writing means not risking: not risking complicated thoughts or language, not risking half-understood ideas, not risking language that has the resonance that comes from being close to the bone" (xix).

If there is time after our discussion, students revise their writing assignments in an attempt to make them more like Stein's writing. At this point, their efforts are usually successful. It's important, however, to highlight the point of our imitative work: the imitation is a means, not an end. I don't want students to write like Stein; I want them to be freed by Stein's radical choices to find their own way. In keeping with that goal, I draw connections between Stein's abstract writings and less obviously experimental work by other writers. Hemingway is an obvious choice, given how his sentence style is a kind of popularization of Stein's rhythms, and the children's book *Goodnight, Moon* also works well.[4] But I typically end up using the first few pages of Jean Rhys's *Good Morning, Midnight*, which is distant enough from Stein's aesthetic to provide a productive comparison and allows us to expand our ideas about rhythm, repetition, and reference while we also, by means of Rhys's concrete prose, trace the complexities of what might at first glance seem so simple.

Whatever texts and authors I choose, all my lessons after reading Stein focus on transfer, on finding our own voices after being liberated by hers. Her work remains a reference point throughout the semester: if students seem to be falling back into old and unhelpful patterns, if they are allowing their assumptions about form and convention to limit their language and imagination, I remind them of Stein's experiments.

How to Read

In an excellent essay on using Stein's texts in a creative writing workshop, Laura Mullen concludes that

> perhaps the first lesson Stein has to teach us is also the simplest: How to read. We think we know that already, yet no one who has sat in on a workshop is unaware of how reading, in that location, is attested to most often not by an accurate description of what is on the page but by a perfect tornado of opinions about what should or could be on the page instead. (207–08)

Stein's lessons on reading are equally valuable for the literature classroom, where an accurate description of what is on the page is both as important and as difficult to come by as it is in a writing class.

In literature courses, I introduce Stein in the same way that I do in writing courses, through an imitation exercise, because when students only read Stein and don't try to imitate her style, they undervalue the difficulty and precision of her particular methods of avoiding and undermining conventional sense. What students need to see right away is not *that* Stein doesn't make sense, but *how* she doesn't make sense.

Sequence is important if a teacher decides to include some of Stein's more abstract texts to explore her place within certain conceptions of modernism (or within groups such as the lost generation writers, literary exiles, women writers, queer writers, etc.). The intuitive approach is to move from some of Stein's more accessible and popular texts toward the more abstract ones, but I've preferred the opposite approach, for a few reasons. The shock effect of writings like "Susie Asado," "If I Told Him," *Tender Buttons*, *How to Write*, etc. can be a valuable pedagogical tool, and I fear weakening this effect by providing context for these writings before students encounter them. And, more important, I find it easier to work toward denotative or referential meaning than to work away from it. Wrestling with the sorts of writings in the selections of Stein's works edited by either

Ulla E. Dydo or Richard Kostelanetz helps students confront assumptions about language and meaning (*Stein Reader* [Dydo]; *Getrude Stein Reader* [Kostelanetz]).[5] Starting with Stein's more difficult texts, we quickly learn that we cannot fall back on typical habits of reading, and must instead develop new strategies.

Introducing Stein can be especially productive for group work. In small groups, students share their impressions of Stein's text or texts, then come up with a list of advice for a reader, a task that always proves challenging because, at this point, students are the ones who themselves would like some advice. For that reason, the content of the lists usually ends up being of limited value, but the process of trying to imagine what such advice would look like is useful, particularly in a group, where students can share their ideas, build on one another's insights, and feel not quite so alone in their befuddlement. The lists typically include such advice as "Read it aloud" and "Don't try to make every word make sense" (perfectly good advice), and in their discussions, students must justify the reading strategies they propose. These group discussions often lead to richer insights. This inductive approach to Stein fits with a key recommendation in James M. Lang's *Small Teaching*: "When you are teaching a new cognitive skill (e.g., writing in a new genre), let students try their hand at it (and receive feedback) before they feel ready" (60).

Learning to read Stein is very much a new cognitive skill, and after students have practiced it, I begin introducing some explications of and critical approaches to her work as a way to help them see beyond what we can come up with on our own. The opposite approach could be stifling—without real experience as readers of Stein, students could too easily defer to the authority of scholars and critics, depriving them of the "unlimited latitude for personal response" that Mina Loy celebrated in Stein's work and in modern art generally (435).

Early readers of Stein's texts often had direct access to the context (literary and otherwise) in which Stein wrote, and especially in a survey course, teachers can provide access to certain contexts for students. There is much value, for instance, in having students look at modern art (of which Stein was an important collector), listen to modernist music (especially Virgil Thompson, with whom Stein collaborated), and read other literature of the period (anything from Dada sound poetry to Hemingway) that provokes productive dialogue with Stein's experiments. Such an approach is enriched with selections of reactions to Stein's work by her contemporaries, many of which are easily available in *The Critical Response to Gertrude Stein*, edited by Kirk Curnutt.[6] With no recourse to the readings of other critics, Stein's early readers and critics had to figure out their own ways to read her work (if they didn't simply dismiss it outright), and the history of how intrepid readers have found ways to read Stein is useful for students after they have themselves grappled with her writings.

Stein can also be a guide to her own work. While some texts such as "Composition as Explanation" and *Lectures in America* are relatively accessible, they are hardly simple guides, and may not be especially useful in courses where Stein is taught for only a few class sessions at most.[7] Dydo offers another approach to understanding Stein, one that could be adapted to shorter and longer class sessions. In the seventh chapter of *Gertrude Stein: The Language That Rises*, Dydo reads some of the essays in *How to Write* alongside short texts Stein was working on at the same time, seeking "to find echoes as much across pieces as chronologically," with the effect that "incomprehensible passages can suddenly connect and open meanings as exhilarating discovery" (337).[8]

Comparing different Stein texts with one another can be illuminating, but in survey courses especially, comparing Stein's techniques to those of other writers with similar goals or perspectives may produce a synergy otherwise unavailable. One of the most productive pairings is with Virginia Woolf, as Rachel Blau DuPlessis proposed in her extraordinary essay "Woolfenstein" (later revised as "Woolfenstein, the Sequel"). DuPlessis finds particular resonance between *Tender Buttons* and *The Waves*: "*The Waves* is Woolf's most Steinian novel and shows Stein's striking reverberations as a maker of an experimental, even drastic, poetics of writing" ("Woolfenstein, the Sequel" 53). In addition to *The Waves*, there is much in Woolf that may be productively compared with Stein, given the attention both writers gave not only to psychology but also to time and objects—*Tender Buttons* pairs at least as effectively with *To the Lighthouse* as with *The Waves*, and I can imagine interesting discussions of objects and repetition when paired with *The Years* as well, given the many repetitions of phrases, objects, colors, and sounds throughout that novel.

Joan Retallack has described Stein as "an experimental literary humanist who developed a fundamentally investigative poetics" whose "work leaves more questions than answers for her readers" (74). Stein's "investigative poetics" and experimental ethos allow students the freedom to broaden their own processes of reading and writing. The writings of Stein cannot be reduced to multiple-choice questions or standardized tests. Instead, Stein's texts demand that we reimagine our expectations of language and writing, and that we broaden our sense not only of what is allowed but also of what is possible.

At the end of one of the most illuminating studies of Stein that I've encountered, *How Reading Is Written*, Astrid Lorange declares that "epistemological anarchism," a concept from Paul Feyerabend, is valuable to the study of Stein. Lorange describes this as an approach where we are not seeking "the one or essential key to Stein, but reading Stein for her exhausting and itinerant suggestions and finding a way to put their generous energies into writing" (247). Such reading leads to writing. This is, perhaps, the ultimate liberation that teaching Stein's works allows: whether we start with writing or start with reading, we must always return to the other, so that our reading process informs our writing process and vice versa, as the two realms are united by a shared practice of experimentation and play.

Notes

1. For other approaches to teaching "If I Told Him" and *Tender Buttons*, see the essays in Esdale and Mix. A substantial list of resources for teaching Stein is available on the companion website for this volume (modwomen.mla.hcommons .org).

2. The decision of whether to mention the flamenco dancer is significant: if my goal is to help students appreciate the sound and shape of words stripped of denotative meaning, then I don't want to say anything that will, for instance, make them search the text for analogues to dancing. I save that sort of discussion for "If I Told Him" and selections from *Tender Buttons*, where the possibility of representation is more clearly offered by the titles.

3. A comparison of Stein's work with instrumental music and abstract painting can also be helpful, as students do not have the same expectation that such nonliterary art forms must be referential.

4. For connections between Stein and Margaret Wise Brown, the author of *Goodnight, Moon*, see Anne E. Fernald's delightful essay "In the Great Green Room: Margaret Wise Brown and Modernism."

5. Dydo's *Stein Reader* comprises experimental and lesser-known writings based on consultation of the manuscripts and presented in the order in which they were written. Particularly useful for teachers is the preface to each text, which offers not only information on the text's composition and publication but also some guidance for reading. Kostelanetz's volume is subtitled *The Great American Pioneer of Avant-Garde Letters*, which the book seeks to substantiate with some of Stein's most experimental and difficult writings, many of them short enough to be practical even for teachers who aren't able to spend a lot of time on Stein. Kostelanetz writes a thoughtful introduction and adds short headnotes for many of the texts to highlight what he sees as their notable features—for example, "'Old and Old' is sustained wordplay. If you think such writing is easy, try it sometime and discover how the constraints can be defeating" (50).

6. W. H. Auden's 1941 review of Stein's *Ida* can be especially useful, as it is difficult to tell whether Auden is being imitative, parodic, or both. Logan Esdale's critical edition of *Ida* includes a section of reviews of the novel from its first release in 1941, including the Auden review (303–05), and these show how common it was for reviewers to attempt parodies of Stein (291–324).

7. Both "Composition as Explanation" and *Lectures in America* are available in the two-volume Library of America edition of Stein's writings (*Stein: Writings*). Also worthwhile is *A Primer for the Gradual Understanding of Gertrude Stein*, edited by Haas, which is out of print but worth tracking down, as it includes not only a helpful 1946 interview with Stein but also short selections from her writings arranged and introduced to provide an approach to reading her work.

8. The problem with following Dydo's approach, though, is that few of the texts she discusses alongside *How to Write* are easily available, and so a teacher would need access to a library with Stein volumes that have long been out of print. Even without access to the specific texts Dydo explores, however, readers can gain much from her example of close reading, and can engage in new analyses of more readily available Stein texts alongside *How to Write.*

Works Cited

Auden, W. H. "All about Ida." Curnutt, pp. 126–27.

Curnutt, Kirk, editor. *The Critical Response to Gertrude Stein.* Greenwood Press, 2000.

DuPlessis, Rachel Blau. "Woolfenstein." *Breaking the Sequence*, edited by Ellen G. Friedman and Miriam Fuchs, Princeton UP, 1989, pp. 99–114.

———. "Woolfenstein, the Sequel." *Primary Stein: Returning to the Writing of Gertrude Stein*, edited by Janet Boyd and Sharon Kirsch, Lexington Books, 2014, pp. 37–56.

Dydo, Ulla E. *Gertrude Stein: The Language That Rises, 1923–1934.* Northwestern UP, 2003.

Elbow, Peter. *Writing with Power: Techniques for Mastering the Writing Process.* 2nd ed., Oxford UP, 1998.

Esdale, Logan, and Deborah M. Mix, editors. *Approaches to Teaching the Works of Gertrude Stein.* Modern Language Association, 2018.

Fernald, Anne E. "In the Great Green Room: Margaret Wise Brown and Modernism." *Public Books*, 17 Nov. 2015, www.publicbooks.org/in-the-great-green-room-margaret-wise-brown-and-modernism/.

Lang, James M. *Small Teaching: Everyday Lessons from the Science of Learning.* Jossey-Bass, 2016.

Lorange, Astrid. *How Reading Is Written: A Brief Index to Gertrude Stein.* Wesleyan UP, 2014.

Loy, Mina. "Gertrude Stein." *Modernism: An Anthology*, edited by Lawrence S. Rainey, Blackwell Publishing, 2005, pp. 432–37.

Mullen, Laura. "Someone Puts a Stein Apple Together: Ways to Widen a Workshop." Esdale and Mix, pp. 202–09.

Retallack, Joan. "Introduction." *Gertrude Stein: Selections*, edited by Retallack, U of California P, 2008, pp. 3–81.

Rhys, Jean. *Good Morning, Midnight.* 1939. W. W. Norton, 1999.
Smith, Hazel. *The Writing Experiment: Strategies for Innovative Creative Writing.* Allen and Unwin, 2005.
Stein, Gertrude. "Composition as Explanation." Stein, *Stein: Writings*, vol. 1, pp. 520–29.
———. *The Gertrude Stein Reader: The Great American Pioneer of Avant-Garde Letters.* Edited by Richard Kostelanetz, Cooper Square, 2002.
———. *How to Write.* 1931. Dover, 1975.
———. *Ida: A Novel.* 1941. Edited by Logan Esdale, Yale UP, 2012.
———. "If I Told Him: A Completed Portrait of Picasso." Stein, *Stein Reader*, pp. 464–66.
———. *Lectures in America.* Stein, *Stein: Writings*, vol. 2, pp. 191–336.
———. *A Primer for the Gradual Understanding of Gertrude Stein.* Edited by Robert Bartlett Haas, Black Sparrow Press, 1971.
———. *A Stein Reader.* Edited by Ulla E. Dydo, Northwestern UP, 1993.
———. *Stein: Writings.* Edited by Catherine Stimpson and Harriet Chessman, Library of America, 1998. 2 vols.
———. "Susie Asado." Stein, *Stein: Writings*, vol. 1, p. 362.
———. *Tender Buttons.* 1914. Edited by Seth Perlow, City Lights, 2014.

Naomi Milthorpe and Robbie Moore

Embracing Modernist Difficulty with Short Fiction by Women Writers

Difficulty is a signature practice of modernist writers and a paradigmatic concern of those who study them. Modernist writers "must be *difficult*," T. S. Eliot said (248). Working through textual difficulty—at the level of experimental language and form or challenging content—is, as Laura Frost argues, one of the pleasures of reading modernist writing, as it can be of education more broadly (Salvatori and Donahue). But getting students to see difficulty as pleasurable can prove challenging. Our students enter the University of Tasmania with diverse abilities and experiences, many from backgrounds of lower socioeconomic status (*Student Experience Strategy*), with little prior exposure to modernism (Fletcher et al.). Their introduction to modernism in their first year is compressed into two weeks, forming a small unit of a broader survey course on literary history. Given the challenges posed in particular by low socioeconomic background, which are common to many smaller or regional universities, difficulty can sometimes become a stumbling block. Many first-year students desire mastery; they want the answers and are wary of appearing a failure in the classroom. By adopting a posture of "not knowing"—by celebrating the radical unknowability of a text and encouraging "insurgent, incomplete meanings" in lectures and discussions (Irving and Moffatt)—we invite students to embrace their own confusion and imperfect understanding as a valuable part of the reading process.

Troped with Eliotic qualities such as hardness or impersonality, modernist difficulty has often, and incorrectly, been gendered male. Until the late twentieth century, modernism's history was largely told through the stories of male poets and novelists: Eliot, Ezra Pound, and James Joyce, the "men of 1914" in Wyndham Lewis's coinage (252). Yet there are multiple narratives of modernism, and its difficult pleasures extend beyond the Eliotic into ranges of difficulty including verbal, affective, and political. As an entry point into modernism, its difficulties, and its pleasures, we introduce our students to the challenges of modernist short prose by women writers. In stories and essays by Elizabeth Bowen, Katherine Mansfield, and Virginia Woolf, students face particular orders of difficulty: the refusal of certainty and resolution, a resistance to New Critical formulations, challenging content, and formal experimentation. In lectures, students learn about the political, social, and economic difficulties of women's lives in the modernist period, whether in the metropolitan centers of London and Paris or on the colonial periphery in Ireland and New Zealand. Discussions and activities are designed to deflect critical analysis away from the teleology of plot toward an appreciation of open-ended form. In keeping with the pedagogical methods expounded by Kay Sambell and colleagues, students are allowed to "rehearse" their responses to modernist short fiction in brief, low-stakes formative assessments that prompt critical reflection on the experience of encountering difficulty (49). Such assessments encourage tentative and provisional attempts at meaning-making.

The focus of Bowen, Mansfield, and Woolf on apparently everyday experiences, together with their refusal of so-called Joycean epiphany, masks the struggles of their protagonists as they embark on parallel odysseys into the heart of modern subjectivity. In this essay, we take a similar journey, reflecting on the challenges and benefits of embracing difficulty from the perspective of our students alongside our experiences as instructors. We examine Bowen, Mansfield, and Woolf as practitioners of unique modes of modernist difficulty, and we offer reading strategies, critical approaches, and classroom activities meant to engage with this difficulty; we also consider the usefulness of difficulty as a pedagogical tool for students of modernism, and of literature more broadly. We begin with our experiences teaching at the first-year level, and then discuss an upper-level course designed with sensitivity to our students' experiences and backgrounds.

Throughout the upper-level course, we encourage emergent readings in class discussions—resisting the urge to explain—in order to foster sustained, satisfying engagements with modernist texts.

Modernism's well-known relation to difficulty was established with Eliot's declaration that modernism—or, more specifically, its authors—"must be *difficult*." Writing in the *Times Literary Supplement* in 1921, Eliot expounded on what he regarded as the imperative of difficulty for literary writers in the early twentieth century: "Our civilization comprehends great variety and complexity, and this variety and complexity, playing upon a refined sensibility, must produce various and complex results. The poet must become more and more comprehensive, more allusive, more indirect, in order to force, to dislocate if necessary, language into his meaning" (248). The violence of Eliot's metaphors here—"to force," "to dislocate"—is obvious and problematic. Eliot's conception of difficulty was driven not only by form: the ideal poet should look not only into the heart or the soul, he argued, but also into "the cerebral cortex, the nervous system, and the digestive tracts" (250). This reconception of the poet's role appears throughout modernism, as a "reconceptualization" of traditional notions of literary pleasure (Frost 27). Morag Shiach has likewise noted the widespread "skepticism about the psychic and social meanings of pleasure" during the modernist period (210). Indeed, the story of modernism's repudiation of pleasure is so commonplace that Liesl Olson wryly comments that "difficulty" in modernism may actually be a "kind of ordinariness" (179). From beautiful images, affirming emotions, moral sublimity, and aesthetic balance to unlovely representations, negating affects, moral conundrums, and aesthetic disharmony: these exist on the same continuum as Eliot's dislocations of language and interest in the digestive tracts. As Lionel Trilling remarks in "The Fate of Pleasure," pleasure—especially sensuous pleasure—came to be regarded as a "specious good" during the modernist moment (182). This was particularly the case with literary pleasure as exemplified in the critical posture of New Criticism, in which the "typical" relation of the reader to the work is one in which the reader is supposed to begin "at a conscious disadvantage, and to wrestle with [the work] until . . . it no longer baffles and resists [the reader]" (178). At that moment of mastery, Trilling comments dourly, "we discover that [the work's] power is diminished" (178). Diminished too, we might add, is its pleasurableness, an idea that seems to lurk beneath Trilling's argument. Trilling's essay stages the difference between satisfaction and satiety: on the one hand, the reader retains an enjoyment of the text by skating along its surface pleasures; on the other, combat and a surfeit of literary activity leaves the reader sickened.

Trilling wrote specifically about the hermeneutic habits of New Critics, but modernism too has a pedagogical reputation. For some readers, this teacherly aspect of modernist literature is stimulating, offering "engaged readers" the opportunity, as Vicki Mahaffey writes, "to interpret more independently, more sensually, more thoughtfully, more joyfully, less deferentially" (vii). For Mahaffey as for many modernist writers and scholars, the difficulties of modernism are also what make this literature most pleasurable. In particular, Mahaffey argues, modernism's challenging fictions constitute at once a repudiation of existing injustices and oppressions, and an embrace of otherness, ethics, and equality (xix). Yet as Michelle Taylor has commented, difficulty as a pedagogical "opportunity" is a "trope so common . . . that it sometimes feels like a generic marker"; in the era of #MeToo, as Taylor remarks, modernism's discomforts all too closely resemble more unsettling, exclusionary "sensations": "when the skin crawls and the heart races—that alerts us to nothing but the fact that where or how we are is some way we'd rather not be. How different is this from the discomfort of reading, from what we feel in front of our books or our peers or our pupils?" Teaching modernist literature, then, offers a set of challenges—which may not be as liberating as teachers would like—to gender, racial, cultural, geographic, and economic inequality.

Our students face many such inequalities: as an island, Tasmania is geographically isolated from the rest of Australia; it has "alarmingly low" rates of educational attainment and general literacy, and "the lowest income rates in the country" (Milthorpe et al. 355). These socioeconomic factors are reflected in the University of Tasmania's student population, which includes a significant number of students who are the first in their families to attend university (Peter Underwood Centre 121). First-generation college students tend to have "lower rates of progression and completion than the broader student body" (*Student Experience Strategy* 8). Sensitive to the needs of this student population, we offer an inclusive, scaffolded approach to modernist pedagogy. Our challenge is to teach modernism in a way that invites an opening-up to difference and an encouragement of provisional readings rather than the imperative expressed in Trilling of mastery followed by impoverishment (or worse, the sense of distance and exclusion felt by Taylor when reading certain modernist texts).

Our first-year students learn about modernism over the span of only two weeks, as part of a survey course on literary history. They arrive at modernism after having studied nineteenth-century realism. In order to think critically about this historical leap, we begin with Woolf's "Modern Fiction." We isolate this essay's concrete imagery—its coat buttons and atoms, gig lamps and halos—in order to unpack Woolf's rhetorical juxtaposition of realism's bulky materialism and modernism's shape-shifting textuality. Woolf's essay pairs well with Mansfield's discussion of realism in her 1908 notebook. "Realism, flesh covered bones . . . is the artists method for me," Mansfield writes, while imagining a form of realism more suited to the age of radiography: "Supposing ones bones were not bone but liquid light" (*Katherine Mansfield Notebooks* 1: 156). This passage allows us to complicate Woolf's juxtaposition of realism and modernism and to think about Mansfield's fiction as making realism difficult from within.

In our discussions, we link back to a previously analyzed realist text (Jane Austen's *Emma*, but other realist texts could work equally well) and examine brief excerpts from both, side by side: these include introductions, representations of place, dialogue, interiority, and moments of epiphany. Trained by having read Austen, students initially want to read Mansfield's *The Garden Party* as a fragmentary bildungsroman in which the prideful heroine learns a moral lesson and is corrected by the social and narrative mechanisms of the text. But the comparative exercise draws students into the details of Mansfield's story and the specificity of the author's reworking of realist tropes. Looked at closely, the functions of these narrative components are more slippery than they first appear. Some students suggest that the story's opening description of the garden decenters the protagonist and offers a vision of the Sheridan family as one of blossoming life in excess; others maintain that the use of free indirect discourse foregrounds the consciousness of Laura Sheridan. Some students argue that Laura describes the world with a moral certainty reminiscent of Austen's Emma, but we also discuss ways in which the story—with its emphasis on the unseen and the nebulous space between seeming and being—makes us distrust our eyes and our initial assumptions.

At the same time, we also dwell on Laura's—and the story's—inability to articulate the lesson that she learns from her confrontation with the dead body of a carter, and the story's consequent refusal of resolution. In this way, the text encourages students to suspend interpretive certainty and to linger on interpretive difficulties. Nancy Gray argues that Mansfield's short fiction allows readers to "occupy narrative spaces that feel uncertain or undefined: they do not tell us what happens but enact the experience of its happening. What emerges are ambiguous glimpses—for us as well as for the characters—into complex possibilities of self and consciousness" (79). Sambell and colleagues make the point that "novices' sense-making in a domain which is 'new' to them is likely to be tentative and provisional at first"; the authors encourage seeding learning communities where "the disposition to try things out, rather than only sharing highly polished performances, is valued" (61). When teaching Mansfield, Gray asks her students not "What happened?" but "What happened to you as you read? When did you first notice that you were troubled, and what happened then?" (80). For some students, that moment in *The Garden Party* is when Laura gently, very gently, bites her mother's ear. Cultivating this affective response, and stepping back from "tidying and ordering the confusing bits into heuristically sound determinations of what lies behind the words" (Gray 80), is the means by which we introduce first-year students to modernist difficulty.

We conclude our discussion of Mansfield by considering the political valence of uncertainty, particularly in relation to the "crumbling certainties of gender roles" and class identities in the 1920s (Kaplan 6). Productive readings also emerge when one considers Mansfield's status as a colonial outsider on the fringes of metropolitan modernism. The story's setting at the colonial periphery is, for our students, deeply familiar; here we find another means of grappling with modernism that allows for connection rather than alienation.

Since developing our approach of embracing difficulty at the first-year level, we have introduced an advanced undergraduate course in modernism. From the outset, this course was meant as an opportunity for English majors to confront, and celebrate, modernism's difficulty. To this end, we developed a course that relied on the rehearsal strategy advocated by Sambell and colleagues, and that framed encounters with critical concepts using manageable texts (poems and short fiction) by a range of both men and women writers: among others, Bowen, Hart Crane, Langston Hughes, Joyce, Nella Larsen, Lewis, Mansfield, Marianne Moore, Pound, Dorothy Richardson, Gertrude Stein, and Woolf.

After reading these authors, students develop original research projects that explore critical concepts in relation to a major modernist text: Eliot's *The Waste Land*, Woolf's *To the Lighthouse*, or Evelyn Waugh's *Vile Bodies*. Critical concepts include high and low (form), center and periphery (space and place), left and right (politics), and inside and outside (interiority and exteriority). These concepts are presented as oppositional pairings in order to spark discussion about the divisive position-taking inherent in modernist movements (and in the history of modernist criticism); to consider how such position-taking can be used constructively to read women writers; and to illuminate how the work of women writers can help disturb such binaries.

In exploring form, for example, students begin by rereading Woolf's "Mr. Bennett and Mrs. Brown," a work familiar to them from their first-year studies. We discuss why Woolf might have chosen her three materialists (Arnold Bennett, H. G. Wells, and John Galsworthy) as straw men. Apart from Wells, most students aren't very familiar with any of these writers, so we first talk about what characterizes their writing (a good moment to remind students about contextual research). We then discuss what might make the author's particular mode of writing irksome to Woolf. This leads to conversations about the ideology of plots and about the ways narrative not only represents the world but also creates and reinforces certain modes of thinking and being. These initial conversations allow us to explore how Woolf's privileging of experimental form could be understood as a gendered response to the masculine conventions of Victorian materialist novels. We read Woolf's essay alongside an extract from Joyce's *Ulysses* (the section known as "Aeolus" [112–43]), partly in order to generate students' awareness of modernism's radical otherness from realist fiction in terms of form. Beginning the course with an examination of the notion of resistance and opposition in the works of Woolf and Joyce enables us to move on to other oppositions that, in our discussions, begin to shade into continuums: popular and elite, reactionary and revolutionary, pleasure and unpleasure.

Frost writes that for many modernists, the "distinctions between high and low, popular and elite, image and word, cinema and literature, are functions of the quality of pleasure produced" (213). In early classes focused on high versus popular culture, we unpack these binary distinctions by thinking through the experiences commonly associated with, for instance, movies versus literature: students are quick to note the stereotypical association of popular cinematic culture with passivity, leisure, and distraction, while literature is associated with activity, work, and concentration. Many students note the problematic gendering of these activities and their associated qualities: passivity and mass culture, for example, are often seen as feminine (this students observe without having read Andreas Huyssen).

To explore modernism's encounter with popular form, and the oppositional pleasures (and unpleasures) of high and low culture, we assign Bowen's sinister story "Dead Mabelle." Described by David Trotter as "one of the finest short stories ever written about movie-going" (1), "Dead Mabelle" follows its protagonist, William Stickford, through a deepening obsession with a silent-film star, Mabelle Pacey. William's mania for Mabelle grows exponentially after her horrible death, reaching its crisis in a bathetic attempted suicide. William, a shy, self-educated bank clerk with a taste for philosophy, decides to go to the movies after "a man with important-looking initials mentioned it in a weekly review as an 'art-form'" (99). In a characteristic reversal, Bowen undoes the usual, pleasurable associations of both modernism and film: movies become an intellectual pursuit, and reading is reduced to "a titillation of the eyeballs" (102).[1] William goes to the cinema expecting an "erotic" experience, but instead finds something quite different: a "stretched sensation of horror and helplessness" brought on by the rush of kinetic imagery and the mechanized whir of the projector (106). The story closes with a repudiation of the melodramatic associations of cinema. Driven to ontological despair by the absent presence of Mabelle—simultaneously "nothing" yet also "more here" than he himself (107, 110)—William tries to end his life. He opens his bureau drawer expecting a convenient pistol, the means to a "conclusively splendid" cinematic catharsis (111), but Bowen forecloses on this promised release, presenting instead banal reality: some trash, a rumpled tie, and a half-written sonnet "litter" the otherwise empty drawer (112).

Reading "Dead Mabelle" alongside the less ambivalent pleasure of two 1920s silent shorts—Buster Keaton's *The Goat* and Charlie Chaplin's *Pay Day*—causes students to struggle with the strange affects (and effects) of Bowen's writing. They report feeling unsettled, uncomfortable, strange; they find the story and its protagonist disturbing. In writing exercises, they note Bowen's repetition of word clusters that intensify key emotions within the present of each paragraph (cf. Moretti 136): "horror," "horrible," and "horrified" (Bowen 97); "abstract," "abstractions" (100); "real," "unreal," and "realness" (108, 109, 110). Students recognize that Bowen's language seems to both represent, in the text, and stimulate, in the reader, particular "ugly" feelings associated with modernity (Ngai): shame, suspicion, anxiety, and paranoia. Yet many also find Bowen's writing strangely moving. They understand that William is quite repellent, yet they sympathize with his anguish. Their struggle with sympathy presents an opportunity to unpack the "panorama of pleasures" offered by modernist reading

(Frost 27). How can something that is hard work or emotionally distancing also be pleasing? How is intimacy promoted by narrative closeness or distance? What does Bowen's story tell us about the affective landscape of the modernist period and the effects of cinema-going on the psyche? By this point in their university careers, many students have begun to embrace the pleasures of difficulty. They are eager to discuss how readerly bliss can result from contradictory and paradoxical means, through "textual challenges, mysteries or riddles": "Reading for modernist pleasure . . . requires an attention to how a text represents, produces, and thwarts bliss at once" (Frost 26).

We deliberately leave the discussion of "Dead Mabelle" open ended—that is, without proffering a definitive reading—in order to highlight the multiple interpretive and affective possibilities available to the reader of modernism. Such openness to multiplicity prepares students for later encounters with the intransigent strategies of Stein's object studies in *Tender Buttons* (some students comment that Stein's poems make them feel uncomfortable), for Mansfield's deliberate refusal of epiphany—and reversal of affective tone—in "Bliss," and for the combination of blurred impressions and "sudden intensity" that characterizes Woolf's *To the Lighthouse* (*To the Lighthouse* 209). Students are invited to devise their own research projects, which present a diverse range of encounters with the prescribed texts and critical ideas. Designing this course with an eye to the rehearsal of concepts, the development of reading strategies, and student-led research, we permit our students to experiment with "insurgent, incomplete meanings" (Irving and Moffatt) that themselves are a feminist challenge to the concept of critical mastery.

Note

1. Bowen's word here recalls Woolf's essay "The Cinema," which describes the brain as "agreeably titillated" by movie-watching (348).

Works Cited

Bowen, Elizabeth. "Dead Mabelle." *"Joining Charles" and Other Stories*, by Bowen, Constable, 1929, pp. 97–112.

Chaplin, Charlie, director. *Pay Day.* First National, 1922.

Eliot, T. S. "The Metaphysical Poets." *Selected Essays*, by Eliot, Harcourt, 1964, pp. 241–50.

Fletcher, Lisa, et al. "The Teaching of English in Tasmania: Building Links Between Senior Secondary and Tertiary Teachers." *English in Australia*, vol. 51, no. 1, 2016, pp. 25–33.

Frost, Laura. *The Problem with Pleasure: Modernism and Its Discontents.* Columbia UP, 2013.

Gray, Nancy. "Un-Defining the Self in the Stories of Katherine Mansfield." *Katherine Mansfield and Literary Modernism*, edited by Janet Wilson et al., Continuum Books, 2011, pp. 78–88.

Irving, Allan, and Ken Moffatt. "Intoxicated Midnight and Carnival Classrooms: The Professor as Poet." *Radical Pedagogy*, vol. 4, no. 1, 2002, radicalpedagogy.icaap.org/content/issue4_1/05_irving-moffatt.html.

Joyce, James. *Ulysses.* Edited by Jeri Johnson, Oxford UP, 2008.

Kaplan, Sydney Janet. *Katherine Mansfield and the Origins of Modernist Fiction.* Cornell UP, 1991.

Keaton, Buster, director. *The Goat.* Metro Pictures, 1921.

Lewis, Wyndham. *Blasting and Bombardiering.* U of California P, 1967.

Mahaffey, Vicki. *Modernist Literature: Challenging Fictions.* Blackwell Publishing, 2007.

Mansfield, Katherine. *The Garden Party.* Alfred A. Knopf, 1922.

———. *The Katherine Mansfield Notebooks: Complete Edition.* Edited by Margaret Scott, U of Minnesota P, 2002. 2 vols.

McLoughlin, Kate, editor. *The Modernist Party.* Edinburgh UP, 2013.

Milthorpe, Naomi, et al. "Blended English: Technology-Enhanced Teaching and Learning in English Literary Studies." *Arts and Humanities in Higher Education*, vol. 17, no. 3, 2017, pp. 345–65. *SAGE*, doi:10.1177/1474022217722140.

Moretti, Franco. *Modern Epic: The World-System from Goethe to García Márquez.* Verso, 1996.

Ngai, Sianne. *Ugly Feelings.* Stanford UP, 2007.

Olson, Liesl. "Everyday Life Studies: A Review." *Modernism/Modernity*, vol. 18, no. 1, 2011, pp. 175–80.

Peter Underwood Centre for Educational Attainment. *Education Transforms: Papers and Reflections.* U of Tasmania, 2015.

Salvatori, Mariolina R., and Patricia A. Donahue. *The Elements (and Pleasures) of Difficulty.* Pearson, 2004.

Sambell, Kay, et al. *Assessment for Learning in Higher Education.* Routledge, 2013.

Shiach, Morag. "'Pleasure Too Often Repeated': Aldous Huxley's Modernity." McLoughlin, pp. 210–27.

Student Experience Strategy, 2016–2020. U of Tasmania, 2015. *University of Tasmania*, www.utas.edu.au/__data/assets/pdf_file/0010/807994/SE-Strategy-v.6.pdf.

Taylor, Michelle. "Discomfort." *Reading "The Waste Land" with the #MeToo Generation*, cluster of *Modernism/Modernity* Print Plus, edited by Megan Quigley, vol. 4, cycle 1, 4 Mar. 2019, doi.org/10.26597/mod.0097.

Trilling, Lionel. "The Fate of Pleasure." *Partisan Review*, vol. 30, no. 2, 1963, pp. 167–91.

Trotter, David. *Cinema and Modernism.* Blackwell Publishing, 2007.

Woolf, Virginia. "The Cinema." Woolf, *Essays*, pp. 348–54.

———. *The Essays of Virginia Woolf.* Vol. 4 (1925–28), edited by Andrew McNeillie, Hogarth Press, 1994.
———. "Modern Fiction." Woolf, *Essays*, pp. 157–65.
———. "Mr. Bennett and Mrs. Brown." *The Essays of Virginia Woolf*, vol. 3 (1919–24), edited by Andrew McNeillie, Hogarth Press, 1988, pp. 384–89.
———. *To the Lighthouse.* 1927. Annotated and introduced by Mark Hussey, Harcourt, 2005.

Lois Cucullu

Assigning Dorothy Richardson's Difficult Modernist Firsts

Imagine a course on modernism at a large, urban land-grant institution that draws an increasingly diverse population of students. Many students on the roster see themselves as pioneers of a new century and millennium. They carry with them a special awareness of coming of age at a momentous juncture—not just the advent of a new historical moment but also of a revolutionary technological epoch. The majority of students in this class are English majors. Their abilities vary: some are seasoned readers with many literature courses to their credit, while others have taken only a smattering, perhaps a British or American survey course, a course on anglophone literature, or a poetry or drama course. Regardless of the experiences these students bring with them, none is familiar with the subject at hand: literary modernism. On the minds of many that first day is, What does *modernism* even mean? Are the texts as difficult to understand as everyone says they are? And more pointedly, Should I even care about these writers? The teacher's challenge becomes how to engage this diverse yet self-aware group with an admittedly arcane and, by its own design, difficult subject. Adding to this challenge is the imperative to counter the received wisdom, now dated but still powerfully felt, that modernism is a field dominated by white men. The goal, then, is to demonstrate modernism's significance and diversity, with the additional ambition of introducing women writers who contributed to modernism—writers whose groundbreaking literary experiments were instrumental in shaping modernism itself.

To tackle these formidable tasks, I propose an English woman modernist as the first representative of the field of modernism. Though largely neglected throughout much of the twentieth century, this writer is credited with many modernist firsts: she not only redefined the literary techniques of the novel but also helped to define modernist literature itself. It is Dorothy Richardson's work, after all, and not that of Richardson's peers James Joyce or William Faulkner or Marcel Proust or even Virginia Woolf, to which the writer May Sinclair in 1918 first applied the term, borrowed from William James, *stream of consciousness*,[1] an honor that belongs to Richardson's monumental saga, *Pilgrimage*. Begun in 1912, as Proust was writing *À la recherche du temps perdu* (*In Search of Lost Time*), Richardson's semiautobiographical *Pilgrimage* spans thirteen chapter-novels, starting with *Pointed Roofs*, published in 1915, and concluding with *March Moonlight*, published posthumously in 1967. Throughout these thirteen novels, Richardson's protagonist and veiled double, Miriam Henderson, leads readers through the labyrinthine experience of a young Englishwoman's encounter with modernity at another significant juncture—the dawn of the twentieth century, a new era marked by technological innovation much as our own time is. Notably, Richardson accomplished her groundbreaking work without the support of a literary avant-garde. No Ezra Pound championed her fiction, and no publishing house, such as the Woolfs' Hogarth Press, guaranteed her publication. Experimenting on her own, however, Richardson nonetheless produced a decidedly modernist style—one that is difficult for the uninitiated. Yet despite the drawbacks of a pioneering work that is rarely straightforward and, at times, barely intelligible, helping students understand the literary and historical context as well as the artistic and political factors that shaped Richardson's experiment enables them to enter the world she created, which spanned the 1890s through to the opening decades of the twentieth century. These are decades laden with change, from the women's suffrage and trade union movements to the upheavals of war and revolution. Richardson's work allows students to find commonality with a young Englishwoman who, on many levels, is very different from themselves. Her work also provides a meaningful introduction to modernism writ large from the distinctive perspective of women.

Ideally suited to a course on modernism is *Pilgrimage*'s fourth novel, *The Tunnel*, an autonomous work depicting Henderson's arrival in London in 1896. *The Tunnel* can serve as an introductory modernist work, pairing well with texts by Richardson's modernist cohort (Woolf, Jean Rhys, Joyce, etc.); as a unit of a survey course on British literature that offers a bridge between nineteenth- and twentieth-century writers (Charles Dickens, George Eliot, T. S. Eliot, Katherine Mansfield); or as an addition to a course on modern women novelists more broadly (from, for instance, Charlotte Lennox to Monique Truong). In my course Modernity and the Metropolitan Novel: Richardson, Woolf, and Joyce, which initially drew many students who wanted to read the works of Joyce and Woolf, students instead came away captivated by Miriam's experience as a young working woman living alone, for the first time, in a great metropolis. "I've never experienced narration quite like this before, so intimate and real," one male student observed after reading *The Tunnel*, the first novel of the semester. "It's as if she were writing for us today," he maintained. He later wrote: "The way Miriam experiences fear, freedom, and exhilaration in the city speaks to how we today as city dwellers still see and interact with the city."[2] In effect, Richardson's *The Tunnel* presents an image of youthful, late Victorian New Woman mobility and interiority from a modernist point of view that was unprecedented in fiction. As Richardson would explain to Vincent Brome in the 1950s, hers was "an attempt to find a feminine equivalent of the masculine realism of people like Balzac, Bennett and Wells" (Brome 29). Thus, Richardson's experiment in *The Tunnel* doesn't shy away from the grim reality of daily working life.[3] Unlike novels of her male contemporaries, however, Richardson's *The Tunnel* singularly captures the thrilling experience of independence, of having a room of one's own, well before Woolf imagined it, though minus a five-hundred-pound legacy. Chapters 3 and 4 in particular, which make up nearly one-quarter of the novel, record both the drudgery and the elation of a single day on the job at an upscale dental practice with every bit of the grim realism of Joseph Conrad's *The Secret Agent*, but transformed to encompass turn-of-the-century modernity from the viewpoint of an intelligent young woman. Accordingly, *The Tunnel* affords students an aperture onto a city and time in flux, a time and place in history that present compelling analogies to students' own, making literary modernism relevant once more.

In keeping with the goal of making modernism relevant to students, the course follows a more organic approach rather than jumping straight into a study of Richardson's novel or of the difficulties of modernist texts.

The course begins by asking students to examine their own situations in this still-new century. Students then consider the situation of Richardson's protagonist, who also lives at the turn of a new century. From there, the course considers modernism's challenge of long-standing literary conventions: why and how did modernists take up Pound's decree to "make it new"? Attention to these literary and cultural contexts ensures a readiness to tackle Richardson's demanding novel and her status as a literary pioneer.

Students begin by reflecting on their own situations: what is challenging and what is exhilarating about coming of age at the turn of a new century? This question can take the form of an in-class exercise (a group or an individual response) or a take-home written assignment. Either way, students' responses are often spirited and lengthy. One common response centers on the notion of living in a time of constant change and great uncertainty: the sense of existing in a time distinct from all others, one marked by technological revolution and the concomitant stresses of fast-paced life, isolation, and transience.[4] Alongside such stresses, students reckon with sizable financial pressures. The challenges of paying tuition and living on a tight budget while keeping up grades and having to manage on one's own constitute some of the most common responses. In general, students' responses give voice to a version of what we understand to be the vicissitudes of modernity, accelerated in this digital age, but ones also expressed by Richardson's protagonist a century ago. Follow-up questions can further the conversation: especially with respect to diversity, instructors may ask whether everyone experiences such stresses equally. Such conversation not only is crucial in itself but also presages the entitlements and privations of Richardson's urban pilgrim.

And, thus, we turn to the situation of Richardson's protagonist, Miriam Henderson. The companion exercise to students' experience of modernity is to ask them to consider the types of challenges a bright young woman living on her own in a modern city at the end of the nineteenth century without the support of family might confront. Here, an overview of Miriam's background is helpful. The privileges and security she and her three sisters enjoyed growing up in an affluent and cultured suburban bourgeois household are abruptly sundered by their father's profligacy and their mother's subsequent mental illness and suicide. Seventeen-year-old Miriam and her sisters are unexpectedly left to their own devices, each to make her way in the world. The paths Miriam's sisters pursue, like Richardson's own siblings, are conventional ones open to well-bred young women without means. Two marry and the third becomes a governess to a wealthy family. Miriam's journey is quite different: Miriam first tries teaching and then serving as a governess before striking out on her own in 1896 London—the opening of *The Tunnel*. Nearly twenty-one at the time, Miriam finds a secretarial position at a respectable dental practice on Wimpole Street in the heart of London with a paltry salary of a pound a week—which she is nonetheless elated to earn.

Equipped with this summary, students begin their own investigations into the pressures this sheltered but gutsy young woman might experience. What types of difficulties would she face? How far would a pound a week go in 1896? What resources would be available to her? What types of responsibilities would she have? What emotions would she experience? What ambitions and fears might she have? And what of London—what would a young woman living alone discover in a city of nearly six million people? Students' research may draw on previous coursework, enlist the recollections or records (e.g., obituaries, diaries, or histories) of family members, or make use of digital resources such as Yale University's *Modernism Lab*, the *Victorian Web*, and the highly informative scholarly website devoted to Richardson, Keele University's *Dorothy Richardson Editions Project* (see also this volume's companion website [modwomen.mla.hcommons.org]). Numerous other sites focus on such topics as female suffrage and the New Woman, working women, trade unions, women and bicycles, female fashion, and inventions from typewriters and Brownie cameras to gramophones and X-rays. To supplement students' research, I recommend assigning two essays: Sally Ledger's "The New Woman and the Crisis of Victorianism," which succinctly introduces the notion of the modernization of women at the fin de siècle, and Georg Simmel's 1903 essay "The Metropolis and Mental Life," which offers a contemporary view of the daily assaults that the modern metropolis of the early twentieth century inflicted on the mental life of city dwellers.[5] Simmel's essay, which emphasizes the psychological afflictions of city life, also provides compelling commentary on the stream-of-consciousness technique pioneered by Richardson.

Having considered Miriam's plight, we then consider the ways modernism challenged long-standing literary conventions. There is no better treatise on modernist fiction than Woolf's 1923 manifesto "Mr. Bennett and Mrs. Brown," the extended version of which is "Character in Fiction." The decisive moments in Woolf's essay make clear what Richardson's novel will enact, what she had indeed already enacted, as Richardson had published seven chapter-novels of *Pilgrimage* by the time of Woolf's essay. The first of these moments is Woolf's claim that "human character changed"—"on or about December 1910," to be precise ("Character" 421). Next is her scathing analysis of the failed representational techniques of the writers Arnold Bennett, John Galsworthy, and H. G. Wells, techniques that Richardson subsequently labelled "masculine realism" (Brome 29). Finally, Woolf also insists that writers must engage anew the perspective of the titular everywoman, whom Woolf calls "Mrs. Brown."

To supplement Woolf's claim about the change in human character, I recommend that students research the 1910 Grafton exhibition in London *Manet and the Post-impressionists.* The formerly outré paintings included in the exhibition and the public outrage they provoked speak to questions explored in Woolf's essay: what constitutes art, who ought to be represented, and in what manner? Such questions elucidate the paradigm shift undertaken by Woolf and her generation of artists. The second major point of Woolf's essay deals with changes in literary representation. As a means of exploring this idea, I recommend a writing exercise in which students closely examine the omniscient narrator of a nineteenth-century novel—such as one by Jane Austen, Dickens, or George Eliot—that includes some form of realist representation. In my class, students read sections of Dickens's *Sketches by Boz* and study these against the backdrop of J. Hillis Miller's essay "The Fiction of Realism" in order to apprehend the limitations of this mode of reproducing the real. One salient point of Miller's essay is the recognition of realism's inherent metonymic properties, its reliance on things on or near characters in order to explain characters' interior lives. This notion helps students to better understand realism's inability, as Woolf states, to truly appreciate Mrs. Brown's sense of reality, to get inside her head in order "to set her in high relations to the world" ("Character" 433). In Dickens's "Meditations in Monmouth Street," for example, it turns out that a set of clothes is all readers need in order to understand the male character who once wore them. Along with Dickens's *Sketches*, I assign Henry James's short story "The Real Thing" to demonstrate how appearances, whether in person or in art, don't always match reality. Discussion of the immaculately attired real couple of the story, the Monarchs, exposes the couple's practically inanimate, static appearance, of no use as the model upper-class pair sought by the narrator-illustrator for a commissioned work. These readings and discussions put into relief the challenge that modernist writers set for themselves: to locate a "realer" realism, to replace an external, supposedly objective realism with a more subjective or psychological realism—this to better capture the volatile conditions individuals encountered at the beginning of the twentieth century, with its modern cult of speed and routinization of sensory overstimulation, as described in Simmel's essay.

This representational shift as narrative technique—Woolf's point that an author must engage Mrs. Brown's perspective—becomes clearer with the introduction of two terms that are critical to modernist literary experimentation: *free indirect discourse* and *stream of consciousness.* In this respect, *The Oxford Dictionary of Literary Terms* provides an invaluable resource. As it explains, free indirect discourse, or style, is

> [a] manner of presenting the thoughts or utterances of a fictional character as if from that character's point of view by combining grammatical and other features of the character's "direct speech" with features of the narrator's "indirect" report. Direct discourse is used in the sentence *She thought, "I will stay here tomorrow,"* while the equivalent in indirect discourse would be *She thought that she would stay there the next day.* Free indirect style, however, combines the person and tense of indirect discourse ("she would stay") with the indications of time and place appropriate to direct discourse ("here tomorrow"), to form a different kind of sentence: *She would stay here tomorrow.* This form of statement allows a third-person narrative to exploit a first-person point of view, often with a subtle effect of irony, as in the novels of Jane Austen. Since Flaubert's celebrated use of this technique (known in French as *le style indirect libre*) in his novel *Madame Bovary* (1857), it has been widely adopted in modern fiction.
> (Baldick, "Free Indirect Style")

Instead of an omniscient narrator who communicates the inner thoughts and actions of characters, free indirect discourse provides characters with a semblance of self-guided thought and action. The shift is subtle but significant. As readers, we move, as it were, from an outside perspective of a character, as realist texts had dictated, to an inside perspective of a character, the modernist technique of knowing a character from the inside out. A character's interiority becomes key to readers' change in perception. An exercise that asks students to take an excerpt of direct discourse from a work by Charlotte Brontë or Dickens and to transform it into free indirect discourse will illustrate readers' newly acquired vantage point.

This representational shift becomes all the more radical, however, when combined with what Joyce called "the broth of thought" (qtd. in Lehrer), and Sinclair, pace William James, termed *stream of consciousness*, the technique par excellence for displaying strikingly the vagaries of the human thought process. *The Oxford Dictionary of Literary Terms* explains *stream of consciousness* thus: "The continuous flow of sense-perceptions, thoughts, feelings, and memories in the human mind; or a literary method of representing such a blending of mental processes in fictional characters, usually in an unpunctuated or disjointed form of interior monologue" (Baldick, "Stream"). This technique endeavors to represent a thought process that is seldom linear and often fragmentary, fleeting, and tenuous. Students can experiment with capturing their thoughts in writing exactly as they come to them, while sitting in a coffee shop or riding a bus, for instance—an exercise that will help students understand stream of consciousness and the difficulties it presented to readers when Richardson first introduced it in her inaugural chapter-novel, *Pointed Roofs*.

Armed with this knowledge, students are ready to engage the prose that employs these innovative techniques and to consider the theoretical and political ramifications thereof.[6] What they soon discover is that these novels no longer have any grounding omniscience—the mainstay of realist fiction. Uncertainty abounds in modernist novels. Time is in flux. Change is constant. Chaos beckons. Protagonists no longer occupy a linear universe understood in terms of past, present, and future. Dickens's ploy of knowing characters through the objects they possess proves insufficient. Unlikely characters emerge, ones that were previously stock figures of pity or romance, if they were present at all: among them the railway passenger Mrs. Brown, a working girl named Miriam Henderson, and an imperial subject such as Molly Bloom—all emblematic of Woolf's cook come out of the basement.[7] The protagonists who narrate these tales are by definition limited and unpredictable. Bastions of realist fiction such as truth, linearity, and normative subjectivity are called into question. Tasked with evaluating the assertions, actions, and truth claims of a novel's characters, readers are required to assume larger roles in the process of meaning-making.

Finally, students come face-to-face with Richardson's *The Tunnel* and the character of Miriam—the year is 1896, the city is London, the setting an upper-story rented room on the fringe of Bloomsbury, the first place Miriam will call *her* home. Everything in the novel is filtered through the perspective of the impressionable Miriam. Despite this seeming limitation, there are numerous ways to examine Miriam's solo foray into this dynamic metropolis. Given the novel's diverse themes and difficult modernist techniques, my suggestion is to start slowly. Ask half the class to trace the often-contradictory emotional shifts that Miriam expresses in chapter 1, while the other half outlines the societal chafing Miriam experiences in chapter 2 during a Sunday get-together at her sister and brother-in-law's home. Then, have the class work together to develop a sense of Miriam's identity and how she experiences events and time. How does Richardson's narrative technique convey the complexity of Miriam's experiences? In chapters 3 and 4, which focus on work, ask students to characterize Miriam's job duties, her attitudes toward them, her perceptions of her surroundings, and her relationships to her coworkers. Next, ask students to describe how the city affects Miriam after she leaves work, as well as in her roles as a pedestrian, diner, and tenant. Can students find examples of straightforward realist depiction and of sense perceptions? Do modes of classical realism work in tandem with stream of consciousness or are they at odds? To test their literary aptitude, ask students whether they detect representational limitations in Richardson's narrative and how these compare to the limitations of realist narration. I suggest introducing the criticism of that formidable adversary of modernism, Georg Lukács. Regardless of whether one chooses to excerpt Lukács's work or to use an intermediary work such as Terry Eagleton's *Marxism and Literary Criticism*, this will lead to a productive discussion about whether stream of consciousness enables a fuller representation of ordinary life, as literary modernists alleged, or whether as Lukács maintains, its use leads to the novel's abandonment of its social function.[8]

As students come to understand, *The Tunnel*'s narrative mode and social function are not, in fact, mutually exclusive. Consider, for instance, Miriam's introduction to literary life, her interactions with her older New Woman pals Mag and Jan, the trauma of her mother's suicide, the social inferiority she experiences in relation to her employer's relatives (who are her intellectual and cultural inferiors), her solitary bicycle vacation, or her governess-sister's depression. Chapter 28 witnesses the arrival of Miss Dear, a nurse suffering from tuberculosis who, it turns out, is determined to marry to gain financial security. As critics have observed, Miss Dear's entrance results in what seems an almost separate work. Indeed, one student perceptively described the novel's shift with Dear's appearance as one that transforms Miriam from protagonist to antagonist. Miriam's complicated attraction to and revulsion of this young nurse offer copious interpretive opportunities: for instance, the idea that Dear functions as Miriam's doppelgänger or that the pair of women is meant to allegorize an ailing "Angel in the House," on the one hand, and the protoprofessional woman on the other.

As with other modernist works, particularly those with multiple episodes or chapters, students are left with the feeling that *The Tunnel* doesn't conclude so much as stop. The novel leaves them wondering about the next chapter for this intelligent working woman, with her newly found literary ambitions, enthralled by the independence and the intellectual life London affords, but hard-pressed to earn a living wage. Yet the uncertainty of Miriam's future at the conclusion of *The Tunnel* paradoxically equips students to make their own informed assessments of the modernist novel and literary modernism. Answers to questions about what modernism means and whether a woman modernist's pioneering work remains relevant today are now within their grasp—as is any canonical modernist novel, be it *Ulysses* or *The Sound and the Fury* or *Mrs. Dalloway.*

Notes

1. First describing Richardson's narrative as "thick and deep" and "fluid" (57), Sinclair famously remarked: "It is Miriam Henderson's stream of consciousness going on and on. And in neither is there any grossly discernible beginning or middle or end. In identifying herself with this life, which is Miriam's stream of consciousness, Miss Richardson produces her effect of being the first, of getting closer to reality than any of our novelists who are trying so desperately to get close" (58).

2. This student's encounter echoes that experienced nearly a hundred years earlier by the writer and editor Bryher (Annie Winifred Ellerman), an early champion of Richardson's work. In a 1959 letter to John Lehmann describing her first encounter with Richardson's work in the early decades of the twentieth century, Bryher recalls the extraordinary effect the work had on her, especially its wonderfully vivid depictions of school and working life, and goes on to name *Pilgrimage* the most important work of her youth. For more on Bryher, see Kane in this volume.

3. See Mattis in this volume for teaching the New Woman, particularly with respect to issues of work.

4. Such issues should be especially relevant to nontraditional students.

5. For a different approach to the effects of urban modernity and place on modernist themes and representations, see Slankard in this volume. For those wishing to explore the class dynamics of Richardson's narrative, I suggest a third reading: Fredric Jameson's "Afterword: A Note on Literary Realism," which understands women's changed relation to public space as connected to their entrance into capitalism.

6. To aid students' reading, I strongly recommend Stephen Ross and Tara Thomson's edition of *The Tunnel.* It not only allows the novel to stand as an autonomous work but also includes valuable supplemental materials that, in addition to an excellent introduction, range from selections of Richardson's own writing to reviews of the novel, among them Virginia Woolf's—all grist for assignment. Along with this edition, I suggest having a copy of George H. Thomson's

A Reader's Guide to Dorothy Richardson's Pilgrimage available to help students manage *The Tunnel*'s often erratic shifts in time and changes in location.

7. The reference here is to the 1910 change of character that Woolf perceives, in which she describes the Victorian cook—a figure we might take as an everywoman—who once "lived like a leviathan in the lower depths, formidable, silent, obscure, inscrutable," and who now slowly emerges as a full-blown character in fiction, "a creature of sunshine and fresh air" ("Character" 422).

8. See Eagleton's discussion of Lukács (27–31).

Works Cited

Baldick, Chris. "Free Indirect Style." *The Oxford Dictionary of Literary Terms*, 4th ed., Oxford UP, 2015, www.oxfordreference.com/view/10.1093/acref/9780198715443.001.0001/acref-9780198715443-e-483?rskey=6I83Rb&result=1.

———. *The Oxford Dictionary of Literary Terms.* 4th ed., Oxford UP, 2015, www.oxfordreference.com/view/10.1093/acref/9780198715443.001.0001/acref-9780198715443?btog=chap&hide=true&page=23&pageSize=20&skipEditions=true&sort=titlesort&source=%2F10.1093%2Facref%2F9780198715443.001.0001%2Facref-9780198715443.

———. "Stream of Consciousness." *The Oxford Dictionary of Literary Terms*, 4th ed., Oxford UP, 2015, www.oxfordreference.com/view/10.1093/acref/9780198715443.001.0001/acref-9780198715443-e-1089?rskey=qdgrHS&result=3.

Brome, Vincent. "A Last Meeting with Dorothy Richardson." *The London Magazine*, June 1959, pp. 26–32.

Bryher. "Letter to John Lehmann regarding 'A Last Meeting with Dorothy Richardson.'" *The London Magazine*, June 1959, pp. 26–32.

Dickens, Charles. "Meditations in Monmouth Street." 1836. *Sketches by Boz*, by Dickens, edited by Dennis Walder, Penguin Books, 1996, pp. 96–104.

Eagleton, Terry. *Marxism and Literary Criticism.* U of California P, 1976.

James, Henry. "The Real Thing." *"The Real Thing" and Other Tales*, by James, MacMillan, 1893. *Project Gutenberg*, www.gutenberg.org/files/2715/2715-h/2715-h.htm.

Jameson, Fredric. "Afterword: A Note on Literary Realism." *A Concise Companion to Realism*, edited by Matthew Beaumont, Wiley, 2010, pp. 279–89.

Ledger, Sally. "The New Woman and the Crisis of Victorianism." *Cultural Politics at the Fin de Siècle*, edited by Ledger and Scott McCracken, Cambridge UP, 1995, pp. 22–44.

Lehrer, Jonah. "The Future of Science . . . Is Art?" *Observe*, isis.artcenter.edu/snowlin/observe/lehreressay.html.

Lukács, Georg. "The Ideology of Modernism." *The Lukács Reader*, edited by Arpad Kadarkay, Blackwell Publishing, 1995, pp. 187–210.

Miller, J. Hillis. "The Fiction of Realism." *Dickens Centennial Essays*, edited by Ada Nesbit and Blake Nevius, U of California P, 1971, pp. 85–153.

Pound, Ezra. *Make It New.* Faber and Faber, 1934.

Richardson, Dorothy. *Pilgrimage*. Dent, 1967. 4 vols.
———. *Pointed Roofs*. Alfred A. Knopf, 1919.
———. *The Tunnel*. 1919. Edited by Stephen Ross and Tara Thomson, Broadview, 2014.
Simmel, Georg. "The Metropolis and Mental Life." 1903. *On Individuality and Social Forms*, edited by Donald N. Levine, U of Chicago P, 1971, pp. 324–39.
Sinclair, May. "The Novels of Dorothy Richardson." *The Egoist*, Apr. 1918, pp. 57–59.
Thomson, George H. *A Reader's Guide to Dorothy Richardson's* Pilgrimage. ELT Press, 1996.
Woolf, Virginia. "Character in Fiction." Woolf, *Essays*, pp. 420–38.
———. *The Essays of Virginia Woolf*. Vol. 3 (1919–24), edited by Andrew McNeillie, Hogarth Press, 1988.
———. "Mr. Bennett and Mrs. Brown." Woolf, *Essays*, pp. 384–89.

Kristina Quynn

Performative Criticism from Virginia Woolf to Shelley Jackson

When teaching Virginia Woolf's *Orlando*, I have often given students the following assignment:

> Write an essay on Virginia Woolf's *Orlando* in which you analyze the moment Orlando changes sex (man to woman). Pay close attention to Woolf's choice of imagery and consider the function of the characters of Purity, Chastity, and Modesty in this scene of Orlando's transformation. Make sure your essay contains a thesis and that you support your argument using concrete examples from the text. Your analysis should be lucid, well organized, and well developed.[1]

Such is a common, and perfectly suitable, prompt for students writing a literary analysis in a course like my Modern Women Writers course at Colorado State University. I have used similar assignments in my classes for years. I still do—although these days with some modifications. The trouble with this particular type of prompt is that it tends to elicit the most standard of essays, ones overflowing with the most general assertions about some of the most intellectually engaging literary texts students may ever encounter.[2] In *Orlando*, for instance, Woolf takes readers on a rollicking romp through more than three hundred years of literary history. From sixteenth-century neoclassicism to Woolf's present day and the era of modernism (which ends in 1928, the same year *Orlando* is published), Woolf's novel stages biographical high jinks spanning the course of hundreds of years, in which the protagonist ages only a few decades, travels the world, befriends queens and "gypsies" alike, falls in love with a Russian princess, marries a sea captain, and changes sex midway through the story. Surely such a literary extravaganza, such a provocative tale—to say nothing of the scene of Orlando's transformation—would elicit the most engaged writing from students.

My experience has taught me that, generally, and unfortunately, this is not the case. This may be because we ask students to write in conventional ways about decidedly unconventional literary texts. For instance, Woolf challenges the formal conventions of biography in *Orlando* to craft a modernist triumph of self-reflexive biographical satire turned novel. The effect of this innovation and play is a delightful, energetic narrative that explores the gendered history of England's aristocracy, the constructedness of biography, and the formal elasticity of the novel. Woolf's work confirms that the borders between creative writing and critical writing are fluid. We can use this fluidity to help students understand different types of literary modes and to bridge some of the formal and cultural distances students experience when reading modernist, postmodernist, and feminist literature.

I have come to question what we often do not—the forms of literary analysis and how certain types of criticism may limit rather than model and foster fresh interpretations of a literary text, particularly unconventional or experimental texts. What if we were to take a critical cue from the very modernist and postmodernist literature we teach in order to revitalize literary-critical practice in our classrooms? What if innovative literary texts are best explored through similarly innovative critical modes? I put forth that they are.

Woolf, Gertrude Stein, Mina Loy, Djuna Barnes, and so many other modernist and postmodernist women writers purposefully experimented with style and form as a means of transgressing conventions (social, political, and artistic) and crafting new types of literature. This formal experimentation served in part as a way to represent women's experiences in new ways—both more truthfully and more thoroughly. If we uphold the work of these authors as innovative in thought and mode—particularly the work of those authors writing explicitly about the nature of writing and of feminism—can we in good conscience (or good pedagogy) limit our own students to traditional modes of literary analysis? I wonder.

But, you argue, students must learn the rules (i.e., demonstrate knowledge) before breaking them. I agree. Just as Woolf, Stein, Loy, and Barnes were exceptionally well-read (if not all formally educated) before they revised or rejected literary conventions, we also want students to demonstrate their knowledge of the texts they read and to produce informed and thoughtful literary analyses. For this reason, I include the option of a performative—or enacted—criticism for essay assignments (usually two to three per semester) in many courses.[3] Performative criticism is a mode of literary analysis in which students make purposeful and strategic choices about the genre and style that will best support their own literary analyses and arguments. It is, in other words, a mode of creative criticism that performs or enacts analysis by engaging with how a text is styled and operates. A play about a play, a story about a story, a poem about a poem, or even a play about a poem would be obvious genre-based examples. Overall, I have found performative criticism to be exceptionally well-suited to teaching (post)modernist women's writing because it allows students to experiment with rhetorical expression and critical forms in order to convey their thoughts in ways that align with the transgressive or revisionary goals of the literary text itself.

An Alternative to Convention: Performative Essay Prompts and Projects

The assigned topics or prompts for the performative criticism option are similar to the conventional essay option presented at the start of this essay, except that the criteria accommodate a self-reflexive critical mode:

> Performative (Enacted) Criticism Option: Consider the best rhetorical or creative approaches for organizing your essay and developing your analysis. You may make use of any number of modes of creative or critical writing. Take care that your performative criticism includes: a main point (thesis), supporting points and examples (close readings of the text that offer critical insights), and a conclusion presenting your findings (a sense of critical significance). Remember that performative criticism is a rigorous approach to literary analysis rooted in close reading of a literary text, not a detour into writing creatively about or around the literary text.

Some of the best essays I have read have come from students bold enough to choose the performative essay option.[4]

In Modern Women Writers, students often use performative criticism to write analyses that center on the notion of storytelling among women, one of the themes of the course. For example, one student employed a prose-poetry style reminiscent of Gertrude Stein's short story "Ada" (*Stein Reader* 100–03) to craft an addition to Emma Donoghue's collection of revisionist feminist fairytales, *Kissing the Witch*. In so doing, the student wished to consider the lifelong importance of women telling empowering stories about and to other women. Another student chose to mimic Ali Smith's narrative criticism in *Artful* in order to consider the relation between biography and temporality in *Orlando*. Other students have developed creative-critical modes to explore representations of otherness in (post)modernist women's writing. As a means of staging the sexually repressed other in Anne Carson's *Autobiography of Red*, one student wrote a three-act play that incorporated Donna Haraway's chimeric cyborg figure in order to clarify how Carson's revisionist novel plays delightfully with symbolism and language. Many students seize the opportunity to engage with literary texts in profoundly personal ways: one student, for instance, wrote a personal letter to Helga Crane, the protagonist of Nella Larsen's *Quicksand*. In the letter, the student detailed Helga's chronic ambivalence about her racial (un)belonging and her tragic acceptance of conventional gender roles. These student analyses are neither dry nor distant, largely because students make their own choices regarding the critical forms used to study and share their understanding of a text.[5]

The works by women authors assigned by many instructors contain more than women-centric ideas, characters, and stories; they often model the innovative styles and sharp-witted critical approaches we hope that students will embrace as lifelong readers. Shelley Jackson, for example, considers the relations among the sexed body, woman, and literary production in her hypertext *My Body—A Wunderkammer*. The reading of a text in Jackson's *Wunderkammer*—itself a collection of textual curiosities—becomes inseparable from the project of writing hypertext and woman anew. Blending literary criticism and literary creation, the narrator of Jackson's text meditates in bold, vivid language on the experience of interpreting James Joyce's *Ulysses* and declares, "my vagina had rewritten Joyce." Jackson reminds us that reading literature and writing criticism are intimate and often revisionist acts. While approaches to fostering critical engagement in the classroom may not always yield such provocative results, it is worth reconsidering how we ask students to engage with (post)-modernist and feminist literature that is often complex and distancing.

The Best Performative Criticism Is Still Rooted in Close Reading

Because of my belief that performative criticism is useful for literature courses, I have made it the focus of a capstone course on reading and writing the avant-garde. My upper-division course Modern Women Writers is open to non-English majors, so I include both conventional essay options and performative writing options for all formal papers (one essay in each of the first two units and one final essay). The course includes three thematic units that introduce students to the work of modern and contemporary writers whose literary or feminist interests include revision and innovation of literary form. Each unit introduces one main literary or theoretical topic that has shaped twentieth- and twenty-first-century women's writing: the techniques and challenges of self-representation, the continual definition and redefinition of woman within particular social and historical contexts, and the value of criticism (in reading and writing) for understanding and articulating intersecting feminisms. The course guides students through familiar genres (fairy tale, myth, autobiography, novel) and accessible stylistic modes (realism, naturalism) into less familiar formal experimentations regarded as typical of modernist and postmodernist literary texts (pastiche, fragmentation, self-reflexivity). In "Reading Woman," the first unit of the course, Donoghue's *Kissing the Witch*, Woolf's *Orlando*, and Stein's *Autobiography of Alice B. Toklas* help us explore the themes and politics of narrative order and revisionism. In "Performing Woman," the second unit of the course, Barnes's *Nightwood*, Larsen's *Quicksand* and *Passing*, Ntzoke Shange's *For Colored Girls*, and Dionne Brand's *No Language Is Neutral* focus our attention on writers' investments in representing subjectivity and desire in women's relationships. In the course's third unit, titled "Critiquing Woman," Jackson's hypertexts *Skin* and *Wunderkammer*, Hélène Cixous's "Laugh of the Medusa," Audre Lorde's "Uses of the Erotic," Kristjana Gunnars's *Rose Garden*, and Smith's *Artful* help us consider how criticism can function as an extension of (post)modernist formal experimentation. The readings in unit 3 serve as critical models, hybrid texts that blur the categories of genre and reveal how critical theory and literary criticism can arise out of the novel form—as in the case of Gunnars and Smith—or out of digital, autobiographical, and creative nonfiction—as in the work of Jackson.

These texts are challenging. The literature we classify as modern and postmodern can be "difficult," "rebarbative and foreboding," and "distancing," to borrow terms used by Charles Bernstein (3), Gail McDonald (18), and Madelyn Detloff (98), respectively.[6] Students are apt to disengage from these texts in a variety of ways, but most commonly, they take one of the following four approaches when contributing to class discussions and writing essays: they ask me to tell them what the reading means; focus on a single element of the story, which leads to a discussion of tangential social phenomena or philosophical abstractions; make broad, knowing statements that suggest that the student has consulted *Wikipedia* or *SparkNotes*; or launch a critique in which they reduce the text to a collection of words—claiming the text has no real meaning or value because the student does not get it.

Detloff reminds us, however, that our students are diverse not only in terms of major but also with respect to background and identity, all of which informs the vast distance between student-reader and modern literary text (98). My classroom at CSU, for instance, is very different (historically, geographically, and culturally) from Larsen's Harlem and Stein's Parisian salons, to say nothing of the transhistorical nature of Woolf's *Orlando*, which spans five centuries and, with them, British literature from Shakespeare to the present (i.e., 1928).[7] Intellectually, students may find it easier to turn away from close reading when faced with uncertainty about making or elaborating a critical connection or when they feel as if they have reached their limits as writers. To maintain student focus and endurance, I require that students read out from the text any claims about the passages they select as evidence. This distance-bridging exercise is the same regardless of whether a student selects the traditional or the performative essay option.

Before students write their formal essays, they complete five to ten close readings that engage with the denotative and connotative elements of a passage. These close reading assignments take place at regular intervals throughout the semester and allow me to provide quick, targeted feedback about how a student focuses on the text. In these assignments, students practice reading a passage closely and contextualizing its placement within and value to the overall piece. Rarely do I experience grading overload with these short, low-stakes assignments: the approximately twenty close readings students write over the course of the semester receive a grade of credit or no-credit, and the formal essays at the end of each of the three units are limited to three to four pages (first two units) and five to six pages (final essay at the end of the third unit).

Close reading can be as engaged and rigorous as it is intimate and personal. Such close readings are not summaries; nor are they general response papers. Rather, they are rich engagements with, and analyses of, a specific passage that students present to the class for discussion. I share Michael Gamer's user-friendly definition of close reading: "When we write literary criticism, we look for textual moments where a specific passage seems to explode with meaning—where the connotations are so unavoidable, so packed with suggestiveness, and so complicated they need to be read especially closely and slowly to understand what is being said (denoted) and what's suggested (connoted)." Such close textual work helps focus class discussions while modeling an attunement to the text students can draw on in their formal critical papers.

My experience has taught me that students develop critical reading skills and endurance quickly. Most of my class sessions open with students presenting a ten-minute close reading of a passage I select from the day's assigned reading. Students' close readings generally include the following: a short (one to three sentences) summary of the passage's context that identifies its placement relative to the narrative or poem as a whole and that includes relevant characters, events, settings, and so forth; key elements in the passage that the student recognizes as important to the text's meaning, techniques, tone, or affect; and connections to overarching themes, characterizations, affect, storylines, and the more general objectives of the text—or at least those connections that may be found within the assigned pages the student will have read to date. The logic of this in-class close reading assignment reproduces the expectations of any literary analysis in which students must ground their interpretations and arguments using evidence from the text. While such a process may be overt in conventionally composed criticism, it is often only implied in performative criticism.

One of the obvious risks of assessing student understanding and interpretation of modernist literature through an aligned creative-critical practice is that students may feel they have unfettered access to creative modes, which can derail a critical reading or obscure (rather than demonstrate) their learning and critical engagement with the literary text. This is not, however, necessarily or exclusively an issue with performative criticism, but rather a challenge inherent to all criticism. Students (and even some scholars) may find it tempting to shy away from or avoid textual interpretation or engagement. Close reading helps students maintain and develop an analytical connection to the text, an idea offered in Jane Gallop's endorsement of close reading. Gallop maintains that literary analysis is always rooted in close reading, and that this distinguishes literary studies from related fields such as cultural studies and history. In the end, close reading is what literary scholars do best.

Pedagogical Benefits of Performative Criticism

To be sure, performative criticism has a theoretical and critical legacy. Stephen Benson and Clare Connors identify a range of creative-critical modes from the past forty years: "post-criticism, deformative criticism, anarcho-scholasticism, ficto-criticism, visionary criticism, Other criticism, philosophic criticism" (2). Drawing on theatrical and literary techniques, Gerry Brenner's collection of fictocriticism "bends the genre by applying inventive rhetorical strategies to interpret individual literary works from the inside" (2). We can spot elements of this critical mode in the rise of reader-response criticism in the 1980s, which shares with performative criticism a personal and intimate engagement with the reader.

More often than not, essays are an attempt to try out or test an argument, an idea instantiated in the Old French *essai*, meaning "the action or process of trying or testing" ("Essay, n. 1"). This definition broadens the scope of the essay form to include modes of writing typically cordoned off as creative or imaginative: lyric, narrative, fictive interviews and letters, and the like assist students in their attempt to try or test an argument. Just as important as encouraging students to incorporate a range of literary techniques to sharpen their analyses is the need to explore new modes of literary criticism in our classrooms. If our goal is for undergraduates to learn, practice, and value literary criticism, we must show them that the persuasive styles and critical forms they employ when crafting their interpretations are inseparable from their ideas about the literary text. Transforming idea into analysis, word into essay, would be impossible without style and structure. Given the current nationwide decline in reading long-form texts (and a corresponding decline in English majors), we must reconsider the practice of criticism itself and the forms through which we ask our students to share in critics' attempts at interpreting a piece of literature. My experience shows that performative criticism is a valuable tool for digging into self-reflexive, women-oriented, genre- and gender-bending texts, and that it can also reinvigorate our teaching of self-reflexive literary greats from

Shakespeare's *Hamlet* to Salman Rushdie's *Midnight's Children* to Ali Smith's new Brexit-themed book series.

Much modernist and postmodernist feminist writing incorporates self-reflection in an attempt to focus on the language, representations, narratives, and historical contexts that give rise to binary understandings of gender and sexual difference, gendered norms, and narratives about woman. At the same time, such formal experimentation reenvisions the very idea of criticism, of narration, and of woman, and suggests that such texts may be best written about using equally exploratory and unconventional means. In course evaluations, students remarked that while the content of course was gendered feminine and the politics of many of the assigned readings were blatantly feminist, the course felt inviting and students felt encouraged to take risks when sharing their textual interpretations. Although I have not tested this theory, I suspect that training students to return to the text to make any claim about a literature that is often transgressive, self-reflexive, and challenging helps them feel more connected not only to the text—literally, to the words on the page—but also to the insights and interpretations shared by their peers in class discussions. A performative criticism rooted in close reading demonstrates the ways modernist literature can open up to include, rather than alienate, readers. Performative criticism allows students to engage more fully, purposefully, and pleasurably with difficult texts and produces an intellectually rewarding and affirmative course. How delightfully modernist!

Notes

1. This essay prompt mimics the opening of Benson and Connors's *Creative Criticism*.

2. See Bernstein's "Is Your Poem Being Difficult?"

3. Courses in which I have incorporated performative criticism include Women Authors (Michigan State University), Modern Women Writers (Colorado State University [CSU]), and a capstone course titled Reading and Writing the Avant-Garde (CSU). In Reading and Writing the Avant-Garde, performative criticism was the only option for the students' final capstone projects. Because Twentieth-Century Fiction and Survey of British Literature II: Romanticism-Contemporary (both taught at CSU) are lower-division courses comprised largely of non-English and non-liberal-arts majors, I offer the performative criticism option conditionally and require that students interested in this option meet with me beforehand to discuss their essay's argument, the passages from the text that they will use to support that argument, and the proposed style of the essay. This requirement helps students take this option more seriously than they might otherwise and prevents them from approaching creative criticism as an escape into creative writing. In

these lower-division courses, approximately 10 percent of students will choose the performative criticism option.

4. Most students still choose the traditional essay option. The 10–30 percent of students who write performative pieces, however, submit papers that tend to demonstrate higher levels of intellectual rigor and closer textual reading and that are consistently a pleasure to read. While I have not conducted a systematic study, I suspect students who select the performative criticism option produce higher quality analyses because those students opt into writing outside the conventional essay box. This kind of criticism is challenging—but the rewards offered in terms of reading and writing (for both teachers and students) are remarkable. In fact, a number of students have submitted their work for this assignment to our department's essay or scholarship competitions; some placed and one student took first prize.

5. I thank the students who have shared their creativity and rich interpretations in my Women Authors and Modern Women Writers courses over the years. Special thanks go to Colton Myhre, Tina Ramirez, and Trevor Wilson, who have allowed me to share their work in this essay.

6. On teaching modernist difficulty and helping students engage with difficult texts, see Milthorpe and Moore as well as Cucullu in this volume.

7. Madelyn Detloff has written with insight and care about how students may feel excluded when reading classics of modernism like *Mrs. Dalloway*. While Detloff uses a cultural studies approach to bridge this distance, I teach self-reflexivity and critical forms.

Works Cited

Barnes, Djuana. *Nightwood*. 1936. New Directions Publishing, 2006.

Benson, Stephen, and Clare Connors. *Creative Criticism: An Anthology and Guide*. Edinburgh UP, 2014.

Bernstein, Charles. "Is Your Poem Being Difficult?" *Attack of the Difficult Poems: Essays and Interventions*, U of Chicago P, 2011, pp. 3–6.

Brand, Dionne. *No Language Is Neutral*. McClellend and Stewart, 2007.

Brenner, Gerry. *Performative Criticism: Experiments in Reader Response*. State U of New York P, 2004.

Carson, Anne. *Autobiography of Red: A Novel in Verse*. 1999. McClellend and Stewart, 2016.

Cixous, Hélène. "The Laugh of the Medusa." *Signs: Journal of Women in Culture and Society*, vol. 1, no. 4, 1976, pp. 875–93.

Detloff, Madelyn. "*Mrs. Dalloway* and the Ideology of Death: A Cultural Studies Approach." *Approaches to Teaching Woolf's* Mrs. Dalloway, edited by Eileen Barrett and Ruth O. Saxton, Modern Language Association, 2009, pp. 97–101.

Donoghue, Emma. *Kissing the Witch*. Picador, 2013.

"Essay, n. 1." *Oxford English Dictionary*, Oxford UP, 2020, oed.com/view/Entry/64470?rskey=lYXeri&result=1#eid.

Gallop, Jane. "The Historicization of Literary Studies and the Fate of Close Reading." *Profession*, 2007, pp. 181–86.

Gamer, Michael. Syllabus for ENG050. Department of English, U of Pennsylvania, Spring 2014. *Course Hero*, www.coursehero.com/file/7858953/Assignment-Close-Reading-Exercise/. Accessed 20 June 2019.

Gunnars, Kristjana. *The Rose Garden: Reading Marcel Proust.* Red Deer College Press, 1997.

Haraway, Donna. "A Cyborg Manifesto: Science, Technology, and Socialist-Feminism in the Late Twentieth Century." 1985. *The International Handbook of Virtual Learning Environments*, edited by J. Weiss et al., Springer, 2006, pp. 117–58.

Jackson, Shelley. *My Body—A Wunderkammer. Electronic Literature Collection*, 1997, collection.eliterature.org/1/works/jackson__my_body_a_wunderkammer.html. Accessed 30 June 2019.

———. *Skin. YouTube*, uploaded by BAMPFA, 7 Mar. 2011, www.youtube.com/watch?time_continue=19&v=viF-xuLrGvA&feature=emb_logo.

Larsen, Nella. Quicksand *and* Passing. 1928, 1929. Edited by Deborah E. McDowell, Rutgers UP, 1986.

Lorde, Audre. "Uses of the Erotic: The Erotic as Power." *Sister Outsider: Essays and Speeches*, by Lorde, Crossing Press, 2007, pp. 41–48.

McDonald, Gail. "Hypertext and the Teaching of Modernist Difficulty." *Pedagogy: Critical Approaches to Teaching Literature, Language, Composition, and Culture*, vol. 2, no. 1, 2002, pp. 17–30.

Shange, Ntzoke. *For Colored Girls Who Have Considered Suicide When the Rainbow Is Enuf.* 1976. Scribner, 1997.

Smith, Ali. *Artful.* Penguin Books, 2014.

Stein, Getrude. *The Autobiography of Alice B. Toklas.* 1933. Vintage Books, 1990.

———. *A Stein Reader.* Edited by Ulla E. Dydo, Northwestern UP, 1993.

Woolf, Virginia. *Orlando.* 1928. Mariner, 1973.

Part III

Genres

Robert Reginio

Questioning Modernist Poetry: Feminist Poetics in the Classroom

Students reading modernist poetry need a graspable context for navigating reading experiences that require a concomitant theorization of language. One might think this difficulty is compounded when one brings feminist literary theory to bear on the reading process—that is, when students interrogate the historical contexts of poems and ask questions about the cultural process of textual transmission. Rather than necessitating two courses—one on theory and one on modernist poetry—this situation is a propitious one for the instructor of modernist women's poetry.

In this essay I argue that Susan Howe's work of literary criticism and poetics *My Emily Dickinson* offers a context for and theorization of experimental poetry. Since Howe and other women writers associated with the Language poetry movement of the 1970s and 80s revised the canon of modernist poetry (e.g., by making the Gertrude Stein of *Tender Buttons* central to their version of modernism), I believe it is sounder to refer to these poets as experimental poets. The term *experimental* fits the way that canonical refashioning (reading against the grain) and innovative poetic practice come together in this version of modernist women's writing.

In what follows I offer an outline of an assignment that allows students to open lines of inquiry in place of producing semantic closure. Such inquiry offers students the opportunity to produce written work that remains true to the deconstruction of lyric subjectivity crucial to such high modernist poets as H.D., Marianne Moore, and Stein, as well as to their experimental followers. This essay draws on my experience teaching an upper-level undergraduate seminar titled Modernist Women Writers; while the first half of the course focuses on high modernist women writers, the second half of the semester centers on books by living poets—*Next Life*, by Rae Armantrout; *Sleeping with the Dictionary*, by Harryette Mullen; *Zong!*, by M. NourbeSe Philip; *Dura*, by Myung Mi Kim; and *Souls of the Labadie Tract*, by Howe.[1] Throughout the course students come to discover how these writers are part of a larger project that explores the possibilities of poetry to interrogate gendered language. Reading these poets leads to crucial questions: are experimental, nonreferential strategies an effective way of subverting patriarchal power structures, or do such strategies fail to consider the historical? When a singular subjectivity needs to be voiced, how can poetry still testify to historical occlusions?

I believe that one should begin with the formal strategies of these poets when considering the intersections of gender and experimentation in poetry. As Harriet Tarlo has argued, "It is too confining to the poets and their work to emphasize feminine or feminist subject matter above all else, in particular above formal experimentation" (63–64). In the end, careful attention to formal strategies is what enables a process of contextualization whereby feminist subject matter becomes the topic of conversation in the classroom.

Throughout the semester, I require students to complete formal written analyses that conclude with students' ideas about the types of questions posed by these poems. These assignments provide an opportunity for students to engage in traditional close reading within the historical context of experimental women's writing. The pedagogical imperative underlying these assignments is to engage with the notion of "poetics." From the perspective of experimental writing, poetics indicates a speculative writing on the nature of (poetic) language itself. Poetics, so understood, encompasses everything from the discursive segments of William Carlos Williams's *Spring and All* and Mina Loy's "Feminist Manifesto" to latter-day incarnations including the various prefaces and prose segments that appear in Howe's collections. Students consider the ramifications of such formal experimentation not just when reading these extrapoetic texts. This theoretical inquiry is at its most powerful when students write their own metatextual commentary on their reading experiences. As Elisabeth Frost writes, "The category of 'women's poetry' in America, for an emphasis on personal voice—and the relatively transparent language that often accompanies it—supports an unspoken assumption that linguistic experimentation has little relevance to feminist writing" (xix). This assumption belies how writing about linguistic experimentation allows students to engage with the major themes of much feminist writing.

Beginning with *My Emily Dickinson*

Understanding how experimental poetics intersects with feminist concerns is the driving force behind my course. The course is intended to help students read often challenging experimental poetry, and it asks students to develop a particularly feminist vocabulary to talk about the connections among the poets on the syllabus. This is accomplished in theory and in practice. Theoretically, the poets we read in the course are concerned with the archive—the archive as a collection of traces, as well as language as an archival medium, one that underpins and denies self-expression (language, always, is determined by a history that precedes our own narratives of self). We therefore examine these poets as working to reveal the historically formed nature of their medium, while mapping out terrain for the shaping of a distinctly gendered language. In this regard, Howe's engagement with the pathbreaking work of Emily Dickinson serves as a touchstone. It is imperative to acquaint students with Dickinson's poetics before moving on to Howe's text. I focus on the poems of fascicle 34; this short collection contains poems such as "My Life had Stood - a Loaded Gun" (a poem Howe subjects to innovative exegesis in *My Emily Dickinson*) and "Essential Oils - are wrung," both of which decidedly serve as statements of poetics. A consideration of these poems as part of a sequence allows for recursive traversals of the sequence and for an introduction to the way experimental poetry uses fragmentation and nonclosure to elucidate themes that are tightly woven into its form.[2]

In the opening of *My Emily Dickinson*, Howe offers this invigorating fusillade: "In the college library I use there are two writers whose work refuses to conform to the Anglo-American literary traditions these institutions perpetuate. Emily Dickinson and Gertrude Stein are clearly among the most innovative precursors of modernist poetry and prose" (11).[3] It is important and helpful to recognize that Howe is positioning herself in this rhetorical gesture as a woman reader. The subversive nature of Stein's and Dickinson's works has an unmistakably gendered hue. This feeling of reading at the margins helps contextualize the more complex parts of Howe's text, such as her proclivity to juxtapose elements from the Dickinson archive and her own poetic pronouncements. Howe keeps sight of the way Dickinson's poetry was domesticated by various editors, a history of occlusion and elision Howe doesn't want to transcend, but rather a history with which she wants to engage dialectically.

Howe proclaims that in "prose and poetry [Dickinson] explored the implications of breaking the law just short of breaking communication with a reader" (11). Howe rejects the notion of an exchange between reader and writer determined by the passivity of the reader in the face of the monovocal text. When Howe insists that "gender difference does affect our use of language," she is quick to qualify this by arguing, "[t]hat doesn't mean I can relegate women to what we 'should' or 'must' be doing. Orders suggest hierarchy and category. Categories and hierarchies suggest property. My voice formed from my life belongs to no one else. What I put into words is no longer my possession. Possibility is opened" (13). In much the same way as Dickinson "break[s] the law," Howe cites a relinquishing of "possession" similar to Stein's radical realignment of the reader's and writer's respective positions vis-à-vis a text. As I insist to my students, when we read a text like *Tender Buttons* for the promiscuous play of meaning-making in Stein, we are engaging with language along with Stein, meaning that her authority is relinquished in favor of a linguistic multiplicity. As Howe writes, Stein "clearly broke the [patriarchal, heteronormative] codes that negated her" (12). A perennial concern of experimental writing—how to break the stultifying codes of language and, at the same time, how to write with the fragmentary remains of language—emerges in the opening sections of Howe's book, which considers the constraints gender places on Dickinson the writer and Howe the reader. As such, *My Emily Dickinson* is exemplary for use in the classroom as a means of tracing innovative subversion as a style back to precursors like Dickinson, and as an ongoing experiment in the work of poets like Howe and her contemporaries.

As readers of Dickinson are continually made aware, a lexical mark in her poetry serves as a site of undecidable possibilities. Howe theorizes that Dickinson's poetics of the "stutter," Dickinson's resistance to semantic coherence and closure through her use of dashes and unexpected enjambment, is rooted in Dickinson's history as a writer who was "eternally on intellectual borders, where confident masculine voices buzzed an alluring and inaccessible discourse" (21). For Miriam Nichols, Howe's theorization of "the stutter" in *My Emily Dickinson* is a "way in which [Howe] indexes alterity" (224). Nichols further asserts that, in relation to a gap-filled history, the experimental woman poet who works with the fragmentary "welcomes the dead into the realm of the living because she accepts (as her poetry performs) the derivative nature of the singular" (268). Frost concludes that the experimental genealogy conceived of by Howe links avant-gardism to the lineage of "women's spiritual and political dissents," and that Howe's poetics "represent a textual form of antinomian resistance" (107). For Howe to recover Dickinson as a poet of "antinomian," avant-garde "resistance" suggests a dual gesture, one of mending (of recovery) and of breaking (of resistance). By way of such productive antinomies, Howe makes the argument that innovative poetry must formally "stutter" or, as she insists, "HESITATE" (21). Howe constructs a genealogy of American experimental poets with Dickinson authorizing a paratactical style over that which buttresses a cohesive subject. Howe's reimagining of the historical site of Dickinson's writing offers students a way to make connections between, say, the hesitation of Marianne Moore's poetry (exemplified by her patient, and often frustrating, accrual of dependent clauses in "Marriage") and the hesitant line endings of H.D. that break potential strands of syntactical meaning in a manner reminiscent of Dickinson.

Howe insists that the radical redefinition of the roles of reader and writer proved an obstacle for Dickinson's "stuttering," or hesitant, poetics to enter into, and potentially disrupt, mainstream literary discourse: Dickinson's "re-ordering of the forward process of reading is what makes her poetry and the prose of her letters among the most original writing of her century" (51). In her exploration of "My Life had Stood - a Loaded Gun," Howe postulates that "[i]n a shorter space (woman's quick voice) Dickinson went . . . coding and erasing—deciphering the idea of herself, dissimulation in revelation" (76). Howe argues, "A poem is an invocation, rebellious return to the blessedness of beginning again, wandering free in pure process of forgetting and finding" (98). Using such language to define Dickinson's writing—which conjures images of shock and subtraction, "finding" and "forgetting"—points to the double nature of the lexical mark as both an archivable, denotative mark and an acoustical echo that allows for a recognition of the figurative. The difficult concept for students to grasp, but which these passages reveal—when singled out by an instructor and carefully considered—is that every mark or trace is an attempt to speak the (feminine) self in a language not its own.

H.D.'s "Fragment 113" and the Questions of Modernist Poetry

As Howe's theorization of the "stutter" implies, the reclamation project of feminist literary criticism and the poetic strategies of experimental poets arguably center on the fragment. The assignment outlined in this section encourages students to discover ways of incorporating the formal self-consciousness of these fragmentary poems into their own analytical writing and extratextual reflections.

Certain women poets—H.D., for instance—serve as examples of poets who embody modernist strategies of collage to emphasize that the fragment (not only a testament to loss but also a trace that has been preserved) is one of the key products of modernity. Rita Felski insists that "[w]omen's experience cannot be seen as a pre-given ontology that precedes its expression, but fractures into a number of often contradictory, albeit connected, strands. . . . Gender is continually in process" (201). The potential for students to see the experiments of Stein or H.D. carried through to women poets of the present emphasizes the power of high modernist poetry to interrogate the still regnant discourses of fixed gender identity. Rachel Blau DuPlessis, a modern-day experimental poet and influential critic, argues that the formal daringness of high modernist women's poetry opposes the utopian claims of male modernist poets to cleanse or purify language and that such opposition should occupy a central place in feminist-experimental poetics. In DuPlessis's words, "let the connotations and the discourses—the appropriate, the inappropriate, the intelligent, the silly—swirl, coagulate" (*Pink Guitar* 53).

Such poetic strategies present challenges when it comes to analyzing the poems that constitute this tradition. And yet assignments that allow for analyses that resist semantic closure, analyses offering a feminist critique of dominant modes of poetic form, can give students the space to craft their own articulations of poetic theory. In so doing, students take part in a conversation actualized by a course that combines high modernist and current experimental poets.

In their papers, students use analytical writing to uncover larger questions a poem is asking of its readers, but in a way that denies a certain kind of closure, making the assignment well-suited to experimental poetry. These papers begin with a short paragraph that identifies one of the poem's main themes. The paragraphs that follow consist of textual analysis that explores that theme. The paper concludes with some of the questions students think the text might be asking. In order to flesh out this assignment, I model how one might write such a paper on H.D.'s poem "Fragment 113."

The recovery of a poet like Sappho and the attention required to read an imagist poem such as H.D.'s "Fragment 113" can be understood as feminist revisions of a male-dominated canon. As I describe it in class, H.D. sought to eliminate ornament from poetry, recollect the fragments of Sappho, and write verse that subverted the expectations of the reader of lyric poetry: these include a clear narrative voice, poetic ornament, heightened emotion, and a clearly articulated transcendence of the enmeshment of the self in language. To read without a fulfillment of these expectations is what it means to read experimental women's poetry.

For this challenging reading experience, we turn to H.D.'s "Fragment 113." We discuss its epigram—the fragment from Sappho, "Neither honey nor bee for me"—which tantalizingly sets up the speaker's resolution in an ambivalent rejection: we can guess that a rejection of honey would mean a rejection of sensuality, but to reject the bee, and its connotations of industriousness, leaves us uncertain as to where the speaker stands. The epigram speaks to a state of being that partakes neither of the bounty of the senses nor of the oblivion of pure industry. This kind of ambivalence—to sit as it were between passivity and activity—is the perfect opening for a poem that proceeds by rejection. It is this ambivalence (the speaker's indecisive relation to the past) that functions as a guiding theme of the poem. "Not honey," H.D.'s poem begins, "not the plunder of the bee,"

> not honey, not the deep
> plunge of soft belly
> and the clinging of the gold-edged
> pollen-dusted feet. (131)

Encouraging attention to the title of the poem could suggest to the class that H.D. brings us into a world of textually mediated poetic experimentation. The image of the pollen-covered bee enwrapped in the folds of a flower could be seen as a trope for the poetry of a self-satisfied, satiated age: the "pollen dusted [poetic] feet" of someone such as Algernon Charles Swinburne, for instance, are rejected. The poem also proceeds by negation. The opening stanza gives us no place on which to stand, but leaves us in anticipation (in hesitation, as Howe would put it) of a determinate statement in response to the rejections that constitute the poem. Only in the poem's fourth and final stanza do we receive the speaker's determinate acceptance of "heat, more passionate / of bone and the white shell /

and fiery tempered steel" (132). The poem enacts a full-scale rejection of the feminine as constituted by a passive sensuality and instead accepts a kind of poetic vision that incises and takes as its subject those objects—"bone" and "white shell"—that have been tempered by the processes of time. It is a poetry that seeks to fix its vision on historical traces (those things recovered from the fire of time). Such a process of recovery could be employed in an experimental poetry alive to the gaps and absences of a gendered canon. A crucial turning point in "Fragment 113" comes at the beginning of its fourth and final stanza:

> not iris—old desire—old passion—
> old forgetfulness—old pain—
> not this, nor any flower,
> but if you turn again,
> seek strength of arm and throat,
> touch as the god;
> neglect the lyre-note. (131–32)

The "forgetfulness," which this poetry is set against, signifies conventional modes of poetic writing in which symbolism "forgets" perceptual reality and the historical forces that produced certain symbolic resonances as natural (woman as flower, for example). "[I]f you turn again," however—if one "tropes" again—it should be a troping or a turning used sparingly, and which is deliberately neglectful of the melodic suffusion of iambic meter that ornaments words with an inessential music. "Figuration," explains Ann Keniston, "does not signal the equivalence between things and ideas, nor does it align the past with the present. Instead it marks the difficulty in understanding a fixed underlying reality," and in experimental poetry, it actually "interrogate[s] equivalence" (153). This focus on formal breakdown and reinvention within the context of a historically minded recuperation of a woman writer makes "Fragment 113" a great starting point from which to begin the class's investigation of an archival feminist poetics within an experimental tradition.

However, it is imperative to note that this interpretation is but one way of engaging with H.D.'s poem. An instructor should also consider the poem's exploration of sexuality, alive as the poem is to representations of the body that defy gendered expectations—in other words, the passive imagery of the scene, suffused with traditional symbols of femininity, is contrasted with a "strength of arm and throat," a line enjoining a reclamation of the body alive to its unadorned potential to evade traditional representations of a heteronormative sexuality.

As a means of concluding the paper based on the interpretation offered above, a writer might ask: is the imperatively voiced "neglect" of H.D.'s poem part of a lament for an occluded past?[4] Or can an act of recovery be refigured as a gesture of radical break and renewal? Is the very occlusion of traces of Sappho in the archival record—a metonym of women's voices—that which lends the fragment its unquestioned power? Is there a way of writing poetry that can attest to these occlusions while forging a recovery of the past that interrogates the language used to stage such projects?

The conclusion of the paper consists of a series of open-ended questions that reflect on the analysis that precedes it. Students are asked to take seriously the implications embedded in the analysis they have produced. The conclusion is where the student practices writing speculatively on poetics.[5] Students are initially apprehensive about thesis-less, exploratory writing, but in my experience they begin to enjoy writing about poetry as a way of uncovering a poem's essential questions. This is especially pertinent for experimental poetry: poems concerned with poetic form as much as with content.

Notes

1. A fuller list of resources is available on the companion website for this volume (modwomen.mla.hcommons.org).

2. To see which poems were ordered into specific sequences and bound into fascicles by Dickinson, see the appendix to *The Poems of Emily Dickinson*, edited by R. W. Franklin.

3. Here and throughout, all citations from Howe are from *My Emily Dickinson*.

4. This line of questioning chimes with the ways students typically understand modernist poetry. T. S. Eliot's *The Waste Land*, a canonical example of modernist poetry, is often interpreted as a lament for and a tentative recovery of the fragments of high culture left in the wake of the First World War. H.D.'s poems are much more ambivalent about restoring certain orders of meaning that have been fractured.

5. I have found the poet Jena Osman's exploration of the legacy of Language poetry, in which she discusses her disillusionment with the traditional lyric, a useful text for introducing students to writing on poetics. Other useful statements of poetics include Myung Mi Kim's "Anacrusis," Howe's "Personal Narrative," M. NourbeSe Philip's "Notanda," and Rachel Blau DuPlessis's "For the Etruscans."

Lynn Keller's interviews with Rae Armantrout, Howe, and Kim are also extremely useful in this context.

Works Cited

Armantrout, Rae. *Next Life*. Wesleyan UP, 2007.

Dickinson, Emily. *The Complete Poems of Emily Dickinson*. Edited by Thomas H. Johnson, Little, Brown, 1960.

———. "Essential Oils - are wrung." Dickinson, *Complete Poems*, p. 335.

———. "My Life had Stood - a Loaded Gun." Dickinson, *Complete Poems*, p. 369.

———. *The Poems of Emily Dickinson: Variorum Edition*. Edited by R. W. Franklin, Belknap Press, 1998.

DuPlessis, Rachel Blau. "For the Etruscans." DuPlessis, *Pink Guitar*, pp. 1–19.

———. *The Pink Guitar: Writing as Feminist Practice*. U of Alabama P, 2006.

Felski, Rita. "Modernism and Modernity: Engendering Literary History." *Rereading Modernism: New Directions in Feminist Criticism*, edited by Lisa Rado, Routledge, 2012, pp. 191–208.

Frost, Elisabeth. *The Feminist Avant-Garde in American Poetry*. U of Iowa P, 2003.

H.D. "Fragment 113." 1921. *Collected Poems, 1912–1944*, edited by Louis L. Martz, New Directions Publishing, 1983, pp. 131–32.

Howe, Susan. *My Emily Dickinson*. New Directions Publishing, 2007.

———. "Personal Narrative." Howe, *Souls*, pp. 12–19.

———. *Souls of the Labadie Tract*. New Directions Publishing, 2007.

Keller, Lynn. "An Interview with Myung Mi Kim." *Contemporary Literature*, vol. 49, no. 3, 2008, pp. 335–56.

———. "An Interview with Rae Armantrout." *Contemporary Literature*, vol. 50, no. 2, 2009, pp. 219–39.

———. "An Interview with Susan Howe." *Contemporary Literature*, vol. 36, no. 1, 1995, pp. 1–34.

Keniston, Ann. *Ghostly Figures: Memory and Belatedness in Postwar American Poetry*. U of Iowa P, 2015.

Kim, Myung Mi. "Anacrusis." *How2*, vol. 1, no. 2, 1999, www.asu.edu/pipercwcenter/how2journal/archive/online_archive/v1_2_1999/current/readings/kim.html.

———. *Dura*. Nightboat Books, 2008.

Mullen, Harryette. *Sleeping with the Dictionary*. U of California P, 2002.

Nichols, Miriam. *Radical Affections: Essays on the Poetics of the Outside*. U of Alabama P, 2010.

Osman, Jena. "After Language Poetry." *UbuWeb*, 2001, www.ubu.com/papers/oei/osman.html.

Philip, M. NourbeSe. "Notanda." Philip, *Zong!*, pp. 189–207.

———. *Zong!* Wesleyan UP, 2008.

Tarlo, Harriet. "'The New Comes Forward': Anglo-American Modernist Women Poets." *Teaching Modernist Poetry*, edited by Nicky Marsh and Peter Middleton, Palgrave Macmillan, 2010, pp. 58–76.

Sarah E. Cornish

Playing Stupid: Self-Taught Women and the Modern Diary-Novel

My institution is a state teaching university that draws a large number of first-generation college students who want to become educators; thus, teaching texts written by women offers an opportunity to put feminist teaching into practice and to model that approach for future educators. Urmila Seshagiri points out that "the process of canon-formation—and deformation, and reformation—constitutes the simplest and yet the most complex act in feminist scholarship about modernism. We can only speak about what we have read." The same is true for feminist teaching. By giving students access to texts written by women, my goal is to give future teachers diverse texts to speak about with their own students. I explain to students that it is my responsibility as a feminist scholar and teacher to ensure a future for feminism by highlighting social justice and equality advocacy, and I do this by exposing students to women writers whose skill and inventiveness create space for underrepresented voices within literary and cultural studies. Those of us who are feminist teachers confront and negotiate the traditional structures of our institutions, structures that are sometimes embedded in the curricula we are asked to teach and the authors we are expected to include on our syllabi. Our students will be more willing to negotiate, resist, refuse, and even alter such structures once they are aware of how their reading tastes are shaped by traditional canonical decisions.

To that end, this essay suggests how the diary-novel—a subgenre of the first-person, homodiegetic, fictional narrative—can be taught in a way that introduces students to the form's feminist possibilities. Instructors may choose to teach several diary-novels together as part of a unit in a course on women writers, or in combination with other texts and contexts in a more general course on modernism. The diary-novel's chief narrative qualities create an impression of the diarist recording her uncensored thoughts about time and place as they occur. Such thoughts include associative flashbacks inspired by the sensory experiences of the diarist in the narrative present—these disjointed, and sometimes contradictory, mental pathways disclose the decision-making processes of the diarist as they unfold and produce an artifice of immediacy that students initially read as confused, uneducated, unreliable, and even stupid. Yet diary-novels featuring a woman narrator have the potential to reveal decisions made by these women that lead to their unconventional, nontraditional educations within the sociopolitical contexts of the interwar period. As students uncover and define the characteristics of the genre based on the texts we read, they also discover contexts that enrich their discourse on modern women in the interwar city: topics such as work, class, education, entertainment, fashion, finances, and consumer culture become especially important. We examine the publication histories of the texts we read, which includes learning about the fashion and culture magazines in which some were first published. Students also consider the likely readership of a work and explore scholarly debates about categories of popular writing, including the middlebrow.[1]

Anita Loos's *Gentlemen Prefer Blondes*; Irmgard Keun's *The Artificial Silk Girl*, which was directly inspired by Loos's novel; and Stevie Smith's *Novel on Yellow Paper* serve as my pedagogical examples for this essay, though they are not prescriptive. These are funny, witty, brainy, biting feminist novels that, through diverse approaches to the diary form, convey urban women's experiences of modernity via the first-person voices of the fictional diarists Lorelei Lee, Doris, and Pompey Casmilus, respectively. All three women must learn to negotiate urban space, teaching themselves how to be modern, progressive women in the public sphere while negotiating traditional patriarchal structures and recording their impressions of these in their notebooks in what results in temporal immediacy. The nationality of each author—American, German, and British—plays a part in the process of contextualization.[2] Despite national differences, however,

Loos, Keun, and Smith all write women characters who provide much-needed voices about issues ranging from education to living and working in an interwar city (New York, Berlin, London and its suburbs).[3]

None of these diary-novels feature episodes of traditional schooling or characters with conventional educational backgrounds. I present my students with the idea that these diarists are autodidacts, a label that invites inquiry into the practices and accessibility of learning, what constitutes education, and how different types of education can produce multiple and gendered forms of literacies. As Loos's Lorelei Lee says, "I seem to be thinking practically all of the time. I mean it is my favorite recreation and sometimes I sit for hours and do not seem to do anything else but think. So this gentleman said a girl with brains ought to do something else with them besides think" (*Gentlemen* 11). Lorelei and the other autodidact diarists under discussion here provide a means for students to interrogate gendered expectations surrounding teaching, learning, and the structures that shape what and how we know. These interwar women characters who strike out alone and make a modernity of their own captivate my students, who must often push against cultural or familial expectations to be in college themselves. Because many of my students are training to be teachers, discussions about nontraditional types of education become philosophically valuable as students develop their own approaches for their future students.

A Place-Based Unit on the Diary-Novel and Weimar Berlin

In a lower-division, introductory course I teach for new English majors, students often need ways to make connections between what they read and their own experiences, especially as many of them have just moved to a new town. Doris, the protagonist of Keun's novel, moves to Berlin from her "mid-size town" to seek new opportunities (1), just like my students have done by coming to college. During the first week of class, I have students respond in writing to the following prompt, which serves as a diagnostic essay: "Write about a place, real or imaginary, that has value to you. Describe it in detail. Include directions to this place. How has this place contributed to your identity? What values do you hold that might connect to this place?" Most students write about a place in their hometowns—a local diner, a park, a skating rink, their own bedrooms. Some will describe a world they're developing in a story. After students have completed the assignment, I ask them to share their narratives with one another. Paying particular attention to the second part of the prompt, I ask them to reflect on how coming to this new place, the university, is contributing to or challenging their sense of identity and their values. This exercise builds a community within the classroom early on; it also helps students anticipate how the places in the assigned texts impact the characters' identities, values, and search for knowledge, as well as how these are expressed through the form and style of each text, especially Keun's diary-novel.

My place-based approach for a unit featuring Keun's *The Artificial Silk Girl* and the culture of Weimar Berlin begins with an in-class discussion about the connotations of the word *diary*. I first ask students to define the term, an exercise that nearly always reveals highly gendered assumptions about the writer and the content. Students maintain that a diary is meant to be private, that it often includes unimportant details about the writer's day and thoughts, that it is usually slapdash and grammatically unsound, and that only girls write them. I then ask them to discuss the word *journal*. Students often suggest that a journal contains important details that can later be culled for scholarly work. Journals, they assert, are written by famous people as a means of documenting history. If students have read any published journals, they are nearly always composed by men.[4]

Because students attribute diary-writing to women and see it as less important than other forms of writing, I often pair Keun with the first section of Christopher Isherwood's *Goodbye to Berlin* (1935), "A Berlin Diary," as a means of comparing representations of place and women's educational experiences. A consideration of prose style highlights the differences in agency between a woman's story (that of Sally Bowles in "A Berlin Diary") as told by a male narrator (Christopher) and a woman's own story as told by the woman herself (Keun's protagonist, Doris). Students initially claim that Doris and Bowles are a natural pair for comparison, but I also introduce Christopher's German women friends, Natalia Landauer, Hippi Bernstein, and Sally, to encourage a more dynamic conversation about the ways Christopher's diary documents each woman's processes of self-fashioning, seeking learning opportunities, communicating decision-making, and navigating the urban environment. In order to promote such a conversation, I split the class into groups and have each group peruse the text for descriptions of each character (Sally, Natalia, and Hippi). Students then consider how Isherwood's women characters relate to Christopher, the narrator, and what attitudes these characters and their experiences—as filtered through Christopher's narrative voice—reveal about the expectations for women in Weimar Berlin. The groups share their findings and we compare these reflections to our interpretations of

Doris's character. One objective of teaching Keun alongside Isherwood is for students to compare Christopher's British-educated narrative voice with the uneducated voice Keun crafts for Doris. Peppered with idioms particular to Berlin, fragmented images, and disarming temporal shifts, Keun's novel is not easy. I ask students to listen to the tone of Doris's words rather than try to discern a clear narrative structure (the same is true for Loos's and Smith's diary-novels). I then ask students to write, either in class or on our online discussion board, a paragraph in which they emulate Doris's writing style. For students, this is a fun, low-stakes activity. At the same time, however, it opens up a conversation about style that leads students to understand the significance of Doris being an autodidact and writing the way she does. I elaborate on generic qualities and narrative theory in a later section in upper-division and graduate courses.

Doris offers a steady flow of observations about her exterior world coupled with her internal feelings and desire to learn about and document everything she sees. Many sentences begin with "And," so the reader experiences impressions abruptly, the way that Doris recalls them as she records them. The overwhelming artifice of immediacy is a stylistic feature of the diary-novel, but it often leads to students' contention that Doris is stupid, especially when she dismisses important things, like finding a safe place to sleep, for creature comforts, like hazelnut torte (63) and dwelling on a stolen fur coat (which incidentally serves as a powerful symbol of class and status throughout the text). However, by working into our discussions the cultural contexts of Weimar Berlin's political situation as the Nazi party began to gain traction, students attach significance to the moments when Doris is searching for knowledge. While I provide context (see Ward; Nicholls; Gay) and include visual material from the 1930s like photographs of women in public spaces, advertisements, expressionist paintings, and archival footage of Berlin, students take responsibility for uncovering additional contexts in breakout research groups. Students use their personal electronic devices to search for contexts in answer to what I refer to as a discovery question. Following are some examples of discovery questions:

What was the status of women's educational opportunity in Weimar Berlin between 1918 and 1933? What changed when Hitler rose to power in 1933?

What sorts of pastimes were popular in the Weimar Republic? [Cinema-going is crucial here as Doris is obsessed with movie stars. Magazine reading and clothes shopping also provide good contexts for understanding Doris's tastes and processes of self-fashioning.]

Doris finds herself swept into a political rally on arriving in Berlin for the first time. What political tensions exist during the early 1930s that might contribute to an understanding of Doris's experiences?

What employment opportunities might a woman in Weimar Berlin have had? [This helps students unpack the depiction of office-girls and prostitutes in the novel and leads to a deeper conversation about money, femininity as commodity, and financial independence.]

Unearthing these types of contexts often helps students understand why Doris can't just get a job, why she is dependent on men to take care of her, and why she is reliant on them for her own self-validation. For me, contexts undergird feminist teaching by illuminating existing social and political structures that contribute to the questions and concerns expressed by the characters. For example, with contextual support, students will be able to interpret the line "I so want to give him my notebook—I want to be a real person—he should read my book . . . I'm Doris—Doris isn't just some piece of dirt" (Keun 153), which suggests that Doris's writing gives her agency, documents her acquisition of unconventional knowledge, and validates her desire to fight limitations placed on her by the cultural conditions in which she finds herself.

Contextual exploration can teach students how to read and annotate scholarly work. Students read Katharina von Ankum's essay "Gendered Urban Spaces," which I use to train them on how to read a scholarly essay. This painstaking work can be done in one or two class periods and serves as a foundation for those students whom I later reencounter in advanced courses. I ask students to contribute additional annotated sources to a shared Google Doc (a wiki page in your learning management system will work, too); I can then suggest additions, edits, and deletions, and ask students to draw from this list for research sources to include in the writing of their essays. Within a longer unit, I include a screening of *The Blue Angel* (1930), Josef von Sternberg's film about a cabaret performer (played by Marlene Dietrich) who can't settle into traditional patriarchal expectations of womanhood. At the end of the unit, students write a comparative essay in which they analyze how cultural contexts inform their reading of the primary texts discussed throughout the unit. Students must include one scholarly essay as well as three of the contextual pieces of information we've amassed as a class. Most students will find additional sources and craft a rich tapestry of evidence to support their textual analysis.

Using the Diary-Novel in Upper-Division or Graduate Courses

In the introduction to her translation of Keun's novel, Ankum explains that in an attempt to address the lack of female representation in German literature by women writers, Keun "set out to write the German answer to" Loos's story of Lorelei Lee (Keun xvi). For this reason, Loos's *Gentlemen Prefer Blondes* and Keun's *The Artificial Silk Girl* seem like a natural pairing. When teaching these two texts in parallel, an instructor might choose to eliminate the focus on Weimar Berlin and focus instead on the style of the two texts as well as their representations of women's self-fashioning, commodity culture, and the search for both educational and financial independence. Like Doris's speech, Lorelei's is replete with lowbrow slang embedded in modernist experimental sentence construction (see Hammill). There are many instances of phonetic spelling in Loos's diary-novel that are humorous to the seasoned reader. Students, however, often believe these moments are the result of printing errors, or that, like Doris, Lorelei is stupid.

I teach Loos's novel in an upper-division senior seminar on women writers. The course employs intermodernism (see Bluemel) as theoretical terrain and the middlebrow as an aesthetic category that reveals women's experiences through fictional representation and through a study of the production history, popularity, and adaptations of the selected authors and their works. While my course is intentional in its selection of a set of texts authored by women that I define as intermodernist and middlebrow and that are underread and understudied, one could include Loos in courses on American modernism, transatlantic modernism, and film history (see Fedirka in this volume).

In this course I also teach Smith's *Novel on Yellow Paper*. This is by far the most challenging text for students because Smith's prose is so fragmentary, experimental, and packed with allusions, references to real or invented historical events, and contradictory statements that continually impel readers to call into question Pompey's trustworthiness, intelligence, and reliability. Smith's poetry appears in many British literature anthologies and may be taught in survey, poetry, and modernism courses, but students will likely not be familiar with her *Novel on Yellow Paper*, a text that requires patience and the ability to contextualize as discussed above. Because Smith interpolates poems into *Novel on Yellow Paper*, instructors can also use Smith's diary-novel as an opportunity to teach her poetry.

During an early discussion of Loos's diary-novel, we briefly consider the implications of the term *diary*, as we do in the lower-division course. We then focus on a theoretical model posed by Lorna Martens that illuminates for readers the relations among the author of the diary-novel, the reader of the diary-novel, the fictive author of the diary, and the presumed or fictive reader of the diary (33). Martens's model also helps us think more intentionally about the world within the diary-novel and how that world might provide extratextual social critique. This attention to form helps students avoid conflating the author with the narrator, not only for this genre but also for many other kinds of literature (see Keen). In the case of *Gentlemen Prefer Blondes*, Loos wrote Lorelei's character as the stereotypical dumb blonde in response to her own frustrations with her friend H. L. Mencken, who "preferred a witless blonde" (Loos, "Biography" 12). To further complicate the relations established within the form, Lorelei's friend and travel companion, Dorothy, can be read as a stand-in for Loos herself, an idea that displaces students' assumptions that the diarist and author are biographically aligned.

In comparing the diary with the diary-novel, Martens writes, "In the diary-novel the author is distinct from the narrator, while in the diary he is not," so that "[i]n the diary-novel, the fictive diarist has no more control over his material and his form than the real diarist. The author, in contrast, has absolute control" (33–34). The author can use the form to undermine and exploit the diarist in order to assert her own agenda. Loos uses Lorelei to assert a strong critique of patriarchal ideologies that privilege beauty over brains and submission to men over self-reliance, and the difference between the author's and diarist's respective ideologies is clear. I introduce Martens's model with Loos's novel so that when we get to Smith's novel, students are prepared to consider the diarist as a foil for Smith's critique of 1930s racism, anti-Semitism, and Fascism.

In contrast to Loos's diary-novel, Smith's novel directly addresses the reader, effectively merging the fictive reader imagined by Pompey and us, the very much alive readers, which results in a sense that to read Pompey's musings is to become complicit in her thoughts and actions. Students are faced with a narrator who is anti-Semitic, which reveals a troubling attitude of the day: "Hurrah to be a goy! . . . I have a lot of Jewish friends. It makes me feel januslike, doublefaced. Nobody knows but me what I think about that thing" (Smith 11). Yet Pompey also exhibits fierce economic independence; strong feminist perspectives; and a disdain for English cultural and educational hierarchies, evidenced by her attacks on "highbrow nonsense" (67). Pompey's contradictory and conflicting ideas serve as a good starting point for a discussion that begins by considering how these ideas have developed in the character and then considers how Smith uses Pompey to advance a feminist critique of female educational limitations in the interwar period. In a senior seminar, I tend to remain silent during discussions to let students take control of their own critical interventions (see Gooblar). Thus, the questions I pose for discussion are loose and flexible. I project them on the board and use them as prompts for the course's online discussion board. Discussion questions might include the following:

How does Pompey's family background inform your understanding of her beliefs and prejudices?

Find and consider two conversations Pompey has during social gatherings. How does she embrace or reject the ideas of her conversation partners? Is there a middle ground for Pompey?

In what ways does Pompey's direct address to you, "Dear Reader," ask you to question the institutions of taste, class, and power she presents through her anecdotes?

Consider the novel's repeated imagery of the "ivory haystack," a play on "ivory tower." How might you interpret this image in relation to Pompey's critique of the limitations placed on female education?

In the senior seminar, students complete a capstone project that consists of a research paper and a subsequent presentation of their research. Because there is little scholarship that focuses directly on the authors I teach, students need to develop research questions motivated by the historical and social contexts that inform cultural production. To keep my objective of reshaping the field of modernism at the forefront of students' research, we look to current debates in feminist-modernist studies about recuperation and recovery. Reading essays that advocate feminist interventions into new modernist studies gives students a sense of truly participating in the current discourse of the field (see Caughie; Detloff; Fernald; Garrity; Laity; Seshagiri). Students share their work in conference-style panel presentations during the last two weeks of classes. They write and post abstracts on a wiki and have the authority to form their own panels based on their topics, which reveals connections I myself may not have made. Students are encouraged to submit their abstracts to our Undergraduate Research Day, and several students have gone on to present at local undergraduate and graduate conferences. Even students who have little to no expectation of going to graduate school report that presenting their material in these miniconferences gives them confidence about their ideas and a sense of accomplishment.

In my experiences teaching these three novels across lower-division, upper-division, survey, and topical courses, I have heard students identify with Doris's, Lorelei's, and Pompey's educational quests for self-definition, independence, new experiences, and the cultivation of taste. Because these characters oscillate between challenging and succumbing to patriarchal structures and because they appear politically disengaged (ignorant, even), these texts offer a valuable inroad into exploring how the heightened liberation afforded to the interwar woman was often at odds with the limitations that persisted as a result of social and cultural expectations of what constituted proper womanhood. At first, students dismiss these characters as playing stupid, and express frustration at Lorelei's material desires and loose ways, Doris's morally ambiguous dip into prostitution, and Pompey's irreverence and anti-Semitism. However, by learning about the various historical, social, political, and cultural contexts that shaped the interwar period, with a focus on education limitations, by means of autodidactic, first-person self-presentation, students gain an essential appreciation for voices outside the male-dominated modernist canon.

Notes

1. On middlebrow literature, see in this volume the essays by Dinsman and Marshik.

2. Because of a rich cultural exchange between Germany and Great Britain during Germany's Weimar period, the German-language bestseller *The Artificial Silk Girl* was translated into English in 1933 by Basil Creighton, who subjected the novel to political editorializing. Keun's novel enjoyed immediate popularity with English-speaking readers on its publication by Chatto and Windus. All German-language copies were destroyed by the Nazis in 1933. A new English translation by Katharina von Ankum appeared in 2002.

3. See also Cucullu in this volume for teaching the representation of women in the modern city using the works of Dorothy Richardson.

4. Instructors who plan to teach students how to use the *Oxford English Dictionary* can have students compare the entries for "diary" and "journal." The definitions are similar, and both contain the other word.

Works Cited

Ankum, Katharina von. "Gendered Urban Spaces in Irmgard Keun's *Das kunstseidene Mädchen*." *Women in the Metropolis: Gender and Modernity in Weimar Culture*, edited by Ankum, U of California P, 1997, pp. 162–84.

Bluemel, Kristin. "Introduction: What Is Intermodernism?" *Intermodernism: Literary Culture in Mid-Twentieth Century Britain*, edited by Bluemel, Edinburgh UP, 2011, pp. 1–18.

Caughie, Pamela. "Lessons Learned." *The Future of Women in Modernism*, special issue of *Literature Compass*, edited by Tory Young and Jeff Wallace, vol. 10, no. 1, 2013, pp. 1–7.

Detloff, Madelyn. "Metics, Methods, and Modernism." *Mind the Gap! Modernism and Feminist Praxis*, cluster of *Modernism/Modernity* Print Plus, edited by Urmila Seshagiri, vol. 2, cycle 2, 7 Aug. 2017, doi.org/10.26597/mod.0023.

Fernald, Anne E. Introduction. *Women's Fiction, New Modernist Studies, and Feminism*, special issue of *Modern Fiction Studies*, edited by Fernald, vol. 59, no. 2, 2013, pp. 229–40.

Garrity, Jane. "Found and Lost: The Politics of Modernist Recovery." *Modernism/Modernity*, vol. 15, no. 4, 2008, pp. 803–12.

Gay, Peter. *Weimar Culture: The Outsider as Insider*. Harper Torchbooks, 1970.

Gooblar, David. "How to Undermine Your Own Authority." *ChronicleVitae*, 18 Jan. 2017, chroniclevitae.com/news/1670-how-to-undermine-your-own-authority.

Hammill, Faye. "'One of the Few Books That Doesn't Stink': The Intellectuals, the Masses, and *Gentlemen Prefer Blondes*." *Critical Survey*, vol. 17, no. 3, 2005, pp. 27–48.

Isherwood, Christopher. "A Berlin Diary." *The Berlin Stories*. 1945. New Directions Publishing, 2008, pp. 389–410.

Keen, Suzanne. "The Undergraduate Literature Classroom." *Teaching Narrative Theory*, edited by David Herman et al., Modern Language Association, 2010, pp. 19–32.

Keun, Irmgard. *The Artificial Silk Girl*. 1932. Translated by Katharina von Ankum, Other Press, 2011.

Laity, Cassandra. "Introduction: Toward Feminist Modernisms." *Feminist Modernist Studies*, vol. 1, nos. 1–2, 2018, pp. 1–7.

Loos, Anita. "The Biography of a Book." 1963. Loos, *Gentlemen*, pp. 11–16.

———. *Gentlemen Prefer Blondes*. 1925. Penguin Books, 1992.

Martens, Lorna. *The Diary Novel*. Cambridge UP, 1985.

Nicholls, A. J. *Weimar and the Rise of Hitler*. 4th ed., St. Martin's Press, 2000.

Seshagiri, Urmila. "Mind the Gap! Modernism and Feminist Praxis." *Mind the Gap! Modernism and Feminist Praxis*, cluster of *Modernism/Modernity* Print Plus, edited by Seshagiri, vol. 2, cycle 2, 7 Aug. 2017, doi.org/10.26597/mod.0022.

Smith, Stevie. *Novel on Yellow Paper*. 1936. New Directions Publishing, 1994.

Ward, Janet. *Weimar Surfaces: Urban Visual Culture in 1920s Germany*. U of California P, 2001.

Steven Ambrose

The Woman Born with a Difference: Teaching the Lesbian Novel in a Modernist Context

A volume devoted to the teaching of modernist women's writing in English must address the portion of that literature that represents women's same-sex desire. As such, this essay focuses on one genre of modernism—the lesbian novel—not only because several modernist authors were, or were thought to have been, lesbians but also because the genre helped imagine the figure of the lesbian into being. Drawing on both my research on the lesbian novel and my experience teaching either courses that focus on the lesbian novel or more traditional courses that integrate such novels into the syllabus, this essay is meant to give instructors a working definition of the genre, some basic background information on the genre, several assignments I've found useful when teaching the lesbian novel, and a bibliography of modernist lesbian novels (a full list of which is available on the companion website to this volume [modwomen.mla.hcommons.org]). In an attempt to situate modernist women's writing—and the lesbian novel specifically—within the broader context of modernism, I've also included some francophone texts as well as lesbian novels not written by women.

Terminology

Part of the difficulty of teaching the lesbian novel begins with its definition. The issue is not only deciding which definition to use. Indeed, finding any definition of the lesbian novel can prove surprisingly difficult. Sherrie A. Inness writes, "Exactly what features make a novel 'lesbian' are difficult to specify. Critics have different ideas about how to define a lesbian novel, but most agree on two points: The author must be a lesbian, and the central character or characters must be lesbians" (491). Inness's point speaks to a larger anxiety in lesbian studies: discerning how the term *lesbian* becomes attached to a given literary genre, be it a novel, a play, or a poem. For the purposes of this essay, Inness's definition suffices. However, I would add my own definition, too: a lesbian novel is "any novel in which female same-sex desire is integral to its narrative or form" (Ambrose 20). Inness's definition emphasizes the author's identity as at least equally if not more important than the content. My own definition—which focuses instead on a novel's representation of same-sex desire—allows for greater latitude in determining what kinds of novels one can interpret to be lesbian. At the same time, it includes novels whose authors may not have been or may not have seen themselves as lesbians.

Why *Lesbian*?

Sapphic is the dominant moniker signaling women's same-sex desire in modernist studies, but I am more inclined to use *lesbian*.[1] On a practical level, *lesbian* is a word with which students are likely more familiar. From a theoretical point of view, the terms *lesbian* and *sapphic* also figure women's same-sex desire in subtly different ways. Same-sex desire has come to be associated with the word *sapphic* because the speaker in Sappho's lyric poetry is assumed to be female (because Sappho is) and because the speaker's object of address is also female. *Sapphic* implies a connection both to the person (i.e., one is "like Sappho") and to her (perceived) desire represented in poetry, to both the poet and her work, collapsed into one. *Sapphic* also signals a connection to a classical (and classed) literary tradition that *lesbian* does not (always). And while *lesbian* is certainly connected to Sappho in the way that it indicates female same-sex desire—it alludes to the island of Lesbos on which Sappho lived and infuses the island with her perceived desire for women—it doesn't call to mind a direct comparison with Sappho as a poet, as a speaker in her work, or as a historical figure. Taken literally, rather than being like a person, *lesbian* signals being of a place, a metaphorical inhabitant of the isle of Lesbos. Thinking of lesbian novels as individual members that make up a constituency—unique yet having shared characteristics—encapsulates how genres coalesce and change over time. Using the term *lesbian* also connects modernist novels that represent women's same-sex desire with novels that emerge later in the twentieth century. For these reasons I prefer *lesbian*. It may, however, be fruitful for students to choose for themselves which term best suits the assigned novels, to consider the limits of each term, and to decide whether one need choose at all.

On Inversion

It would prove challenging to teach a modernist (or any) lesbian novel without an understanding of sexual (also known as "congenital") inversion. This concept, disseminated by sexologists contemporary with modernism such as Havelock Ellis and Richard von Krafft-Ebing, describes what we now call homosexuality in terms of having the body of one sex with the soul or essence of the opposite sex, a conception that persists in medical narratives of trans experiences in our own contemporary moment. Discerning the degree to which this concept was part of the medical or even public discourse in the modernist period is difficult; its place in Radclyffe Hall's *The Well of Loneliness* as well as in works like Djuna Barnes's *Ladies Almanack* or Lucie Delarus-Mardrus's *The Angel and the Perverts* (*L'ange et les pervert*s) did make inversion a central trope throughout lesbian novels of the twentieth century and beyond by means of the figure of the masculine or mannish lesbian. Exceptions can be found, especially in French novels—Marcel Proust's *In Search of Lost Time* (*À la recherche du temps perdu*) and Violette Leduc's *Therese and Isabelle* (*Thérèse et Isabelle*) come to mind. Whether or not instructors choose to assign the work of Ellis or Krafft-Ebing, introducing the idea of inversion allows a discussion of just how recent the idea of sexuality-as-identity is in the longer history of human sexuality. Volume 1 of Michel Foucault's *History of Sexuality* might be useful as a way to introduce the idea that homosexuality as a state of being is a historical phenomenon. For many students, this idea will be mind-blowing, as they have likely only ever been taught that sexuality-as-identity is a scientific fact, not a historical construction. However one chooses to address inversion—whether as a mini-lecture, in the form of supplemental reading, or as a class discussion—I recommend having a conversation early on about the historical production of homosexuality; this will allow students to see how lesbian novels played a role in creating the idea of "lesbian," which allowed readers themselves to identify as lesbians.

Texts and Approach

There are numerous factors to consider when it comes to text selection: the course's learning goals, one's feminist politics, the availability of a given work, and, by extension, its affordability. Will the lesbian novel be a singular addition? A unit of two or three novels? An entire course on the topic? Will the course prioritize a historical-biographical approach or a more formalist approach? Having taught several modernist lesbian novels in a variety of courses, I have a handful of recommendations. Hall's *The Well of Loneliness* is iconic, arguably archetypal, for the genre.[2] Instructors can trace conventions from this novel through to those of several other lesbian novels written later in the twentieth century, and it is also the text early-twentieth-century lesbians cite as the first instance in which they see themselves reflected in a work of literature.[3] Hall's novel is useful as part of an author-centered approach, as well as a great example of a novel influenced by both Victorian and modernist conventions, and, as such, illustrates how style is fluid across literary periods. Barnes's *Nightwood* is useful for questions of style and what makes a work modernist, as well as for considerations of formal aspects beyond plot.[4] While admittedly not a page-turner, Natalie Barney's *The One Who Is Legion*—nearly forgotten and reprinted only once in the past century—offers all kinds of vectors for analysis: biographical (it was inspired by Renée Vivien's suicide and is a collaboration with Romaine Brooks); linguistic; generic (gothic, memoir, epistolary, drama); visual; and philosophical. Additionally, it presents an opportunity for feminist praxis. This lesser-taught novel is difficult to obtain, but assigning it may aid its survival.

In my own approach, I shy away from a historical-biographical methodology, especially when teaching multiple lesbian novels. Particularly when novels are difficult to understand, students may turn to an author's life as *the* hermeneutic for interpreting a novel rather than look to it as one of many possible methodologies. Students' investment in the novel's mimetic dimension—their desire to know what parts of the novel's content really happened—can overshadow the imaginative dimension. As anyone who's read *The One Who Is Legion* can attest, it is a lot easier and even more pleasurable to read about Barney and Vivien's relationship, locating its echoes in the text, than it is to address the novel's confusing plot and the way it mixes conventions of multiple literary genres. However, modernist texts offer opportunities to challenge notions of fixed generic conventions and strengthen students' abilities to form their own interpretations. There is a utility and politics to using an author's life to apprehend a text's subtle homoerotics, but I instead pose questions like, "How are gender and sexuality represented in this text?" or "Where are you seeing desire?" or "How are generic conventions and erotics working together or against each other in this work?" I've also taken the perhaps more political approach of assuming homosexuality, rather than heterosexuality, as the default and have framed discussion not around whether a work is lesbian, but how it is lesbian, and how we come to apprehend its lesbian quality. Whatever the approach, text selection is always intimately connected to the learning goals of the course.

An Initial Assessment: The Lesbian *Pinterest* Board

An initial assessment is key to the success of a course or unit on the lesbian novel. My initial assessment, a collaborative *Pinterest* board, is intended to determine students' understanding of what *lesbian* means. After I create a *Pinterest* account for the class and a board titled "Lesbian," the directions students receive are simple: "Using the log-on information provided, pin three to five images that illustrate what *lesbian* means to you. Along with each pin, write a description that explains why you chose this image." I project the *Pinterest* board in the classroom and we discuss the images students selected. In our discussions, I encourage students to explain their reasoning for choosing particular images. We then look at all images and ask if any patterns are discernible. This leads to a common definition of *lesbian* and also teaches skills like pattern recognition, which can later be applied to the reading of lesbian novels as we look for similarities and differences in how each novel represents women's same-sex desire. This also provides an opportunity to demonstrate how something like a photograph—a medium we all presume to be mimetic in nature—does not necessarily represent reality as it is so much as how we imagine reality to be (kind of like novels).

Two Approaches, Two Final Projects

Whether one adopts a historical-biographical approach or an approach that focuses on text or genre, I suggest two final research projects that have been successful in the past: a biopic and a definitional essay. The directions for the biopic are as follows:

> For your final project, create a ten-minute biographical documentary on a largely forgotten lesbian author. Your project should include a proposal explaining why you want to research the author in question and why you think it's important that she not be forgotten, the video itself, and an annotated bibliography of all sources used to create your video (including sources of any images you include). Upload the completed video to *YouTube.*

For this assignment, I always include a handout on the generic conventions of documentary; a guest lecture by an instructor in film studies may be an option. Throughout the semester, I also incorporate weekly vlog assignments in which students reflect on their learning; each week students learn a new basic editing technique meant to provide them with the technical skills needed for the larger biopic assignment. I also dedicate at least one class session to individual progress meetings as part of the course grade. I allow students to research authors outside the modernist period for the sake of variety; however, instructors can stipulate that students connect the work of a nonmodernist author to what the class has studied about modernism, modernist novels, or the modernist lesbian novel. The political charge of this project emerges as students work against the erasure of lesbian authors and lesbian representation by producing artifacts that will exist publicly on the Internet (possibly forever). Students have made videos about authors such as Liane de Pougy, Monique Wittig, and Natalie Clifford Barney; one student, Sydney Ford, created a particularly effective video entitled "Pat Parker: The Poet of Generations," which is available on *YouTube.*

The definitional paper is more straightforward in terms of directions but far more difficult conceptually. It is perhaps better suited to a course that assigns multiple lesbian novels. The directions are as follows:

> Using only close readings of primary texts (novels), create a definition of both *lesbian* and *lesbian novel.* Your reading should attend to the obvious and, most especially, the less obvious moments where you sense lesbianism at play, as well as any generic conventions around which you organize your definition.

I recommend having students include in this essay one other modernist lesbian novel not covered in class. Though fewer opt for this route, a through line in the definitional essay is the palpable limitations the number of examined novels places on the thoroughness of the definition. In one paper, a student made the wonderful inference that extrapolating what *lesbian* is based on the lived experience of a small set of lesbians represents a similar constraint. Only one student noted how the overwhelming whiteness of both authors and characters, particularly in lesbian novels published in the early twentieth century, problematizes the very foundation of the genre. It therefore seems particularly important to foreground the impact of racism on the selected lesbian novels, particularly in a modernist context.

Concluding Polemic; or, Why I Stopped Assigning Canonical Texts

One of the most common concerns expressed by queer graduate students and faculty members is that their classes have become "too gay." I have felt this pressure both from within and from without when faculty members in positions of authority have told me to "tone it down" in terms of queer content. Luckily, my classes to date seem to have only gotten queerer. As someone who strongly identifies as a queer scholar and feminist ally, I feel an obligation to do more than pay lip service to the politics I espouse. This requires teaching traditional literary skills while also using texts that challenge racism, sexism, heterosexism, and bourgeois classism. One of the ways I've done this is by teaching noncanonical texts whenever I can, novels by lesser-known authors, and books that, at times, have only had one printing. This tactic is not new to modernist studies; consider the recuperation of Gertrude Stein or the significance of Shari Benstock's work. While our politics and pedagogy are naturally not limited to the classroom, if intersectional politics aren't reflected on our syllabi, if we don't actively assign texts that represent marginal experiences, without fear, without apology, without the need for justification, what are we even doing here?

Notes

My title nods to Djuna Barnes's *Ladies Almanack*: "And not nine Months later, there was heard under the Dome of Heaven a great Crowing, and from the Midst, an Egg, as incredible as a thing forgotten, fell to Earth, and striking, split and hatched, and from out of it stepped one saying 'Pardon me, I must be going!' And this was the first Woman born with a Difference. After this the Angels parted, and on the Face of each was the Mother look. Why was that?" (24–26).

1. Shari Benstock is credited with coining the term *sapphic modernism* in her foundational *Women of the Left Bank*, a trend in modernist studies we can trace through the work of such scholars as Jaime Hovey, Erin G. Carlston, Diana Collecott, Robin Hackett, Laura Doan and Jane Garrity, Sashi Nair, and Jasmine Rault, to name a few. Elizabeth English's *Lesbian Modernism: Censorship, Sexuality and Genre Fiction* is a notable exception—English links her deviation in terminology to a break with exclusively high modernist literary objects—as is Elisabeth Ladenson's *Proust's Lesbianism*, a work situated within a French literary studies context.

2. See Marshik in this volume for another approach to teaching *The Well.*

3. See the oral histories in Nestle's *The Persistent Desire.*

4. On teaching Barnes, see in this volume the essays by Kopley and Tate.

Works Cited

Ambrose, Steven. *Lesbians: How Novel.* 2017. Michigan State U, PhD dissertation.

Barnes, Djuna. *Ladies Almanack.* 1928. Dalkey Archive Press, 1992.

———. *Nightwood.* 1936. New Directions Publishing, 2006.

Barney, Natalie Clifford. *The One Who Is Legion; or, A.D.'s After-life.* 1930. U of Maine Printing Office, 1987.

Benstock, Shari. *Women of the Left Bank: Paris, 1900–1940.* U of Texas P, 1987.

Carlston, Erin G. *Thinking Fascism: Sapphic Modernism and Fascist Modernity.* Stanford UP, 1998.

Collecott, Diana. *H.D. and Sapphic Modernism, 1910–1950.* U of Durham P, 1999.

Doan, Laura, and Jane Garrity, editors. *Sapphic Modernities: Sexuality, Women and National Culture.* Palgrave Macmillan, 2006.

English, Elizabeth. *Lesbian Modernism: Censorship, Sexuality and Genre Fiction.* Edinburgh UP, 2015.

Ford, Sydney. "Pat Parker: The Poet of Generations." *YouTube*, 1 May 2014, www.youtube.com/watch?v=CJ1GahnqCbE. Accessed 20 June 2019.

Foucault, Michel. *The History of Sexuality: An Introduction.* Translated by Robert Hurley, vol. 1, Vintage Books, 1990.

Hackett, Robin. *Sapphic Primitivism: Productions of Race, Class, and Sexuality in Key Works of Modern Fiction.* Rutgers UP, 2004.

Hall, Radclyffe. *The Well of Loneliness.* 1928. Anchor Books, 1990.

Hovey, Jaime. "Sapphic Primitivism in Gertrude Stein's *Q.E.D.*" *Modern Fiction Studies*, vol. 42, no. 3, 1996, pp. 547–68.

Inness, Sherrie A. "The Novel: Lesbian." *The Gay and Lesbian Literary Heritage: A Reader's Companion to the Writers and Their Works, from Antiquity to the Present*, edited by Claude J. Summers, rev. ed., Routledge, 2002, pp. 490–94.

Ladenson, Elisabeth. *Proust's Lesbianism.* Cornell UP, 1999.

Nair, Sashi. *Secrecy and Sapphic Modernism: Reading Romans à Clef Between the Wars*. Palgrave Macmillan, 2011.

Nestle, Joan, editor. *The Persistent Desire: A Femme-Butch Reader*. Alyson, 1992.

Rault, Jasmine. *Eileen Gray and the Design of Sapphic Modernity*. Routledge, 2016.

Melissa Dinsman

Adapting Women's Writing: Melodrama and the Second World War

To teach students about British literature of the Second World War and more specifically about Britain's transatlantic and transmedial push for American intervention in the war, I turn to modernist women's writing—high and middlebrow—and its adaptation as Hollywood melodrama. While some critics dismiss melodrama as an overly sentimental form of writing by and aimed at women, my course teaches students that melodrama is both the driving narrative form of fiction and film as well as a powerful narrative mode that is highly persuasive because of its alignment of fiction with propaganda. That fiction, specifically modernist fiction, and propaganda share formal qualities is not an original argument (see Wollaeger). For students new to modernist studies, however, *modernism* and *propaganda* are big, amorphous terms, and the relation between the two is not immediately obvious. By analyzing texts and media from the Second World War with an eye to the melodramatic, students find concrete evidence of the connections between propaganda and modern literature.

As Linda Williams states, "Melodrama is the fundamental mode of popular American moving pictures" and "the foundation of the classical Hollywood movie" (42). Similarly, Peter Brooks argues that melodrama is "a central fact of the modern sensibility" (21), and he locates the mode across modern literature and art. Through the juxtaposition of hero and villain, the reliance on happenstance, the portrayal of extreme emotional states, and the search for a stable center that remains elusive, the melodramatic form connects not only film and literature but also art and propaganda, especially in a time of war. Thus, a gothic middlebrow text like Daphne du Maurier's *Rebecca* relies on many of the same tropes as Elizabeth Bowen's *The Heat of the Day* and the Ministry of Information propaganda documentary *London Can Take It*. When they identify and analyze transmedial forms of melodrama, students are able to recognize differences across texts included under the broad term of *modernism*. This practice also gives students the tools to challenge traditional distinctions between high and middlebrow literature, and, especially during the Second World War, between art and propaganda.

By pursuing a transmedial or multimodal approach—by including literature, film, radio broadcasts, poster campaigns, and documentaries centered on the domestic as well as everyday activities performed by ordinary people—I present students with subjective experiences of a total war that caused massive disruptions to civilian routines and an extensive loss of life. Instead of the battlefields that students expect to read about in my course, students encounter the quotidian (rationing, cooking, dance halls, auxiliary service, family life) and the dangers (air raids, Mass Observation, Ministry of Information propaganda campaigns, fifth columnist spies) that were part of the home front (that is, feminine) experience. By the end of the semester, students have a better understanding of the history and culture of the Second World War from a British perspective, are able to dissect propagandistic rhetoric across media forms, and can identify the features of melodrama underlying wartime propaganda and literature. As a result, students learn that in the modern era, social, cultural, industrial, domestic, and narrative structures were used to transmit wartime propaganda, and that this transmission was very much a part of modernist women's writing during the war.

A list of primary texts, films, and other media objects that I have used in some combination on three different occasions teaching this course, as well as a link to the course website, is available on the companion website to this volume (modwomen.mla.hcommons.org) and provides a sense of the breadth of the course. This list is not meant to be exhaustive but may be a helpful resource for those wanting to teach a course on British literature and culture of the Second World War or to include a segment on the Second World War as part of a survey course on modernism.

Framing the Course: History, Adaptation, and Close Reading

One of the hurdles to teaching the literature and culture of the Second World War is the vast amount of historical and formal knowledge students need for contextualization. One could argue that this is true of any course, but there are some unique challenges to teaching the literature and film of this era in particular. First, the Second World War is so much a part of our cultural memory that students imagine they understand the complexities of the war, when in reality they know very little about the experiences of Americans, let alone how people outside the United States experienced the war. At the same time, there is too much historical ground to cover in one semester. One cannot do justice to the western and eastern military fronts, the North African campaign, the French Resistance, Japanese internment, the bombing of London, the carpet bombings of Germany, the Holocaust, and the atomic bomb in sixteen weeks, and I'm up front with students about what the course can reasonably cover in terms of depth and breadth. In a literature course, where students are required to gain both formal and historical knowledge, I tend to favor depth over breadth, focusing on representations of the British home front during the Phoney War of 1939–40 and the Blitz of 1940–41. I narrow the course's focus even more by leaning heavily on women middlebrow authors, such as Jan Struther, Daphne du Maurier, Phyllis Bottome, Vera Brittain, and Mollie Panter-Downes, many of whom played major roles both within the popular literary scene and as part of the war effort. Their fiction addresses the complexities of Britain's participation in the war and was written with a broad reading public, including Americans, in mind. Thus, their work is not only historically enlightening but also accessible to students new to the study of the period. Assigning texts that were widely read during the war also gives students a means to challenge the questionable dichotomy—discussed by Virginia Woolf in her essay "Middlebrow"—between the popular (literature written for money) and the highbrow (literature written for the sake of literature). Read alongside Woolf's *Three Guineas* or Bowen's *The Heat of the Day*, these middlebrow novels express many of the same wartime concerns and do so using similar melodramatic tropes.

During the first few weeks of the course, students focus on the lead-up to the war: they need an understanding of Britain's appeasement policy in the late 1930s and of how the looming shadow of the First World War led to this policy in the first place. To this end, students read literary texts, such as Jan Struther's *Mrs. Miniver* and Phyllis Bottome's *The Mortal Storm*, alongside newspaper articles of the time; watch educational videos on the Second World War available on *YouTube*; and acquire historical information provided in lectures. We discuss the events directly mentioned or alluded to in Struther's and Bottome's works in the light of the historical events that led up to the war. As the course moves into a consideration of the Phoney War and the Blitz, students read literary accounts of the time, many of which only indirectly mention the war; these fictional writings are paired with historical materials, such as Humphrey Jennings's documentaries, Mass Observation reports, propaganda posters, Ministry of Food recipes, and rations books. The goal is for students to learn about the lived experience of the war and the everyday responses to the crises of late modernism not only through reading but also through cultural objects. Seeing the expansiveness of Britain's total war state—which influenced how people thought about things such as food, transportation, clothing, family, work, and entertainment—allows students to begin to contemplate how such massive changes also impacted literary form, which increasingly relied on the melodramatic mode to express the uncertainty of survival and emotional instability of the time.

This shift by modernist women writers to address the struggles of Britain's home front and the fight against Fascism, both abroad and at home, made their texts very attractive to Hollywood. Due to the widespread appeal and timely topic of these middlebrow texts, Hollywood studios like MGM bought the adaptation rights. Yet despite the popularity of these domestic, women-centered narratives, the role of the woman protagonist in each of the movies is altered—sometimes drastically, as in the case of *The Mortal Storm*—to better meet the demands of the Classical Hollywood form, the visions of male directors, and the expectations of American audiences. The result of these transmedial and transatlantic adaptations are films that look little like their original sources and often frame Britain's struggle even more melodramatically than the popular print versions.[1] While students might be media-savvy, they need training in how to read and analyze film adaptations; therefore, I introduce adaptation theory early (about four weeks into the semester). Before students watch the first adaptation, they tell me what their favorite adaptations are and why. Fidelity is almost always their answer to what makes a good adaptation. To develop an understanding of adaptation theory, I assign manageable secondary readings, such as excerpts from Brian McFarlane's *Novel to*

Film (3–11) and Linda Hutcheon's *A Theory of Adaptation* (1–32). After about a week of discussing adaptation theory, students watch the film versions of our primary texts and reflect on how and why the text and its film adaptation might be different. We take these films slowly, working on one film a week for a junior- or senior-level course for English majors. Here, McFarlane's three categories of adaptation—transposition, commentary, and analogy (10–11)—prove fruitful for class discussion, as students debate which category might be applied to each film. *Mrs. Miniver* is a particularly good film for this segment, as the movie at first seems to resemble the book in name only. It also surprises students that a text so devoid of overt or explicit political discussion was transformed into one of the most famous propaganda films of the Second World War. By looking at the Hollywood adaptations of British middlebrow novels, students come to appreciate the scope of British wartime propaganda, which travelled across both oceans and media.

The study of different media forms also provides students with an opportunity to practice close reading. When students perform a close reading of a film, I want them to be able to explain not only what is happening on screen but also how it is happening. To facilitate this, I assign excerpts on select film forms from David Bordwell and Kristin Thompson's *Film Art: An Introduction*, which we then use in our close readings of film adaptations. By the end of the semester, students are able to analyze a film for its mise-en-scène, camera distance, and shot length. Moreover, because we are discussing adaptations that are exemplary of Classical Hollywood cinema, students are expected to be able to explain what this genre looks like at a formal level and how its formal requirements affect narrative changes in the transition of a work from text to screen. For example, students complete worksheets, like the one on *Mrs. Miniver* in table 1, to help them think about how an adaptation conforms to Classical Hollywood cinema.

I find that restricting this course to texts and films of the Second World War—ones that are often written by and centered on women—helps students focus on form. For example, for most of the semester, the class discusses Ministry of Information propaganda messaging and how this messaging was altered for an American audience.[2] Because students are looking for these specific messages, as well as elements of melodrama, they are able to zero in on how late modernist plot or form mimics, as well as challenges, public and state-sponsored British home front messaging as it appeared on both sides of the Atlantic.

Table 1. Student worksheet on *Mrs. Miniver*, adaptation, and Classical Hollywood cinema

Classical Hollywood Form	Representation in Film (*Mrs. Miniver*)
Plot is driven by characters (not by the war)	Kay Miniver is concerned about keeping her domestic space intact and not about fighting the war.
Main character is goal-oriented	Kay Miniver does whatever it takes to keep her family and community intact.
Obstacles	The war; class structure (Lady Beldon)
Process of change for main character	Kay Miniver is hesitant to let her son (Vin) fight; she fights a Nazi; she learns to cope with loss.
Cause and effect	Clem Miniver buys a new car at beginning of film; Carol Miniver (Vin's wife) dies in the same car at the end.
Closure	Sense of unity in the closing church scene

Assessing Student Learning: Propaganda and Cultural Projects

In addition to completing a variety of low- and high-stakes writing assignments, students are also expected to create their own forms of digital propaganda with messaging aimed at a domestic Second World War audience. Working on this digital project provides students means of demonstrating their understanding of course material, apart from discussion and writing. Through the process of creating a piece of propaganda, students reflect on the best medium or platform (whether a tool or apps) for their messaging, and they think about how one might use content and form to persuade British or American women and men of the 1940s to support the war effort. As a result, this project also asks students to reflect on the transmedial process of adaptation—recreating messaging made for analog forms using digital media.

For students to complete this project, a great deal of scaffolding is needed. Students are made aware of the project on the first day of the course and, within the first month, are provided with a written description of the project's requirements (a group proposal, the project itself, and a presentation) and grading criteria. As students are introduced to propaganda messaging through novels, films, and other media, we discuss how such messaging is presented and brainstorm potential ways to digitally re-create or adapt it. By the sixth week of the course, students pick the type of propaganda they would like to make from among the following forms: documentary, radio program or play, song, comic book, poster series, or newspaper article. I then form groups based on students' choices. Throughout the rest of the semester groups are given some class time to meet and discuss their projects; however, I expect most of this work to be done outside class. By mid-semester break, groups submit a proposal for their propaganda project, which details the specific type of messaging they will be using, how they plan to execute this messaging (in terms of content, form, tools or apps needed, labor division, timeline), as well as the primary audience for their messaging (e.g., housewives, children, the elderly, etc.). Groups meet with me throughout the remainder of the semester to discuss the development of their projects or to learn how to use a new tool or app.

Finally, students present their propaganda projects during an end-of-semester 1940s-themed celebration. During the presentation, groups are expected to display their projects, briefly explain how their projects relate to the course, and lay out the design process and the roles each participant played in the project's development. Although presenting is often a high-stress event, the environment in which students exhibit their projects is intended to be a celebratory one that reflects the cultural knowledge students have gained throughout the course. During each previous week of the semester, we will have discussed a particular cultural object or experience alongside a novel or film in order to develop cultural knowledge. For example, students read about rationing and cooking alongside *Mrs. Miniver* or learn about proper attire and clothing hacks while reading *The Heat of the Day.* Throughout the semester, students also create three to four blog posts on cultural topics such as food (one post detailed students' experiences cooking and eating a Ministry of Food recipe), propaganda posters, music, and finally clothing and makeup.[3] During the end-of-semester celebration, we revisit these blog posts and students' experiences researching and writing them. I bring in historically appropriate (but tasty) food and play popular music of the period by Vera Lynn, Glenn Miller, and the Andrews Sisters, music about which students have previously written. The goal of the final day, aside from being an opportunity for students to present their newly acquired knowledge, is to emphasize that everyday objects and activities also illustrate the stresses of wartime and thus serve as fitting vehicles for the transmission of propaganda.

Although my course, especially in the first half of the semester, focuses on late modernist women's writing and its cinematic adaptations, the components of the course are transferrable and can be adjusted to teach a broader or narrower range of texts and media objects. The pedagogical methods used to teach history, adaptation, genre, and close reading are techniques that I use in other courses, especially those that have a film component. Smaller modules deploying literary texts, cultural objects, and media fit well within a survey. For example, teaching *Mrs. Miniver* in a course that also features Woolf's *Mrs. Dalloway* could lead to interesting discussions about the evolution of food and entertaining in the early twentieth century. Such a course might be designed around units devoted to cultural activities rather than literary-historical representation. Or, one might pair poets of the First World War with Vera Brittain's diary entries in *Wartime Chronicle* and Mollie Panter-Downes's *New Yorker* articles (collected as *London War Notes*) in order to emphasize the evolution and expansion of the war front in the early twentieth century. And while instructors might eschew a larger, semester-length project like my digital propaganda assignment, they could incorporate smaller cultural projects. For example, in a segment on food and entertaining, students could be asked to prepare a dish of the period and write about the environment in which their dish might be served, as my students do for their first cultural blog post. Such an assignment would give students a hands-on approach to learning and enable them to practice their analysis of texts and cultural objects. One could also expand the emphasis on adaptation described here to look at how approaches to filmic adaptations of women's writing have evolved throughout the twentieth century.

Regardless of whether women's literature of the Second World War is a course segment or the focus of the course itself, the teaching of women's literature in conjunction with more popular or state-sponsored media objects provides students with a historical context through which they can approach their reading of primary texts. Moreover, when working across media, and more specifically with adaptations, students are given the chance to see more clearly that written texts are media too, a fact that many often overlook. Finally, students grasp not only that women authors are writing within a specific historical context but also that they are restrained formally by the medium in which they choose to write, or which they have available to them. By the end of the semester, students have begun to understand that the form of the medium affects the content of the narrative or the argument, a point amplified by the inclusion of adaptations.

Notes

1. Vera Brittain, for example, disdainfully comments in her wartime diary on the "sentimentality" of Hollywood's adaptation of *Mrs. Miniver*, but also admits that the film "moved one despite the propagandist intention of the whole thing" (169).

2. I have found Nicholas John Cull's *Selling War* very helpful for students as they pinpoint specific propagandist messaging in literature, film, and other cultural objects. Examples of this messaging include, for instance, British fortitude (as in the famous propagandist phrase "Keep Calm and Carry On") and the dissolution of class lines.

3. Student blogs and digital projects are posted to the course website and made available for public viewing.

Works Cited

Bordwell, David, and Kristin Thompson. *Film Art: An Introduction*. 10th ed., McGraw-Hill, 2012.

Bottome, Phyllis. *The Mortal Storm*. 1937. Edited by Phyllis Lassner, Northwestern UP, 1998.

Bowen, Elizabeth. *The Heat of the Day*. 1948. Anchor Books, 2002.

Brittain, Vera. *Wartime Chronicle: Vera Brittain's Diary, 1939–1945*. Edited by Alan Bishop and Y. Aleksandra Bennett, Victor Gollancz, 1989.

Brooks, Peter. *The Melodramatic Imagination: Balzac, Henry James, Melodrama, and the Mode of Excess*. Yale UP, 1995.

Cull, Nicholas John. *Selling War: The British Propaganda Campaign against American "Neutrality" in World War II*. Oxford UP, 1995.

Du Maurier, Daphne. *Rebecca*. 1938. William Morrow Paperbacks, 2006.

Hutcheon, Linda. *A Theory of Adaptation*. 2nd ed., Routledge, 2012.

London Can Take It. Directed by Humphrey Jennings and Harry Watt, GPO Film Unit, 1940. *YouTube*, uploaded by Nuclear Vault, 5 Mar. 2011, youtu.be/yoS-CQKvAZA.

McFarlane, Brian. *Novel to Film: An Introduction to the Theory of Adaptation*. Clarendon Press, 1996.

Mrs. Miniver. Directed by William Wyler, performances by Greer Garson and Walter Pidgeon, Metro-Goldwyn-Mayer, 1942.

Panter-Downes, Mollie. *London War Notes, 1939–1945*. Edited by William Shawn, Farrar, Straus and Giroux, 1971.

Struther, Jan. *Mrs. Miniver*. 1939. Mariner, 1990.

Williams, Linda. "Melodrama Revisited." *Refiguring American Film Genres: History and Theory*, edited by Nick Browne, U of California P, 1998, pp. 42–88.

Wollaeger, Mark. *Modernism, Media, and Propaganda: British Narrative from 1900 to 1945*. Princeton UP, 2006.

Woolf, Virginia. "Middlebrow." *The Essays of Virginia Woolf*, vol. 6 (1933–41), edited by Stuart N. Clarke, Hogarth Press, 2011, pp. 470–79.

———. *Three Guineas*. 1938. Annotated and introduced by Jane Marcus, Harcourt, 2006.

Beth Wynstra

From Page to Stage: Dramaturgy and the Women's Voices of the Provincetown Players

In his book *Ghost Light: An Introductory Handbook for Dramaturgy*, Michael Mark Chemers titles his introduction "What the #%@ Is a Dramaturg?" For theatergoers and even for dedicated theater patrons, the term *dramaturg* and the work of a dramaturg are likely mysteries. Chemers defines the role thusly: "A dramaturg is a member of the artistic team of a production who is a specialist in the transformation of a dramatic script into a meaningful living performance" (5). Indeed, dramaturgs are a vital part of any production as they help establish the context, history, and significance of the work for the artists, as well as prepare an audience to see the work. Lawrence Switzky offers that dramaturgy is "concerned with opening up a production and endorsing multiple simultaneous audiences to the same performance or exposing the latent fecundity of a specific word or detail" (176). In Switzky's estimation, dramaturgy ensures an audience's engagement with and understanding of a dramatic work and helps an actor or director with elements like the meaning of words or phrases from the script. Anne Cattaneo provides a series of helpful questions that any dramaturg should be able to answer in order to generate a compelling production where both artists and audience are fully engaged with the material on stage. Questions include the following: "What type of stage was the play written for? What kind of acting? Who were its audiences? More importantly, what was the play's function?" (7). I see the dramaturg as the official researcher for any theater production. Directors rely on dramaturgs to provide research material, and to define historic references or nebulous phrases or words in a script, all of which leads to an effective production. Dramaturgical work may also result in such artifacts as an audience guide—a guide that provides contextual material—on a theater company's website, a preshow talk or postshow discussion led by the dramaturg, or notes in the program meant to prepare an audience for what it is about to see. In approaching a play and preparing an artistic team to stage or an audience to see that play, dramaturgs act as historians, anthropologists, and sociologists. Their multifaceted methodology, which brings a theatrical work from page to stage, is not only vitally important—it also provides an excellent model for students as they approach dramatic texts in the classroom.

For educators who have taught dramatic literature, a significant challenge can be getting students not only to think about a play as a work meant to be performed but also to consider the play from the audience's, actor's, and director's points of view. Instructors may feel hesitant about incorporating a play into a literature syllabus if they do not have experience with theater production or the tools for guiding students to imagine a play off the page and on the stage. The practice of dramaturgy brings to the classroom elements of theater production that anyone, experienced theater artists or theater neophytes, can access and use to study a play and unlock its production possibilities. By supplementing classroom discussion and work with dramaturgical assignments, students consider the historical framework, (auto)biographical elements, and current relevance of a given dramatic text. Furthermore, students' interactions with a theater director, which the assignments necessitate, get students to imagine the script they are working with as performed by actors. When students take a dramaturgical approach to a script and are expected to use their research and writing in the service of a theatrical production, they enter a professional sphere where their work resembles that of specialists. Students' expertise is not only necessary but also valued: they become the experts on a dramatic text and have the opportunity to teach and share what they have learned with others. Such an experience can be empowering for students, as they learn new ways to approach dramatic literature and see the direct results of their engagement with literature.

In 2015 fourteen Babson College students performed in *Provincetown Four*, a collection of four one-act plays first produced by the Provincetown

Players over one hundred years ago. The commemorative production, held in Babson's rustic campus pub, enjoyed a sold-out run; Boston's NPR station covered *Provincetown Four* with a lengthy article on its website. Similar to undergraduate performances at most universities, *Provincetown Four* involved students at every level of production: as actors, as assistant directors, as stage managers, and as light and soundboard operators. Unique, however, was the production's use of student dramaturgs; the faculty directors of the one-acts were each aided by a group of student dramaturgs from my course Modernism and the Making of the New.

The dramaturgical assignment I created gave students the ability, like real-world dramaturgs, to assist the artists and audience of a production. The dramaturgical work was necessary for several key reasons. Despite their contributions and revolutionary and influential practices, the Provincetown Players are not well-known in American theater history. A course on American modernism might include a play by Eugene O'Neill or Susan Glaspell but likely not a work by the Provincetown Players, the very group that launched the careers of O'Neill and Glaspell. The faculty directors of *Provincetown Four* at Babson College, all of whom work in professional theater, benefitted from the historical research their dramaturgs provided about the Provincetown Players and their important legacy and contributions to modernism. Dramaturgical work was also vital because each play presented as part of *Provincetown Four* is over one hundred years old. Although the plays in many ways feel surprisingly fresh and relevant for today's audiences, there were still many references, phrases, and lines that needed research and contextualization. The dramaturgical team assigned to each play performed the necessary work to make the script accessible to the artistic team. Finally, dramaturgs were necessary to get our mainly undergraduate audiences excited about plays that were unfamiliar. As part of their assignments, dramaturgs had to consider the audience's expectations and gaps in knowledge as they prepared materials and notes for the program. Dramaturgs had to imagine the theatrical experience of the audience and craft resources accordingly.

In recounting her theater-going experiences at the start of the twentieth century, the Pulitzer Prize-winning American playwright Susan Glaspell wrote, "We went to the theatre and for the most part came away wishing we had gone somewhere else. Those were the days when Broadway flourished almost unchallenged. Plays, like magazine articles, were patterned. . . . [S]eldom did they open out to . . . where it surprised or thrilled your spirit to follow. They didn't ask much of you, those plays"

(190). A group of artists, writers, and performers would revolutionize American theater in 1915. This group, which lived and worked together in New York City's Greenwich Village, included the journalists Mary Heaton Vorse and John Reed; Floyd Dell, the editor of *Masses*, and Max Eastman, one of its contributors; the theater designer Robert Edmond Jones; the novelists Hutchins Hapgood, Neith Boyce, and Susan Glaspell; and Glaspell's husband, George Cram Cook, an erstwhile professor of classics (Black 1). These Greenwich Villagers vacationed in Provincetown, Massachusetts, during the summers, and in 1915 their days were spent not only in worried conversations about the outbreak of war in Europe but also in discussing the role art, specifically theater, could play in addressing serious political, social, and economic issues. In a rented cottage that summer, an unassuming performance of two new one-act plays, Boyce's *Constancy* and Cook and Glaspell's *Suppressed Desires*, was enthusiastically received by the vacationing artists and writers. The Provincetown Players were born. The group would go on to produce nearly one hundred new plays by American writers over the next eight years.

The Provincetown Players are perhaps best known for launching the careers of O'Neill and Glaspell, as well as those of Djuna Barnes, Edna St. Vincent Millay, and Wallace Stevens. The group broke new ground in American drama by presenting works that experimented with expressionistic, futuristic, and surrealistic forms and that explored important political and social issues. The Provincetown Players were also revolutionary in the way that their ensemble-based group celebrated and promoted the work of women: many of the company's members were women, as were nearly half of its twenty-nine founders. Women were also involved as executive committee members, playwrights, set designers, and directors.[1] In the Provincetown Players' rich eight years, the plays by women addressed significant yet underexposed issues like gender inequality, roles in marriage, free love, birth control, and women in the workplace. In other words, the Provincetown Players, and its women artists in particular, are largely responsible for bringing modernist concerns, modes, and themes to the American theater.

The Provincetown Players' refusal to produce works that resembled popular Broadway fare, namely melodramas and frothy romantic comedies, aligned them with other companies that emerged as part of the little theater movement of the first part of the twentieth century. The little theater movement was spearheaded by small companies that sought to produce more realistic and avant-garde works.[2] Two companies in particular, the Little Theater of Chicago and the Washington Square Players in New York, helped introduce European playwrights to American audiences and cultivated a following for more realistic drama. In plays by August Strindberg as well as works by other prominent European and Russian playwrights like George Bernard Shaw, Henrik Ibsen, and Anton Chekhov, audiences witnessed realistic characters struggling with social and cultural ills outside their control. The project of the Provincetown Players—to create serious drama for and by American playwrights—was guided by the group's transatlantic roots. If drama is a unit of study in a modernism course, works by Chekhov or Strindberg would be likely additions to a syllabus; instructors might consider the inclusion of an early Provincetown Players work to extend the discussion of the impact of Chekhov or Strindberg on modernist drama while situating new American theater in a global context. Another important precursor to the founding of the Provincetown Players was an American tour of Dublin's Abbey Players in 1911. This theater company was dedicated to producing original plays by Irish playwrights such as William Butler Yeats, John Millington Synge, and Lady Gregory, and to presenting "simplified staging methods and naturalistic acting style," a change from the exaggerated acting seen in British and American melodramas during this time (Murphy 3). Glaspell would later write that "quite possibly there would have been no Provincetown Players had there not been Irish Players" (qtd. in Murphy 4). Indeed, the Irish Players' dedication to a new kind of acting, and their loyalty to homegrown playwrights, provided a clear model for the writers and artists who would form the Provincetown Players.

The Provincetown Players moved to Greenwich Village in 1916 and occupied two different theaters there. In these spaces they produced ninety-seven new plays written by forty-seven American playwrights. They experimented with surrealism and expressionism, and they presented acting that was naturalistic and did not overshadow important messages about political and societal ills. The first plays were penned by women, and the examination of feminist issues and concerns by women playwrights would be an important hallmark of later works by the Provincetown Players. Boyce's *Constancy*, Cook and Glaspell's *Suppressed Desires*, and Rita Wellman's *Funiculi Funicula* all focus on couples who are interested in and engage with new movements and philosophies such as free love, open marriage, psychoanalysis, and avant-garde art and literature. In all these plays, however, the women who try to take part in or enjoy these hallmarks of early-twentieth-century modernity are punished.

Constancy, *Suppressed Desires*, and *Funiculi Funicula* make visible the tension between liberatory social movements often seen as part of modernism and the actuality of bringing such movements to life, particularly when it is women who attempt to engage with and enjoy such movements. Boyce based *Constancy* on the real-life tumultuous romance between the heiress and famed salon hostess Mabel Dodge and John Reed. The play explores differing notions of faithfulness, or "constancy," held by men and women. In this inaugural play of the Provincetown Players, a woman is seen as unable or unwilling to participate in open marriage and free love.

Cook and Glaspell's comedy *Suppressed Desires* centers on Henrietta and Stephen Brewster, a married couple living in Greenwich Village, and includes Henrietta's visiting sister Mabel. At the start of the play, Henrietta, a devotee of psychoanalysis, tries to persuade a resistant Stephen to learn about the new science and urges him to go to Dr. Russell, her analyst. Henrietta's admiration for psychoanalysis is so intense that she does not hear Stephen's pragmatic protestations; she believes instead that Stephen's annoyance with and lack of interest in the subject of psychoanalysis is because of "some sort of complex" (35). Henrietta persuades her sister Mabel to see Dr. Russell with somewhat more ease. However, when Mabel learns at her appointment that she has a subconscious desire for her brother-in-law Stephen, and Stephen discovers at his appointment his desire to leave Henrietta, Henrietta gives up on psychoanalysis entirely. Although it is clear that Glaspell and Cook are skeptical of psychoanalysis, an emerging and popular trend in Greenwich Village at the time, the play also suggests that women face certain obstacles in their access to realms such as this new science, obstacles that result from the cultural restrictions of women's place in the domestic sphere and that men do not face.

In Wellman's 1917 play *Funiculi Funicula* Alma is a woman wrestling with the obligations of a household despite her artistic desires. Alma is in a domestic partnership with a fellow artist, Taddema, and the two have a baby girl named Bambi. The play opens as Alma is meeting with Dr. Collins, who has come to her filthy Washington Square apartment to care for a very sick Bambi. Although it seems that Alma does not hear Dr. Collins's stern lecture and warnings about Bambi, it becomes apparent when Taddema returns home that Alma has absorbed much of what the doctor has said. When Taddema discovers that Alma has put the sick child in their bed to rest, he asks, "And where am I supposed to sleep . . . you might have thought of me" (171). The child eventually dies and, even in death, remains a kind of magnet, keeping Alma inside the apartment instead of enjoying the bohemian life of Greenwich Village. Taddema, however, is able to move on in a way that Alma cannot.

Babson College produced *Constancy* and *Suppressed Desires* as part of *Provincetown Four*, and these two plays provide excellent opportunities for student dramaturgical work. While *Funiculi Funicula* was not part of the production, it is a work ripe for dramaturgical examination in the classroom. When students examine these plays through a dramaturgical lens—thinking critically about the performance of the plays and the steps necessary to prepare a director, actor, and audience to access them—they see the plays as performative texts and as living works that reveal much about the world in which they were created.

The dramaturgical assignment I designed has three components. As part of the first component, students meet with the director of their assigned play (for classes not assisting a live production, students could meet with a faculty member in the theater department or with a local director). The director, who should be contacted ahead of time by the faculty member and who should be aware of the parameters of the assignment, meets with the dramaturgical team to discuss how they plan to produce the play. The director shares the vision and goals for the production. This initial discussion is an illuminating experience for the student dramaturgs because it presents a unique opportunity to learn what a director considers when readying a play for production. As part of the assignment, request that the director ask three questions about the play for the dramaturgs to research and answer. For the Babson College project, my students reported that the director of *Constancy* asked the dramaturgs the following questions:

> Who were John Reed and Mabel Dodge? What was their romance like?
>
> Who was Weininger? What does the line "It is true, as Weininger said, women have no soul, no memory" mean (Boyce 62)? Why is this line important for the characters and the world of *Constancy*?
>
> On page 57, Rex uses the following quotation: "Love is not love that alters when it alteration finds or bends with the remover to remove."[3] Where does this quotation come from? Why is it significant? And how does it connect to Rex and his objectives?

Such questions focus on the complexities of relationships between men and women, particularly when the boundaries of such relationships are not easily agreed on. The goal of this component of the assignment is to give students an experience that resembles the work of professional dramaturgs, that demonstrates how directors help move the script from page to stage, and that reveals the research required to create compelling, viable productions.

The second component involves dramaturgical work on behalf of the actors. Each student team is responsible for finding ten phrases, words, or expressions in the script that are unfamiliar or need further clarification. The team then writes five to ten sentences that describe the phrase, word, or expression; its context; and the reasons it is included in the script. After this, the team gives the list to the director of the play to approve before presenting the annotated list to the actors.

The third component of the project, dramaturgical work meant for the benefit of audience, is a two-part assignment. First, students create a "Dramaturg's Note" for the production's program. This note is three pages long and contains information about the playwright(s), the production history and reception of the play, important historical moments that influenced the playwright's approach to crafting the work, and the work's significance today. Second, students create a poster for the play to be displayed in the front lobby during the production. During the Babson production, members of each dramaturgy team stood in front of their respective posters and answered questions or engaged in discussions about the plays before the show and during intermission.

Some of the major learning goals of my course include an ability to synthesize the tenets of modernism and its major cultural, political, and artistic trends; a recognition of how the literature, art, and drama of the twentieth century relate to one another in a historical context; and an appreciation of how these arts can illuminate social problems and injustices. The work of the Provincetown Players, particularly the work done by the group's women artists, was influenced by and in turn impacted modernist thought and aesthetics. When students examine this work as dramaturgs, they reach the goals of the course through active engagement and thoughtful research. And I believe that the Provincetown Players' great experiment becomes all the more significant as a result.

Notes

1. As Cheryl Black reports, "More than 120 women were associated with the Provincetown Players. Of those, approximately 40 were important, regularly active members who performed a multiplicity of functions. Thirteen of the company's 29 founders were women; 16 of its 51 playwrights were women; 7 of its 19

executive committee members were women; 6 of its 28 scenic designers were women; its leading costume designer was a woman; its leading actor was a woman; and its leading director was a woman" (3).

2. See Snyder in this volume for more on drama.

3. Here, Rex quotes, practically verbatim, from Shakespeare's sonnet 116.

Works Cited

Black, Cheryl. *The Women of Provincetown, 1915–1922.* U of Alabama P, 2002.

Boyce, Neith. *Constancy.* Ozieblo, pp. 52–63.

Cattaneo, Anne. "Dramaturgy: An Overview." *Dramaturgy in American Theater: A Sourcebook*, edited by Susan Jonas et al., Harcourt Brace College Publishers, 1997, pp. 3–15.

Chemers, Michael Mark. *Ghost Light: An Introductory Handbook for Dramaturgy.* Southern Illinois UP, 2010.

Cook, George Cram, and Susan Glaspell. *Suppressed Desires.* Ozieblo, pp. 34–51.

Glaspell, Susan. *The Road to the Temple: A Biography of George Cram Cook.* Ernest Benn, 1926.

Murphy, Brenda. *The Provincetown Players and the Culture of Modernity.* Cambridge UP, 2005.

Ozieblo, Barbara, editor. *The Provincetown Players: A Choice of the Shorter Works.* Sheffield Academic Press, 1994.

Switzky, Lawrence. "Dramaturgy as Skill, Function, and Verb." *The Routledge Companion to Dramaturgy*, edited by Magda Romanska, Routledge, 2015, pp. 173–78.

Wellman, Rita. *Funiculi Funicula.* Ozieblo, pp. 166–78.

Part IV

Places and Races

Tamara Slankard

Teaching American Modernism and Place

At the small, midwestern liberal arts university where I teach, my biannual senior seminar on American modernism must accomplish multiple objectives. In addition to fostering more sophisticated textual analysis skills and guiding students through advanced research techniques, the course often serves as the first introduction to literary modernism for a handful of English majors and minors. The prospect of adding another topic to an already packed syllabus seemed too daunting to consider. Yet engaging with place through concepts in environmental psychology facilitates the teaching of literary modernism. Doing so makes some of modernism's basic thematic tenets—the tendency to focus on interiority, a pervasive sense of alienation and disillusionment, the exploration of individual anxiety in an increasingly fragmented and mechanized world—more accessible for students. It also frees me to teach the "expansion" Douglas Mao and Rebecca L. Walkowitz describe in their formulation of the new modernist studies within the confines of sophomore-level surveys and upper-level undergraduate courses (737). Teaching modernism and place expands the parameters of literary modernism thematically and geographically, opening dialogue between urban and regional modernisms and between the formal and the popular. It also complicates the concept of modernist subjectivity as women writers draw attention to the necessity of thinking outside the self.

Environmental psychology emerged as an interdisciplinary field of study in the early seventies as a means of understanding the relation between people and their physical worlds. Scholars like Harold M. Proshansky, whose work helped define the discipline, were interested in how individuals are shaped by their natural and constructed surroundings, particularly in urban settings. In his 1978 article "The City and Self-Identity," Proshansky establishes "place-identity" as a foundational theory of environmental psychology, arguing that who we are is determined by where we live, work, and play as much as by our race, gender, and class. Why, Proshansky wondered, did both insiders and outsiders tend to have such negative views of the city and city dwellers, even as society was becoming increasingly urban? For environmental psychologists, the answers to this still-pertinent question are essential in determining the influence of city life on social interactions and understanding the complexities of our thinking about subjectivity.

More recent theorists, including urban sociologists, are interested in the complementary but inverse relation between individuals and their environments. Not only does place contribute to the construction of individual identity, but people "invest places with meaning and value in order to make sense of their world" (Borer 180). Neither cities, nor small towns, nor office cubicles have innate and unalterable identities. Rather, they are constantly made and remade by the people who exist within them. People construct place actively and socially through "the flux of human dialogue" in an attempt "to make sense of their locatedness" (Dixon and Durrheim 32, 40). People also construct place simply because there is no "there" without the "normally unnoticed phenomenon of person-or-people-experiencing-place" (Seamon 11). In other words, people do not merely define place. People are place. How they act and interact leads to central questions about the essence of humanity as well as the experiences of modernity.

We can apply theories of environmental psychology to the teaching of literary modernism and place even though—or perhaps precisely because—as Anthony Giddens argues, "[m]odernity 'dis-places'" its subjects (140). Wesley A. Kort suggests that scholars of modern fiction would do well to consider issues of "place and space" as much as "time and temporality" (1), as one defining characteristic of modernity might very well be the widening distance between "vast urbanization" and "subjectivity" (207, 208).

Asking students to begin with the presupposition that modernism entails restlessness invites conversation about how these works depict anxiety and mobility. By focusing on characters' interactions with their physical environments, students see how modernist writers were simultaneously describing and defining modernity for their imagined readers—how some were, in effect, creating what environmental psychologists might call built or even virtual environments by setting the parameters of high modernism. Bringing the background—that is, bringing place—to the fore and shifting the focus away from high modernist subjects can also establish key distinctions between urban and rural or regional modernisms without creating reductive hierarchies.

Teaching literary modernism through environmental psychology creates a space for genre fiction within modernism. The turn toward new modernist studies has meant that the generic boundaries of modernism continue to expand in scholarship and the classroom. David M. Earle has argued that genre novels written by established modernist authors like William Faulkner and Ernest Hemingway call into question "the long-standing tradition of seeing modernism as antagonistic to popular culture" (346). Paula Rabinowitz writes on a subgenre she calls "pulp modernism" and sees mid-century cheap paperbacks as "part of a larger process by which modernism itself . . . spread across America" (22). I will not spend time reestablishing the legitimacy of applying modernist labels to works of genre fiction. It is no longer unusual to find detective novels or noir alongside more traditional texts on syllabi. And yet these spots are frequently taken by men who have entered the canon, such as Raymond Chandler and Dashiell Hammett. The Femmes Fatales series, published by the Feminist Press, makes many mid-century pulp novels written by women readily available to students, thereby giving instructors the ability to teach the tensions within the male-dominated noir genre and between women's genre fiction and traditionally defined modernism.

One tension has to do with how women writers imagine the relations between character and environment as more symbiotic, less deterministic, and less fatalistic than other modernist depictions. Their characters appear more adaptable, more able to learn to navigate spaces. Despite this, Patricia Highsmith, master of the psychological thriller, whom Gore Vidal once called "[o]ne of our greatest modernist writers" (qtd. in Schenkar 511), claimed that she wrote male protagonists almost exclusively because "[w]omen are tied to the home, tied to somebody, not as independent to travel," whereas "[m]en can do more, like jump over fences" (qtd. in Dupont).

The globe-trotting heroine of Dorothy B. Hughes's *The Blackbirder*—a noir novel I teach in my American modernism seminar and discuss below—suggests otherwise (as does Highsmith's own biography), but still other works like Vera Caspary's *Laura* seem to purposefully demonstrate how women are socially and psychologically confined to certain spaces. Thus, environmental psychology allows students to work through how what we think we know about what modernism was and did is under constant revision.

What follows is a description of my own most recent revision: the addition of a four-week "Modernism and Environmental Psychology" unit to my American Modernism senior seminar. The course began with an introductory unit ("WTF Is/Was Modernism?!") before we jumped into the idea of modernism and place. Malcolm Bradbury's "The Cities of Modernism" and Eric Homberger's "Chicago and New York: Two Versions of American Modernism" established a critical framework for urban modernity and the inextricability of the city from a particular view of modernist subjectivity. Homberger's article initiated discussion of the differing identities, sensibilities, literary histories, and subsequent mythologies of two American cities, allowing us to begin with a shared understanding of place as central to literary modernism, and facilitating a branching out into theoretical concepts of environmental psychology with which students would be unfamiliar. Students read these two articles alongside three poems: T. S. Eliot's "The Love Song of J. Alfred Prufrock," Claude McKay's "Harlem Shadows," and Gwendolyn Brooks's "Kitchenette Building."

We began with "Prufrock," a poem decidedly of the faceless modern city, with a speaker whose just-on-the-fringes urban desires indicate, if not catalyze, his alienation and anxiety. I teach this poem in American literature survey courses as part of a unit on modernism, but students tend to have difficulty understanding just why Prufrock is so awkward and insecure, which can (ironically) contribute to their own frustrations about feeling like outsiders with respect to literary modernism. When we looked at the poem in the context of environmental psychology, however, students—some of them the very same students who had taken the twentieth-century survey course with me just one semester earlier—were able to more clearly see how Prufrock's anxieties are a representation of his relation to place. The "yellow fog," the "pools that stand in drains," and the "soot that falls from chimneys" are not simply Eliot's dark vision of modernity (lines 15, 18, 19). These lines are indicative of Prufrock's sense of himself as threatened by a dirty and tainted outside, urban world. The "women

[who] come and go / Talking of Michelangelo" are not simply "[i]n the room," they are the room (13–14). Prufrock's every self-flagellation can be traced back to his desire not just to be with these women but also to be where they are. And if this is the case, then Prufrock's anxieties—and those of the modernist subject more generally—go far beyond the gendered concerns of a fragile masculinity.

Liesl Olson proved a valuable addition to our discussion of "Harlem Shadows" and "Kitchenette Building," particularly in her juxtaposition of the modernisms of New York and Chicago (*Chicago Renaissance* and "When Chicago"). Each poem has as its subject a distinct city—New York's Harlem for McKay and the South Side of Chicago for Brooks—and each explores the relation between (racial and gendered) modernist subjectivity and place. Students compare the poems' treatment of African American women and their association with either the nighttime streets of Harlem or the cramped apartment space, particularly as those images are communicated through different gendered voices. McKay's male speaker is voiced boldly in the first person and teeters on the edge of either sympathy for or judgement of the "little dark girls" whose "prowling through the night from street to street" is either indicative of or instrumental to his "fallen race." Conversely, Brooks's weary woman speaker begins from the position of a collective "We," recognizing the concerns of the many. Thereafter, "Kitchenette Building" oscillates between the concrete and the abstract, between "yesterday's garbage ripening in the hall" and "a dream sent up through onion fumes," and so connects the physical environment to individuals' inner lives.

With this groundwork in place, students read two essays on environmental psychology: Proshansky's "The City and Self-Identity" and Per Gustafson's "Place Attachment in an Age of Mobility." These essays develop key questions that guide discussion for the remainder of the unit (and semester). Students also used the following questions as they wrote literary analyses, and as a guide for a take-home midterm exam that asked them, in part, to discuss how one or two of the texts we read engaged with literary modernism and place through the lens of environmental psychology:

How is place depicted in a particular work?
Is it important whether a place is urban or not? Why?
How do characters use, or learn to use, their environments—and for what purposes?
In what ways do characters instill places with meaning?

How do places help shape characters' personalities or internal monologues (i.e., their relationship to the self)?
In what ways does place determine how characters are defined by other characters?
How do characters exhibit place-attachment or place-aversion? How does this affect the meaning of the story and reflect the story's engagement with the ideologies of literary modernism?
What effect does place have on relationships between characters?
How do places influence characters' actions?
Do some characters seem hopelessly mired in one place? What is the significance of this?
How does gender affect characters' relations to their environments?
In what ways are characters, even background characters, depicted as part of a place or environment? How are some characters depicted as decidedly separate from a place? How is this distinction important to the project of literary modernism?
If we begin with the presupposition that modernism is restless and that placelessness and isolation are characteristic of modernist subjects (both people and characters), then what do we, as literary critics, make of the depiction of place in a particular work or works?
How might reading a work through the lens of environmental psychology help us better understand that work's engagement with the central concerns of literary modernism?

Establishing these key questions as parameters allowed us to venture away from canonical modernist works without losing sight of the connections to them. Two weeks into this unit we began Hughes's mid-century spy thriller, *The Blackbirder.* At least two main challenges emerge in the teaching of noir fiction and modernism—both have to do with style. Undergraduates often struggle to grasp the intersections between form and function in modernist works, just as they often get lost in the highly stylized dialogue and tone on their way to apprehending the twists and turns of the noir plot. Both concerns are remedied by teaching noir as modernism because, in many respects, the form is the function in mystery and detective fiction. When students prioritize style over structure, they see noir as a vehicle for expressing such modernist concerns as mid-century disillusionment, the plight of the individual among masses and machines, and the breakdown of gendered and socioeconomic boundaries.

I acknowledged at the start of this essay that women's genre fiction was an unusual choice for a course on American modernism. Even more peculiar is that, despite Hughes's genre-defying style and her interrogation of gendered assumptions in both *The Blackbirder* and *In a Lonely Place*, the author herself "loathed the term 'feminist'" (Villarejo 210). With my apologies to Hughes, I found that the simplest place to start a discussion of gender and modernism in *The Blackbirder* is with the novel's obvious but understated feminism. The double-identity heroine, Julie Guille / Juliet Marlebone, escapes the gestapo and the FBI and kills only for the greater good. When the helpless man in need of saving turns out to be a traitorous *homme fatal*, Julie mourns for about half a page before literally fighting fire with fire against a Nazi henchman. The novel invites discussion of gender performance in mid-century America; at times, Julie notes how her options and freedom of movement are restricted by the gendered perceptions of others. While she searches for the elusive Blackbirder in that modern fount of information—the cocktail bar—she thinks to herself, "[i]f she were a man" she could come and go at will and with confidence. But "[a]s it was she could enter upon occasion, sip and listen" (46). Julie also knows that momentarily playing the dutiful and attentive woman can sometimes help her save the day, as when she discovers that her secret husband is actually a Nazi smuggler: "she could appear trusting," Hughes writes, for "she too had learned to act a part" (186). In the end Julie chooses the active, traditionally male role of fighting in order to end the need for fighting, rather than sitting at home and waiting to help in the "woman's way" by nurturing the men who return and "helping the children to forget" (205). And in so doing, Hughes imagines a postwar world in which gendered boundaries are far more nebulous—even though the author herself claimed that feminism "is for the birds" (qtd. in Villarejo 234).

To highlight the interconnectedness of urban modernism, place, and environmental psychology, students identified scenes in which a character is depicted as being part of a characteristically modern environment. For example, Julie begins her journey westward to escape her pursuers by first stopping to collect her thoughts and eat a breakfast special at the 42nd Street Automat, before taking the bus down to 34th Street because it will be "[s]afer to buy clothes in a mammoth department store" (15–16). Julie knows that she will always "be safer in a city" like New York, where anonymity allows her a measure of comfort and cover, whereas in a "sinister" and "grim little town" like Santa Fe she is in constant danger because "the smallness of the village trap[s] her" (44). Gustafson's article was useful in our discussions of place versus placelessness in modernity because it asks, "What happens to people's emotional bonds with place in a highly mobile society?" (37), which turns a potential contradiction into an analytical question. The answer for Gustafson is that when "roots" become "routes," a multitude of "places may be meaningful as expressions of a person's individual trajectory and identity" (39). This framing concept helped students articulate how the development of Julie's character is tied to her cross-country movements. It also helped us contrast and define a more decidedly stationary, static regional modernism through two short stories we discussed in the remainder of the unit: Willa Cather's "The Sculptor's Funeral" and Katherine Anne Porter's "Noon Wine."

Each of these two stories is set firmly in a specific geographic location—Cather's fictional "little Kansas town" (168) and Porter's "Small South Texas Farm" (222). Depiction of place and its influence on individual and group psychology is in large part the point of each story, as each author explores the problematics of place-identity for modernist subjectivity. Cather's "The Sculptor's Funeral" lambasts the small town as insidiously stifling and suffocating (somewhat surprisingly, given the author's other romanticized portrayals of plains people). Students identified the lengthy opening description of a "group of townspeople" (168) huddled en masse against the cold and, implicitly, against the Bostonian outsider accompanying Harvey Merrick's body back "home" (169) on the "night train" (168) as immediately establishing both the closed physical and ideological borders of Sand City and the mandated group identity of its inhabitants. Cather presents the psychologically patrolled borders of the small town, "sentinelled" by "long lines of shivering poplars," as completely at odds with a modern desire for movement and change, indicated by the "number of lanky boys" who are called to attention by the train whistle, "the world-wide call for men" (169). But it is the battle to define Harvey Merrick, to figuratively "take charge of the body" (169), that most clearly portrays a regional modernist anxiety, seeing as the men of Sand City label and isolate anyone who dares not validate their perception of the place that defines them. While they sit up with Harvey's corpse, they reassure themselves by reconstructing an image of "Harve" as a weakling who was always either unwilling or unable to do real work. They are disdainful of his art and of any education beyond "some first-class Kansas City business college" (175). All would have been as it should be, they speculate, "[i]f Harve had stayed at home" (174).

Students initially read Porter's "Noon Wine" as a more forgiving portrayal of place because, although the story ends with two murders and a suicide, much of the plot suggests the possibility of change. Mr. Thompson is at first suspicious of "the stranger" (223), clearly some kind of "forriner" (225) who shows up at his dairy farm looking for a job, but is quickly won over by Mr. Helton's work ethic and quiet, unassuming demeanor. After a few years, Helton is no longer an outsider but "the hope and prop of the family" (241). It is most certainly this adopted familial relationship that leads Thompson to kill the fugitive hunter he believes is about to murder Helton, and this defensive act seems to suggest that allegiance to people trumps allegiance to place and that place-identity is malleable. But Thompson ultimately cannot escape the place that defines him. His suicide can be read as a succumbing to that particular brand of modern isolation that is universal and decidedly regional: though the courts had ruled him innocent, Thompson is consumed by the feeling that his neighbors "didn't believe he was not a murderer" (262), and so he makes an exhausting and futile attempt to convince his neighbors of his innocence because he cares more for appearances and the opinions of others than for his own life. He can define another man by his character, but cannot extricate his own self-identity from the ideology of place. In this way, both Cather and Porter depict one facet of regional modernity in which people are mired not only within the borders of a specific geographic place but also within the psychological gray area between place-attachment and place-aversion.

Reading literary modernism through the multifaceted lenses of place-identity and place-attachment theories broadens students' understanding—and our own—of the relation between modern subjects and spaces. Doing so also contributes to the expansion of modernist studies, as place bridges distances among otherwise disparate modernisms. When we talk about modernism and place, we also facilitate a more concrete conceptualization of modern alienation, mobility, and placelessness. But the relation between literary modernism and environmental psychology is not unidirectional. Literary modernism also complicates some key theories of environmental psychology because modernist poetry, like Brooks's "Kitchenette Building," shows how space and subjectivity are constructed differently for women. Regional modernist writers like Cather and Porter reveal the potentially destructive effects of place-attachment. And works of genre fiction like Hughes's *The Blackbirder* at times suggest not only that people are the environment but also that the individual's very survival depends on joining the crowd. Likewise, engaging with the work of colleagues in other disciplines enriches teaching opportunities at every institutional level. Reaching across those spaces can also help ensure the continued relevance of literary studies.

Works Cited

Borer, Michael Ian. "The Location of Culture: The Urban Culturalist Perspective." *City and Community*, vol. 5, no. 2, pp. 173–97.

Bradbury, Malcolm. "The Cities of Modernism." Bradbury and McFarlane, pp. 96–104.

Bradbury, Malcolm, and James McFarlane, editors. *Modernism: A Guide to European Literature, 1890–1930*. Penguin Books, 1978.

Brooks, Gwendolyn. "Kitchenette Building." *The Essential Gwendolyn Brooks*, edited by Elizabeth Alexander, Library of America, 2005, p. 1.

Caspary, Vera. *Laura*. 1942. Feminist Press, 2005.

Cather, Willa. "The Sculptor's Funeral." 1905. *The Norton Anthology of American Literature*, 9th ed., vol. D (1914–45), edited by Robert S. Levine et al., W. W. Norton, 2017, pp. 168–77.

Dixon, John, and Kevin Durrheim. "Displacing Place-Identity: A Discursive Approach to Locating Self and Other." *British Journal of Social Psychology*, vol. 39, 2000, pp. 27–44.

Dupont, Joan. "Criminal Pursuits." *The New York Times Magazine*, 12 June 1988, www.nytimes.com/1988/06/12/magazine/criminal-pursuits.html.

Earle, David M. "The Modernist Genre Novel." *A History of the Modernist Novel*, edited by Gregory Castle, Cambridge UP, 2015, pp. 345–68.

Eliot, T. S. "The Love Song of J. Alfred Prufrock." 1915. The Waste Land *and Other Poems*, by Eliot, Signet, 1998, pp. 5–11.

Giddens, Anthony. *The Consequences of Modernity*. Stanford UP, 1990.

Gustafson, Per. "Place Attachment in an Age of Mobility." Manzo and Devine-Wright, pp. 37–48.

Homberger, Eric. "Chicago and New York: Two Versions of American Modernism." Bradbury and McFarlane, pp. 151–61.

Hughes, Dorothy B. *The Blackbirder*. 1943. Feminist Press, 2004.

———. *In a Lonely Place*. 1947. New York Review Books, 2017.

Kort, Wesley A. *Place and Space in Modern Fiction*. UP of Florida, 2004.

Manzo, Lynne C., and Patrick Devine-Wright, editors. *Place Attachment: Advances in Theory, Methods and Applications*. Routledge, 2014.

Mao, Douglas, and Rebecca L. Walkowitz. "The New Modernist Studies." *PMLA*, vol. 123, no. 3, May 2008, pp. 737–48.

McKay, Claude. "Harlem Shadows." *Harlem Shadows: The Poems of Claude McKay*, Harcourt Brace, 1922, p. 22.

Olson, Liesl. *Chicago Renaissance: Literature and Art in the Midwest Metropolis*. Yale UP, 2017.

———. "When Chicago Was the Real Literary Capital of the United States (According to H. L. Mencken, Anyway)." *Literary Hub*, 18 Sept. 2017, lithub.com/when-chicago-was-the-real-literary-capital-of-the-united-states/.

Porter, Katherine Anne. "Noon Wine." 1937. *The Collected Stories of Katherine Anne Porter*, Harcourt Brace, 1965, pp. 222–68.

Proshansky, Harold M. "The City and Self-Identity." *Environment and Behavior*, vol. 10, no. 2, 1978, pp. 147–69.

Rabinowitz, Paula. *American Pulp: How Paperbacks Brought Modernism to Main Street.* Princeton UP, 2014.

Schenkar, Joan. *The Talented Miss Highsmith: The Secret Life and Serious Art of Patricia Highsmith.* St. Martin's Press, 2009.

Seamon, David. "Place Attachment and Phenomenology: The Synergistic Dynamism of Place." Manzo and Devine-Wright, pp. 11–21.

Villarejo, Amy. Afterword. Hughes, *Blackbirder*, pp. 209–35.

Emily M. Hinnov

Teaching the Harlem Renaissance: Hannah Höch, Marita O. Bonner, and Nella Larsen

The New Negro movement, known also as the Harlem Renaissance, is a phenomenon of Black modernism with transatlantic influence within the broader modernist movement—a phenomenon resplendent with the cross-pollination of Black and white cultural expression in art, literature, and popular culture. This chapter offers an intersectional approach to teaching this phenomenon by placing writers of the Harlem Renaissance era—the novelist Nella Larsen and the essayist, playwright, and short story author Marita O. Bonner—in conversation with the Dada artist Hannah Höch. Höch's photomontages from the 1920s provide co-texts for Bonner's multigeneric essay "On Being Young—a Woman—and Colored" (1925) and Larsen's *Quicksand* (1928). Creating a space in which these women artists might be considered together gives students the opportunity to view Bonner's and Larsen's texts as well as Höch's montages as feminist critiques of fragmented, displaced, even tormented Black female identity within an avant-garde, modern, cosmopolitan context. Furthermore, these texts lend themselves to an affective analysis of various twentieth-century art forms.[1] My ultimate aim is for students to understand how the work of these global modernist women artists invites readers and viewers to reconcile the space between self and other.[2]

To draw together seemingly disparate cultural texts such as Höch's photocollages, Bonner's essay, and Larsen's novel, I begin with a brief presentation on the Harlem Renaissance using Claude McKay's poem "The Harlem Dancer." McKay's poem celebrates the beginnings of the Harlem Renaissance, a period in the 1920s in which Black culture flourished. McKay's sonnet presents a counterpoint to any purely celebratory vision of this period such as we might see in Alain Locke's introduction to *The New Negro* (1925), which reflects Locke's confidence in the commitment of young Black artists to representing Black America in new and progressive ways. The figure of the Harlem dancer in McKay's poem embodies both the pride and the ambivalence embedded in the Black American (female) experience and has much in common with Larsen's and Bonner's complex versions of New Negro womanhood. As the focal point of the Harlem club depicted in the poem, the dancer "seemed a proudly-swaying palm" who inspires the admiration of "even the girls" (lines 7, 11). All those under her spell "devoured her shape with eager, passionate gaze" (12), while beneath the surface of the dancer's expression, "her falsely-smiling face" proves to the speaker that "her self was not in that strange place" (13, 14). The Harlem dancer must "wear the mask" of primitivism similar to that of the poet Paul Laurence Dunbar's minstrel show, while striving to maintain an inner power that cannot be penetrated by her applauding onlookers. Writers such as Bonner and Larsen in particular negotiate the dual impulse of Harlem Renaissance literature to celebrate Black cultural forms and to avoid denigrating or primitivizing the Black experience—especially in writing for a predominantly white audience whose gaze produces what W. E. B. Du Bois termed a "double consciousness" experienced by Black artists of the era (*Souls* 3). Black women writers leave us with no simple version of the period now known as the Harlem Renaissance.

After discussing McKay's poem, I show students a series of Höch's images, which I contextualize by providing information on primitivism within the modernist era. Höch fits into our conversation about the transatlantic reach of the Harlem Renaissance, and her work gets students to think about women modernists' engagement with the trope of primitivism. An originator of the photomontage form, Höch took photographs from magazines, juxtaposing the modern German woman with the colonial woman in ways that were often jarring. In doing so, she, like Bonner and Larsen, challenged cultural representations of women in the modernist period, raising questions regarding sexuality and gender roles in modernity. As described in "A Few Words on Photomontage, 1934," photomontage represented for Höch "a new, magical territory, for the discovery of which freedom is the first prerequisite. . . . Here more than anywhere else, these beauties, wandering and extravagant, obligingly enrich our fantasy" (qtd. in Lavin 220). Many of Höch's pictures still appear astonishingly current.[3]

After providing students with a short outline of Höch's biography, I ask them to consider the fantastical nature of Höch's photocollages. I begin with *Monument I* (1924). In this composition, Höch furnishes a disturbingly primitive sculpture with the body parts of a contemporary woman whom we can presume is German. I find it necessary to situate Höch's problematic use of the primitive in a classroom discussion about primitivism and modernism, especially given that Larsen and Bonner recognize that primitivism is part of the appeal of the Harlem Renaissance for both artists and audiences. In order to teach the complex interrelation between primitivism and modernism, instructors may also wish to refer to Pablo Picasso's 1907 painting *Les Demoiselles d'Avignon* (*The Young Women of Avignon*) and read against the Eurocentric gaze of the image and its racist cultural appropriation. Feminist art historians such as Suzanne Preston-Blier have strongly rejected the widespread notion of a pure aesthetic encounter in this piece: "Picasso visualises a colonial regime of the gaze, artistically mapping out a scientific evolutionary model by hierarchically arranging the five women according to their skin colour" (qtd. in Edenheiser and Rodatus). Picasso's work demonstrates that Höch was not the only European modernist to incorporate primitivist imagery into their art. Introducing Locke's *The New Negro* alongside Josephine Baker's *danse sauvage* ("wild dance") shows students how Black artists grappled with the trope of primitivism as well.

Sieglinde Lemke's *Primitivist Modernism* and more current scholarship such as Ben Etherington's *Literary Primitivism* provide an overview of the link between Black and white cultural expressions in the development of a global modernism. Lemke argues that "the ideological base of the Harlem Renaissance follows th[e] . . . pattern of finding one's identity through one's cultural other" (191). This is a particularly useful point about the production of modernist texts. By encouraging students to think about how they, too, might imagine and then achieve the vital task of sympathetically connecting with the experience of another person, we come closer to achieving the learning goal of affective literary analysis.

When I ask students what first strikes them about Höch's *Monument I*, they often comment on how the abstract head of the figure tilts downward, digging her chin into her chest and clenching her hands as she shrugs in discontent. The torso of the female figure includes the elongated breasts of an African sculpture; stemming from the torso are the leg of a female dancer and the arm of a man. I then ask students why they think Höch chose to use fragments of other pieces of art to construct her photomontages rather than create something more one-dimensional, such as a photograph, and students respond that they appreciate the multimodal nature of these images. They agree that the message is more complex than it would be with a single or uniform image. When asked if they find Höch's artwork engaging in its bizarre aesthetic or absurd, off-putting, or even meaningless, I've found that students are almost never disengaged; with this piece in particular, they often value the presence of a kind of dark humor in the midst of a turmoil and anxiety surrounding gender identity.

Next we look at Höch's *Abduction* (1925), which depicts another modern German woman within an even more explicitly primitive scene. Four figures—two males and two females—are seated on top of a wooden sculpture of an animal. The head of the first female figure is replaced with the contrasting white face of a modern German woman. This female figure is facing backward on what seems to be a journey forward, and while the other faces appear calm, her mouth is open as if she is hollering. Students consider how this image positions us as viewers. In an attempt to realize the goal of an affective and intersubjective interpretive practice, I ask students if they see, as Lavin argues, that this work suggests the "replacement of an image of the Other with one of self" (170). If students concur that Höch intends to present her figures as other, then students may be asked to dismantle the concept of otherness by attempting to bridge the gap between self and other. Students often agree that Höch's message suggests a sense of dislocation or abduction from the familiar, the result of which is an unnerving feeling for women in her time and place and the ensuing possibility of empathy for the plight of this female figure.

I finish the sequence of Höch's photocollages with *Sadness* (1925), which presents another portrait of misshapen female identity. In an image of unstable gendered and racial selfhood, the upper set of hands of the composite figure is raised in a gesture of futility and resignation. The somber quality of the facial expression on the mask, combined with the dark tones of the background, contribute to the photocollage's nihilistic mood. Students are drawn to this image because of the figure's hybrid racial appearance. As we discuss, despite the montage's reliance on primitivist characteristics, we can agree that something about the female figure's readily apparent suffering suggests that we are meant to connect or empathize with her.

The Harlem Renaissance was a global movement that initially portended widespread celebration of an African American perspective on arts and culture, but the color line remained, and some of the movement depended on exploiting the attraction of white artists and audiences to the primitive—a trend that Black women writers of the era are extremely critical of. Höch's photomontages let us teach the place of primitivism within modernism because they illuminate the phenomenon of a cosmopolitan, transatlantic version of modernism that Bonner and Larsen challenge. At this point in the course, I reemphasize the idea that the concept of primitivism is integral to an understanding of the Harlem Renaissance, and that Höch holds a vexed position with respect to the use of primitivism. Her ethnographic series belies any overt criticism of contemporary attitudes on race, and critics of her artwork might well contend that she focuses too narrowly on white European ideas about gender. We might even fault Höch's ethnographic photocollages as "romanticized necrophilia" (Lavin 163). Some students are upset by her apparent cultural insensitivity; I have responded by pointing out the importance of her use of irony, which could function as an implicit judgment of otherwise primitivist points of view. At the very least, the unsettling nature of Höch's photomontages raises questions about how gender and race are represented within a modernist framework. The following are questions I offer for students to consider in our comparison of these texts: To what extent have these modernist women artists created empowering critiques of interlocking systems of dominance? And further, do these modernist women imagine their subjects succeeding outside the framework of conventional sexist and racist primitivism? Ultimately, by highlighting the relationship among these three women artists of the Harlem Renaissance era, instructors can teach the inarguable place of primitivism within this movement, and, more importantly—with an eye toward critique—generate transformative intersectional thinking on the part of students.

Before we delve into Larsen's *Quicksand*, we look at Bonner's grueling delineation of the life of the downtrodden race woman of the 1920s. An imagistic admixture of manifesto, episodic narrative poem, bitter social commentary, and memoir, Bonner's "On Being Young—a Woman—and Colored" enables an intersectional and intertextual approach to teaching primitivism and modernism. In a character portrayal that parallels that of Helga Crane in Larsen's *Quicksand*, Bonner sardonically narrates the doubly disadvantaged perspective of the young Black woman. Bonner writes bitterly about the weight of oppression she endures, but argues that with critical thinking, she might overcome it. The central obstacle to enlightenment is the prevailing racist and sexist stereotype projected onto African American women; some might say Höch's photomontages are evidence of this. Bonner asks, "Why do they see a colored woman only as a gross collection of desires, all uncontrolled?" (111). Like Larsen's protagonist and McKay's Harlem dancer, Bonner points to the internalized social mask of primitivism, what she calls out as "[a]n empty imitation of an empty invitation. A mime; a sham; a copy-cat. A hollow re-echo" (111). Because students have already been introduced to the Harlem Renaissance and its connection to primitivism, a few recognize a link between the suffering female figures rendered in Höch's photocollages and the sensibility of the speaker/narrator of Bonner's piece. Bonner expresses how a Black woman is perceived by the dominant white culture—as well as the inner turmoil that results from this culture's circumscribed gaze. I use this discussion as another opportunity to encourage an intersubjective understanding of these texts.

Bonner urges other Black women to call into question the image of the Black female other. She counsels her own generation of Black women to let go of the idea of the Old Negro, to relinquish those "[o]ld ideas, old fundamentals" because "they are useless to you in Their world" (111). Bonner contends that the best response to the forces of white supremacist, capitalist patriarchy is the creation of a protective outer shell that renders you "steely and brittle" yet mentally astute (111). With this inner resolve, subversively coupled with an outer compliance and a gendered expectation of calm, Bonner argues that young Black women can position themselves in a way that allows them to analyze the world around them. Bonner speaks fiercely about the intellectual domination that has silenced Black women. In the end, she recommends that young Black women remain silent while doing the intellectual work necessary to resist the dual oppressions of race and gender: "So—being a woman—you can wait . . . quiet. Like Buddha—who, brown like I am—sat entirely at ease, entirely sure of himself, motionless and knowing, a thousand years before the white man knew there was so very much difference between feet and hands" (112). She then refers to the enduring wisdom of women with the remark, "Perhaps Buddha is a woman" (112). Bonner concludes that a woman of the 1920s, especially a Black woman, must "with a smile . . . draw understanding into [her]self" and summon inner power for "when Time is ripe" (112).

At such time, she will "swoop to [her] feet" in a "single gesture" of freedom that will conquer this double inequality (112). Students find this piece demanding yet empowering for the ways Bonner navigates the challenges faced by young women of color in her own time.

Finally, we explore how Bonner's and Höch's work as cultural representations of the New Negro and New Womanhood, respectively, are further complicated by pivotal scenes in Larsen's *Quicksand*. For a luxuriant but brief time during her first visit to New York City, Larsen's protagonist Helga Crane, a biracial woman, feels a sense of wholeness within her community in the "primitive jungle" of "Harlem, teeming black Harlem" (43). An example of this feeling of wholeness occurs in the Harlem nightclub scene, which we examine closely: "[Helga] was drugged, lifted, sustained, by the extraordinary music" but then "the shameful certainty that not only had she been in the jungle, but that she enjoyed it . . . began to taunt her" (59). In this scene, Helga, like Bonner, resists being categorized as savage and oversexed; her total abandon in the dance would only reinscribe the sensationalized stereotype of the primitive and exotic female (as in some of Höch's photocollages).

As we trace similar scenes throughout the novel, we note that Helga constantly struggles with her racialization as an exoticized woman, a construction produced by the whiteness of her surveyors. From the moment she arrives in Copenhagen, she behaves as a "silent, unmoving," exotic museum piece (65), reminiscent of Höch's figures. As a kind of token for the aptly named Anglo artist Axel Olsen and her Danish relatives in Copenhagen, Helga at first relishes the feeling of freedom that Danish culture allows her, and dresses in vibrant clothing that emphasizes her ability to "make an impression, a voluptuous impression" (74). Helga participates—although with reticence—in the literal construction of her body as sexual, exotic, and available to men. Helga's impending romance with Olsen, who paints her portrait, further emphasizes her status as an unspeaking, captivating prop. As a mute object of the white male gaze, she is at once approvingly surveyed by and silenced by Olsen: "Helga . . . had a stripped, naked feeling under his direct glance" (86). Olsen's finished portrait of her literalizes her status as a thing to be admired for its foreignness and sexual appeal. Silent and estranged by her position as outsider in Copenhagen, Helga remains an art object until finally finding her voice of protest.

At this point in the discussion, we return to Höch and her photocollage *Strange Beauty* (1929), whose title and composition questions norms of feminine beauty and initiates the notion of the white woman's gaze. The photocollage presents a nude, white European female body joined with an alien face—here, a shrunken head with superimposed, enlarged spectacles. The magnified eyes on the shrunken head emphasize the reciprocal gaze; this female figure is on display, yet she also peers back at her onlooker. Höch wrote of this work: "I want to blur the firm boundaries that we as people tend self-assuredly to draw around all that we can achieve" (qtd. in Lavin 167). This statement, together with the image's reciprocal gaze, helps me reemphasize the goal of viewing these modernist works as spaces to imagine the encounter between self and other. Students who are already fans of Höch love this piece, which suggests that since beauty is strange and even grotesque, traditional notions of attractiveness are just as arbitrary.

After this, I cannot help but turn to Höch's *The Sweet* (ca. 1926), where the female figure appears to be on stage, an idea that is emphasized by a contrasting colorful backdrop. The figure's mismatched parts culminate in an elongated tribal mask—whose one-eyed glance askance suggests fragmented selfhood—and awkward yet pretty white dancing legs. In this tortured performative dance, the disproportionate female form seems uncomfortably aware—as evidenced by her wringing hands—that she is on perpetual display. Students connect this to the scene in which Helga is profoundly disturbed by Olsen's portrait. At the unveiling of the portrait, she observes, "It wasn't . . . herself at all, but some disgusting sensual creature with her features" (Larsen 89). I ask students whether Helga's refusal to accept Olsen's offensive attitude reveals a kind of feminist resolve that is reflected in Bonner's strong declaration of Black female selfhood or in Höch's complex images of modern women. Some students find Höch's pieces effective as a critique of society and the conflicts that women experienced in the modernist period, and many have connected her work to oppressive images of women in the media and popular culture in our current political moment. Larsen's Helga rejects a formulaic primitivist version of herself. Unfortunately, however, Helga's construction (and that of the female figure in *The Sweet*) as a sensual creature seems the only one afforded her within a racist and sexist culture where she is subject to the white male *and* female gazes. It is this culture and these gazes that continually obstruct her access to any kind of whole existence.

I always conclude this discussion with a consideration of the sorrowful ending of *Quicksand*, which brings us closer to the intention of bridging the gap between self and other. Hampered by a profound silence that renders her incapable of communication, it becomes evident that Helga lacks the language to articulate her desires or any vision of a full self. She appears increasingly alienated from herself, and, ultimately, her reading audience. Helga is nothing like the quiet, emancipated image of Buddha described by Bonner, and students often perceive her character as self-sabotaging and remote. I hope students will understand that her unrealizable need of imagining a balanced sense of self with regard to race and gender insists that audiences fill in this seeming impasse through an affective reading. If we can imagine convergence between self and other in contending with these texts, then perhaps we can recognize and empathize with the complexities of Helga's personal quicksand (and then we might even learn to hone such skills in our everyday life encounters). Our assessment of Larsen's novel, sparked by short writing assignments based on close textual analysis, intense discussion, and collaborative critical thinking about the various forms of primitivism and modernism we have studied, attempts to accomplish just that.

Notes

1. I take the concept of affective analysis from Jerome Bump's study of Toni Morrison's *The Bluest Eye*, in which he outlines the value of "emotive literary criticism" (148).

2. Instructors grappling with the intersections of modernism and primitivism might consult the following: Baker; Davis; Du Bois ("Criteria"); Gilroy; Hackett; Hutchinson ("Nella Larsen" and *Harlem Renaissance*); Kramer; Marcus; Monda; Nenno; Patton and Honey; Silverman; Tate.

3. See the companion website to this volume for the images discussed here (modwomen.mla.hcommons.org).

Works Cited

Baker, Houston A., Jr. *Modernism and the Harlem Renaissance.* U of Chicago P, 1987.

Bonner, Marita O. "On Being Young—a Woman—and Colored." Patton and Honey, pp. 109–12.

Bump, Jerome. "Racism and Appearance in *The Bluest Eye*: A Template for an Ethical Emotive Criticism." *College Literature*, vol. 37, no. 2, Spring 2010, pp. 147–70.

Davis, Thadious M. *Nella Larsen: Novelist of the Harlem Renaissance: A Woman's Life Unveiled.* Louisiana State UP, 1994.

Du Bois, W. E. B. "Criteria of Negro Art." Patton and Honey, pp. 47–51.

———. *The Souls of Black Folk.* 1903. Johnson Reprint, 1968.

Dunbar, Paul Laurence. "We Wear the Mask." *Poetry Foundation*, 2021, www.poetryfoundation.org/poems/44203/we-wear-the-mask.

Edenheiser, Iris, and Verena Rodatus. "'The Savage Hits Back' Revisited: Art and Global Contemporaneity in the Colonial Encounter." *Third Text: Critical Perspectives on Contemporary Art and Culture*, Aug. 2016, www.thirdtext.org/domains/thirdtext.com/local/media/images/medium/The_Savage_Hits_Back_1.pdf.

Etherington, Ben. *Literary Primitivism*. Stanford UP, 2017.

Gilroy, Paul. *The Black Atlantic: Modernism and the Harlem Renaissance*. Cambridge UP, 1993.

Hackett, Robin. *Sapphic Primitivism: Productions of Race, Class, and Sexuality in Key Works of Modern Fiction*. Rutgers UP, 2004.

Hutchinson, George. *The Harlem Renaissance in Black and White*. Harvard UP, 1995.

———. "Nella Larsen and the Veil of Race." *American Literary History*, vol. 9, no. 2, 1997, pp. 329–49.

Kramer, Victor A., editor. *The Harlem Renaissance Re-examined*. AMS Press, 1987.

Larsen, Nella. Quicksand *and* Passing. Edited by Deborah E. McDowell, Rutgers UP, 1986.

Lavin, Maud. *Cut with the Kitchen Knife: The Weimar Photomontages of Hannah Höch*. Yale UP, 1993.

Lemke, Sieglinde. *Primitivist Modernism: Black Culture and the Origins of Transatlantic Modernism*. Oxford UP, 1998.

Locke, Alain. *The New Negro*. 1925. Touchstone, 1999.

Marcus, Jane. *Hearts of Darkness: White Women Write Race*. Rutgers UP, 2004.

McKay, Claude. "The Harlem Dancer." *Harlem Shadows: The Poems of Claude McKay*, Harcourt Brace, 1922, p. 42.

Monda, Kimberly. "Self-Delusion and Self-Sacrifice in Nella Larsen's *Quicksand*." *African American Review*, vol. 31, no. 1, 1997, pp. 23–39.

Nenno, Nancy. "Femininity, the Primitive, and Modern Urban Space: Josephine Baker in Berlin." *Women in the Metropolis: Gender and Modernity in Weimar Culture*, edited by Katharina von Ankum, U of California P, 1997, pp. 145–61.

Patton, Venetria K., and Maureen Honey, editors. *Double-Take: A Revisionist Anthology of the Harlem Renaissance*. Routledge, 2001.

Silverman, Debra B. "Nella Larsen's *Quicksand*: Untangling the Webs of Exoticism." *African American Review*, vol. 27, no. 4, 1993, pp. 599–614.

Tate, Claudia. *Psychoanalysis and Black Novels: Desire and the Protocols of Race*. Oxford UP, 1998.

Amanda Golden

Digital Landscapes: Mapping Global Modernist Women Writers

In Marianne Moore's poem "An Octopus" the transparent, "[d]eceptively reserved and flat" tentacles are part of a glacier's "unimagined delicacy" (72). In a different context, yet one that sheds new light on Moore's image, Gabriel Hankins has recently described the "fragile geographies" (570) of modernist digital humanities as part of the "weak conjunctions between digital method and modernist field" (576). The relation between modernism and digital humanities is flexible, yet labored, not unlike the "glass that will bend" in Moore's poem (72). Discussing the effort that shapes Moore's verse, Natalia Cecire notes Cristanne's Miller's discussion of Moore's "The Plumet Basilisk": "Like the poem itself, the basilisk that 'you' see . . . is a work of art, a moral guide, every bit as much as it is a creature scientifically observed and precisely rendered onto a page" (qtd. in Cecire 87). The glass tentacles in "An Octopus" are similarly wrought, and the design of a digital map can reflect a logic inherent to the map's subject. Such projects can work against the assumption, as Marlo Starr puts it, that digital representations "attempt to tame the messiness of experience or to flatten information to a single plane of data" (198). In doing so, mapping projects should "reveal the particular human details that slip through big-data representations" (198). Whether one plots points or relations among them, the adaptability of maps and their various formats make the medium a fitting one for interpreting the experiments presented by modernist texts.

Mapping projects sustain students' attention and prompt them to interpret language and media by approaching the specificity with which modernist women writers and their characters navigate geographic, historical, and psychological terrains.[1] This essay focuses on a mapping project in Global Digital Modernisms at the Georgia Institute of Technology. Like other writing courses that first-year students complete at Georgia Tech, the structure emphasized WOVEN (written, oral, visual, electronic, and nonverbal) communication, and students learned to develop arguments demonstrating "multimodal synergy," which combines different modes of communication to different ends (Burnett and Cooper). Geared toward students working in STEM fields, the course included a series of multimodal projects designed to strengthen communication skills.[2] During and after class, students completed shorter activities and assignments designed to scaffold these projects, and that enabled testing of software with peers and close reading of texts. While students were encouraged to experiment with forms of technology or software of interest to them or relevant to their other courses, they were not assessed on their technical skills; their projects were graded using a rubric that emphasized the overall strength of the argument made, accounting for the ways various parts of the project worked together. Moreover, the accessibility of applications like Google Maps means that the interface provides students with familiarity, something that the modernist texts they read do not.

The title of the course, Global Digital Modernisms, signals an effort to better understand individual texts and their relation to wider ideas of global, transnational, and planetary modernism, and what using digital tools can contribute to this process.[3] As this essay addresses, the course undertook this task on a small scale, bringing together writers from a range of nationalities, some of whose paths intersected. Because this was an introductory course, such intersections helped familiarize students with broader stylistic concepts and how writers and artists redefined them and responded to one another. To consider global modernisms, the course was largely organized by country, and the travels and networks of the writers under study were taken into account. The course's global dimensions could be further expanded: an instructor might choose to anchor the course in a less familiar modernism, one to which students could contribute fresh interpretations in print and digital media. Hankins proposes that "[t]he next generation of work on spatial modernist studies has the prospect of a greatly enlarged geographic field" (577). If this becomes the case, students could place more weight on the design of future maps and could harness new digital possibilities to best represent individual texts' formal and stylistic characteristics as well as their relation to more expansive conceptions of global modernism.[4]

My approach in the course and the adaptability of mapping enable an introduction to the process in which, as Eric Hayot and Rebecca L. Walkowitz put it, "intellectual paradigms we've long associated with modernism—such as tradition, antiquity, style, classic, and translation—are transformed" (2). In their projects, students can contribute to what Hayot and Walkowitz call "the archive of works that imagine other worlds and other versions of the world" (2). My course sought to engage the untranslatable elements of global texts, the words and cultural dimensions that complicate the concept of reading, and to consider them together. Responding to Jonathan Arac's description of the ways that national and colloquial definitions of words have been elided in world literature, Emily Apter argues that what Arac describes as

> [*v*]*erkehrte Weltliteratur*, or screwed-up literature, has precisely the right impertinent coding. For in standing the world on its head, it encourages the literatures of the world to mess with World Literature, turning it into a process of translating untranslatably. It beckons one to run the experiment of imagining what a literary studies contoured around untranslatability might be. (18)

While Apter's use of the word "coding" appears neutral, a code is also a language. She later acknowledges Franco Moretti's references to "systems" as another form of the "[u]ntranslatable, a loose name for a practice of World Literature shaped by quantitative analysis and computational skills" (45), adding that these methods lead to a "contraction of the economy of interpretation" (56). Instead of simplifying interpretation, the expansive potential of maps leads to new layers, attending to the language of texts and the experiences of characters. While by definition untranslatable elements of texts and cultures remain as such, the question of how digital forms can better speak to these aspects presents an opportunity for new approaches and interpretations.

My course focused on writers for whom cities like London and Paris served as literary and artistic hubs (for a link to the course site, see the companion website to this volume [modwomen.mla.hcommons.org]).

A broader conception of global modernism would adopt less traditional British and European starting points, but beginning with these cities also shaped our assessment of streets throughout the texts that we read, from Jean Rhys's *Good Morning, Midnight* to Mulk Raj Anand's *Untouchable.* We began with England (E. M. Forster and Virginia Woolf), followed by the United States (Nella Larsen), France (Rhys), the Caribbean (Rhys, Claude McKay, and Una Marson), Ireland (James Joyce), and India (Anand and Sarojini Naidu). Our first assignment was a mash-up called "The Society Machine Stops" in which students worked in groups to consider Forster's story "The Machine Stops" and Woolf's story "A Society" together. Each text looks toward the future in different ways, one set in space and one set in London, and reconsiders issues relating to family politics, gender, education, knowledge, and communication.

We then turned to Larsen's New York and Chicago in *Passing*, followed by Rhys's Paris in *Good Morning, Midnight.*[5] Students mapped sections of both texts in groups, interpreting how each protagonist navigates the city. As we read *Good Morning, Midnight*, students wrote about passages from the novel in the light of Charles Baudelaire's "Painter of Modern Life" and subsequently considered Sasha's flânerie as they mapped her journeys throughout Paris. An assignment requiring students to plot the landscapes of Larsen's and Rhys's novels brought into relief the particularity of the characters' journeys, which included sidewalks, rooms, cafes, and city streets with long histories.

Each group created and annotated maps using Google Maps. Groups could also use such software as Prezi or PowerPoint.[6] Students were required to explain their design choices and the arguments of their maps in a five-hundred-word essay. One group addressed *Good Morning, Midnight*'s representation of Sasha's flânerie by night and day. This group used the Seine to divide the map into two parts and then considered Sasha's different paths in each. These students added a color-coded overlay, with the Right Bank in yellow and the Left Bank in gray, which made day and night visible. They connected the sites Sasha visited on each side of the Seine using blue and black. By mapping, the students realized that there was an order to how Sasha spends her time, of which she herself may not be aware. Ultimately, the challenges of mapping *Passing* and *Good Morning, Midnight* reflect the differences in both novels' relations to geography. Set in New York during the Harlem Renaissance, Larsen's novel depicts fewer explicit addresses than Rhys's novel does. Larsen's descriptions reflect a certain fidelity to place—for instance, the area of Harlem where the protagonist Irene Redfield resides and where Larsen herself lived contained shorter buildings at the time, not unlike the six-story building where the novel's final scene takes place. Other references are obscured; Larsen mentions, for example, the Drayton Hotel in Chicago (8), which critics believe may be the Drake Hotel. Rhys, by contrast, notes innumerable cafes, bars, and streets that existed and in some cases still exist, many of which were investigated by students.

The structure of each novel also informed how students represented events. When set against a map of Chicago, the orderly sections of *Passing* could be seen to take shape in the corners of one group's map. Another group similarly depicted Irene's later encounter with Clare's husband, John Bellew, at the intersection of the New York street corner to which Irene gestures in the novel. By contrast, students observed that Rhys's novel is less cohesive in its reflection of Sasha Jensen's thoughts, memories, and meanderings. When designing their maps, students recognized patterns. While one group rendered Sasha's flânerie by night and day, another created a Prezi to organize the progression of Sasha's thoughts in relation to the places she visits. Interpreting the novels in this fashion enabled students to combine modes of communication, displaying text and depicting arguments, which provided for comparisons of both texts' navigation of city spaces.[7] *Good Morning, Midnight* invited students to approach the stream-of-consciousness technique that has anchored aesthetic understandings of canonical modernism, and as Hankins puts it, such a practice "remain[s] largely within the paradigm of 'modernist consciousness,' focusing our view on the spatial dimensions that located that consciousness" (577). Because Rhys's fragmentary narrative can be difficult for students to follow, the novel works well for mapping projects. Tracing Sasha's path through Paris becomes a means for students to make their own way through the novel.[8]

By combining different formats, including Prezi and Google Maps, students exercised creativity and flexibility in giving voice to characters' lives. We practiced using these formats in class, and students worked in groups to test out options in preparation for their projects.[9] This type of experimentation replicates in different media the reconceptualization of form that Rhys and Larsen achieve in their novels, and helps students engage with this dimension of the authors' work.[10] Ultimately, students create forms that reflect their conclusions; in doing so, they work toward an understanding of digital media as adaptable, and are better able to display or visualize data and information. As Miriam Posner and Lauren F. Klein have argued, "[o]bjects or tables" are not "mere containers" (4).[11] Considering what it means for data visualization to be feminist, Posner and Klein underscore that the display of data is itself an argument. Becoming more conscious of this idea shapes not only students' projects but also their future interpretations.[12]

When students map *Good Morning, Midnight* and *Passing*, they attend to the spaces that women inhabit, including the domestic spaces with which women have been associated in fiction.[13] Students located floor plans of hotels like the Drake in Chicago, photographs of the rooms in hotels where Sasha may have lived, and cafes and bars where she spent time. By doing so, students represent the spaces that, as Deborah L. Parsons points out, "conceal [women] . . . from the urban map" (125). In their experimentations, students also continue Rhys's efforts in *Good Morning, Midnight*; as Parsons argues, "Rhys is attempting to do something different, observing rather than reflecting the state of wandering and using it to plot a female psycho-geographic map" (132). When transferred to a digital plane, Parson's argument allows for commentary and illustration that combine psychology and landscape. While Rhys's novel demonstrates this synthesis, digital mapping presents a means of interpretation that allows students to combine written, oral, visual, electronic, and nonverbal forms of communication. Ideally, they do so in a way that does not compromise the novel but instead provides an interpretive lens.

Plotting the landscapes of Larsen's and Rhys's novels illuminates the uniqueness of the journeys undertaken by their characters. Because students wrote about *Good Morning, Midnight* in relation to Rhys's memoir *Smile Please*, they also considered how Rhys's perspective may be reflected in that of her protagonist. But unlike Anna in Rhys's novel *Voyage in the Dark*, Sasha is not from the Caribbean—or, if she is, Rhys does not make readers aware of it.

Sasha's London and Paris are the product of Rhys's imagination. Anna Snaith argues that "[w]hen writers like Jean Rhys . . . 'wrote' London, they were, inevitably, writing transnationally, writing the colonial space and refiguring the relationship in between" (12). Students could consider how this idea plays out in Rhys's novel, and how one might digitally render the similarities and differences between author and character. If I gave this assignment again and assigned a broader range of texts, I would ask students how the form of maps could be altered digitally to speak more to Snaith's contention that for "networks of colonial peoples in modernist London," "[n]ew maps are not just laid over the old; they act to reconfigure existing terrain" (9).[14] Using this idea, students could address how writers or protagonists alter this landscape, and how best to represent it.

As the course progressed, students gained experience interpreting difficult textual experiments and completing projects that combined research, organization of materials, and close reading. After finishing their map projects, students composed essays addressing the ways that women in both novels navigate the city, and these papers engaged the texts and concepts in greater depth because students built on the research they conducted while creating their maps. Students' digital work encouraged immersion, and their essays developed the interpretation of the patterns that they identified in their maps. In the second half of the course, students composed scripts—which they then recorded or filmed as podcasts or videos—that interpreted the role of language, history, geography, or a combination of these elements in Joyce's *A Portrait of the Artist as a Young Man* and Anand's *Untouchable*. These projects were wide-ranging in format, from interview podcasts to animated videos.[15] As in the mapping project, this assignment emphasized communication and analysis of texts over technological expertise. Students were encouraged to use available recording tools on phones or computers, but neither the instructor nor the students needed specialized training to complete this project. Joyce and Anand enabled students' discussions of subjects such as imperialism, colonialism, and the caste system, and broadened the course's overall treatment of global modernism. The structure of this project was malleable: students could write scripts for interviews, documentaries, or anything else they desired.[16] As they learned to adapt the form of their interpretations, as they had done with their maps, students gained more control in their use of different forms of communication and media.

Creating digital projects motivates students to become more informed readers of modernism and the lives of modernist women. When instructors consider less traditional texts and regions, they also invite students to interpret using new media the work of writers who have been underexplored in modernist studies. Moore's "glassy octopus symmetrically pointed" (77) can have tentacles that reach in unanticipated directions. As a result, students craft forms that respond to the depths of women's words.

Notes

1. Virginia Woolf's *Mrs. Dalloway* experienced early popularity as a subject for student maps. See Hussey; Crowther; and Croxall, which is also available on the companion website to this volume.

2. See Burnett and Cooper. See also Kamen, a 2015 alumna of my course Victorian Technology and Art, on the value of communication in writing courses at Georgia Tech.

3. For an extended discussion of digital humanities and the use of digital tools in teaching modernist women's writing, see part 7 of this volume.

4. See Hayman and Lewis for case studies. See Berman for approaches to global modernism. Gabriel Hankins discusses Alex Christie's experiments in creating maps that reflect texts' formal characteristics (576–77).

5. For more on Larsen, see in this volume Tate; Quynn; Hinnov; and Mattis. For more on Rhys, see the essays by Sorensen and Chalk in this volume.

6. For examples, see this volume's companion website.

7. For images, see this volume's companion website.

8. See Golden, "Mapping," also available on the companion website to this volume.

9. See the course website for Global Digital Modernisms, the link to which can be found on this volume's companion website.

10. See Elkins's work on teaching modernist craft.

11. Sketching the possible contours of "feminist data visualization," Catherine D'Ignazio notes that such projects include "the perspectives of oppressed groups including women, minorities and others [who] are systematically excluded from 'general' knowledge." For an example, see Angel David Nieves's Soweto Historical GIS project, a link to which is available on the companion website to this volume.

12. Reflecting on her experience teaching a course on Victorian literature and culture in which students from a range of majors, including engineering, created their own steampunk artifacts, Kathryn Crowther asks whether "more innovative pedagogy—pushing the boundaries of my own knowledge and comfort—could inspire students to do the same in their own work."

13. D'Ignazio and Klein address the work of Mei-Po Kwan, whose "design principles" include using mapping practice to account for narratives of struggle and the quotidian.

14. In her keynote at the Annual International Conference on Virginia Woolf on 30 June 2017, Susheila Nasta displayed a static map of colonial writers in London that could be interpreted in critical contexts to consider ways the city differed from various writers' perspectives.

15. A later version of this assignment addressing Joyce's *The Dead* and Anand's *Untouchable* is available on the course website for Global Digital Modernisms; see the companion website to this volume.

16. The assignment was based on one that Anne Sexton gave at Colgate University in 1972 in which she asked students to craft an imaginary interview with her; see Golden, "Mock Interviews."

Works Cited

Anand, Mulk Raj. *Untouchable.* 1935. Penguin Books, 1940.

Apter, Emily. *Against World Literature: On the Politics of Untranslatability.* Verso, 2013.

Baudelaire, Charles. "The Painter of Modern Life." 1863. *Charles Baudelaire: Selected Writings on Art and Literature*, translated and introduced by P. E. Charvet, Penguin Books, 1993, pp. 390–435.

Berman, Jessica. *Modernist Commitments: Ethics, Politics, and Transnational Modernism.* Columbia UP, 2012.

Burnett, Rebecca, and L. Andrew Cooper. "Multimodal Synergy: The Synergy of Modes and Media in Academic and Professional Communication." *Georgia Tech* WOVENText *Supplement*, pp. 26–56, canvas.instructure.com/courses/866713/pages/georgia-tech-woven-text-supplement. Accessed 18 Aug. 2020.

Cecire, Natalia. "Marianne Moore's Precision." *Arizona Quarterly: A Journal of American Literature, Culture, and Theory*, vol. 67, no. 4, 2011, pp. 83–110.

Crowther, Kathryn. "Punking the Victorians, Punking Pedagogy: Steampunk and Creative Assignments in the Composition Classroom." *Journal of Victorian Culture Online*, 6 Sept. 2012, jvc.oup.com/2012/09/06/punking-the-victorians-punking-pedagogy-steampunk-and-creative-assignments-in-the-composition-classroom/.

Croxall, Brian. "Mapping *Mrs. Dalloway.*" *Introduction to Digital Humanities: English 389 at Emory University*. www.briancroxall.net/dh/assignments/mapping-mrs-dalloway/. Accessed 29 Apr. 2020.

D'Ignazio, Catherine. "What Would Feminist Data Visualization Look Like?" *Medium*, 22 Jan. 2017, medium.com/@kanarinka/what-would-feminist-data-visualization-look-like-aa3f8fc7f96c.

D'Ignazio, Catherine, and Lauren F. Klein. "Feminist Data Visualization." *Kanarinka*, www.kanarinka.com/wp-content/uploads/2015/07/IEEE_Feminist_Data_Visualization.pdf. Accessed 19 Aug. 2020.

Elkins, Amy E. "Teaching." *Amy E. Elkins*, updated Spring 2019, amyelkins.net/teaching/.

Forster, E. M. "The Machine Stops." 1909. *Selected Stories*, by Forster, edited by David Leavitt and Mark Mitchell, Penguin Books, 2001, pp. 91–123.

Golden, Amanda. "Mapping *Jacob's Room.*" *TECHStyle*, 12 Nov. 2013, techstyle.lmc.gatech.edu/mapping-jacobs-room/.

———. "Mock Interviews with Contemporary African American Writers." *TECHStyle*, 18 Apr. 2014, techstyle.lmc.gatech.edu/mock-interviews-with-contemporary-african-american-writers/.

Hankins, Gabriel. "The Weak Powers of Digital Modernist Studies." *Modernism/Modernity*, vol. 25, no. 3, 2018, pp. 569–85.

Hayman, Emily, and Pericles Lewis. "Can There Be a Global Modernism?" *The Bloomsbury Companion to Modernist Literature*, edited by Ulrika Maude and Mark Nixon, Bloomsbury Academic, 2018, pp. 329–48.

Hayot, Eric, and Rebecca L. Walkowitz, editors. *A New Vocabulary for Global Modernism*. Columbia UP, 2016.

Hussey, Mark. "Digital Woolf." *A Companion to Virginia Woolf*, edited by Jessica Berman, Wiley, 2016, pp. 263–75.

Joyce, James. *The Dead*. 1914. Edited by Daniel R. Schwarz, Bedford / St. Martin's, 1994.

———. *A Portrait of the Artist as a Young Man*. 1916. Penguin Books, 2006.

Kamen, Brighton. "Do Not Disparage Your English Class at Tech Just Yet." *Technique*, 15 Sept. 2017, nique.net/opinions/2017/09/15/do-not-disparage-your-english-class-at-tech-just-yet/. Accessed 1 June 2019.

Larsen, Nella. *Passing*. 1929. Edited by Carla Kaplan, W. W. Norton, 2007.

Moore, Marianne. "An Octopus." *New Collected Poems*, edited by Heather Cass White, Faber and Faber, 2017, pp. 72–78.

Nasta, Susheila. "The Bloomsbury Indians." Keynote presentation. Annual International Conference on Virginia Woolf, Reading, England, 30 June 2017.

Parsons, Deborah L. *Streetwalking the Metropolis: Women, the City, and Modernity*. Oxford UP, 2003.

Posner, Miriam, and Lauren F. Klein. "Editor's Introduction: Data as Media." *Data*, special issue of *Feminist Media Histories*, edited by Posner and Klein, vol. 3, no. 3, 2017, pp. 1–8.

Rhys, Jean. *Good Morning, Midnight*. 1939. W. W. Norton, 1999.

———. *Smile Please*. Penguin Books, 1995.

Snaith, Anna. *Modernist Voyages: Colonial Women Writers in London, 1890–1945*. Cambridge UP, 2014.

Starr, Marlo. "Slow Writing: Archival Research in the Digital Age." *PMLA*, vol. 133, no. 1, Jan. 2018, pp. 197–98.

Woolf, Virginia. "A Society." 1921. *The Complete Shorter Fiction of Virginia Woolf*, 2nd ed., edited by Susan Dick, Harcourt Brace Jovanovich, 1989, pp. 124–36.

Bridget Chalk

Teaching Jean Rhys and Present-Day African Women's Fiction

Complex but immensely pleasurable to read and to teach, Jean Rhys's novels exemplify modernism's aesthetic responses to urban modernity and imperialism. In my Roots: Literature course, an introductory survey for mostly non-English majors, the focus on modernism's interaction with colonialism provides a geopolitical through line for teaching present-day African literature. By forging connections between periods, students come to understand the longer history of exploitation and globalization of which more recent postcolonial texts are a part. This course provides an overview of modern literature roughly from the early modern period to the present, organized by a theme of the instructor's choosing. The theme of my course is literature, empire, and race, and we move from Shakespeare's *Othello* to *We Need New Names*, a 2014 novel by the Zimbabwean writer NoViolet Bulawayo. Rhys's *Voyage in the Dark* serves as a central text in the course because it revisits important themes of texts that came before it (e.g., *Othello*, Aphra Behn's *Oroonoko*, and Joseph Conrad's *Heart of Darkness*) and also prefigures later novels (e.g., J. M. Coetzee's *Disgrace* and Bulawayo's *We Need New Names*). The historical and political implications of Rhys's novel allow us to dismantle narratives of Western male supremacy by looking to African literature that combines political statements with literary experimentation. The sweep of the course illustrates the value of teaching modern-day literature as the inheritance of aesthetic modernism and its geopolitics, or as part of what David James and Urmila Seshagiri have termed "metamodernism," defined as the "burgeoning dialogues between literary present and literary past [that] reveal twentieth-century modernism's complex—but still undertheorized—appeal for the ambitions of twenty-first-century novelists" (88).

In my course, we turn to recent African literature to see how postcolonial voices and stories emerging from the continent respond to and refigure the racist colonial imperatives structuring earlier narratives. In particular, dynamic female writers illustrate the legacy of Rhys; works by such writers as Chimamanda Adichie, Taiye Selasi, Yaa Gyasi, and Marie NDiaye examine migration and neo-imperialism alongside gender oppression tied to systems of social inequality. In the past few iterations of this course, I have ended with *We Need New Names*, which serves as a clear and powerful present-day counterpart to *Voyage in the Dark*.

Literature, Empire, and Race

To contextualize Rhys's connection to modern-day African women writers, I will outline my Roots: Literature, Empire, and Race course. In the wake of reignited racial tensions in the United States, the Black Lives Matter protests of 2020, and the ideological polarity exacerbated by the 2016 presidential election, teaching literature in the context of empire and race became more charged and, in my view, more crucial. On the first day of class, I provide an overview of the age of European empires, focusing on British colonial rule in the Caribbean and Africa. I turn to Ta-Nehisi Coates's definition of racism: "The need to ascribe bone-deep features to people and then humiliate, reduce, and destroy them" (7). Coates continues: "Difference in hue and hair is old. But the belief in the preeminence of hue and hair, the notion that these factors can correctly organize a society and that they signify deeper attributes, which are indelible—this is the new idea" (6–7). In order to approach literature concerning the British Empire through a revisionary lens, our semester begins as we think about how racial difference has been made to mean things, how it has been endowed with specific registers of significance, throughout the modern history of imperialism and slavery. The course considers the historical ways Blackness, brownness, and whiteness have been represented, and therefore invested, with particular, lasting meaning. Within a global system of empire, basic “difference in hue and hair” has been and is used as a means of oppression, dominance, and organization within society.

Our first three readings—*Othello*, *Oroonoko*, and Hannah More’s “The Sorrows of Yamba”—all feature African protagonists who live within predominantly European societies, and serve as illustrations of the negative constructions of the other in the context of the European drive to empire. Importantly, these texts demonstrate the complex nature of such constructions. Beyond racism, the works grapple with the inhumanities and tragedies engendered by racism. A major focus of the course is the rise of racist language and logic in texts between the early modern period and the twentieth century. Students often assume that the Western treatment of race has become progressively better and more equal, when these texts in fact demonstrate the opposite. While suffused with racist assumptions, Shakespeare’s play and Behn’s protonovella highlight the exceptionality and extraordinary nature of their protagonists of color. It is not until we get to Conrad’s *Heart of Darkness*, which I teach alongside Chinua Achebe, that students see gross dehumanization and objectification of the African body.

These readings set up *Voyage in the Dark* thematically and aesthetically.[1] Alongside discussions of race and empire, we note the treatment of gender and the subversion and containment of characters like Desdemona and Imoinda in *Oroonoko*. In Rhys’s novel, Anna Morgan’s story highlights the exploitation of women while providing a revision of racial and colonial dynamics previously encountered. Anna is a white, relatively wealthy colonial of the plantation class in the Caribbean, but in England she is a poor, single girl, marked by colonial difference and unable to identify with the white privilege by which one might expect her to be defined. Students see how a consideration of the geopolitical frame of British colonialism in the Caribbean produces a symbolic reading in which Anna represents the colony, and the wealthy older men who exploit her represent the imperial power. Anna’s passivity and the lack of sympathy she engenders in the reader raises questions about the colonial victim’s complicity, an ambiguity also seen in our reading of W. B. Yeats’s poem “Leda and the Swan.”

Like *Voyage in the Dark*, Yeats’s poem features a symbolic pregnancy replete with political implications. After our next reading, Coetzee’s *Disgrace* (which likewise contains a politically charged pregnancy), we end with *We Need New Names*, which follows the protagonist, a young girl named Darling, from Zimbabwe in the 2000s to the United States in the early 2010s. These texts and the important issues they address allow students to gain an understanding of the connections between politics in far-flung areas of the world and the privilege buttressing white, upper- and middle-class European and American life.

Pairing Rhys and Bulawayo

Voyage in the Dark illuminates the contours of modern-day African women's writing. Migration, sexual abuse, and exploitation; how gender inequity compounds racial difference; the limitations on and implications of social and geographic mobility for women—all are framed by Rhys's novel both formally and thematically. *Voyage in the Dark* tells the story of Anna Morgan, a poor, teenage creole émigré to London from the island of Dominica. Orphaned, abandoned by her stepmother, and earning a paltry living as a chorus girl at the novel's beginning, Anna spirals down a continuum of respectability, from the daughter of a plantation-class colonial to a prostitute. The novel ends as she nearly dies from an abortion. (See also Kopley and Sorensen in this volume.) Throughout the novel, Rhys uses flashbacks and interpolated memories to sketch the outlines of Anna's childhood as an unhappy white colonial islander.

We Need New Names focuses on Darling, a Zimbabwean girl who suffers through the effects of Robert Mugabe's dictatorship in the 2000s and emigrates to the United States. The novel's African scenes address the continued complexity of racial identity and property rights in Zimbabwe, while the American scenes underscore the alienation and anxiety of the undocumented immigrant. Both Rhys and Bulawayo employ autobiographical details, specifically as concerns their own migratory routes: Rhys, like Anna, was born and raised on the island of Dominica and came to England as a teen, and Bulawayo was raised and finished high school in Zimbabwe before moving to Michigan, where she began college. Bulawayo's novel subverts the narrative of upward mobility conventionally associated with migration from the Global South to the Global North in its depiction of the cold, dark Midwest and the general unhappiness Darling experiences there. Darling's life as a teen in America does not tend to extreme forms of violence or deprivation, but she does experience isolation, casual racism, and the poverty of the undocumented working class as she cycles through friends and jobs, growing increasingly disconnected from her family back in Zimbabwe.

Our most important early discussion of Rhys involves the moment when Anna, walking with a friend, encounters her future lover Walter Jeffries for the first time and casually allows him to buy her stockings. We talk about why this feels odd to the reader, and how the exchange relates to other items a stranger might purchase for a young woman, and their implications. What obligations, if any, does a woman have when a man buys her a coffee, a drink, or dinner? The raucous conversation that ensues demonstrates the sexual dynamics of exchange underwriting students' daily encounters and helps them see the pervasive commodification of women's bodies in the novel as well as in their own social worlds. This prompts definition and discussion of the male gaze and its constitution of Anna through consumerism and sexual objectification. We consider moments such as when Anna suffers from "the shop-windows sneering and smiling in your face" and when she recalls, regarding Walter, "I was so nervous about how I looked that three-quarters of me was in a prison, wandering round and round in a circle. If he had said that I looked all right or that I was pretty, it would have set me free" (Rhys 25, 76). Rhys's novel moves from the dynamics of colonialism to those of gendered oppression, which shows students how Rhys conjoins these systemic forms of exploitation.

In the second session on *Voyage in the Dark*, I ask students to work in small groups to locate two moments in which Anna feels alienated; when we reconvene as a class, we list these moments on the board and extrapolate the categories of Anna's identity that contribute to these moments: nationality, gender, class, age, socioeconomic status, and race. Students often select the moment when Anna says, "I always wanted to be black" (31), which telescopes the novel's exceedingly complex construction of colonial psychology. Anna is legibly white, though her Creole blood leads her stepmother to cast aspersions on her character's (specifically sexual) "unfortunate propensities," and she was resented by her former Black servant, Francine, whom she loved. We discuss Salman Rushdie's concept of "double unbelonging," or the state of alienation experienced by the (former) colonial living in the (former) imperial center, to articulate Anna's position within this world (*East* 141 and *Joseph Anton* 54). Ultimately, Anna's dark and destructive London experiences demonstrate the liabilities of both the colonial and the woman in a world structured by patriarchy and imperial capitalism.

Broadly speaking, Rhys shows students how the individual story can open out to comment on vast systems structuring our world. During our concluding discussion of *Voyage in the Dark*, we consider the novel's ending and use certain elements of the book to construct a possible symbolic reading. The following are examples of questions I pose to students: If Anna is the colony, and the men encountered throughout her life represent imperial power, then what might her aborted fetus suggest about the future (or lack thereof) of the global system? What does it mean that the ending is ambiguous regarding Anna's own future? How does our readerly sympathy (or lack thereof) contribute to our interpretation of Rhys's political commentary? Because there are no easy answers to these questions, students often make the most ambitious interpretive leaps during this conversation.

We begin *We Need New Names* by focusing on connections to Rhys's text. Bulawayo's novel spends more time than Rhys's does on the youth of its protagonist, in postcolonial Zimbabwe in the case of Bulawayo's novel, and includes episodes that reveal the complexity of anti-colonial sentiment there. The first chapter, "Hitting Budapest," which won the Caine Prize for African Writing in 2013 as a short story, addresses the gross inequities in Zimbabwe through the starving young children (including a twelve-year-old impregnated by her grandfather) who trespass into an upscale housing development to steal guavas. In the housing development, the children encounter a wealthy woman from England, eating pizza and throwing away the crust, and gawk "at her pretty peeking feet, at her big jewelry, at her large eyes, at her smooth brown skin that doesn't even have a scar to show she is a living person, at the earring on her nose, at her T-shirt that says 'Save Darfur'" (Bulawayo 10–11). By blithely asking the children if she can take their picture, the woman comes to embody what James Arnett calls the "dynamics of the uneven exchange of humanitarian aid for the performance of suffering" (169). The wealthy woman, with family ties to Zimbabwe, is from the Global North and performs a kind of poverty tourism.

Another scene in the novel that underscores the significance of such spectacle concerns an NGO charity outfit that arrives with a truck of goods for Darling's neighborhood. The dynamics of the scene sketch out a Western neo-imperial gaze that objectifies the children in particular in order to advance the cause of the charity. Darling recalls the aid workers thus: "They just like taking pictures, these NGO people, like maybe we are their real friends and relatives. . . . They don't care that we are embarrassed by our dirt and torn clothing, that we would prefer they didn't do it; they just take the pictures anyway, take and take" (54). This scene leads to a spirited class discussion of the ethical quandaries that result when these children are constructed as abject others in need of help from the wealthy

West, if only in order to generate capital to provide them with goods and services. Several students typically defend the larger cause and suggest that the end goal of charitable giving justifies the means, while others vehemently denounce the more systemic geopolitical inequities that give rise to organizations dependent on a fundamental condescension.

Both Rhys's and Bulawayo's novels offer insights into their specific geopolitical contexts. The connections between the two texts make for a valuable case study in connecting modernist and postcolonial literary periods. Each text features a young female protagonist that migrates from a (post)colonial space to a (neo)imperial country, and rewrites the bildungsroman as a fragmented, stunted plot of aging rather than a story of development and social integration. The narratives are instead driven by events of displacement and its reverberations.

The exploitation of girls in both novels serves as a metaphorical means for thinking about political exploitation, particularly its bearing on the future through episodes involving pregnancy. While Anna's abortion seems to signal what Seshagiri describes as "a violent literalizing of Anna's psychic disunity and her exile from the domains of imperial modernity" (499), the twelve-year-old Chipo's pregnancy in *New Names* functions rather differently. What begins as a horrific case of incestuous abuse in a poor neighborhood marked by the disappearance of men transforms after the birth of the child (whom Chipo names "Darling," ostensibly after the protagonist) into a symbol of the family connection and intimacy in Zimbabwe that Darling has lost access to. Darling's experience in the chapter titled "Destroyed, Michigan" likewise parallels Anna's misery in London: both destinations, supposedly the better, richer locations, are dark, cold, and serve up specific forms of deprivation. Darling laments, "I mean, coldness that makes like it wants to kill you, like it's telling you, with its snow, that you should go back to where you came from" (Bulawayo 150). This moment connects to the beginning of *Voyage*, in which Anna complains, "I couldn't get used to the cold" (Rhys 7). This similarity helps students see how Rhys and Bulawayo subvert narratives of uplift and deliverance that conventionally inflect migration stories from the developing world to the West. This subversion and the reality to which it gestures often surprises some American college students, who expect adverse conditions elsewhere in the world, but assume life in England or the United States would be an improvement over anything immigrants from the Global South have experienced. The visceral homesickness experienced by Rhys's and Bulawayo's protagonists, as well as their psychological struggles of dislocation and alienation, demonstrates to students how double unbelonging underwrites the economic and material promises of a new world associated with mobility. Throughout the semester, students come to see that Rhys's rewriting of Conrad's colonial narrative, in which the European man travels to Africa and discovers its primitive, brutal truths, sets the stage for much postcolonial and contemporary literature, which seeks to redress widespread misapprehensions about the relation between the developing and developed worlds.

Students have an opportunity to explore the relation between these texts and among all of our texts by means of roundtable presentations as well as short in-class writing prompts, which I use to begin class sessions. I begin one session, for example, with a short freewriting prompt that asks students to examine the similarities between *Voyage* and *New Names*, and that draws out students' ideas on the respective political frameworks and the novels' relation to gender and poverty. In roundtable sessions, six to eight students serve as panelists who prepare a discussion topic connecting multiple readings; these students are also responsible for responding to their fellow panelists and keeping discussion lively and forward-moving. For the final paper, I give students the option to write a creative dialogue between Anna and Darling in which they discuss their experiences in a way that builds on similarities and illuminates differences. For this assignment, I require at least ten footnotes of explication (Why have you included this detail? How specifically has it emerged from the text for you?). Many assignments and topics of discussion stress the use of gender as a proxy symbolic economy that addresses the issue of imperialism and neo-imperialism, a trope that runs through Rhys, Yeats, Coetzee, and Bulawayo.

According to our college's catalog, Roots: Literature teaches Western literature, and my version of the course focuses largely, if also critically, on British representations of imperialism. The turn toward global literature written in English toward the end of the semester, then, risks restricting students' understanding of African literature to a Eurocentric framework. Rhys, however, provides an example of a transnational modernist whose work seeks to destabilize the Eurocentric imperialism that secures conventional Western canonicity; in using *Voyage* as a fulcrum, the course therefore asks students to not only read Western literature but also grapple with the problematic category of "the West." Moreover, the connections between Bulawayo's work and that of Rhys illuminate a postcolonial genealogy of literature that traces the rejection of Eurocentrism and dual attention to the global and the local back to the early twentieth century, which belies the notion that postcolonial aesthetics are reactionary and indebted to Anglo-European paradigms.

Seshagiri contends that *Voyage in the Dark* is a "pivotal text in the transition between the downturn of British experimental modernism and the crescendo of postcolonial literature" and that it "look[s] back to the techniques that demarcated high modernism" while "also look[ing] ahead to the historical crises that shape later novels by Chinua Achebe, V. S. Naipaul, and Salman Rushdie" (488–89). Seshagiri's placement of this text as a fulcrum between modernist and postcolonial literature extends to recent anglophone fiction coming out of Africa and the subcontinent. While I have focused on one example here, Rhys's foundational subversion of patriarchal Western imperialism (or illustration of the tragedies of its dominance) can be usefully connected to new voices in global literature. Indeed, other modernist women writers like Katherine Mansfield, Elizabeth Bowen, and Una Marson, whose work engages with colonial journeys and imperial metropolitan spaces, might similarly provide formal and thematic grounds to explore present-day global anglophone literature by women. In particular, recent narratives of migration that refuse to position Europe or the United States as the destination of deliverance or promise (Selasi's *Ghana Must Go*, NDiaye's *Three Strong Women*, Dinaw Mengestu's *How to Read the Air*, Kiran Desai's *The Inheritance of Loss*, Jhumpa Lahiri's *The Interpreter of Maladies*) can be usefully predicated for students by looking back to modernism and the challenges posed to world systems by its aesthetic experimentation.

Note

1. For teaching Rhys's novel in the context of global modernism, see Rosenberg in this volume.

Works Cited

Arnett, James. "Taking Pictures: The Economy of Affect and Postcolonial Performativity in NoViolet Bulawayo's *We Need New Names.*" *Ariel: A Review of International English Literature*, vol. 47, no. 3, 2016, pp. 149–73.

Behn, Aphra. *Oroonoko*. Oxford UP, 2009.

Bulawayo, NoViolet. *We Need New Names*. Back Bay Books, 2014.

Coates, Ta-Nehisi. *Between the World and Me*. Spiegel and Grau, 2015.

Coetzee, J. M. *Disgrace*. Penguin Books, 2000.

Conrad, Joseph. Heart of Darkness *and the* Congo Diary. Penguin Books, 2007.

Desai, Kiran. *The Inheritance of Loss.* Grove Press, 2006.

James, David, and Urmila Seshagiri. "Metamodernism: Narratives of Continuity and Revolution." *PMLA*, vol. 129, no. 1, Jan. 2014, pp. 87–100.

Lahiri, Jhumpa. *The Interpreter of Maladies.* Mariner, 2000.

Mengestu, Dinaw. *How to Read the Air.* Riverhead Books, 2011.

More, Hannah. "The Sorrows of Yamba." *The Romantics and Their Contemporaries*, Pearson, 2011, pp. 262–67. Vol. 2A of *The Longman Anthology of British Literature*, 5th ed., general editors, David Damrosch et al.

NDiaye, Marie. *Three Strong Women.* Translated by John Fletcher, Vintage Books, 2013.

Rhys, Jean. *Voyage in the Dark.* 1934. W. W. Norton, 1994.

Rushdie, Salman. *East, West.* Vintage Books, 1994.

———. *Joseph Anton.* Random House, 2012.

Selasi, Taiye. *Ghana Must Go.* Penguin Books, 2014.

Seshagiri, Urmila. "Modernist Ashes, Postcolonial Phoenix: Jean Rhys and the Evolution of the English Novel in the Twentieth Century." *Modernism/Modernity*, vol. 13, no. 3, 2006, pp. 487–505.

Shakespeare, William. *Othello. The New Oxford Shakespeare: The Complete Works: Modern Critical Edition*, edited by Gary Taylor et al., Oxford UP, 2016, pp. 2111–94.

Yeats, William Butler. "Leda and the Swan." 1924. *The Collected Poems of W. B. Yeats*, edited by Richard Finneran, Palgrave Macmillan, 1989, p. 214.

Part V

Modernist Cultures

Celia Marshik

Teaching Modernism and the Middlebrow Using the Artist-Novel

The list of modernist novels that focus on or contain artists is extensive: James Joyce's *A Portrait of the Artist as a Young Man* and *Ulysses*, Willa Cather's *The Song of the Lark*, Virginia Woolf's *To the Lighthouse*, Jessie Redmon Fauset's *There Is Confusion*, and many other titles come to mind. Popular literature of the period was equally interested in the figure of the artist, as writers from E. M. Delafield to W. Somerset Maugham focused their fiction on characters that write or paint to various degrees of success. Reading these novels side by side, one immediately notices immense differences in characterization and tone: no two artists are alike, of course, but different registers regard this most modern of figures with various attitudes.

For the past three decades, scholars such as Joan Shelley Rubin, Janice A. Radway, Nicola Beauman, Nicola Humble, Lisa Botshon and Meredith Goldsmith, Robert Scholes, Jaime Harker, and Faye Hammill have worked to recover authors who have been critically ignored and to draw attention to the unstable boundary between modernism and the so-called middlebrow: a type of popular literature contemporary with modernism that eschewed the latter's stylistic experimentation, antiestablishment stance, and cultivation of an elite audience. The proliferation of work on the middlebrow (and the pulps) has been a notable part of the evolution of modernist studies, a result of the vertical expansion of the field described by Douglas Mao and Rebecca L. Walkowitz:

> Quite sharp boundaries between high art and popular forms of culture have been reconsidered; . . . canons have been critiqued and reconfigured; . . . works by members of marginalized social groups have been encountered with fresh eyes and ears; and . . . scholarly inquiry has increasingly extended to matters of production, dissemination, and reception. (738)

Despite these important changes in our scholarship, it is often difficult to add middlebrow texts to syllabi for courses on modernism. No matter the type of institution, faculty members may feel pressured to introduce students to the classics of our field. And yet a diversification of our courses along vertical lines can help students come to terms with modernist fiction precisely by placing it on a continuum with other modern novels. In this essay I argue that an instructor's choice to include middlebrow works on a syllabus helps clarify the assumptions, ambitions, and experiments of modernist women writers. Middlebrow works also provide students with a sharper sense of what early-twentieth-century fiction looked like and how writers of all stripes came to understand themselves vis-à-vis the lowbrow, middlebrow, and highbrow. This essay reflects my experiences teaching a whole course on artist-novels, but I highlight three works that can be productively taught side by side in a unit of a more general course on modernism.

When including middlebrow works on a syllabus, I have found it helpful to supply brief definitions of the term. The difficulty, as the attributives *low*, *middle*, and *high* suggest, is that *middlebrow* is a relational term: it is a cultural register that depends on its location between two extremes of artistic production. Moreover, critics who work on the middlebrow disagree on whether the term should be applied to individual authors, works, readers, publication venues, or experiences of reception. Given its relational identity and that the definition of *middlebrow* is up for debate, I find it most useful to expose students to a range of short definitions and to then lead them in a discussion of what these definitions share. The *Middlebrow Network* project offers a set of short quotations that address the middlebrow, and the works from which these quotations are drawn provide more in-depth treatment of the term ("Defining the Middlebrow").[1] Instructors can ask students to read the project's "Defining the Middlebrow" page and to discuss, for instance, the adjectives and emotions that predominate in the range of definitions; the possible reasons why the page states that the British humor magazine *Punch*'s use of the term is "rather more revealing" than other instances; and whether more recent scholars of the middlebrow define the term more positively than those who took it up earlier in the twentieth century. I find that these discussions enable students to approach both middlebrow and modernist fiction with open minds. In contrast, when I have taught Woolf's infamous 1932 essay "Middlebrow," I have found that students end up disliking Woolf or the subject of her piece. Although "Middlebrow" illuminates Woolf's feelings about the middle of the cultural spectrum, it's important to note that Woolf is concerned in this essay with not only popular literature but also a range of cultural practices and historical conditions including education, consumption, and class differences. The *Middlebrow Network*'s list of definitions, in contrast, focuses more specifically on the ways in which the category of the middlebrow operates as a literary register.

I have taught modernist and middlebrow fiction in many of my courses, but students reaped the greatest benefit from a vertical expansion of the syllabus in an upper-division elective that focused on modernism and the artist-novel. This class included canonical modernist fiction by men and women (Joyce's *A Portrait of the Artist as a Young Man*, Woolf's *Orlando*, Ernest Hemingway's "The Snows of Kilimanjaro"), lesser-known fiction by modernist writers (George Orwell's *Keep the Aspidistra Flying*), and three novels that have generally been received as middlebrow even though they were targeted at different reading publics (Delafield's *The Provincial Lady in London*, Radclyffe Hall's *The Well of Loneliness*, and Maugham's *The Moon and Sixpence*). Together, these novels helped illustrate that assumptions about artistry as rooted in individual genius sometimes cross cultural registers: Joyce's, Maugham's, and Hall's protagonists are all depicted as solitary but brilliant minds who must write or paint and who succeed (or, in the case of Joyce's Stephen Dedalus, promise to succeed) by dint of devotion to their craft and an iconoclastic approach to family. By beginning the class with Joyce and Maugham, this prototype of the artist is ingrained in students. Orwell's novel illustrates what happens to an impoverished would-be poet who tries to follow the same pattern, and students enjoy debating whether the protagonist of *Keep the Aspidistra Flying* is really an artist and what sacrifices individuals should be prepared to make in the name of their avocation.

While reading across registers of artist-novels by and about men has benefits, novels by women do a great deal more to highlight cultural assumptions about who an artist is and what their career and life look like. Hall's, Woolf's, and Delafield's novels all feature women writers as protagonists. All deal with the process of artistic creation, the reactions of reading publics, and the economic or critical success of specific works. When read side by side, however, each novel reveals significant differences in the protagonists' (and authors') attitudes toward artistic production and literary audience. For example, Woolf's Orlando, a character widely known for their mid-novel sex change, is also a lifelong writer whose work eventually garners critical respect. While Woolf amusingly chronicles the character's youthful excesses in style and material—and students can be asked to discuss why Woolf highlights the protagonist's amateur productions—Orlando eventually comes to express many highbrow or modernist attitudes: these include Orlando's vow to write for personal reasons; the manuscript's seemingly independent desire for a readership; and the character's lack of interest in literary prizes and profits. The novel's sense that poetry is "a secret transaction, a voice answering a voice" (*Orlando* 325) reflects modernism's overt (if often fictive) disdain for public recognition. Moreover, readers may be startled to discover in the final pages of the novel that Orlando has become a wildly successful writer:

> Fame! (She laughed.) Fame! Seven editions. A prize. Photographs in the evening papers (here she alluded to the "Oak Tree" and "The Burdett Coutts" Memorial prize which she had won; and we must here snatch time to remark how discomposing it is for her biographer that this culmination and peroration should be dashed from us on a laugh casually like this; but the truth is that when we write of a woman, everything is out of place—culminations and perorations; the accent never falls where it does with a man). (312)

Having read to this point in the novel, students will have already noticed the indirect treatment of what most readers assume to be significant events in a character's life. They can be encouraged to discuss why major occasions, such as the birth of Orlando's son and the winning of the literary prize, are scarcely discussed in the text as well as why the biographer (like Orlando) does not pay them much attention. The biographer attributes the slight treatment of fame and success to Orlando's sex, and students can unpack the assumptions behind this logic: namely, that women writers are not supposed to win prizes and did not do so historically. It's important to encourage students to connect this passage with the kind of artist Orlando is: one who has given up the search for fame. "Bad, good, or indifferent, I'll write, from this day forward, to please myself," Orlando vows earlier in the novel (103). Students can discuss whether Woolf herself seemed to have the same attitude (letters and diary entries can be helpful here), as well as what a modernist writer like Woolf might have gained by publishing a novel in which the artist-protagonist turns their back on fame, prizes, and financial remuneration.

The style and form of Hall's *The Well of Loneliness* immediately strikes students as worlds apart from *Orlando*.[2] The plot of Hall's novel is linear; character development is conventional; and the narrator remains stable and in control throughout the text. Some basic information about Hall's career—her earlier novels *The Forge* (1924) and *Adam's Breed* (1926) made bestseller lists, for example—can help students understand that Hall already had a reputation for popular success before she became the author of a succès de scandale. Students can examine the relation between the conventional form of *The Well* and the book's larger project of generating sympathy for homosexual and transsexual characters; they might debate, for example, whether a fictional biographer, like the one in *Orlando*, could have served as the book's narrator. While an examination of the different formal qualities of these novels helps sharpen students' understanding of differences between modernist and middlebrow style, students should also be asked to consider similarities between the content of the books: both authors associate being nonbinary with artistic talent, both create writers who draw inspiration from rural sources, etc. What do these parallels suggest the authors assumed about who might become a (good) writer or about what modern writers might choose as their subjects?

While *Orlando* and *The Well* thus share some assumptions about authorship, their very different treatment of fame and critical success can help students understand the distinctions between modernist and middlebrow authors and audiences. While Orlando laughs at the wide readership that has embraced *The Oak Tree*, Hall's protagonist Stephen Gordon publishes both commercially and critically successful novels. Gordon's former governess, Puddle, reflects that "the long-limbed creature who lounged by the fire had suddenly sprung into something like fame thanks to a fine first novel" (Hall 210). Here and throughout Hall's novel one encounters characters that take book reviews and sales quite seriously, a facet of *The Well* that demonstrates the middlebrow's sense that wide audiences and fame were "reward[s] for genuine achievement" (Hammill 15). Once students think about the different ways Woolf and Hall represent authorial success, they can try their hand at analyzing Stephen Gordon's work. Hall's novel details the contents of the protagonist's first book, *The Furrow* (213–14), which allows students to consider whether the book was likely to be received as modernist or middlebrow. Even Gordon's final book project, a novel that would generate sympathy for "inverts," the period's term for nonbinary and homosexual individuals, lends itself to this discussion. In this regard, students can examine the advice Stephen receives about the importance of artistic work by and about inverts: Adolphe Blanc, a designer and fellow invert, tells her, "the whole truth is known only to the normal invert. The doctors cannot make the ignorant think, cannot hope to bring home the suffering of millions; only one of ourselves can some day do that" (390). This passage and others are in sharp contrast with Orlando's view of writing as a "secret transaction" as *The Well* demonstrates the middlebrow's interest in pointedly didactic writing that would reach a wide public.

I conclude the semester with Delafield's *The Provincial Lady in London*, the second in Delafield's series of novels about a provincial middle-class wife and mother who struggles to write. These books, which had their roots in light serials Delafield created for the feminist periodical *Time and Tide*, are written in diary form and offer a humorous account of the Lady's struggles to manage her household and navigate her local community even as she longs for wider social and intellectual stimulation.[3] While it may seem strange to introduce students to Delafield's world using the second, rather than first, book in the series, the protagonist has become a published author by this volume, and thus her status as an artist is evident. The first diary entry introduces this theme: "Life takes on entirely new aspect, owing to astonishing and unprecedented success of minute and unpretentious literary effort, published last December, and—incredibly—written by myself" (Delafield 1). Here and throughout the novel, the Lady displays the humility and lack of pretension that characterize a great deal of popular fiction, and while Delafield's character will always minimize her talents and successes in her diary, the book itself gently mocks other characters who make light of the Lady's achievements. Many of her neighbors display a

> [c]urious and rather disturbing tendency to suspect me of Putting Them into a Book. Our Vicar's Wife particularly eloquent about this, and assures me she recognized every single character in previous literary effort. She adds that she has never had time to write a book herself, but has often thought that she would like to do so. Little things,

> she says—one here, another there—quaint sayings such as she hears every day of her life as she pops round the parish—Cranford, she adds in conclusion. (4)

Such passages not only complicate the sound of the middlebrow—Delafield's comic tone is more in line with *Orlando*'s satire than with Hall's earnestness—but also allow students to consider some of the assumptions at work in the register. The Lady will never make grand claims about the importance of her "literary effort," but she—and we as readers—are bemused by the attitude of friends and family, who assume that her work must be autobiographical and thus requires little talent. In addition, the reference to Elizabeth Gaskell's mid-Victorian novel *Cranford* draws readers' attention to the kinds of literary references the Lady and her neighbors share. While Orlando hobnobs with Alexander Pope, Jonathan Swift, and other canonical poets and pamphleteers, and Woolf expected her audience to know something about these figures, Delafield's frame of reference is nineteenth-century novels by Charles Dickens and Jane Austen as well as contemporary middlebrow authors like Hugh Walpole and even Hall (106). Students may know little more about Walpole than about Pope, but they can consider why Delafield's characters think so fondly of the Victorians (and the middlebrow) while Woolf reaches back to the seventeenth and eighteenth centuries—and to male writers—in her account of her protagonist's development. Delafield's Lady, for her part, seems unable to find any authors who are like-minded souls: when she attends a conference of writers, she is shocked by the behavior of the other attendees and repeatedly offended by one who "enquires whether I intend to spend my life between the nursery and the kitchen" (39). The Lady, we find, may be as iconoclastic in her world as Orlando and Stephen Gordon are in theirs, but in the case of Delafield's novel, the author's outsider status is due precisely to her conventional role as a wife and mother.

In fact, the nursery and the kitchen take up a good deal of the Lady's time and energy. Her struggle to write a second book is painfully detailed: time that might have been spent writing goes instead to finding a suitable school for her daughter, replacing the few domestic servants she employs, shopping for groceries, paying bills, and making appointments for family members. Throughout the novel, Delafield emphasizes the work women must undertake to keep a middle-class family clothed, fed, and educated, and the many discussions of bank balances and overdue bills serve as a point of contrast with the wealth and independence Hall's and Woolf's protagonists enjoy. Most readers do not pause to consider the role of money and well-trained (and plentiful) servants in the artistic success of Orlando and Stephen Gordon. The Lady presents a striking foil for these characters, and her difference obliges students to debate the question of the relation between class and artistic opportunity. The Lady's duties as a wife and mother do not keep her from writing, but Delafield's novel insists that readers understand and sympathize with her struggle to find time for work. As a result, as Hammill writes, "Delafield's narrator articulates a . . . democratic concept of authorship as something of which 'all' are potentially capable" (185). *The Provincial Lady in London* helps students examine and challenge their own assumptions about who can be a real author or artist.

Although an entire course on artists may not be in the cards for every instructor who teaches modernism, I hope I have shown the benefits students reap if they are able to study at least a few modernist and middlebrow authors side by side. As Alison Light points out, "Cultural and literary evaluations [are] dialectical judgements—the labels 'high' and 'low' only make sense in relation to each other" (x). Making this dialectic available in our courses can be as simple as teaching one or two middlebrow works alongside the canonical writers that fill anthologies and generally populate syllabi. The most important principle of selection, I have found, is to make sure that modernist and middlebrow texts on the syllabus have some point of contact in terms of content, whether with regard to their treatment of artists; the representation of marriage, travel, or sexuality; or any number of other topics. Such contact ensures that the texts can be compared and contrasted, and students are sure to find shared assumptions as well as obvious differences. While many students come away from my courses with a preference for the popular literature they have studied, a surprising number instead embrace modernism's difficulty and unconventionality precisely because middlebrow works allow them to see what other narrative and stylistic choices were available to authors of the time.

Notes

1. See the companion website to this volume (modwomen.mla.hcommons.org) for a link to the *Middlebrow Network* website, which includes these resources.

2. For a discussion of teaching *The Well* as a lesbian novel, see Ambrose in this volume.

3. For teaching the diary-novel, see Cornish in this volume.

Works Cited

Beauman, Nicola. *A Very Great Profession: The Woman's Novel, 1914–39.* Virago, 1983.

Botshon, Lisa, and Meredith Goldsmith, editors. *Middlebrow Moderns: Popular American Women Writers of the 1920s.* Northeastern UP, 2003.

"Defining the Middlebrow." *Middlebrow Network*, www.middlebrow-network.com/DefiningtheMiddlebrow.aspx. Accessed 27 June 2019.

Delafield, E. M. *The Provincial Lady in London.* 1933. Academy Chicago Publishers, 1983.

Hall, Radclyffe. *The Well of Loneliness.* 1928. Anchor Books, 1990.

Hammill, Faye. *Women, Celebrity, and Literary Culture between the Wars.* U of Texas P, 2007.

Harker, Jamie. *America the Middlebrow: Women's Novels, Progressivism, and Middlebrow Authorship between the Wars.* U of Massachusetts P, 2007.

Hemingway, Ernest. "The Snows of Kilimanjaro." 1936. *The Norton Anthology of American Literature*, 7th ed., vol. D (1914–45), edited by Nina Baym et al., W. W. Norton, 2011, pp. 1983–99.

Humble, Nicola. *The Feminine Middlebrow Novel, 1920s to 1950s: Class, Domesticity, and Bohemianism.* Oxford UP, 2004.

Joyce, James. *A Portrait of the Artist as a Young Man.* 1916. Penguin Books, 2006.

Light, Alison. *Forever England: Femininity, Literature and Conservatism between the Wars.* Routledge, 1991.

Mao, Douglas, and Rebecca L. Walkowitz. "The New Modernist Studies." *PMLA*, vol. 123, no. 3, May 2008, pp. 737–48.

Maugham, W. Somerset. *The Moon and Sixpence.* Heinemann, 1919.

Orwell, George. *Keep the Aspidistra Flying.* 1936. Mariner, 1969.

Radway, Janice A. *A Feeling for Books: The Book-of-the-Month Club, Literary Taste, and Middle-Class Desire.* U of North Carolina P, 1997.

Rubin, Joan Shelley. *The Making of Middlebrow Culture.* U of North Carolina P, 1992.

Scholes, Robert. *Paradoxy of Modernism.* Yale UP, 2006.

Woolf, Virginia. "Middlebrow." *The Essays of Virginia Woolf*, vol. 6 (1933–41), edited by Stuart N. Clarke, Hogarth Press, 2011, pp. 470–79.

———. *Orlando.* 1928. Mariner, 1973.

Sarah Fedirka

Refining the "Bozarts": *Gentlemen Prefer Blondes*, Advertising, and the Mainstream Appropriation of Modernism

Near the middle of Anita Loos's comic novel *Gentlemen Prefer Blondes* (1925), the gold-digging protagonist, Lorelei Lee, schemes to keep a diamond tiara purchased for her by Sir "Piggie" Beekman, a wealthy admirer. When Piggie's wife learns of this extravagance, she confronts Lorelei and Lorelei's street-smart friend, Dorothy. Lady Beekman demands, unsuccessfully, that the American girls give her the tiara, an exchange as farcical as it is ineffectual. Not easily deterred, Lady Beekman hires two French lawyers—the "charming" father and son (89), Robber (Robert) and Louie—to steal the tiara from Lorelei. Lorelei counters with a plan of her own: she secures the real tiara in a safe at the Ritz, replacing it with an imitation, a paste that she keeps carelessly in her handbag. She then seduces Robber and Louie, not with a glimpse of her stocking, but with glimpses of what they believe to be the tiara. Lorelei writes in her diary, "Dorothy and I could get them . . . to spend quite a lot and every time they seemed to get discouradged [sic], I could open my hand bag, and let them get a glimpse of the imitation of a diamond tiara" (89).

This ruse occupies a central position both in Loos's slim volume and in my approach to teaching it. While sex and gender are essential to any discussion of *Blondes*, especially if the book is taught alongside the 1953

Howard Hawks film starring Marilyn Monroe and Jane Russell, this scene reveals another important aspect of the novel: the question of imitation versus authenticity. How does one discern a paste from a real diamond tiara? a refined lady from an uncultured one? highbrow culture from the "bozarts"?

In this essay I describe my experience teaching *Gentlemen Prefer Blondes* in an undergraduate literature course on twentieth-century modernism. While my students and I considered modernist literature's portrayal of sex and gender (and watched the 1953 Hawks adaptation of Loos's novel), these discussions were situated within the larger context of early-twentieth-century marketing and advertising. With its examples of product placement, *Blondes* is a study in consumerism, and the book's satire reveals the permeable border that separates crass commercialism from highbrow refinement. Lorelei from Little Rock is refined through a largely modernist education. In modernism's canonical cities—New York, London, Paris, Vienna—she is educated by the likes of Charlie Chaplin and Sigmund Freud. Lorelei thus comes to embody a middle-class appropriation of modernism, a co-option further evidenced by the book's overwhelming popularity. Loos's audience was in on the joke.[1]

"The Biography of a Book"

Prior to its publication by Boni and Liveright, *Gentlemen Prefer Blondes* was serialized in *Harper's Bazaar* under the title "Gentlemen Always Prefer Blondes: The Illuminating Diary of a Professional Lady." As Loos recalls in "The Biography of a Book," the introduction to the 1963 edition of *Blondes*, she got the idea for the story while traveling from New York to Los Angeles with a group that included her husband, John Emerson; Douglas Fairbanks, Jr., for whom she wrote scenes; and H. L. Mencken, her "idol" (12). The brunette Loos observed on the train that Mencken "preferred a witless blonde" to herself (12). Lorelei Lee, whom the author intended "to be a symbol of the lowest possible mentality" (13), was born in mock revenge. Dashed off on her "yellow pad" (13), the initial story is described by Loos as "merely a short sketch" (14). On Mencken's suggestion, Loos would later send the story to *Harper's Bazaar*, where Mencken assured her, "it'll be lost among the ads and won't offend anyone" (15). Hardly. The serialized story found success with the magazine's readers, doubling and then tripling sales on the newsstand (15). In November 1925, Boni and Liveright published a vanity edition of the collected sketches.

By January, *Blondes* was in its seventh printing (Schrader 5). In addition to mainstream readers, the book was also popular with many of Loos's literary contemporaries, including Sherwood Anderson, James Joyce, Edith Wharton, and William Faulkner, who wrote to Loos, "Please accept my envious congratulations on Dorothy" (32). Despite its original popularity, Loos's satire has been largely overlooked within modernist studies and is typically absent from modernist course syllabi. Critics suggest one reason for this absence is that, rather than being lost among the ads, *Blondes* has been lost among the blockbuster literary class of 1925, which includes F. Scott Fitzgerald's *The Great Gatsby*, Gertrude Stein's *The Making of Americans*, William Carlos Williams's *In the American Grain*, Theodore Dreiser's *An American Tragedy*, Virginia Woolf's *Mrs. Dalloway*, Alain Locke's *The New Negro*, and W. B. Yeats's *A Vision* (Hegeman 525).

Blondes's commercial and critical success complicates its place in the canon. Canon formation requires clear categories; Loos's novel is not easily categorized. Does it belong to highbrow or popular culture? Faye Hammill argues it belongs to both, noting, "Loos works the border between high and popular culture, never fully identifying herself with either" (28). According to Hammill, "[Loos's] books are apparently aimed at a fairly educated audience, since their primary satiric target is a semiliterate, philistine lowbrow, but they also satirize the pretensions of highbrow culture" (28–29). "Undervaluing" the book, some critics dismissed it (and by extension its author) as insignificant (28). Among these were Mencken himself, who Loos believed thought of her as "a cute kid that wrote a book" (qtd. in Schrader 3), and Wyndham Lewis, who considered her "a small mercenary practitioner of the school of Stein" ("'Time'-Children" 61). Lewis's choice of the word "mercenary" here is significant, as it attributes to Loos a characteristic frequently applied to Lorelei, and thereby conflates author and protagonist. Loos herself seems to have encouraged this blurring of boundaries. As Sarah Churchwell notes, to promote the sequel *But Gentlemen Marry Brunettes*, "Loos began appearing in the pages of *Harper's* in a series of self-advertisements that promoted and simultaneously disavowed her resemblance to her characters" (154). In these ads, "the author [is turned] into an advertisement for her fiction and her fiction into an advertisement for herself" (156). Loos was perhaps willing to be identified with Lorelei because she did not see herself as a real writer. In "The Biography of a Book," she twice distinguishes herself from "real novelist[s]" (12, 13) "such as Sherwood Anderson, Dreiser,

Faulkner or Hemingway" (13). Here Loos equates "real" with the highbrow and, by implication, associates the popular with imitation.

Critical reception of *Blondes* reflects an early-twentieth-century cultural anxiety—an anxiety at the heart of the novel itself. As a growing middle class with increasing spending power bought entrée into the cultural elite (or at least bought quality facsimiles of cultural artifacts), the boundaries of the high-, middle-, and lowbrow were transgressed. Lorelei's wealthy male suitors likewise buy her entrée into a fictionalized (and satirized) highbrow, and notably modernist, culture. The novel can thus be read as representative of a particular twentieth-century moment—a moment in which modernism, advertising, and consumerism converge. In what follows, I offer an example of how to teach the novel through this lens.

"People All Get Together in the Evening and Improve Their Minds"

I taught *Gentlemen Prefer Blondes* as the final text in an upper-level English course on twentieth-century literature offered at a private, comprehensive university in northwestern Ohio. The course, titled Picture This: Literary Modernism and Visual Culture, ran as a senior seminar. Over sixteen weeks, we considered the connections among visual and literary modernisms and how modernist representations challenged traditional perspectives of reality and genre. To guide our inquiry, I divided the course into four units: magazines and manifestos; visual modernism (i.e., painting and sculpture); modernist photography; and modernist cinema. In addition to *Blondes*, we read Lewis's *Blast One*, Woolf's *To the Lighthouse*, Stein's *Picasso*, John Dos Passos's *Manhattan Transfer*, and Nathanael West's *Day of the Locust* as well as primary and secondary texts on painting, photography, film, and advertising. My intention for the course mirrored Lorelei's description of a French *salo* ("salon"): "people all get together in the evening and improve their minds" (*Gentlemen* 23).

Of the eleven students in the class, five were English majors. Given my students' wide-ranging experiences with literary analysis and my own constructivist approach, I did not require them to write an end-of-semester paper. Instead, I assigned what I called Make It New projects; students completed one project for each of the four units. For these projects, students researched a modernist piece from which they drew inspiration and then created an artifact in the same medium; they wrote manifestos, created advertisements, took photographs, and made films. Students submitted written reflections analyzing the original work and their own, commenting on everything from the process of production to the final product. At the end of the semester, artifacts, which were digitized as necessary, were collected in individual electronic portfolios that included a cumulative reflection situating the contents both within the course and with respect to modernism. As I communicated to students, my goal with these inquiry-based projects was to give them the chance to develop their understanding of the modernist period by investigating and experimenting with modernism's arts, styles, and technologies. I kept the projects intentionally open-ended to allow students to engage with modernist texts and concepts in individually meaningful ways. Because I did not want such freedom to create anxiety, students were able to brainstorm their projects in class; drafts were peer workshopped, and final versions could be revised.

"All of the Famous Historical Names, like Coty and Cartier"

For all students, even those who were English majors, this course provided their first prolonged exposure to modernism. To get to *Blondes* by week fifteen, much scaffolding was required. I began by situating modernism within a context that was familiar to students. For them, *The Great Gatsby* had always been on high school reading lists and Van Gogh's *Starry Night* had always been on T-shirts. With apologies to Alan Golding, I introduced modernism as "classic" before challenging students to see it as "outlaw." During week one, I shared twentieth- and twenty-first-century print ads that incorporated modernist authors, texts, or styles. For example, the Reebok "Cubist Classic" ad (2001), part of the Bartle, Bogle, and Hegarty (New York) Reebok Classic campaign, reimagines the body of a fit, naked Caucasian woman as if in a cubist painting ("Cubist Classic"). Gazing directly at the viewer, the woman holds a pose similar to the central figures in Pablo Picasso's *Les Demoiselles d'Avignon* (1907; *The Young Women of Avignon*). Her most notable features are her eyes, her breasts (the least cubist part of her body), and her sneakers. I also presented ads for La-Z-Boy's "Gatsby Sofa"—which urges viewers to "[g]ive your TV something interesting to look at for a change" ("Gatsby Sofa")—and for the Ernest Hemingway Collection by Thomasville. An advertisement for the Hemingway bedroom suite promises, "Though you may not be able to trace his footsteps, you can still experience the world through his eyes" ("Ernest Hemingway"). These advertisements served multiple purposes in the course. Foremost, they introduced modernism to an audience that had only a superficial knowledge of it. Many of the students had seen the ads before; most had read Hemingway or seen a cubist painting. Additionally, the Reebok ad prompted discussion of sexual stereotyping and the male gaze, while the Hemingway Collection invited conversation about masculinity and gender norms. Collectively, the advertisements led to a consideration of modernism as a commodity, a mass-produced classic that traded on a twenty-first-century middle-class nostalgia for the 1920s and a related belief that refinement could be purchased through conspicuous consumption—the very ideas Loos satirizes in *Blondes* updated for a new millennium.

I linked discussion of these ads to the second Make It New project, which asked students to research and experiment with a modernist visual style or technique (e.g., cubism or collage). One student, inspired by Picasso's cubist period, created an advertisement for Aesop Rock's album *Bestiary.* He chose this album because it includes the song "Ego Death," which features the line, "Hit the corner like the devil is a cubist" (Busdriver). In his reflection, the student observes how experimental artistic movements "are often captured, repurposed, and utilized in the world of advertisement." He saw his ad "as a reminder that cubism is still influencing artists today, and that this influence is not limited to visual artists." Aesop Rock, he writes, "took advantage of the fact that people who understand cubism know it's largely defined by its use of sharp, well-defined corners." In this, the singer is not unlike Loos, who similarly capitalized on her readers' being in the know. Another student, recognizing the irony inherent in selling the idea that one should desire to live like Gatsby or Hemingway, created a series of satiric print ads using quotations from modernist texts. In one ad, she used lines from T. S. Eliot's "The Love Song of J. Alfred Prufrock" ("Time to turn back and descend the stair, / with a bald spot in the middle of my hair—" [lines 39–40]) to sell Rogaine, a choice reflecting her awareness that "[m]odernism has evolved over the years from the avant-garde to mainstream media," from outlaw to classic.

These early exercises with print advertisements helped prepare students for *Blondes* in week fifteen. They framed our discussion of commodification, imitation, and authenticity in relation not only to modernism but also to the novel's publishing history and content. As Churchwell claims, "*Blondes* is pervaded by contemporary anxieties about cultural capital, advertisement, imitation, and the middlebrow" (135). These anxieties, she suggests, arise from a belief that "'the real thing' transcends commodification, and the commodity is a mere reproduced imitation of real value" (139). To allow for interrogation of these arguments, we read Loos's novel alongside excerpts from both the original sketches in *Harper's Bazaar* and Magdalen King-Hall's fictitious *Diary of a Young Lady of Fashion in the Year 1764–1765*, another overlooked text by a woman writer of this period.[2]

As originally published in *Harper's Bazaar*, *Blondes* provides striking visual evidence of the novel's link to advertising: story and advertisement share space on the page. Churchwell observes, "Reading *Blondes* in the context of *Harper's*, one finds satire and its target literally side by side, as Loos mocks Lorelei for buying what the reader of *Harper's* is told to fantasize about" (143). This becomes salient for students who have mocked contemporary advertisements that sell fantasized versions of modernism. The Thomasville ad for a Hemingway Collection bedroom suite differs only in kind from an advertisement for the Elgin A. Simonds Furniture Company that appears in the June 1925 issue of *Harper's*. Both ads appeal to the reader's desire to possess an original or at least a quality reproduction. The Thomasville ad reminds viewers that "Hemingway had a tremendous appetite for life," "a quality" the furniture maker and the reader (implied in the ad's use of "we") "also bring to the table" ("Hemingway"). The Simonds's copy informs one that furniture of the type being sold was previously available only as an "inheritance from stern Pilgrim forebears." Now, however, "All America is . . . heir to these gallant traditions" ("Simonds"). Similarly, buying a piece from the Hemingway Collection makes twenty-first century Americans heirs to modernism.[3] Issues of imitation and authenticity repeat with a difference in the *Harper's* advertisements that feature women models. Often in cloche hats and wraps, these women bear resemblance to Ralph Barton's drawings of Lorelei and Dorothy, which also appeared in the magazine, and to later representations of Loos herself.[4] The novel even practices product placement, which, though satiric, nonetheless advertises the Ritz ("I really love the *Majestic* because you would not know it was a ship because it is just like being at the Ritz" [*Gentlemen* 43]) and Coty and Cartier ("in only a few blocks we read all of the famous historical names, like Coty and Cartier" [78]). *Blondes* thus invites students to consider how advertisements, like novels, are a fiction and how novels, like advertisements, can sell products, even though novels are considered a more authentic art form than advertisements.

Alongside *Blondes*, I introduced students to *The Diary of a Young Lady of Fashion*, by Cleone Knox (a pseudonym for Magdalen King-Hall). Published in January 1926, two months after *Blondes*, *The Diary* chronicles Knox's adventures on the grand tour. Though little known today, *The Diary* was a popular success at the time of its publication, receiving "a long and enthusiastic review" in *The Sunday Times of London* (Maxwell) and going through "nine U.S. editions in two months" ("Admiral's Daughter"). Legend even has it that Winston Churchill "excused his late arrival at a dinner party by saying he had had to finish the *Diary* before coming" (Maxwell). Shortly after publication, however, the text was revealed to be a hoax, an imitation of an authentic eighteenth-century diary. Cleone Knox was in actuality a thoroughly modern twentieth-century teenager, Magdalen King-Hall, who confessed to writing "the book in a few weeks" ("Admiral's Daughter").

Many similarities exist between Loos's and King-Hall's diaries and their fictitious authors, making them a rich point of comparison. Both books masquerade as "intimate, gossipy journal[s]" (Katsoulis), and a description of Cleone's diary as "the casual and intermittent record of a racy love affair and the Grand Tour" could be applied to *Blondes*—though the plural "affairs" would be more accurate (Davison). Both Cleone and Lorelei share "a naughty awareness which is at once suspicious and delicious" (Davison), and one reviewer, seemingly unaware of the hoax, notes that while not "a modern lady in the sense that she is all leg exhibition and lipstick," Cleone "is as modern as a post war flapper" (qtd. in Maxwell). One reviewer of *Blondes* makes an explicit connection between the two texts, suggesting that Lorelei's "confidences should be read in connection with that diverting hoax, *The Diary of a Young Lady of Fashion in the Year 1764–65* by 'Cleone Knox'" in part because Lorelei "covers much the same ground as 'Cleone' did" ("Moronese"). While Cleone meets Louis XV and Voltaire, Lorelei meets the Prince of Wales and "Dr. Froyd."

Cleone and Lorelei even share a similarly irreverent style. Near the end of *The Diary*, Cleone indignantly reports that her brother, Ned, had run off with a nun. Her description of the situation could be that of Lorelei:

> What seems to me so strange in this affair is that if Ned had merely continued to be the lover of this Nun all would have been well, for they are permitted to carry on intrigues and lead lives of great immorality; but to attempt to become her lawful husband was it seems an Unpardonable Sin, and thus poor Ned is to suffer for the first Respectable thing I have ever known him to do! (Knox 238)

Lorelei provides a similar kind of logic when speaking about her suitor Gerry Lamson: "So it seems that Gerry has had quite a lot of trouble himself and he cannot even get married on account of his wife. He and she have never been in love with each other but she was a suffragette and asked him to merry her, so what could he do?" (*Gentlemen* 29).

Revelation of *The Diary* hoax was front page news. "Cleverest Hoax of the Century" ran as the headline of London's *Daily Express*, while *The New York Times* claimed, "Girl Tricks the World with Literary Hoax, Intended as Joke" (qtd. in Maxwell). That the diary was a hoax appears not to have hurt sales of the book. One review in *The New Republic* suggests, "But what did all this matter [the identity of the author of *The Diary*] in an age of salesmanship and credulity? Cleone Knox enjoyed her little day. She was even annexed by the department stores, her inelegant phrases being turned to use in the advertisements of lingerie" (L. M. N. 281).

"The Name of a Word Which Means Imitations"

On learning that paste is "the name of a word which means imitations" (*Gentlemen* 78), the usually ebullient Lorelei Lee becomes depressed. She confesses in her diary, "So it really makes a girl feel depressed to think a girl could not tell that it was nothing but an imitation" (78). In this way, Loos's seemingly witless protagonist articulates the anxiety of the moment: How does one determine what is real, original, or authentic? What does it say about cultural distinctions if after only one day spent in the museums of Munich, "get[ting] full of kunst," the German word for *art*, a girl like Lorelei "could be a high brow" (113)? When taught in the context I have described here, *Gentlemen Prefer Blondes* challenges students to consider such questions. As they reason through their answers, students arrive at a deeper understanding of Loos's novel and of modernism's own Lorelei-like transition from disruptive outsider to conspicuously consumed insider, a recognition that invites students to consider modernism's continued relevance in the present day.

Notes

The title of this essay alludes to the American writer and critic H. L. Mencken's essay "The Sahara of the Bozart." Mencken coined the term *bozart*, a play on *beaux arts*, or "fine arts," to suggest that the New South was as "sterile, artistically, intellectually, culturally, as the Sahara Desert." In her introduction to *Blondes,*

Loos suggests erroneously, as far as I can tell based on the versions of Mencken's essay I have read, that Mencken "branded" Arkansas in particular with this term ("Biography" 13). Loos chose Little Rock as the hometown of her unrefined protagonist because the city "lives up to" what Loos claims was "Mencken's choice as a nadir in shortsighted human stupidity" (14).

1. Wyndham Lewis dismisses Loos's novel as a punchline "for the benefit of the middle-class public," which is "able to chuckle over the dish of bad grammar and naughtiness to their hearts' content" ("'Time'-Children" 62).

2. This work appears as both *The Diary* and *A Diary*.

3. Such furniture ads call to mind Virginia Woolf's definition of the middlebrow, which, as Sarah Churchwell notes, "defined the middlebrow by what it bought: 'Queen Anne Furniture (faked, but none the less expensive)'" (139).

4. See Churchwell 143–46 for a reading of Barton's illustrations against advertisements in the magazine.

Works Cited

"Admiral's Daughter." *Time*, vol. 7, no. 24, 14 June 1926, p. 14.

Busdriver. Lyrics to "Ego Death." Featuring Danny Brown and Aesop Rock. *Genius*, genius.com/Busdriver-ego-death-lyrics. Accessed 18 June 2019.

Churchwell, Sarah. "'Lost among the Ads': *Gentlemen Prefer Blondes* and the Politics of Imitation." *Middlebrow Moderns: Popular American Women Writers of the 1920s*, edited by Lisa Botshon and Meredith Goldsmith, Northeastern UP, 2003, pp. 135–64.

"Cubist Classic." *Vanity Fair*, 1 June 2001, p. 115.

Davison, Edward. "A Charming Hoax?" *The Saturday Review of Literature*, 6 Mar. 1926, p. 610.

Dos Passos, John. *Manhattan Transfer*. 1925. Mariner Books, 2003.

Eliot, T. S. "The Love Song of J. Alfred Prufrock." 1915. The Waste Land *and Other Poems*, by Eliot, Signet, 1998, pp. 5–11.

"Ernest Hemingway: The Collection of a Lifetime." *LeAnna Graves Creative*, www.leannagraves.com/hemingway.html. Accessed 20 June 2019.

Faulkner, William. *Selected Letters of William Faulkner*. Edited by Joseph Blotner, Random House, 1977.

"Gatsby Sofa." *Country Home Magazine*, Jan./Feb. 2001, p. 25.

Golding, Alan. *From Outlaw to Classic: Canons in American Poetry*. U of Wisconsin P, 1995.

Hammill, Faye. "'One of the Few Books That Doesn't Stink': The Intellectuals, the Masses, and *Gentlemen Prefer Blondes*." *Critical Survey*, vol. 17, no. 3, 2005, pp. 27–48.

Hawks, Howard, director. *Gentlemen Prefer Blondes*. Twentieth Century Fox, 1953.

Hegeman, Susan. "Taking *Blondes* Seriously." *American Literary History*, vol. 7, no. 3, 1995, pp. 525–54.

"Hemingway Had a Tremendous Appetite for Life." *Country Home Magazine*, Nov.-Dec. 2000, pp. 2–3.

Katsoulis, Melissa. *Telling Tales: A History of Literary Hoaxes.* Kindle ed., Constable, 2013.

Knox, Cleone (Magdalen King-Hall). *The Diary of a Young Lady of Fashion in the Year 1764–1765.* D. Appleton, 1926.

Lewis, Wyndham. *Blast One.* 1914. Facsimile ed., Gingko Press, 1982.

———. "'Time'-Children: Miss Gertrude Stein and Miss Anita Loos." *Time and Western Man*, edited by Paul Edwards, Black Sparrow Press, 1993, pp. 58–62.

L. M. N. "An Invented Young Lady." *The New Republic*, vol. 46, no. 594, 21 Apr. 1926, pp. 281–82.

Loos, Anita. "The Biography of a Book." 1963. Loos, *Gentlemen*, pp. 11–16.

———. *Gentlemen Prefer Blondes.* 1925. Penguin Books, 1992.

Maxwell, Richard Perceval. "Background to the Publication of *The Diary of a Young Lady of Fashion, 1764–65*, by Magdalen King-Hall." *King Hall Connections*, sites.google.com/site/kinghallconnections/6940---wife-and-daughters-of-george-king-hall/diary-of-young-lady-of-fashion. Accessed 18 June 2019.

Mencken, H. L. "The Sahara of the Bozart." *New York Evening Mail*, 13 Nov. 1917. *The Archive of American Journalism*, thegrandarchive.wordpress.com/the-sahara-of-the-bozart/. Accessed 3 June 2020.

"Moronese." *Time*, vol. 7, no. 8, 22 Feb. 1926, p. 41.

Schrader, Richard J. "'But Gentlemen Marry Brunettes': Anita Loos and H. L. Mencken." *Menckeniana*, no. 98, Summer 1986, pp. 1–7.

"Simonds." *Harper's Bazaar*, June 1925, p. 122.

Stein, Gertrude. *Picasso.* 1938. Dover, 1984.

West, Nathanael. *The Day of the Locust.* 1939. Miss Lonely Hearts *and* The Day of the Locust, by West, New Directions Publishing, 2009, pp. 59–185.

Woolf, Virginia. *To the Lighthouse.* 1927. Harcourt Brace Jovanovich, 1981.

Vicki Tromanhauser

Dining at the Modernist Table: Teaching Food in Women's Interwar Writing

When Andrew Solomon remarks that the richness of Virginia Woolf's writing, "like chocolate," requires rationing lest he grow "emotionally obese" on its decadent substance, he identifies the connection between Woolf's aesthetics and the gustatory. The emotionally and sensuously saturated moment that is a hallmark of Woolf's prose, like that of many of her high modernist contemporaries, does not always go down easily. A unit I have created on women's gastronomical modernism, which may be used within a variety of teaching contexts, treats the food writing of the interwar years, a period shaped by the rationing of the World Wars, as a vital moment of creativity and formal experimentation. Patriotic calls to action, like the Eat Less Meat campaign of the First World War and the Dig for Victory gardening movement of the Second, and the formation of a centralized Ministry of Food in the United Kingdom, with its bureaucratization of food production, distribution, and preparation, transformed food in the interwar period into a matter of geopolitical significance. More than a concern of private sustenance or gustatory pleasure, food became central to larger questions of national security, social justice, and sustainable agriculture.

At the regional comprehensive university where I teach, I have found this unit pedagogically rewarding and readily adaptable to general education courses for nonmajors like Women in Literature, sophomore-level introductions to the English major, and more specialized upper-level courses in modernist literature. Through a comparison of the overt rhetorical strategies and implicit modes of representation we observe in different kinds of culinary writing, we can help students make sense of how women writers navigate the shifting categories of class, gender, ethnicity, and species in the interwar period. By including popular and quotidian forms of cultural production, those that reside within a kind of everydayness, as part of the frame of our discussion of women's interwar prose, instructors create a hospitable space inside the literary studies classroom for the interdisciplinarity that invigorates new modernist studies. At the same time, instructors begin to separate modernism from the highbrow or from a canon and the expectations engendered by that canon. In this essay I elaborate a method for engaging texts across different genres—including recipes, household primers, dietary guides, and culinary memoirs—for challenging the hierarchies of literary value that attend them, and thus for enlarging our sense of what constitutes the literary. The diversity of form and style in women's modernist food writing, which is both aesthetic and practically oriented, comprises what Amy L. Tigner and Allison Carruth call "vernacular literary practices," which involve modes of writing that are "variously empirical, sensory, instructive, interactive, and intergenerational" (3). The gastronomical-pedagogical approach I propose provides an entry into conversations with students about how modernism is construed, especially as the field has shifted in recent years toward more flexible understandings of its temporal, geographic, and generic limits.

An approach to modernist studies through the lens of the gustatory leverages the momentum of literary food studies. Kyla Tompkins and Timothy Morton, for example, have offered engaging treatments of food in nineteenth-century American literature and Romantic literature, respectively, and a recent special issue of *Resilience: A Journal of the Environmental Humanities*, edited by J. Michelle Coghlan, addresses gastronomical modernism across media and cultures. The collection *Modernism and Food Studies: Politics, Aesthetics, and the Avant-Garde*, edited by Jessica Martell and colleagues, takes up authors as varied as Katherine Mansfield, Ford Madox Ford, James Joyce, and Langston Hughes and includes considerations of futurism and film.

In order to think about what food means, students should first learn to appreciate how it matters. To facilitate an understanding of the cultural and ethical stakes of who consumes what or whom, and how, I begin with selections from food theorists and ethicists of the present moment: Carol J. Adams's *The Sexual Politics of Meat* (35–55), Jonathan Safran Foer's *Eating Animals* (21–41), and Michael Pollan's *The Omnivore's Dilemma* (1–11, 287–303). Students new to feminist food studies may find the complexity of Adams's argument daunting at first; I alert them to these challenges up front. An awareness of how discourses of speciesism and sexism overlap and how the processes by which bodies (whether women's or animals') routinely objectified as meat are erased provides us with a conceptual paradigm applicable to modernist women's writing. David Foster Wallace's "Consider the Lobster" offers a witty exploration of how considerations of taste and cultural tradition intersect with social class, animal ethics, and the pressures generated by industrial food production. Before students encounter the fiction of Anglo-Irish writer Elizabeth Bowen, it's helpful to read Jonathan Swift's "A Modest Proposal," which, in satirically recommending the cannibalization of Irish youth, succinctly and powerfully exposes students to how food production and consumption are bound up with the history of colonialism, constructions of ethnic difference, and conceptions of human and nonhuman agency. By beginning with this framework, we sharpen students' interpretive responses to the ethical stakes of eating so that when we turn to matters of aesthetics—that is, how writers represent encounters with food—they are able to approach the formal aspects of modernist gastronomical writing, where aesthetic discernment and ethical judgment meet, with greater nuance and sophistication.

The recipe, at once an artifact and a minigenre addressed predominantly to women, provides an object lesson in the contingencies of material circumstances, cultural traditions and their transmission, and the politics of taste. When students read recipes closely for the values they suggest—economic, social, aesthetic—modernism's formal contortions are made more accessible. At the same time, students learn to appreciate the psychological and affective challenges of noncombatant life in the interwar period—whether experienced as an interval of peace, a time of plenty, or as a time of traumatic expectation determined by impending violence, scarcity, and loss. The "anticipatory syndrome" of the 1920s and 1930s, as Paul K. Saint-Amour describes it, reimagines the interwar period not simply as a retroactive designation assigned with the advantage of hindsight but as an experience of expectant dwelling in which the most quotidian of spaces and encounters is already invaded by a rending awareness of imminent catastrophe, the prospect of conflict and loss to come (13).

Woolf famously located modernism's cultural and aesthetic watershed four years prior to the outbreak of the First World War, "on or about December 1910," and identified as its protagonist the figure of the cook, whose Georgian incarnation surfaces from the obscure depths of the Victorian kitchen "to borrow the *Daily Herald*," promising to become a reader as much as a potential author ("Character" 422). What Sandra M. Gilbert identifies as a distinctive "culinary poetics" in the early twentieth century gives form to the ordinary, immediate, and material aspects of food rather than the sacred and transcendent notions of cuisine, and finds expressive value in the sensuous fullness of daily consumption (124). This modernist culinary poetics emerges in response to shifting protocols of the table and changing systems of household management, including the progressive erosion of the servant class and, inversely, the growth of a female professional class; the development of new kitchen technology advertised in women's periodicals; the rise of the restaurant and its status as a public space; the advent of national food control; and the introduction of tinned and packaged, ready-to-eat food (Gilbert 118). In order to bring this historical perspective into focus and excavate its gastronomical textures, we consider the wartime narrative *How We Lived Then, 1914–1918*, by Constance Dorothy Peel (known to her readers as Mrs. C. S. Peel), who directed the women's service of the Ministry of Food during the First World War and wrote a series of cookbooks for the war ration economy. Chapters 6 and 7 of *How We Lived Then* elaborate with a documentarist's precision the swift transformation of the entire food network from farm to table introduced by the strenuous regulatory measures of the British Ministry of Food. Peel's meticulous record of long rationing queues, meat scarcity, nutritional studies, and wartime recipes eerily evokes the mid-war sensibility of the interwar period—a troubling presage of privations to come. At the same time, such historical context demonstrates how alimentary experience becomes a matter of wide-ranging intellectual, scientific, and aesthetic interest during the interwar period.

With historical context in place, we proceed with a handful of recipes from the interwar period. We start by considering the food writing of the American gastronome M. F. K. Fisher, whose career began in the interwar period. Fisher's brief essay "The Anatomy of a Recipe" helps frame our discussion of the recipe as a form situated on the margins of the literary and historical archive. Suspended between the performative and the aesthetic, between gustatory and intellectual consumption, the recipe—or *receipt* in its archaic form derived from the Latin, as Fisher reminds us ("Anatomy" 4)—is an interactive text that depends on its reception and, shaped by the available stock in the cook's pantry, invites improvisation and variation. If it is in essence a formula consisting of a name, ingredients, and instructions in method—"a little of this, some of that, baked long enough, and then served forth" (4)—then the recipe as micronarrative at times bends toward another concentrated, condensed literary form—the lyric. Fisher admonishes us, "There can be no frills about it, no ambiguities . . . and above all no 'little secrets'" (10). Yet where the staple cookbook of the Victorian kitchen, *Mrs. Beeton's Book of Household Management* (1861), featured comprehensive instructions in the preparation of dishes, including the best methods of slaughter and of choosing and carving different cuts and kinds of meat, we pay special attention in class to how and why modernist recipes, by contrast, court the rhetorical properties of ambiguity or even opacity, symbolic figuration, and semantic multiplicity, against the purely pragmatic considerations that determine how a dish will turn out. Fisher's late modernist satire of wartime dietary guides *How to Cook a Wolf* evades the monotony of Second World War rationing (which continued in Britain until 1954) with advice about "how to distribute your virtue" (14) or "how to be cheerful though starving" (80) like her friend Sue, an example of "inspired oblivion to the ugliness of poverty," who develops an improbable cuisine of forageable weeds, cactus leaves, and sea kelp that manages to keep the famished wolf at bay while delighting her guests' palates with an "intense romantic strangeness" (84). Such therapy counsels the hungry through wit and gusto to retain culinary dignity and sensual entertainment in the mind if not in the kitchen. Several selections pair well with "The Anatomy of a Recipe" (*How to Cook* 14–25, 80–85).

Two competing aesthetic modes come out of the food writing of the interwar period, and our sampling of recipes that are exemplary of these opposed culinary practices enables us to identify tensions between the values of sacrifice for the collective good and pleasure for its own sake; between doing one's bit and relishing the sensually exquisite moment; and between bracing for conditional future disaster and holding crisis in reflective suspension. As part of a day-long symposium at the Culinary Institute of America, I presented wartime and interwar recipes to a group of student chefs who, in comparing these recipes, readily appreciated the contrasting attitudes they represented toward meat and its preparation. When I'm not talking to chefs, however, I find this makes for a good in-class writing exercise. It is especially important to emphasize how the same formal attention to descriptive language that students in the literature classroom bring to a lyric poem applies to a recipe as a text. In other words, practical considerations of preparation do not preclude questions of tone and style. The four recipes I use, which I explain in more detail in what follows, may be found on this volume's companion website (modwomen.mla.hcommons.org). Group discussion of this exercise gives students an opportunity to reflect on how matters of personal taste, culinary skill, and familial or cultural traditions inform how they approach culinary writing from a different historical period.

The austerity of food writing under wartime rationing is characterized by a principle of economical precision that scorns waste and insists democratically on the substitutability of scarce ingredients. Its style is evocative of sparsity and frugality; it privileges thrift over taste and pleasure; and it emphasizes nourishment, stripping dishes down to nutritional essentials. Marion Harris Neil's recipe for "Army Broth" in the *Thrift Cook Book*, published in 1919 (when England was still in the throes of rationing that would continue until 1921), is marked by privation and an intent to rein in excesses at a time of limited resources: "For this broth," Neil advises, "scraps of all kinds can be used up" and "[a]ny vegetables in season may be used"; the resulting broth can be served with dumplings or toasted bread (24). Reveling in the ingenuity of its culinary recycling, Neil's recipe for the pluckily titled "'Hard Times' Pie" conserves both ingredients (calling for unspecified meat or fish) and fuel (by baking in a "quick oven" [324]) and betrays its allegiance to culinary economy over enjoyment: "This is excellent, and in addition to using up remains of cold meat or fish, it also helps to make stale bread appetizing" (324–25). It is hard to fathom how cold remains of meat or stale bread might produce something appetizing, but in forsaking enjoyment for the self-abnegation of the kitchen front the recipe teaches new wartime values—ones that Stella Rodney learns in Bowen's *The Heat of the Day* (1948) when she commits the gaffe of forgetting to bring her own butter ration to tea with her lover's family and thus finds the gathering leeched of pleasure by the patriotic impulse to sacrifice.

By contrast, the fashionable food writing of the post-rationing era celebrates the diet of decadence. This highly stylized culinary writing is characterized by sublime descriptions that yield a sensual and intellectual pleasure akin to the gustatory satisfaction promised at the table. Ruth Lowinsky's surrealist *Lovely Food: A Cookery Notebook*, which includes table decorations illustrated by her husband, features associative suggestions for dishes and a menu for a "dream party of some of the most celebrated people of the day, whom one can never hope to meet, or, if met, be remembered by" (54), one that includes people such as Woolf, Albert Einstein, Charlie Chaplin, Benito Mussolini, and Sigmund Freud (54–55). Much of the pleasure of such unabashedly extravagant dishes derives from the whimsical combination of foods and artful recommendations for hosting. Prizing culinary style over clarity, Lowinsky, who didn't learn to cook until after the Second World War (Humble 284n), neglects to specify quantities of ingredients or even, in the case of the "tomates à l'espagnol" ("Spanish tomatoes"), the kind of cheese (which would have an appreciable effect on the flavor); fails to give a cooking time for the "saumon en surprise" ("salmon surprise"), which might yield a surprise indeed; and is often keener to elaborate the arrangement of a dish like "poulet aux choux" ("chicken with cabbage") on the serving plate than its method of preparation.

These opposed perceptions of food—as elegantly and sometimes ingeniously reduced nutritive medium or as rarified art form, the occasion for the lavish, even ostentatious display of culture—characterize the food writing of the interwar period. While the influence of these culinary modes is particularly marked in women's writing because such works address the mistress of the house as chief domestic officer, I make clear that sensitivity to the sexual, cultural, and species politics of food and consumptive practices is not an exclusively feminine prerogative—the "Lestrygonians" episode in Joyce's *Ulysses* (124–50) proving as alert as Mrs. Ramsay's dinner scene in Woolf's *To the Lighthouse* (85–114) to what Jacques Derrida calls the "carno-phallogocentrism" (113) at the heart of Western conceptions of human subjectivity.

When we turn to gustatory fiction like Woolf's *To the Lighthouse* and Bowen's *The House in Paris*, narratives that pivot on a decadent meal, we examine how these competing modernist approaches to cuisine are interfused within the novels, often playing against each other to subversive effect. An exercise in what the nineteenth-century French gastronome Jean Anthelme Brillat-Savarin dubs "transcendental gastronomy," which promises social communion through sublime and artful fare, occurs when Mrs. Ramsay serves an heirloom dish of "boeuf en daub" ("beef stew") that effects a transformation of her dinner guests, who partake, in no uncertain terms, "of eternity" (Woolf, *To the Lighthouse* 107). Mrs. Ramsay's culinary triumph—or more precisely, that of her cook Mildred—appears to defy its own material substance as a Provençal stew and transport its diners to gustatory Elysium. Ambrose Heath's *Good Food* pays tribute to Woolf's dish with a recipe from the French chef Auguste Escoffier, but takes exception to William Bankes's use of a knife and fork where epicures would prefer a spoon, noting that the dish is known in some parts of France as "boeuf à cuiller" ("spoon beef"; 185). In a blogging assignment that builds on our in-class writing, students compare Heath's recipe with the dinner scene in *To the Lighthouse*. Woolf's lyrical rendering of the effects of the dish, when read alongside a recipe such as Heath's, raises a host of textual questions: Why doesn't Mrs. Ramsay prepare the beef herself? Why doesn't Mr. Ramsay share with Lily a technique for blanching bacon rind? And, for that matter, why doesn't Charles Tansley offer to pitch in with the dishes? For the text is also keen to remind us of the excised bits of social tension that stubbornly assert themselves, refusing to be digested in the metaphysics of the carnivorous feast: the labor of the Ramsays' hired cook, Mildred; the sardonic laughter that threatens to erupt in the younger generation; Lily Briscoe's refusal to renounce her love of painting in favor of Mrs. Ramsay's mania for marriage; or the proffered sacrifice of victims to come (the engaged young couple, Paul and Minta, and the Ramsays' eldest children and heirs).

The most devastating formal articulation of these indigestibles are the square-bracketed passages in "Time Passes," a textual innovation that does a kind of violence in and to the novel. The contents of the square brackets—which announce with such terse economy the deaths of characters and thus the undoing of the values that reigned in the Ramsays' dinner—are analogous to the stylistic reduction that we see in the rationing discourse of the time, which without sentimental ado braces its readers for the subtraction of ingredients or their substitution with more available ones. The narrative shocks delivered by those seven bracketed passages in "Time Passes" and another unsettling moment in the novel's last section send us back to revisit the dinner scene that had delivered such an appetizing portrait of Edwardian familial and cultural cohesion, this time to witness its incipient fractures.

Bowen's gustatory novel *The House in Paris* shares the tripartite structure of *To the Lighthouse* and likewise turns on a multicourse French meal, but locates this central scene in a restaurant in Boulogne, where an ill-fated affair begins between Max and Karen, both of whom are engaged to other partners. The novel's longest, central section, "The Past," flanked by two sections titled "The Present," anxiously projects a catastrophic future, even to the extent of experiencing that future as capable of inflicting injury in advance and thus of inhabiting the "future conditional anxiety" that Saint-Amour attributes to much interwar literature (7). Expectant trauma or "dread," a word that appears over forty times and about every five pages in *The House in Paris*, permeates times past and present (Bennett and Royle 61). Bowen's conspicuously ornamental diction throws the material properties of language into relief and thus arrests our conceptual digestion of words into sense. Bowen's mannered prose, the inclusion of decorative or nonreferential descriptions, produces what Susan Osborne has identified as a "queer, opaque style that realizes itself not solely as a style to be looked *through* but as a style to be looked *at* as well" (194). In a second blogging assignment, students draw connections between the in-class exercise that asked them to compare Neil's and Lowinsky's recipes and the verbal style of the restaurant passage in *The House in Paris.*

Karen and Max enter Mony's restaurant like partially digested food particles, a sense of expectation having "made [Karen] hollow" (*House* 144) and left Max feeling depleted by what the domineering matriarch Madame Fisher's "wit ate out" of him (150). In contrast to Woolf's emphasis on serving and tasting the meal, Bowen's scene refocuses attention on culinary remains, the orts, scraps, and fragments of the meal's endings rather than the bounty of its beginnings: drained glasses of wine, cantaloupe rinds, husks of hollowed-out rolls, and fish gone cold. Amidst the couple's halting conversation, the narrator tells us: "Karen, moving despairingly, caught an edge of the cloth between her knees and the table, pulling the knives crooked, some wine splashed from his glass" (153). The peculiar twists of Bowen's agrammatical syntax are jarring in a way reminiscent of Woolf's bracketed announcement of Mrs. Ramsay's death. Bowen's fiction is invested in compositional arrangement; it prefers opacity to plain intelligibility as a kind of aesthetic *en surprise*. Through a series of accreting verbal clauses, Karen loses her place as subject of the sentence to Max's upset wine glass. The syntax oddly evacuates Karen's agency while the surrounding objects (tablecloth, knives, glass) become correspondingly animated as the bearers of the scene's emotional agitation. While the supercilious French waiter straightens the creases in the tablecloth and throws a napkin over the wine stain, the stain remains, lurking beneath as a prefiguration of Max's eventual suicide after he learns of the son that issues from his and Karen's affair. The mess left by the meal, like the mess of the couple's erotic entanglement, provides a different insight into the gustatory that illuminates the costs of our personal and cultural appetites.

What I seek to model for students is a practice of horizontal reading that thinks along the surfaces of prose whose rhetorical and syntactical perplexity doesn't readily dissolve or translate into the strictly representational. Like Lowinsky's Bohemian menu, such ornamental or decorative choices obtrude as a form of commentary on the narrative's action. And yet, by teaching women's interwar writing through food, we make such complex interpretive operations at once tangible and pleasurable for students of many tastes and stripes, from English majors to general education students. To reinforce this gastronomical approach to modernism, I often end our discussion of Woolf's and Bowen's gustatory novels with a writing assignment that asks students to analyze competing representations of eating: students may pair Mrs. Ramsay's dinner or Mr. Ramsay's comparatively spartan bag lunch with Cam, James, and the Macalisters on the boat to the lighthouse with Bowen's French restaurant scene, Karen's lunch with a roughish Irish woman on the ship bound from Cork to England, or Karen's lunch with Max and his fiancée, Naomi Fisher, at the Adelphi Hotel in London. In so doing, students consider how the social and cultural values we discuss shape the formal aesthetic practices they see at work in such passages by employing one of the archival or critical texts we read earlier (Peel; Adams; Fisher) as a historical lens or conceptual framework for their argument.

Finally, to underscore the literary afterlives of gastronomical modernism in today's vital and continually evolving forms of food writing, I close this unit with examples of the foodoir (the food memoir), food journalism, and the recipistolary (a narrative interposed with recipes) from the later twentieth and early twenty-first centuries like Fisher's *The Gastronomical Me* (31–39, 171–79), Bee Wilson's *First Bite* (37–64), and Linda Furiya's *Bento Box in the Heartland* (1–17). Students explore their own gastronomical selves as foodoirists, food bloggers, or, for the kitchen-savvy among them, recipistolists. This creative exercise includes an analytic component in which students identify their literary precedents and make structural and stylistic connections to modernism's innovations in gastronomical letters.

When we ask students to read major works of women's modernist experimental narrative alongside everyday texts from the interwar period like recipes and household primers, we not only hone their close reading skills but also empower them to reimagine the modernist archive by recognizing how formal experimentation in popular and quotidian genres of writing is integral to modernism's aesthetic invention. Moreover, by approaching modernism through food, we bring the material culture of the early twentieth century to life for twenty-first-century students while providing them with a more nuanced means of understanding the shifting structures of relationality—at once social, ethical, corporeal, and sensual—that make up modernism's movable feast.

Works Cited

Adams, Carol J. *The Sexual Politics of Meat: A Feminist-Vegetarian Critical Theory.* Rev. ed., Continuum Books, 2000.

Bennett, Andrew, and Nicholas Royle. *Elizabeth Bowen and the Dissolution of the Novel: Still Lives.* St. Martin's Press, 1995.

Bowen, Elizabeth. *The House in Paris.* 1935. Anchor Books, 2002.

Brillat-Savarin, Jean Anthelme. *The Physiology of Taste; or, Meditations on Transcendental Gastronomy.* 1825. Translated by M. F. K. Fisher, Everyman's Library, 2009.

Coghlan, J. Michelle, editor. *Resilience: A Journal of the Environmental Humanities.* Vol. 2, no. 1, Winter 2014.

Derrida, Jacques. "'Eating Well'; or, The Calculation of the Subject." Translated by Peter Connor and Avital Ronell. *Who Comes after the Subject?*, edited by Eduardo Cadava et al., Routledge, 1991, pp. 96–119.

Fisher, M. F. K. "The Anatomy of a Recipe." *With Bold Knife and Fork.* 1969. Counterpoint Press, 2002, pp. 1–14.

———. *The Gastronomical Me.* 1943. North Point Press, 1954.

———. *How to Cook a Wolf.* 1942. North Point Press, 1954.

Foer, Jonathan Safran. *Eating Animals.* Little, Brown, 2009.

Furiya, Linda. *Bento Box in the Heartland: My Japanese Girlhood in Whitebread America.* Seal Press, 2006.

Gilbert, Sandra M. *The Culinary Imagination: From Myth to Modernity.* W. W. Norton, 2014.

Heath, Ambrose. *Good Food.* Faber and Faber, 1932.

Humble, Nicola. *Culinary Pleasures: Cookbooks and the Transformation of British Food.* Faber and Faber, 2005.

Joyce, James. *Ulysses.* 1922. Vintage Books, 1986.

Lowinsky, Ruth. *Lovely Food: A Cookery Notebook.* Nonesuch Press, 1931.

Martell, Jessica, et al., editors. *Modernism and Food Studies: Politics, Aesthetics, and the Avant-Garde.* UP of Florida, 2019.

Morton, Timothy. *Poetics of Spice: Romantic Consumerism and the Exotic.* Cambridge UP, 2006.

Neil, Marion Harris. *The Thrift Cook Book.* David McKay, 1919.

Osborne, Susan. "Reconsidering Elizabeth Bowen." *Modern Fiction Studies,* vol. 52, no. 1, 2006, pp. 187–97.

Peel, C. S. (Constance Dorothy Peel). *How We Lived Then, 1914–1918.* John Lane / The Bodley Head, 1929.

Pollan, Michael. *The Omnivore's Dilemma: A Natural History of Four Meals.* Penguin Books, 2006.

Saint-Amour, Paul K. *Tense Future: Modernism, Total War, Encyclopedic Form.* Oxford UP, 2015.

Solomon, Andrew. "Andrew Solomon: By the Book." *The New York Times*, 26 Sept. 2013, www.nytimes.com/2013/09/29/books/review/andrew-solomon-by-the-book.html.

Swift, Jonathan. "A Modest Proposal." 1729. Gulliver's Travels *and Other Writings*, edited by Louis A. Landa, Houghton Mifflin, 1960, pp. 439–46.

Tigner, Amy L., and Allison Carruth. *Literature and Food Studies.* Routledge, 2018.

Tompkins, Kyla. "Consider the Recipe." *Journal of Nineteenth-Century Americanists*, vol. 1, no. 2, 2013, pp. 439–45.

———. *Racial Indigestion: Eating Bodies in the Nineteenth Century.* New York UP, 2012.

Wallace, David Foster. "Consider the Lobster." *"Consider the Lobster" and Other Essays*, by Wallace, Back Bay Books, 2006, pp. 235–54.

Wilson, Bee. *First Bite: How We Learn to Eat.* Basic Books, 2015.

Woolf, Virginia. "Character in Fiction." *The Essays of Virginia Woolf*, vol. 3 (1919–24), edited by Andrew McNeillie, Hogarth Press, 1988, pp. 420–38.

———. *To the Lighthouse.* 1927. Annotated and introduced by Mark Hussey, Harcourt, 2005.

Part VI

Radical Women

Ann Mattis

Introducing New Womanhood and Intersectionality through the Threshold Concept Approach

Throughout my teaching career, I have investigated the modern woman worker in special topics courses on gender and literature as well as in units in American literature survey courses. As an instructor whose specialization straddles literary studies and women's studies, I find that many lessons, including the one on the New Woman described here, are applicable in different pedagogical contexts. In each setting, I invite students to generate materialist-feminist analyses of texts that consider how socioeconomic and cultural forces shape representations of, and mythologies surrounding, the so-called New Woman. My goal is for students to consider how New Womanhood was shaped by the historically specific variables of class, race, gender, and sexuality, as well as by hegemonic ideologies that naturalize the profits extracted from all wage workers, but disproportionately so from women and people of color. In order to get at this discursive complexity, I present students with a diversity of literature, film, and archival materials that illuminate how representations are inevitably sites of ideological negotiation.[1] As a class, we explore how texts relate to real efforts of modern women seeking to productively transform the terms of their labor and social relations with others. Students are prompted to engage with the gaps between representations and the lived experiences of women working in a variety of industries, including domestic service, factory work, shop work, and clerical work. As each of these had different meanings and social implications for working women in the United States, the focus on different industries helps students situate work and modern womanhood within a variable matrix of class, gender, and race.

Initially, many students observe that early-twentieth-century depictions of working women in the United States reveal how far women have come. However, this simplistic narrative of social progress is at odds with the decidedly challenging endeavor of unpacking modern femininity as a multivalent social construct or a technology of gender that intersects with other technologies of race, class, and sexuality. As an instructor, I have been overwhelmed by the task of making this critical apparatus more accessible to students. In this essay, I explain how I have learned to effectively scaffold complex analyses of New Womanhood through early lessons that use visual texts and a threshold concept approach that clarifies the process of deciphering historically specific images for novice undergraduates.

A deep analysis of New Womanhood requires students to comprehend a number of "threshold concepts," or what Jan H. F. Meyer and Ray Land describe as "a concept [that] can be considered as akin to a portal, opening up a new and previously inaccessible way of thinking about something" (3). For Meyer and Land, the threshold concept "represents a transformed way of understanding, or interpreting, or viewing something without which the learner cannot progress" (3). By using threshold concepts to guide a lesson, instructors cultivate practical, skill-based knowledge that allows students to interpret material in a specialized manner. The threshold concept model is particularly useful when introducing students to a feminist-critical paradigm.[2] Christie Launius and Holly Hassel clarify key feminist threshold concepts for introductory-level women's and gender studies courses; these concepts include "the social construction of gender," "systems of privilege and oppression," and "intersectionality" (4). In a modernist studies course that focuses on analyzing and historicizing texts, these concepts provide students with a critical context for grounding cultural representations in relation to power structures and the dominant culture. Whether they are introduced within a classroom focused on gender or not, these concepts position students to interpret modern cultural texts in relation to early-twentieth-century norms, ideologies, practices, and institutions.

Though I use Launius and Hassel in an Introduction to Gender, Sexuality, and Women's Studies course, their underlying pedagogical emphasis on feminist threshold concepts has helped me in a variety of contexts. In order to provide literature students with an explicit conceptual foundation for analyzing representations of working women, I devote one lesson to the concept of intersectionality. The concept of intersectionality is indispensable to contemporary feminist analysis because it underscores the overlapping nature of race, sexuality, gender, and other identity markers. An intersectional feminist approach accounts for multiple axes of oppression and privilege that are essential to an understanding of the ideological underpinnings of cultural representations.[3] By isolating intersectionality as an interpretive portal to New Womanhood, I am able to help students adopt a critical apparatus that is decidedly unfamiliar to many of them. By discerning learning roadblocks and isolating threshold concepts, I introduce New Womanhood in ways that make the multifaceted critical moves of feminist-modernist studies more accessible to students.

Critical Trends in New Woman Studies

Women's entry into the public workforce is a social phenomenon that figures prominently in modernist texts, and this theme is a useful frame for either a course or unit that serves to illuminate the ideological and cultural complexity of gender, modernity, and modernism more broadly. When introducing early-twentieth-century literature, I invite students to regard literary texts written by men and women modernists as complicated responses to modern social relations, especially those pertaining to gender, class, and race. This emphasis on the complex and ambivalent implications of social phenomena underlies how I frame literary depictions of the New Woman. I rely on Marianne DeKoven's insight that modernism reflects an "irresolvable ambivalence toward empowered femininity" (174). By extension, my pedagogical approach invites students to complexify their notion of modernity itself. Modernity, as Rita Felski defines it, "embraces a multidimensional array of historical phenomena that cannot be prematurely synthesized into a unified Zeitgeist" (15). Felski argues that, given the multidimensionality of modernity, we must also reconsider how we interpret gender in modernist texts; accounts of gender, like modernity, are diversified and multivocal responses to various social phenomena (21).

This critical emphasis on ambivalence and multivocality has extended to studies of the New Woman. Feminist-modernist studies has shown that

New Womanhood encompasses more than white, middle-class, or elite women's transgressions of Victorian ideals through their entry into the labor market or their seizing of other traditionally male prerogatives. Intersectionality allows students of modernism to explore how modern ideologies of gender, race, class, etc. converge in New Womanhood; representations are thereby situated within a complex cultural and historical moment. It is in fact impossible to disentangle gender from other identity categories when we analyze the New Woman, a figure that often confounded many different ideologies of class and race. For instance, Ann Ardis argues that in addition to subverting the doctrine of the separate spheres, the New Woman "challenges the cultural ideology that naturalizes the bourgeois patriarchy by appropriating 'Woman' as the symbol of its rightful dominance" (26). New Women writers transformed signifiers of womanhood by creating literary representations of women who were repudiating traditional domesticity and learning to navigate a modern public sphere. More than a mere reflection of a monumental and progressive shift in women's labor history, the New Woman, in Rosemary Hennessy's words, signals a "crisis of subjectivity" that is "overdetermined by the general composition of capital in the west between 1880–1920" and "an index of disruption and containment of the hegemonic bourgeois ideology of the feminine" (105). Though she catalyzed conservative backlash on account of her disruption of the separate spheres, the New Woman, as many critics have shown, was hegemonic in her own right. As a site of various contradictions, including wage exploitation, ethnic pride, racial and gender progressivism, and eugenic and patriarchal anxieties, New Womanhood encompassed different meanings for many different social groups.

In unpacking the New Woman in cultural texts, contemporary feminist scholars continue to resist a singular narrative of modern women's progress and empowerment by highlighting intersectionality and ideological complexity. Feminist studies has shed light on the social diversity inherent in New Womanhood and the idea of "the Modern Girl," and has thereby accounted for regional, ethnic, and sociopolitical nuances that shaped new modes of agency and identity emerging at the turn of the century.[4] Martha Patterson historicizes the political and sociopolitical processes that generated this prolific feminist trope in an American context, arguing that the New Woman trope was ambivalently deployed by an array of ethnic and social groups with specific political interests. Given this diversity, Patterson calls for scholarship to widen its focus to reveal how marginalized writers redeploy the New Woman icon, which signals "at once a protest for, anodyne for, and an appeasement to the ideological imperatives of the dominant icon" (3).

Determining Learning Roadblocks and Dispelling Cultural Myths

In my initial lesson on the New Woman, I use prints and advertisements from the late nineteenth and early twentieth centuries to show shifts in the mediation of womanhood in modern culture. Through trial and error, I have learned that merely exposing students to a diverse visual archive of the New Woman trope does not result in an ability to unpack the historical and cultural complexity of those images. Despite my efforts to introduce New Womanhood through a series of advertisements and paintings that highlight women's diversity with respect to class, race, and geography, students tend to have many misconceptions about modern femininity that are at odds with critical trends in the field. Students often remark that the visuals confirm how "all women" became more liberated with the advent of modernity. They interpret representations of modern working women as mimetic reflections of an era far removed from their own. Students struggle with the capacious and complex vehicle of modern femininity and rely on the familiar, dominant paradigm of cultural progress. In other words, students tend to view New Womanhood as part of a monolithic narrative that equates women's entry into the workforce with emancipation and agency.

This learning roadblock exists because unpacking the historical signification of New Womanhood is a disciplinary-specific procedure that falls into the category of "troublesome knowledge," or knowledge that appears "counter-intuitive" or even "alien" to the novice student (Meyer and Land 5). Indeed, the task of interpreting the New Woman requires students to possess an understanding of gender as a social construct as well as an ability to interpret cultural texts through the lens of intersectionality. Challenging students' default narrative of New Womanhood involves a series of pedagogical steps that scaffold the important threshold concept of intersectionality. Before I define intersectionality, students examine commonplace assumptions about women's agency and modernity. I begin the unit with slides entitled "You've Come a Long Way, Baby." On these slides, I include statements such as "All women were oppressed housewives until they entered the public workforce." This exercise prompts students to begin a metacognitive journey that calls for a reexamination of commonplace understandings of gender, work, and progress. Once we have challenged this overarching myth of the woman worker, I present students with a cultural geography of women's labor as it shifted in the early decades of the twentieth century. In a Women in Literature course on the theme of the woman worker, students read Joan W. Scott's essay "The Woman Worker," as well as selections from Alice Kessler-Harris's *Out to Work: A History of Wage-Earning Women in the United States.* In a survey of American literature, I condense this information in a PowerPoint. Scott's essay is useful because it explains how the woman worker was always a discursive figure, as opposed to one that reflected material or historical reality. Scott explains how modern debates over the "dilemma" of women workers between work and home obscures the diversity of working women, as such debates assume that all women workers were middle-class and disposed to marriage and motherhood. This assumption informed and buttressed the feminization of cheap labor that restricted working women's earning potential and employment opportunities (401). This historical lens provides students with a frame for interpreting a varied archive of highbrow and lowbrow literary and visual texts that represent women workers. By obviating the gaps between the historical map of modern women's labor and its cultural depictions, this initial process prepares students for interpreting New Womanhood as a cultural phenomenon as opposed to a mimetic truth. This initial lesson sets up a framework for an interdisciplinary feminist analysis that is scaffolded by threshold concepts used to interpret gender as a social construct, in the light of women's intersectional identities.

Highlighting Intersectionality

Once I have demonstrated how representations of working women are discursively and socially constructed, I introduce the threshold concept of intersectionality. Using Launius and Hassel as a touchstone, I emphasize how an intersectional feminist lens accounts for multiple axes of identity oppression and privilege in an analysis of the woman worker. Visuals are a useful way to immerse students in this concept because they lay bare the striking array of positionalities that women have occupied at different moments in history. They also reveal how class and race are relational identity markers that inevitably underpin representations of the New Woman. Through a variety of images, I underscore how different groups benefit from, or are disadvantaged by, institutional structures and ideologies of domesticity and work.

Before delving into modern images of working women from the early twentieth century, students examine the prehistory of the Modern Girl. First, I show students images from fashion plates from the late 1880s depicting leisure-class white women in elaborate dresses, petticoats, and corsets who entertain guests in their parlors. Students are very adept at noting how the clothes not only constrict women's mobility but also highlight a woman's status and decorative function. I also share slides that showcase the cult of true womanhood, highlighting the ways middle-class white women were idealized as icons of Christian virtue and domesticity in the dominant culture. I include an illustration entitled "The Sphere of Woman" from the popular nineteenth-century magazine *Godey's Lady's Book*, which presents the common image of a mother nestled with her children in a cozy parlor ("Sphere"). I also provide images of working-class women in the Victorian era—images of servant women in liveries who lace up wealthy women's corsets. For instance, I share the image "Boudoirscene (Maid Laced a Lady the Corset)" and the famous image of Hattie McDaniel (portraying Mammy) tightening the corset of Vivien Leigh (as Scarlett O'Hara) from the film *Gone with The Wind* ("Mammy"). I ask students to identify or describe the versions of femininity that are embodied by these images. I often ask, "Is one of the subjects portrayed in this image more of a woman than the other?" and "What does the fact that these images are so distinct tell us about ideals of womanhood or gender in general?" In analyzing these images and answering such questions, students get a glimpse of how womanhood is inherently inflected by the social relations of race, class, status, and labor. These images also provide students with a foundation for understanding how systems of privilege and oppression are interlocking and relational.

After we discuss these images, I show students an excerpt from Sojourner Truth's famous "Ain't I a Woman" speech from 1851:

> That man over there says that women need to be helped into carriages, and lifted over ditches, and to have the best place everywhere. Nobody ever helps me into carriages, or over mud-puddles, or gives me any best place! And ain't I a woman? Look at me! Look at my arm! I have ploughed and planted, and gathered into barns, and no man could head me! And ain't I a woman? I could work as much and eat as much as a man—when I could get it—and bear the lash as well! And ain't I a woman? I have borne thirteen children, and seen most all sold off to slavery, and when I cried out with my mother's grief, none but Jesus heard me! And ain't I a woman? ("Modern History Sourcebook")

This excerpt provides a dramatic counterpoint to the images of Victorian womanhood that precede it. In Truth's powerful resignification of womanhood, students see how the privilege that stems from class and race informs default notions of womanhood. At the same time, Truth's speech allows us to articulate the feminist concept of intersectionality in terms that effectively frame an exploration of other visual texts—those that introduce the notion that women's relation to labor has always been contingent on their positionality.

Once I have illustrated the threshold concept of intersectionality, I show a variety of sketches by Charles Dana Gibson; I include images of upper-class Gibson Girls from his late-nineteenth-century series, as well as those of working-class women from his Social Ladder series ("Gibson Girls' America"). Finally, I immerse students in the highly saturated and diverse visual archive of Modern Girls in the 1920s: flappers, the New Woman in cars, John Held covers from *Life* magazine, factory workers in high heels, and images from *The Modern Girl around the World*, which features a global archive of modern femininities that highlight the similarities and differences of this iconography across cultures in this era (see Weinbaum et al.). We compare, for instance, depictions of American flappers to women in modern Japanese advertisements, who were called the *modan garu* ("modern girls"), and photographs of the actress Jahanara Kajjan, who embodied Modern Girlhood in India. In analyzing these images, students see how modern conceptions of femininity were the result of complex global economic transformations that took place under capitalism. In order to challenge students' assumption that Western (i.e., American) images of femininity shaped those of non-Western cultures, I show students an image of Josephine Baker, whose haircut became popular among white Parisian women (Image), as well as an advertisement for an Egyptian face powder advertised in *The Crisis* ("Alluring Perfection"). These images often prompt students to discuss how nonwhite femininities are commodified within contemporary American beauty culture through celebrities such as Jennifer Lopez and Beyoncé.

After adapting my introductory lesson on New Womanhood in order to foreground the threshold concept of intersectionality through visuals, I found that many students analyzed literary representations in more sophisticated ways. Visuals allowed me to explicitly foreground the learning portals through which I expected students to engage with the concept of New Womanhood in literary texts. For instance, students were able to see how the flapper cartoons by John Held in *Life* resonated with F. Scott Fitzgerald's portrait of Judy Jones in "Winter Dreams," but not with the working women in the popular New Woman stories in Maureen Honey's *Breaking the Ties That Bind* ("John Held Jr."). Visual signifiers of class, leisure, and labor became more evident to students, which resulted in their ability to zero in on those nuances in stories that materialized the subjectivities of different classes of women workers. Visual representations illuminate the symbolic charges of specific worker figures such as the typist or the secretary, who are prominently represented in modern(ist) texts. Though these industries may have signaled progress in mainstream images, New Woman stories that focalize particular industries ask us to consider the material, emotional, and social conditions under which women labored. For example, Dorothy Parker's "Mr. Durant," a story about a young woman who becomes pregnant by her married boss, reveals the psychosexual power dynamics and exploitation that undergirded secretaries' experiences. While this narrative exposes the sexism of workplace culture, other popular depictions of typists tended to represent female office workers as sexually dangerous or else as homewreckers.[5]

An exploration of how particularities of race and class inflect modern womanhood becomes more accessible when students are exposed to a variety of images that provide discomfiting narratives. For instance, by reviewing images of Martha Murray Washington alongside the Gibson Girl, students are able to see how women's gender identities are inextricably bound to their class and racial positionalities. I share with students many Hollywood images of Black female servants, including Louise Beavers in John M. Stahl's 1934 film *Imitation of Life*. These visuals bring into stark relief how a modernist text such as Zora Neale Hurston's "Sweat" resignifies the sexuality of Black women, including Black female domestics, in relation to hegemonic ideologies that either desexualized them or denounced them as jezebels. The intersectional connotations of race, class, and labor are further illuminated as we discuss Fannie Hurst's and Hurston's complicated friendship, which was muddled by the power dynamics of white patronage and employer-worker relations. Hurston's depiction of Black women engaging in domestic work is very different from Hurst's stereotypical depiction of Delilah, the Mammy figure who is the literary basis for Beaver's character in Stahl's *Imitation of Life*. Dorothy West's depiction of a Black typist in "The Typewriter" provides further contrast to the hegemonic visual culture that sutured Black womanhood to domestic service. By viewing reified images of Black female domestics and prostitutes within the dominant white culture, students are also able to get a clear sense of how Harlem Renaissance authors such as West, Hurston, Jessie Fauset, and Nella Larsen were burdened by the racism and sexism that conflated Black women with certain industries and roles. My decision to define and model the threshold concept of intersectionality through such visuals allows me to lay bare the building blocks of intersectional feminist knowledge, and provides students with a multifaceted critical understanding of New Womanhood, an essential component of new modernist studies.

Notes

1. Some of these materials have included Charlotte Perkins Gilman's "Women and Economics"; Gertrude Stein's *Three Lives*; Zora Neale Hurston's "Sweat"; Dorothy West's "The Typewriter"; Winnifred Eaton's *Me: A Book of Remembrance*; Karyn L. Hollis's *Liberating Voices*; Dorothy Parker's "Mr. Durant" and "Big Blonde"; Maureen Honey's edited collection *Breaking the Ties That Bind*; Anita Loos's *Gentlemen Prefer Blondes*; Fannie Hurst's *Imitation of Life*; Sophie Treadwell's *Machinal*; Ann Petry's *The Street*; Gwendolyn Brooks's *Street in Bronzeville*; James M. Cain's *Mildred Pierce*; and Connie Field's feminist documentary *The Life and Times of Rosie the Riveter*.

2. Christie Launius and Holly Hassel argue that "foregrounding the 'learning roadblocks' that many students encounter as part of the learning process helps circumvent and move quickly past those misconceptions that keep students from progressing in their understanding of Women's and Gender Studies" (viii). The threshold concept model makes feminist analysis more accessible to undergraduate students because it prompts their metacognition of interdisciplinary praxis in the field of gender studies. By isolating threshold concepts, I am able to lay the building blocks of materialist-feminist analysis.

3. See Goodspeed-Chadwick in this volume for another approach to teaching modernist women writers and new modernist studies that focuses on intersectionality, a term coined by Kimberlé Crenshaw.

4. In using the term *Modern Girl*, I refer to the American New Woman's global counterpart, which the Modern Girl around the World Research Group explores in its eponymous study of a geographically diverse archive of modern femininity (Weinbaum et al.).

5. For more on depictions of typists in literature, see Rainey.

Works Cited

"Alluring Perfection." *The Crisis*, 1928. *U of Washington*, www.washington.edu/news/2009/04/23/uw-professors-follow-the-modern-girl-around-the-world-in-new-book/.

Ardis, Ann. *New Women, New Novels: Feminism and Early Modernism*. Rutgers UP, 1990.

"Boudoirscene (Maid Laced a Lady the Corset). About 1880. Stereo Photograph." *Getty Images*, www.gettyimages.com/detail/news-photo/boudoirscene-about-1880-stereo-photograph-boudoirszene-um-news-photo/166523412.

Brooks, Gwendolyn. *A Street in Bronzeville.* Harper and Brothers, 1945.

Cain, James M. *Mildred Pierce.* Alfred A. Knopf, 1941.

Crenshaw, Kimberlé. *On Intersectionality: Essential Writings.* New Press, 2019.

DeKoven, Marianne. "Modernism and Gender." *The Cambridge Companion to Modernism*, edited by Michael Levenson, Cambridge UP, 1999, pp. 174–93.

Eaton, Winnifred. *Me: A Book of Remembrance.* 1915. UP of Mississippi, 1997.

Felski, Rita. *The Gender of Modernity.* Harvard UP, 1995.

Field, Connie, director. *The Life and Times of Rosie the Riveter.* Clarity Films, 1980.

Fitzgerald, F. Scott. "Winter Dreams." *The Best Early Stories of F. Scott Fitzgerald*, edited by Bryant Mangum, Modern Library, 2005, pp. 230–52.

"The Gibson Girls' America: Drawings by Charles Dana Gibson." *Library of Congress*, www.loc.gov/exhibits/gibson-girls-america/the-gibson-girl-as-the-new-woman.html.

Gilman, Charlotte Perkins. "Women and Economics: A Study of the Economic Relation between Men and Women as a Factor in Social Evolution." 1898. *"The Yellow Wallpaper" and Other Writings*, introduced by Lynne Sharon Schwartz, Bantam Books, 1989, pp. 124–83.

Hennessy, Rosemary. *Materialist Feminism and the Politics of Discourse.* Routledge, 1993.

Hollis, Karyn L. *Liberating Voices: Writing at the Bryn Mawr Summer School for Women Workers.* Southern Illinois UP, 2004.

Honey, Maureen, editor. *Breaking the Ties That Bind: Popular Stories of the New Woman, 1915–1930.* U of Oklahoma P, 1992.

Hurst, Fannie. *Imitation of Life.* 1933. Duke UP, 2004.

Hurston, Zora Neale. "Sweat." *The Norton Anthology of African American Literature*, 3rd ed., vol. 1, edited by Henry Louis Gates, Jr., and Nellie Y. McKay, W. W. Norton, 1997, pp. 999–1007.

Image of Josephine Baker. *National Women's History Museum*, www.womenshistory.org/sites/default/files/styles/main_image/public/images/2018-07/Josephine_Baker_LOC_07816v%20square.jpg?itok=TCqzMspi.

"John Held Jr." Collection by Bob Wale. *Pinterest*, www.pinterest.com/bobwale/john-held-jr/. Accessed 9 Sept. 2020.

Kessler-Harris, Alice. *Out to Work: A History of Wage-Earning Women in the United States.* Oxford UP, 1982.

Launius, Christie, and Holly Hassel. *Threshold Concepts in Women's and Gender Studies: Ways of Seeing, Thinking, and Knowing.* Routledge, 2015.

Loos. Anita. *Gentlemen Prefer Blondes.* 1925. Penguin Books, 1992.

"Mammy, played by Hattie McDaniel, tightens Scarlett O'Hara's (Vivien Leigh) corset strings in *Gone with the Wind.*" *History Daily*, historydaily.org/those-dreaded-corsets. Accessed 13 July 2020.

Meyer, Jan H. F., and Ray Land. "Threshold Concepts and Troublesome Knowledge: An Introduction." *Overcoming Barriers to Student*

Understanding: Threshold Concepts and Troublesome Knowledge, edited by Meyer and Land, Routledge, 2006, pp. 3–18.

"Modern History Sourcebook: Sojourner Truth: 'Ain't I a Woman?', December 1851." *Internet History Sourcebooks Project*, sourcebooks.fordham.edu/mod/sojtruth-woman.asp. Accessed 25 Sept. 2017.

Parker, Dorothy. "Big Blonde." 1924. *Project Gutenberg*, gutenberg.ca/ebooks/parkerd-bigblonde/parkerd-bigblonde-00-h.html.

———. "Mr. Durant." 1929. *The Collected Stories of Dorothy Parker*, The Modern Library, 1942, pp. 101–20. *Internet Archive*, archive.org/stream/in.ernet.dli.2015.184951/2015.184951.The-Collected-Stories-Of-Dorothy-Parker_djvu.txt.

Patterson, Martha. *Beyond the Gibson Girl: Reimagining the American New Woman, 1895–1915*. Illinois UP, 2005.

Petry, Ann. *The Street*. 1946. Houghton Mifflin, 1991.

Rainey, Lawrence S. "Eliot among the Typists: Writing *The Waste Land*." *Modernism/Modernity*, vol. 12, no. 1, 2005, pp. 27–84.

Scott, Joan W. "The Woman Worker." *Emerging Feminism from Revolution to World War*, edited by Geneviève Fraisse and Michelle Perrot, Harvard UP, 1993, pp. 399–426. Vol. 4 of *A History of Women in the West*, general editors, Georges Duby and Perrot.

"The Sphere of Woman." *Godey's Lady's Book*, vol. 40, Mar. 1850, p. 209. Uncle Tom's Cabin *and American Culture: A Multi-media Archive*, U of Virginia, utc.iath.virginia.edu/sentimnt/gallgodyf.html.

Stein, Gertrude. *Three Lives*. 1909. New Directions Publishing, 1933.

Treadwell, Sophie. *Machinal*. 1928. Nick Hern Books, 1993.

Weinbaum, Alys Eve, et al., editors. *The Modern Girl around the World: Consumption, Modernity, and Globalization*. Duke UP, 2008.

West, Dorothy. "The Typewriter." *The Wiley Blackwell Anthology of African American Literature*, edited by Gene Andrew Jarrett, vol. 2 (1920 to the Present), John Wiley and Sons, 2014, pp. 245–50.

Carey Snyder

Teaching *Votes for Women* and Suffrage Propaganda in the Modernist Classroom

On 13 October 1905, the suffragettes Christabel Pankhurst and Annie Kenney were imprisoned for heckling politicians and spitting in a police officer's face, thus initiating the militant phase of the women's suffrage movement. Making headlines and provoking debate about women's rights and roles, suffrage militancy was a crucial part of Anglo-American modernity. Yet even as it powerfully articulates modernist themes of social and political rupture, suffrage literature remains at the margins of modernist studies—only intermittently addressed in scholarship and generally excluded from the classroom.[1]

To redress this omission, I have incorporated Elizabeth Robins's popular play *Votes for Women* into my courses on modernism, using visual propaganda as an inroad into the topic. *Votes for Women* centers on the radicalization of Vida Levering, an attractive, mysterious woman with a past who hobnobs with aristocrats and statesmen. Ten years prior to the action of the play, we learn, Vida was pressured by her ex-lover, the aspiring politician Geoffrey Stonor, into having an abortion in order to avoid embroiling him in scandal and depriving him of his inheritance. Anguished at having succumbed to his pressure, Vida goes abroad. The play rejects the clichéd fallen-woman narrative that would fashion Vida as a figure of tragedy, instead presenting her as an empowered character whose painful past motivates her fight for the vote, which she comes to see as the first step in remedying the "helplessness of women" (472). In act 1, Vida reencounters Stonor, now running for Parliament and engaged to the young Jean Dunbarton, the niece of Vida's close friend Lady John Wynnstay. In act 2, Robins ambitiously recreates a Trafalgar Square suffrage rally where, before a heckling crowd, Vida delivers her first political speech. The ingenue Jean is at once inspired by Vida's courage and distressed to intuit that her fiancé must be the man in Vida's past. In the final act, Vida threatens to recruit Jean into the movement unless Stonor pledges to campaign for women's suffrage, rationalizing that "the man who served one woman—God knows how many more—very ill, shall serve hundreds of thousands well" (472).

With its focus not only on the fight for suffrage but also on a broader feminist struggle for independence, self-expression, sexual freedom, and self-worth, Robins's play resonates with many other modernist works. For example, Vida tells Stonor, "There's a value in women apart from the value men see in them" (486), a point Virginia Woolf echoes in *A Room of One's Own*: "women, like men, have other interests besides the perennial interests of domesticity" (82). The challenge faced by writers like Robins and Woolf mirrored that faced by women more generally—to find a bigger stage and more varied parts for women to play, both in life and in fiction. When teaching *Votes for Women*, I stress that the suffragettes' revolt is part of a much larger upheaval of traditional gender roles and sexual norms that reverberates in numerous modernist works, including, for example, Woolf's *To the Lighthouse*, Dorothy Richardson's *Pilgrimage*, E. M. Forster's *Howard's End*, and George Bernard Shaw's *Mrs. Warren's Profession*.

Biographical and Historical Background

I begin this unit with background on Robins and her involvement in the British suffrage movement. Born in Kentucky in 1862, Robins moved to London in 1888 to pursue a career as a stage actress. Frustrated with the dearth of interesting dramatic roles for women, she joined forces with the actress Marion Lea in 1891 to produce and star in Henrik Ibsen's *Hedda Gabler* and went on to play leading roles in five other Ibsen dramas. Thus, Robins's early theatrical work not only helped bring the Norwegian playwright's work to prominence in England but also enabled modern drama to engage with social issues in new ways. From Nora's slamming of the door in *A Doll's House* to Hedda's ferocious yet ultimately futile revolt, Ibsen's heroines struggle against patriarchal oppression, and because Robins's reputation was closely tied to these rebellious characters, she became prominent as a New Woman. A ubiquitous figure in both fact and fiction at the turn of the century, the New Woman rejected traditional gender roles in pursuit of higher education, professional opportunities, and political rights. In 1902 Robins gave up the stage to devote herself to writing novels and plays and, from 1906 to 1912, to advocating for the suffrage cause, first joining the National Union of Women's Suffrage Societies, founded in 1897 to pursue the vote through petitions and other pacifist means. Becoming skeptical of methods that had been tried for four decades without success, Robins joined Emmeline Pankhurst and her daughter Christabel's militant organization, the Women's Social and Political Union (WSPU), founded in 1903 with the provocative slogan "Deeds not words." The *Daily Mail* dubbed the militants "suffragettes" to distinguish them from their constitutional counterparts, the suffragists, and the Pankhursts and their followers embraced the term.[2]

While attending eight suffrage meetings between July and October 1906, Robins took copious notes that lent her depiction of the Trafalgar Square demonstration the accuracy of documentary reportage. She captured the early years of suffrage militancy, before 1909, when suffragettes began to go on hunger strikes and were met with the government's brutal response of force-feeding—which turned militants into martyrs.[3] Although Robins defended militancy in the early years of the movement, she refrained from directly participating in it. Instead, she saw her role as that of a propagandist and campaigner: she became president of the Women Writers' Suffrage League in 1909 and wrote a series of articles for the WSPU publication, *Votes for Women*. She showed respect for both constitutional and militant approaches by dividing her proceeds from the play *Votes for Women* between the National Union of Women's Suffrage Societies and the WSPU, but became disenchanted with the more extreme militancy of the last phase of the movement (1912–14), which included breaking windows, slashing paintings in galleries, and committing arson.

Suffrage Propaganda

After establishing this historical and biographical background, I segue into a discussion of suffrage propaganda by pointing out that *Votes for Women* was at once a successful play—premiering at Harley Granville-Barker's fashionable Court Theatre in April 1907 and performing to sold-out audiences until the season closed in June—and a work of propaganda, as its subtitle, "A Dramatic Tract," underscores. Its theme, and its goal, is conversion. This success prompted Robins to expand the play into a novel, fittingly titled *The Convert*, and inspired a flourishing new genre of suffrage drama.[4] Pro-suffrage artists and playwrights like Robins sought not only to persuade audiences to fight for the franchise but also to redefine the roles and rights available to women. To do so, they had to counter negative stereotypes pervading anti-suffrage propaganda that represented activists as hysterical women, bitter spinsters, viragoes, and negligent wives and mothers. Taking advantage of new advertising methods made possible by an exploding print culture, pro-suffrage artists advanced the cause by designing visual art for posters, postcards, banners, and other print media. In her influential study on suffrage and spectacle, Lisa Tickner argues that the imagery of the suffrage campaign was "not an afterthought or illustration but an integral part of the fabric of social conflict with . . . its own power to shape thought, focus debates and stimulate action" (ix). In our own image-saturated society, students are savvy when it comes to analyzing visual propaganda and having them do so is an effective way to highlight the clashing ideologies concerning how women should be or act that are on display in the suffrage debate.

For the purposes of this unit, I focus on four images.[5] The first, *A Suffragette's Home* (1912), designed by John Hassall for the National League for Opposing Woman Suffrage, depicts a manual laborer returning, as the captions reads, "After a Hard Day's Work!" to find that his wife has abrogated her duties as wife and mother: one child lies prone, cradling its doll in a pathetic invocation of the absent mother's role as nurturer; the other, kneeling on a stool with holey socks on view, sobs into a pile of neglected laundry. The negligent mother has pinned a hurried "Back in an hour or so" note to a *Votes for Women!* poster—making the problem here clear—and the husband looks tired, exasperated, and vaguely menacing (students note his clenched fist and stern expression). When asked what negative stereotypes of suffragettes the poster conveys, students remark that suffragettes are presented as bad wives and mothers who engage in politics while their husbands do what is deemed the real work of providing for them and their families. A suffragette's home is represented as a sad, anarchical place because the suffragette meddles in politics, abandoning her supposedly natural role as homemaker. Our analysis of this image paves the way for a discussion of how Robins's play negotiates the stereotypical opposition between political activism and motherhood.

The next two images illustrate the stereotype of the angry spinster. The first, *Down with Man!*, is an anonymous postcard with a relatively straightforward message. This satirical image clearly conveys the stereotype of the angry, plain, man-hating suffragette through its caricature of a crowd of spinsters at a suffrage rally. As a class, we tease out the significance of the paired posters on display in this image, which endorse contradictory messages: "Down with Man!" and "Husbands for Old Maids!" Through our discussion, students come to recognize that the cartoon implies that what really motivates the struggle for enfranchisement is not only women's hatred for men (what the women say) but also their sexual frustration (what they secretly desire). If these women were to marry, they would lose their desire for the vote—or so the cartoon seems to tell us. Robins's character Lord John articulates this idea in a somewhat less offensive manner, calling unmarried women's interest in philanthropic projects "a form of restlessness" (382).

Our discussion of a 1912 poster designed by Harold Bird, *The Appeal of Womanhood*, expands on the stereotype of the angry spinster. Bird's image foregrounds a curvaceous, obliging, placid woman holding a banner that politely declines the vote ("No Votes, Thank You"). This icon of traditional womanhood is contrasted with the figure of an angry virago in the background who wields the iconic hammer of suffrage militancy against a silhouette of the British Houses of Parliament, a symbol of the realm she seeks to invade and destroy. While the window-breaking suffragette postdates Robins's play, the image nonetheless usefully distills many stereotypes of militancy that were already operative and that are expressed by the play's anti-suffrage characters. We begin by brainstorming the ways these two figures differ: one is graceful, beautiful, maternal, sober, docile, and sweetly adorned, the other angular, plain, nonreproductive (skinny and boyish), hysterical, angry, and bent on violence. The former is the epitome of appealing womanhood; the latter, abhorred. This trio of anti-suffrage images spotlights the negative stereotypes that pro-suffrage artists and writers needed to combat to win public favor.

The last image we discuss is an instance of pro-suffrage propaganda and a direct riposte to Bird's poster. Designed by Louise Jacobs for the Suffrage Atelier in 1912, this image is also captioned *The Appeal of Womanhood*—signaling that those for and against women's suffrage were engaged in a battle over what constituted the feminine. Here, another image of classical womanhood is presented as politically engaged: she holds aloft a banner listing the social reforms the vote would enable her to promote. These reforms require some explanation: students may not be familiar with the concepts of "sweated labor," which refers to underpaid, physically grueling work such as factory jobs or work in a professional laundry, or "white slavery," which indicates forced prostitution or sex trafficking (Robins also wrote the 1912 novel *Where Are You Going To . . . ?* on the topic of white slavery).[6] Huddled behind the suffrage activist are representatives of two of the most grueling forms of sweated labor—a chain maker and a laundress—along with a mother and a prostitute, among other exploited women. When I ask how the central figure represents the suffrage activist in a positive light, students remark on her classical beauty, apparent strength, and altruistic motives. We discuss how these motives are traditionally feminine: the suffragist depicted in this poster wants the vote to protect the vulnerable, including women and children, a desire that casts her in the role of a maternal figure. This argument is echoed in *Votes for Women* in the Working Woman's comment that politics is "just 'ousekeeping on a grand skyle" (427). As impeccably dressed ladies, the Pankhursts embodied the militant who was also womanly, and they encouraged their foot soldiers to do the same, with dress codes for demonstrations and fashion columns in the WSPU magazine. Militant groups like the Women's Freedom League, an offshoot of the WSPU, also engaged in postcard campaigns showing leaders engaged in domestic tasks like making jam, which emphasized that womanliness and militancy weren't incompatible. As students come to understand, correcting negative stereotypes of the shrill, plain, unwomanly suffragette was one of Robins's main objectives.

Votes for Women

Like Jacobs's pro-suffrage iconography, Robins's play aims to justify and, to an extent, glamorize militancy. We discuss how Robins scrutinizes negative stereotypes of suffragettes in order to dismiss them as unfounded. Mr. St. John Greatorex, a liberal MP and guest at the Wynnstay house, forcefully expresses his hatred of "political women," whom he dismisses as "discontented old maids and hungry widows" (*Votes* 387). Not realizing that Vida is on the verge of joining the WSPU, he makes repeated sexual passes at her (413–14), ironically undermining his own stance that only "plain" and "unsexed" women are involved in the movement (386, 414). We explore how Robins satirizes anti-suffrage views like those espoused by Greatorex while more subtly defending militant methods in the exchange between the suffragist Mrs. Freddy and the budding suffragette Vida concerning the "rowdy" women who were arrested for disrupting a meeting in the House of Commons (386). A proponent of gradualism, Mrs. Freddy believes that the behavior of "a handful of hysterical" militants has "put back the reform a generation," to which Vida retorts that "the well-behaved women had worked for forty years and made less impression on the world than those fiery young women made in five minutes" (418). Through Vida, Robins presents the argument that militancy—which put women's suffrage in the headlines—was a valid and necessary method of fighting for the vote.

We spend time considering the construction of Vida's character as a counterimage to the plain, shrill, sexually frustrated suffragette stereotype, starting with the stage directions, which underscore the importance of her womanly appearance: "*an attractive, essentially feminine, and rather 'smart' woman of thirty-two, with a somewhat foreign grace; the kind of woman about whom men and women alike say, 'What's her story? Why doesn't she marry?'*" (383). Students observe that Vida's beauty, grace, and sex appeal all effectively refute the stereotype. Although at thirty-two Vida would technically be considered a spinster, Robins is at pains to show that Vida's single status is elective, given that men (Farnborough, Greatorex, and, historically, Stonor, who still considers her remarkably attractive) continually proposition her or refer to her sexual allure (as when Lord John calls her a "*nice* creature," only needing "some 'nice' fella to marry her" [382]). Students notice that even the female characters suggest that Vida's power over men is rooted in her unmistakable sexual appeal, as when Mrs. Herriot quips, "She certainly knows how to inveigle money out of the men" and Lady John responds, "It would sound less equivocal, Lydia, if you added that the money is to build baths in our shelter for Homeless Women" (381). We productively debate whether Robins overcompensates for the pejorative stereotype of the ugly, frigid spinster by emphasizing Vida's sex appeal as a means to her activism. As a counterpoint, I point out that both Vida and Robins must maneuver within a set of social constraints to have their messages heard; Vida's physical allure may well be regarded as a "necessary concession" to theatrical and social conventions.[7]

We also discuss how the play invokes the bitter spinster stereotype, which is evident in Lady John's response to Jean's scheme to force Stonor to marry Vida: Lady John cautions, "Intelligent women don't nurse their wrongs and lie in wait to punish" the men who wrong them (477). Robins not only challenges the frustrated spinster type but also rewrites the conventional fallen-woman narrative: within the latter framework, Vida would be a tragic figure, seduced and abandoned by her vicious aristocratic lover.[8] Stonor, however, is no villain, nor is Vida a hapless victim. Instead, Robins emphasizes that personal suffering can motivate political conscience. We discuss how Vida's painful past—especially her unwanted abortion—enables her to empathize with others, which ignites her desire to improve conditions for women. Like the womanly militant in Jacobs's poster, Vida thinks of the "sweated girls of the slums" and "the army of ill-used women whose very existence I mustn't mention," and believes that the franchise will help rectify the economic and social inequities that all women face (471). By identifying with women across the class divide, Vida comes to recognize broader patriarchal structures that hamper women—economic, social, and political—and this becomes the basis of her appeal for feminist solidarity: as she declares in her rousing speech in act 2, "women must learn to work for one another" (450).[9]

In discussing the play's ending, we return to the opposition between motherhood and political activism established by anti-suffrage propaganda. Vida's closing remarks to Stonor—"Jean's ardent dreams needn't frighten you, if she has a child," for "the little, little arms" of children "[subdue] the fiercest of us" (491)—seem to reinforce the idea that the maternal woman can't—or perhaps shouldn't—be political. The implication that women are bound to choose between domestic and political allegiances potentially undermines the work of pro-suffrage propaganda that insists that these two realms are not mutually exclusive. One student, Joshua Davis, pointed out that it is a realistic and still relevant point that motherhood (and fatherhood) encroaches on the time one has available for other commitments. The conclusion of *Votes for Women* may thus be read as a concession to realism or, alternatively, as another instance of Robins appeasing her audience—at a time when anxiety about declining birth rates was pervasive and often tied to anxieties about the New Woman.

The women's suffrage movement lurks in the margins of modernism—figuring in seldom-taught works like Woolf's *Night and Day*, Ford Madox Ford's *Parade's End*, May Sinclair's *Tree of Heaven*, and H. G. Wells's *Ann Veronica*. Given its centrality to the social and political upheavals of the period, women's suffrage literature warrants a place in the modernist classroom. Robins's goal in writing—namely, "to correct the false ideas about women which many writers of the past have fostered" (qtd. in Farfan 70)—was one shared with many modernist women writers. The themes addressed in Robins's work resonate with students, because although the vote has been won, the quest for public respect, for control over one's own body, and for a voice is still relevant today.

Notes

1. Key studies on modernism and suffrage literature include those by Miller; Green; Lyon; and Chapman.

2. For more on WSPU militancy, see Rosen; Tickner.

3. See in this volume Tate's discussion of Djuna Barnes's "How It Feels to Be Forcibly Fed."

4. For two excellent resources for these plays, see *Suffrage Drama*, edited by Cockin, and *The Methuen Drama Book of Suffrage Plays*, edited by Paxton. For a critical discussion of suffrage drama, see Stowell.

5. The first image discussed here, John Hassall's *A Suffragette's Home*, can be found in Lisa Tickner's *The Spectacle of Women*, in the color plates section between pages 210 and 211. The other three images are available on this volume's companion website (modwomen.mla.hcommons.org).

6. Robins's 1912 novel was published in the United Kingdom as *Where Are You Going To . . . ?* In the United States it was published as *My Little Sister* (1913).

7. Renee Benham, a former graduate student of mine, offered this apt phrase during a teaching demo of this material. See Farfan for further discussion of Robins's navigation of negative stereotypes.

8. For a discussion of the play in relation to this tradition, see Eltis.

9. During the early years of the WSPU, the organization welcomed working-class participation, but these ties were broken in 1907 when Emmeline Pankhurst resigned her membership in the Independent Labor Party, after which the organization began consciously fashioning its image as respectably middle-class. See Farfan for a discussion of the way the play reflects the early years' optimism about cross-class alliances in the movement.

Works Cited

Chapman, Mary. *Making Noise, Making News: Suffrage Print Culture and U.S. Modernism*. Oxford UP, 2014.

Cockin, Katharine, editor. *Suffrage Drama. Women's Suffrage Literature*, edited by Cockin et al., vol. 3, Routledge, 2004.

Eltis, Sos. "The Fallen Woman in Edwardian Feminist Drama: Suffrage, Sex, and the Single Girl." *English Literature in Transition, 1880–1920*, vol. 50, no. 1, 2007, pp. 27–50.

Farfan, Penny. "From *Hedda Gabler* to *Votes for Women*: Elizabeth Robins' Early Feminist Critique of Ibsen." *Theatre Journal*, vol. 48, no. 1, Mar. 1996, pp. 59–78.

Green, Barbara. *Spectacular Confessions: Autobiography, Performative Activism, and the Sites of Suffrage, 1905–1938*. St. Martin's Press, 1997.

Lyon, Janet. *Manifestoes: Provocations of the Modern*. Cornell UP, 1999.

Miller, Jane Eldridge. *Rebel Women: Feminism, Modernism and the Edwardian Novel*. U of Chicago P, 1994.

Paxton, Naomi, editor. *The Methuen Drama Book of Suffrage Plays*. Methuen, 2013.

Robins, Elizabeth. *Votes for Women*. *Writing for the Vote*, edited by Sowon S. Park, Routledge, 2004, pp. 367–491. Vol. 1 of *Women's Suffrage Literature*, general editors, Katharine Cockin et al.

Rosen, Andrew. *Rise Up, Women! The Militant Campaign of the Women's Social and Political Union, 1903–1914*. Routledge, 1974.

Stowell, Sheila. *A Stage of Their Own: Feminist Playwrights of the Suffrage Era*. U of Michigan P, 1992.

Tickner, Lisa. *The Spectacle of Women: Imagery of the Suffrage Campaign, 1907–14*. U of Chicago P, 1988.

Woolf, Virginia. *A Room of One's Own*. 1929. Annotated and introduced by Susan Gubar, Harcourt, 2005.

Nancy Berke

Teaching Modernist Women's Poems of Protest

Poetry presents a pedagogical opportunity to shed canonical requirements in favor of themes and ideas that resonate with students. One such theme I have integrated into my poetry courses is protest, a theme that strikes a special chord with the students of color and working-class and immigrant students whom I teach. I use modernist women's poems of protest to engage students in the demands of reading poetry. Students learn about modernism's connections to early-twentieth-century struggles relating to women's rights, workers' rights, and the rights of people of color, and how these issues shaped poetic expression.

When we teach a poetry that centers on the experiences of women, people of color, and the working class, students encounter modernism not only as a form of feminist expression but also as a radical artistic movement enmeshed in other forms of social and political radicalism.[1] Students learn that while modernist writing is itself a protest against outmoded forms of versification, language, and expression, certain poets were also inspired to make protest a modernist subject. Such poems present modernism as a cultural movement that is not only about form but also about the social conditions that exist outside the formal and linguistic innovations that define modernist practice.

The poems introduced below exemplify the rage and defiance of early-twentieth-century social struggles in America and thus are powerful teaching tools. Each poem manifests an aspect of American modernism, from the emergence and flourishing of modernist verse in the 1910s and 1920s, to the 1930s, when modernist poets began to observe the devastating effects of a global depression and embrace the cultural zeitgeist behind the popular front, a coalition of left-wing groups united against Fascism. I teach these poems in chronological order to situate them within their historical contexts. We begin with "Bread," a poem written by the Irish-born Lola Ridge. First published in October 1917 in the *New York Call*, a Socialist Party newspaper, "Bread" depicts a women's protest against rising living costs. We then move on to "A Southern Road," an impressionistic representation of the lynched body written by Helene Johnson, an affiliate of the Harlem Renaissance, in response to waves of lynchings in the South. Johnson's poem was first published in *Fire!!*, a one-off journal from 1926 edited by Wallace Thurman that featured art and literature by important early modernists from Harlem, such as Zora Neale Hurston, Aaron Douglas, Gwendolyn Bennett, and Langston Hughes. Finally, students read Ruth Lechlitner's "Lines for an Abortionist's Office"—first published in the author's 1937 collection *Tomorrow's Phoenix*, the poem offers a critique of church and state interference in women's reproductive lives at a time when one out of every four pregnancies was terminated.

These works challenge students to see an expanded modernism in which poetic innovation is coupled with issues of gender, race, and economic critique. I use visuals—a timeline of important events accompanied by images—to introduce modernism, thereby emphasizing the importance of social context—how the social world influences poetic creation, both consciously and unconsciously. After this, we begin to discuss the issue of protest: what it meant during the period; what it means today. Students complete low-stakes writing assignments, one that asks them to reflect on what protest means to them, a second that requires them to discuss an example of protest they have encountered in literature. I include clips from Clover Hope's multimedia piece for *Vibe*, "Eleven Great Hip-Hop Protest Songs"; drawing a connection to students' own encounters with a culture of protest provides a frame to introduce the three poems. "Bread" describes an actual protest; "A Southern Road" constructs an image of horror as a sign of protest; and "Lines for an Abortionist's Office" uses traditional verse structure to criticize traditions that disempower women.

Although I discuss "Bread," "A Southern Road," and "Lines for an Abortionist's Office" as part of one unit over several class periods, I unpack each poem individually using close reading assignments. Two of the three poems are written in free verse. I discuss the significance of free verse for modernist writing and emphasize the individual life of the word and the structural rhythm of the line as opposed to content-oriented rhyme, which students often hear in music. Yet, because what makes these three poems unique is their experimentation with important social themes, it is necessary to begin with the poems' historical context and to present documentary evidence of the events they describe before we unpack what makes each poem poetry.

To this end, I pair each poem with a supplemental reading: a 1917 *New York Times* report on food rioting, "Women in Bread Riot," complements Ridge's poem; Robert Zangrando's piece on lynching is paired with Johnson; and Meridel Le Sueur's 1932 *New Masses* article "Women on the Breadlines" aids students in their reading of Lechlitner. I make it a point to build in review time with a set of questions drawn from the ancillary readings and multimedia. Students also work together in groups to review historical context and poetic devices.

Students begin their study of poetry with an attention to three key elements: theme, structure, and language. With these elements in mind, students develop their poetry-reading skills as they work in small groups. I supply students with a worksheet that includes questions about identifying voice, setting, tone, word choice and word order, imagery, structure, and form. I also provide them with a handout on poetic devices and a photocopy of the "On Prosody" appendix from Helen Vendler's *Poems, Poets, Poetry* (659–74). Students bring in a one- or two-sentence summary of the poem they have read for homework; in class they paraphrase the poem in order to uncover its theme. They also identify the poem's structure: its layout on the page, rhyme scheme, and stanzas. With free verse poems students focus on the movement of the ideas and images from line to line, and I emphasize the line as the essential distinguishing feature of a poetic work.

"Bread"

Students begin their group work on Ridge's "Bread" by considering the poem's parenthetical epigraph: "(Women's demonstration against the high cost of living, N.Y. City Hall, December, 1916)." I point out that Ridge was an immigrant, activist poet, and inform students about her early experiments with imagism—a modernist movement in poetry that sought clear expression using precise images. Students focus on the poem's language of activity. Ridge's highly visual description of women's bodies thronging the steps of the city hall depicts these bodies as sites of struggle:

> Shawled women,
> Trickling like a sluice out of alleys and side streets;
> Swelling, irresistibly growing—
> Pouring like an addled river
> Through stalled crowds and vehicles cluttered like curses—
> And a cry in their lifted throats. (lines 1–6)

As students discuss "Bread," I project historical photographs of New York's Lower East Side from the 1910s: the shawled protesters and assorted street scenes with pushcarts depict a neighborhood economy largely controlled by women. Students use their phones to research vocabulary specific to Ridge's own history and the historical action she records. For instance, Ridge describes the women protesters "trickling like a sluice out of the alleys." *Sluice* may be an unfamiliar word for many students, but it is significant to Ridge, who grew up around gold mining; students contemplate how Ridge, a feminist poet, uses the language of male labor to represent women's action. Students also think about how Ridge transforms conventional poetic devices such as simile and metaphor. The words *like* and *as*, for example, appear seven times in this forty-two-line poem.

I also assign a comparative analysis essay in which students contrast Ridge's modernist, visual style with a more conventional poem on the same topic: for example, "The Food Riots," by the feminist, genteel poet Marguerite Wilkinson. "The Food Riots" is a metrical ballad-like chant complete with chorus that romanticizes the beauty of harvests, setting these against the urban realities of high food prices. Whereas Wilkinson's poem rhapsodizes the rural pastures that grow the grain, Ridge's employs a poetics of rage as the women shout "curses" (line 5), wave "frenzied fists" (9), and let out "hag-worn" cries to match their "bloodied gown[s]" (34, 41). Students scrutinize Ridge's use of language and image and consider how her focus on women's anger represents a new mode of feminist poetic expression in this period.

"A Southern Road"

I begin class discussion of "A Southern Road" by projecting images from James Allen's exhibit *Without Sanctuary*—Allen's controversial collection of lynching photographs and postcards. I warn students of the severity of the images beforehand, and ask them to consider how the immediate impact of the photographs differs from the process of reading "A Southern Road" and uncovering meaning through the poem's imagery and symbolism. Students will have already reviewed a digitized copy of *Fire!!* in which Johnson's poem first appeared, and which is available on the Web from the *Poc Zine Project* (poczineproject.tumblr.com). Thus, we focus on the journal's upstart reputation as aesthetically and sexually transgressive, as well as on its inclusion of women artists who were seen as important contributors to the Harlem Renaissance.

"A Southern Road" describes a solitary walk along a country lane, shifting readers' expectations as it moves from images of a lush natural landscape toward "a dangling figure,__ . . . / Swinging alone, / A solemn, tortured shadow in the air." As they read "A Southern Road," students take note of the poem's vocabulary, its emphasis on color, and its religious allusions:

> A blue-fruited black gum,
> Like a tall predella,
> Bears a dangling figure,—

It is Johnson's use of juxtaposition that leaves its mark on the reader: the combination of lush country road and a lynched corpse "dangling" from a tree presents an element of visual shock and trauma. As a contrast, we look at canonical imagist poems such as Ezra Pound's "In a Station of the Metro," which also uses juxtaposition. Yet while such a comparison is instructive, it also reveals how "A Southern Road" goes one step further by infusing its images with a social message, thus emphasizing Johnson's rage in the face of unspeakable human crimes. My aim is to get students to think about how juxtaposition may function as a form of stylistic innovation, a social statement, or both, depending on the poet's purpose and audience.

"A Southern Road" also pairs well with Claude McKay's "The Lynching," a politically charged yet conventionally structured Shakespearean sonnet. An essay assignment asking students to compare these two poems would require students to think about how Johnson and McKay, writing on the same topic at around the same time, construct their poems both thematically and aesthetically. It is worth noting to students that Johnson's poem was shared among a coterie of young Black radicals, whereas McKay, then an active Communist, shared his poem with the more mainstream reading public of *Poetry* magazine. Thus, in their essays, students can also be asked to defend the stylistic choices of each poet based on their audiences.

"Lines for an Abortionist's Office"

"Lines for an Abortionist's Office" is challenging for students on several fronts. The topic of abortion often elicits strong emotions. Recent threats to legal abortion in the United States establish a connection between the poem's Depression-era setting and the lives of our students. Adding to the difficult subject matter is that the poem is written in a loose iambic trimeter with an alternate rhyme, which means that students must think about what ends the structure serves as a form of modernist women's protest.

Students have read, and also review in class, Le Sueur's "Women on the Breadlines," which, in a lively, familiar style, recounts Le Sueur's 1932 visit to the women's section of a "free employment bureau." I teach students about the Great Depression and show them well-known images such as Dorothea Lange's photograph *Migrant Mother* and Margaret Bourke-White's *At the Time of the Louisville Flood.* I also hand out a very brief article on the history of birth control (Mintz and McNeil).

Before students break into groups, we discuss the poem's tone and speaker. I point out the poem's somber mood and the speaker's justification for abortion, which was then illegal but widely sought. We also reflect on the double meaning of the poem's title, which connects lines of verse with lines of impoverished women waiting to terminate pregnancies. Students then work in groups, discussing the poem's trimeter, rhyme scheme, and ordered stanzas before moving on to its vocabulary. They identify figures of speech such as the apostrophe in the poem's first line, "Close here thine eyes, O State." Then they focus on the effect of specific stanzas, such as the second, which reveal Lechlitner's political stance and skill at constructing her justification:

> Know that they dare defy
> The words of law and priest
> (Better to let the unborn die
> Than starve while others feast.)

Lechlitner's poem may seem less characteristically modernist to students when compared to "Bread" or "A Southern Road," yet "Lines for an Abortionist's Office" is rhetorically important to Depression-era consciousness and women's protest. To show students how Lechlitner asserts her difference from the male modernists whose work she admired and sometimes emulated, I also have them read William Carlos Williams's poem "A Cold Front," in which a woman asks her doctor for an abortion. Indeed, Lechlitner's glowing review of Williams's *Complete Collected Poems* appeared in the same September 1939 issue of *Poetry* in which "A Cold Front" was first published. I project the original cover of the magazine issue, which allows students to connect the two poets. Though the subject is the same, "A Cold Front" is stylistically very different from "Lines for an Abortionist's Office." Williams's poem is written in free verse, from the male doctor's perspective. Its language is more colloquial and less polemical than that of Lechlitner's poem. Students consider how Lechlitner's contrasting use of tone, rhyme scheme, and figures of speech redefine modernism as a search for new forms of equality rather than new forms of experimentalism.

By the end of the unit, students understand that both style and subject matter move poetry forward, that the injunction to "make it new" is about more than just the reinvention of language—it is also about expressing a new social and political consciousness. Students who take a special interest in this poetry may use these poems as part of research and rhetorical writing assignments. They may decide, for instance, to connect "Bread," "A Southern Road," or "Lines for an Abortionist's Office" with present-day issues such as food insecurity, the Black Lives Matter movement, or abortion rights. In this scenario, students could write an argument from the perspective of their chosen poem's author, considering what Ridge, Johnson, or Lechlitner would say about the issue based on their poems. In what ways might each poem resonate today?

Although I teach "Bread," "A Southern Road," and "Lines for an Abortionist's Office" in a theme-based introductory course, these poems and their authors could also be discussed in more advanced courses on modernism or modern American poetry, or in surveys of American literature. "Bread," for example, is not just a poem about a women's protest against rising food prices; it is also a product of a world at war. Thus, "Bread" can be paired with other First World War poetry, thereby exposing students to a variety of styles, registers, and topics within the canon of war protest literature. I cull selections from the edited collections of Mark Van Wienen and Jon Silkin. Van Wienen's collection includes poems on women's suffrage, pacifism, race, and labor, among other topics. Silkin's collection contains Edna St. Vincent Millay's "Conscientious Objector" (236) and Mina Loy's "Der Blinde Junge" (157–58), which present the theme of war protest in markedly different styles. Posters from the Library of Congress's digital collection such as *Don't Waste Food While Others Starve!* (Clinker and Dwyer), which was produced during wartime for the United States Food Administration, help students connect the visual power of propaganda with the theme of war resistance.

In addition to its relevance to a course on the Harlem Renaissance, "A Southern Road" can be clustered with a series of poetic responses to lynching. Anne P. Rice's *Witnessing Lynching: American Writers Respond* comprises poetry, fiction, and reportage about this uniquely American extralegal violence. Rice's poetry selections include more ambiguous poems such as Angelina Weld Grimke's "Tenebris" (251) and Anne Spencer's "White Things" (235), as well as Ridge's lyric collage about Leo Frank, "Morning Ride" (247). Diverse works of art such as Paul Cadmus's expressionist drawing *To the Lynching!* and Isamu Noguchi's abstract bronze sculpture *Death* complement these poems and expand students' awareness of the ways in which anti-racist politics and modernist aesthetics merged in the 1920s and, especially, in the 1930s.

To expand the discussion of poetry's place in politics, this lynching unit might be extended to examine poems about "legal lynching." The Sacco and Vanzetti case and the Scottsboro case, for instance, produced thousands of literary responses. To highlight women's protest and the modern poet's sense of social responsibility, I focus on two Sacco and Vanzetti poems: Millay's "Justice Denied in Massachusetts" and Ridge's "Two in the Death House," the latter published in *America Arraigned!*, a poetry anthology dedicated to the Sacco and Vanzetti case. Millay and Ridge protested the historic trial not only in verse but also in real life: the two were arrested for picketing the Massachusetts State House in Boston during the trial and execution.[2] To provide students with a visual and historical context for these poets' activism, photographs of Millay on a picket line, and a detective escorting Millay and Ridge to jail, can be shown. Students might also look at Ben Shahn's painting *The Passion of Sacco and Vanzetti*, which can be accessed on the Whitney Museum's website along with information about the trial and Shahn's response to it. The opening pages of Katherine Anne Porter's essay *The Never-Ending Wrong*, in which Porter recalls the protest, add a dramatic touch. Together, the poems, images, and recollections relate the emotion of the trial, and students might discuss how the characteristic detachment of much modernist verse is complicated by these texts and images.

As a significant event of the Great Depression—one that united disparate groups of activists, writers, and intellectuals—the Scottsboro trial provides another opportunity for clustering poetry. Students might be asked to read newspaper reports from journals such as *The Crisis*, or poems by Langston Hughes. The American modernists Kay Boyle and Muriel Rukeyser ("The Trial" [*Collected Poems* 28]) also composed Scottsboro protest verse based on their own activism, as did the British modernist Nancy Cunard, whose reportage appeared in her eclectic *Negro Anthology*. Radical journals published highly evocative graphic art pertaining to the case—for instance, Hugo Gellert's *Bourgeois Virtue in Scottsboro*, which appeared in the June 1931 issue of the *New Masses*—can be used to support the literary material.

A unit on Scottsboro might be extended to include women's rights in a time of national suffering. Charlotte Nekola and Paula Rabinowitz's anthology *Writing Red* includes poetry, fiction, and reportage that place gender at the forefront of the socially conscious modernism of the 1930s. Lechlitner's "Lines for an Abortionist's Office" and selections from *Writing Red* highlight two important issues at stake in modernist women's protest: the social control of women's bodies and the need for women's agency, the latter as seen in Tillie Olsen's "I Want You Women Up North to Know" (Nekola and Rabinowitz 179–81) and Rukeyser's tribute poem "Ann Burlak" (Nekola and Rabinowitz 135–38). Students might also study the convergence of modernism and documentary in Rukeyser's "Ann Burlak" and "Absalom" (Rukeyser 139–41).

During the height of the 1970s women's poetry movement, some activists believed that a woman writing poetry was itself a political act. What I have presented here are a few examples of the poems of protest that women wrote about the many social and political upheavals that coincided with the period of high modernism. Such poetry offers students another perspective on what we define as modern and what we understand as aesthetically modernist. These poems also provide, as a former student of mine noted, a "much-needed history lesson."

Notes

A special thank you to Nina Bannett, Linda Grasso, Carol Quirke, and Phyllis Van Slyck for their insightful comments on various drafts. A grant from the Professional Staff Congress / City University of New York helped fund this essay's completion.

1. See Reginio in this volume for another approach to teaching modernist women's poetry; see the essays by Snyder and Foster in this volume for teaching other forms of modernist women's activism: the suffrage movement and pacifism, respectively.

2. See Newcomb for more on teaching Millay's poem.

Works Cited

Allen, James. *Without Sanctuary: Photographs and Postcards of Lynching in America*. Twin Palms, 2000, withoutsanctuary.org.

Bourke-White, Margaret. *At the Time of the Louisville Flood*. 1937. *Museum of Modern Art*, www.moma.org/collection/works/46797.

Boyle, Kay. "A Communication to Nancy Cunard." *Collected Poems of Kay Boyle*, Copper Canyon Press, 1991, pp. 66–70.

Cadmus, Paul. *To the Lynching!* 1935. *Whitney Museum of American Art*, whitney.org/collections/works/2779.

Clinker, L. C., and M. J. Dwyer. *Don't Waste Food While Others Starve!* 1917. *Library of Congress*, www.loc.gov/item/2002708925/.

Cunard, Nancy, editor. *Negro Anthology*. Wishart, 1934. *The New York Public Library Digital Collections*, digitalcollections.nypl.org/items/294108d0-4abd-0134-e9a7-00505686a51c.

Gellert, Hugo. *Bourgeois Virtue in Scottsboro*. *The New Masses*, vol. 7, no. 1, June 1931. *Marxists.org*, www.marxists.org/history/usa/pubs/new-masses/1931/v07n01-jun-1931-New-Masses.pdf. Accessed 19 June 2019.

Hope, Clover. "Eleven Great Hip-Hop Protest Songs." *Vibe*, 19 Aug. 2014, www.vibe.com/2014/08/ferguson-protests-11-great-hip-hop-protest-songs.

Johnson, Helene. "A Southern Road." *Fire!!: Devoted to Younger Negro Artists*, Fire Press, 1926, p. 17. *ISSUU*, issuu.com/poczineproject/docs/poczp_fire_1926_readview. Accessed 27 July 2020.

Lange, Dorothea. *Migrant Mother, Nipomo, California*. 1936. *Museum of Modern Art*, www.moma.org/collection/works/50989.

Lechlitner, Ruth. "Lines for an Abortionist's Office." *Gender in Modernism: New Geographies, Complex Intersections*, edited by Bonnie Kime Scott, U of Illinois P, 2007, p. 116.

Le Sueur, Meridel. "Women on the Breadlines." *The New Masses*, 1932. *The History Muse*, historymuse.net/readings/womenonbreadline.html. Accessed 19 June 2019.

McKay, Claude. "The Lynching." 1922. *Poetry Foundation*, www.poetryfoundation.org/poems/56983/the-lynching. Accessed 19 June 2019.

Millay, Edna St. Vincent. "Justice Denied in Massachusetts." *Edna St. Vincent Millay: Selected Poems*, edited by Colin Falck, HarperPerennial, 1992, pp. 76–77.

Mintz, S., and S. McNeil. "The Struggle for Women's Suffrage: Birth Control." *Digital History*, 2016, www.digitalhistory.uh.edu/disp_textbook.cfm?smtID=2&psid=3210. Accessed 19 June 2019.

Nekola, Charlotte, and Paula Rabinowitz, editors. *Writing Red: An Anthology of American Women Writers, 1930–1940*. Feminist Press, 1986.

Newcomb, John Timberman. "A Poem and the Times: Teaching 'Justice Denied in Massachusetts' in Context." *Teaching Modern Poetry*, special cluster of *Modernism/Modernity* Print Plus, edited by Emily Setina, vol. 1, cycle 1, 2 Mar. 2016, doi.org/10.26597/mod.0013.

Noguchi, Isamu. *Death*. 1934. *The Noguchi Museum*, www.noguchi.org/artworks/collection/view/death/.

Porter, Katherine Anne. *The Never-Ending Wrong*. Little, Brown, 1977.

Pound, Ezra. "In a Station of the Metro." 1913. *Poetry Foundation*, www.poetryfoundation.org/poetrymagazine/poems/12675/in-a-station-of-the-metro. Accessed 19 June 2019.

Rice, Anne P., editor. *Witnessing Lynching: American Writers Respond*. Rutgers UP, 2003.

Ridge, Lola. "Bread." Van Wienen, pp. 192–93.

———. "Two in the Death House." *America Arraigned!*, edited by Lucia Trent and Ralph Cheyney, Dean and Company, 1928, p. 78.

Rukeyser, Muriel. *The Collected Poems of Muriel Rukeyser*. McGraw-Hill, 1982.

Shahn, Ben. *The Passion of Sacco and Vanzetti*. 1931–32. *Whitney Museum of American Art*, whitney.org/collection/works/1022.

Silkin, Jon, editor. *The Penguin Book of First World War Poetry*. Penguin Books, 1979.

Van Wienen, Mark, editor. *Rendezvous with Death: American Poems of the First World War*. U of Illinois P, 2002.

Vendler, Helen. *Poems, Poets, Poetry*. Bedford / St. Martin's Press, 1997.

Wilkinson, Marguerite. "The Food Riots." *The Masses*, May 1917, p. 33. *Brown University Library*, repository.library.brown.edu/studio/item/bdr:528570/PDF/.

Williams, William Carlos. "A Cold Front." 1939. *Poetry Foundation*, www.poetryfoundation.org/poetrymagazine/browse?contentId=22429. Accessed 19 June 2019.

"Women in Bread Riot at Doors of City Hall." *The New York Times*, 21 Feb. 1917, www.nytimes.com/1917/02/21/archives/womem-in-bread-riot-at-doors-of-city-hall-with-babies-in-arms-they.html.

Zangrando, Robert L. "About Lynching." *Modern American Poetry*, maps-legacy.org./poets/g_l/lynching/lynching.htm. Accessed 19 June 2019.

Part VII

Digital Humanities

Elizabeth Willson Gordon and Helen Southworth

Women Making Modernism: Digital Humanities and Modernist Women's Innovations

The student danced in the library—for she had discovered that "C." stood for "Caroline," that "C." was a woman! An undergraduate writing a biography of C. J. M. Hubback—a name located in J. Howard Woolmer's *A Checklist of the Hogarth Press, 1917–1946* and a figure about whom almost nothing was previously known—had made her first substantial discovery. The student's quest for clues and traces of a life was wide-ranging: she visited libraries, wrote to archivists for copies of letters, perused indexes, and searched online. Eventually, a narrative emerged of a woman who worked as a translator for Sigmund Freud, who had made other contributions using only her initials, who led a courageous life, and who was also an actual descendant of Jane Austen. The student felt not only admiration for Hubback but also a different sort of connection, a sense that Hubback was important, and that she, the student, had a responsibility to make something of Hubback's story known to the world. This discovery mattered.

Because modernist women's writing was often collaborative, sometimes anonymous or pseudonymous and undertaken behind the scenes, and frequently so newfangled that it was hard to categorize, much of it remains unknown and uncelebrated. Digital humanities (DH) has enormous potential for uncovering the work of forgotten women writers. At the same time, DH offers new ways for instructors and students to engage with the work of canonical women authors and artists, illuminating, for example, the networks they participated in and the many interventions that made their publications possible.

In terms of subject and approach, our exemplary course, Women Making Modernism, highlights the work, entrepreneurship, innovation, and DIY spirit that shaped modernist print culture in the hands of women. This course models exciting new work at the intersections of digital humanities, modernist studies, and women's studies. Its goal is for students to learn about the work of modernist women and to emulate their creativity as they experiment with DH tools and build DH projects.

Our focus reflects Douglas Mao and Rebecca L. Walkowitz's perspective on the expansion characteristic of new modernist studies, a field "in which scholarly inquiry has increasingly extended to matters of production, dissemination, and reception" (738), and extends this perspective to show that DH has essential work to do. The course makes use of existing DH sites and archives that have opened up access to information about modernist women's work in magazines, publishing houses, bookshops, book clubs, and salons, and about readership (e.g., full-text versions of works and ephemera connected to institutional contributions). As Stephen Ross and Jentery Sayers have shown, DH has much to offer modernist studies regarding the versatile representation of multiple versions of texts, the provision of manipulable geospatial frameworks, and the preservation and dissemination of fragile materials, among other things. Digitization enables students to view materials at a scale otherwise unavailable, a fact that resonates with Alan Liu's perceptive question: "What kinds of humanistic phenomena appear only at scale?" (qtd. in Ross and Sayers 630).

Emphasis in this course is on the making and doing of modernism. We follow the "humanities lab" model, defined by Sean Latham and Robert Scholes as one in which "similarly collaborative networks of researchers and institutions . . . lend their collective expertise to textual objects that would otherwise overwhelm a single scholar" (530). Latham describes his own role in the classroom as "like [that of] a lead researcher, [helping] point students to new areas, and then [giving] them the structured space for experimentation and discovery" (qtd. in Churchill, "Modernist Periodicals" 222). In this way, students are "[inserted] into research communities from the start" rather than having to undergo a lengthy theoretical apprenticeship away from the site of discovery (Burdick et al. 126). This does not mean that students do not engage in traditional scholarly research:

the tools of DH are complementary to hands-on work in libraries, archives, and special collections. Our goal is to show DH at work, to explore teaching and learning with, rather than about, DH. Taking this two-pronged approach, we respect concerns of feminist DH scholars like Jacqueline Wernimont about the need for attention to recovery and to the capacity of users to participate in those efforts by producing content and building their own skills.[1] When students create material for (digital) archives, they are left with a greater understanding of the constructed nature of knowledge and a sense of their own responsibility and role in making change. Students have, for example, choice in both topic and approach when writing interpretive essays for Yale University's *Modernism Lab* or biographies for the *Modernist Archives Publishing Project*, judging what contribution is important to make.

Parts 1 and 2 of the course look at women's roles in two important modernist institutions: magazines and publishing houses. The modernist period saw more women taking up editorial positions in these traditionally male spaces. As Barbara Green suggests, modernist periodical studies, heavily imbricated with advances in DH, is an "emerging and vibrant field . . . where recovery projects and the 'woman writer' meet new methodological challenges and opportunities" ("Recovering Feminist Criticism" 54). Part 3 explores these institutions in terms of hidden labor, covering lesser-known work by well-known modernist women as well as groundbreaking work by now-forgotten women in a whole range of creative and less-studied professions. In parts 4 and 5, students learn about women and book arts (design, cover art, and illustration) and women and book business (marketing, advertising, and consumption), respectively. In the final week of class, we recreate a modernist salon. This course is aimed at advanced undergraduates and graduate students of modernism, digital humanities, or print culture, but can be modified or used selectively for a range of audiences, including introductory classes, composition classes, and senior seminars. Each unit can stand alone or might be expanded or supplemented to focus on one specific creative industry, such as publishing or theater.

The course aims to foster experimentation and invention in students, and in this respect it mirrors the groundbreaking work of modernist women. Suggesting that DH may prompt students to think in different ways, Suzanne Churchill and her collaborators on *Mina Loy: Navigating the Avant-Garde* illustrate the kind of revolutionary reading enabled by the itinerant quality of DH: "If a digital project can enable peripatetic reading and writing not constrained by genre, geography, or period, then it may bring us closer to post-canon literary studies that is not always reading women writers against a presumed norm for a genre, period, or movement but engages with their work on its own terms" ("Work"; see this volume's companion website [modwomen.mla.hcommons.org] for the link to *Mina Loy*). We endorse such a creative impulse in this course, which demonstrates how uncovering the creativity of modernist women might spur innovation in the classroom.

Part I: Modernist Magazines

During the modernist period, women played important roles—as editors, writers, and readers—in a revolutionary wave of little magazine production spurred by a need to find publishing venues for avant-garde material. Women founded and contributed to not only "suffrage papers, avant-garde feminist journals, feminist literary reviews, [which] give researchers a glimpse into the intersection of gender and discourses of modernity" (Green, "Feminist Periodical Press" 191) but also middlebrow publications such as *Good Housekeeping* and *Vogue*.[2] The *Modernist Journals Project* (*MJP*) offers full-text scans of Jane Heap and Margaret Anderson's *The Little Review* (1914–22), Dora Marsden's *The Freewoman* (1911–12), Harriet Monroe's *Poetry* (1912–22), and, in its 1910 collection, single copies of *Good Housekeeping* and *Ladies' Home Journal*, to name but a few. An instructor might focus, for example, on the earlier work of Jessie Redmon Fauset, a novelist and the literary editor of *The Crisis* (1919–27), using the *MJP*'s scans for 1910–22.[3] Another resource is Princeton University's more international *Blue Mountain Project*, which we use for full-text scans of the editor and poet Lola Ridge's *Broom*.[4]

Instructors should explore the special collections at their own institutions, as they may be surprised by the breadth of available resources. In preparation for a special collections and library stacks visit to look at intact, bound copies of journals, students read Scholes and Clifford Wulfman's chapter "How to Study a Modern Magazine," which provides a step-by-step guide to reading a modernist magazine. We also encourage students to explore the *MJP* website, which offers a variety of reading methods, from reading for audience based on advertisements to performing a close reading of bibliographic codes. This initial work provides an important foundation, as the *MJP* offers a well-curated resource to which students will return. The *MJP* focuses on primary documents and accessing those documents either in special collections or online, and students might be encouraged to write a short reflection piece about how access, or the lack thereof, impacts interpretation. Students can select strategies from among those Scholes and Wulfman discuss—such as reading advertisements, editorials, or using a checklist to anatomize a magazine—based on their interests and apply them either to different issues of a single journal or different journals from a single year. Class time could be spent on group discussions of Scholes and Wulfman's reading strategies. The instructor provides a sample analysis and students follow with group presentations of their findings based on their own analyses.

Part 2: Modernist Book Publishing

In part 2 we focus on women in book publishing, using our own *Modernist Archives Publishing Project* (*MAPP*) as a resource. *MAPP* is a critical-digital archive focused on twentieth-century publishing houses. Its goal is to curate, display, and describe the various documents that go into making a book, and to document the labor of a book's creators. We use *MAPP* in the classroom to look at Virginia Woolf's dual role as a writer and an editor at the Hogarth Press, which led to Woolf's famous claim that she was the "only woman in England free to write what I like" (*Diary* 3: 43).

MAPP also enables students to access layers of heretofore invisible labor at the Hogarth Press. Included in the database are women employees, including managers such as Eileen Burch; book travelers such as Alice Ritchie, who was also a Hogarth Press author; translators like Hubback; and artists like Enid Marx. *Woolf Online* provides an excellent supplementary online resource. *HathiTrust* and the *Internet Archive* have many scans of Hogarth Press first editions, for example Ruth Manning-Sanders's 1922 *Karn*.

Other figures in modernist publishing covered in this part include expatriates Sylvia Beach, Nancy Cunard, and Laura Riding. Beach's Paris-based bookshop and publishing house Shakespeare and Company's first edition of James Joyce's *Ulysses*, and several subsequent editions, are available at the *Modernist Versions Project*. Another excellent resource that highlights Beach's role as a bookseller is Joshua Kotin's *Shakespeare and Company Project*.

The poet and heiress Nancy Cunard launched the Hours Press with Henry Crowder in 1924, despite warnings from the Woolfs—who published Cunard's poetry collection, *Parallax*, in 1925—that her "hands would always be covered with ink!" (Cunard 8). The full text of Cunard's hard-to-find *Negro Anthology* is available as part of the *New York Public Library Digital Collections*. Among those authors published by both Cunard and the Woolfs was the poet Laura Riding, whose Majorca-based Seizin Press, run with Robert Graves, in turn published Gertrude Stein and Len Lye as well as Riding's and Graves's own work.

Part 3: Networks of Obscurity and Celebrity

In the third part of the course, we develop the foundational work undertaken in parts 1 and 2 to consider issues pertaining to celebrity and obscurity. We interrogate the value of hidden labor, of anonymity, which was the fate of Woolf's "mute and inglorious Jane Austen" and of avant-garde artists often doomed to fade away into obscurity (Room 45). We remind students, as Patrick Collier has argued, that "there is more urgent (or at least as much) need for mapping the much larger, nonmodernist locales of the vast landscape of early twentieth-century print culture than for filling the blank spots on the well-sketched map of modernism" (99).

Mixing materials from the above-noted resources with other library and Internet finds, we focus first on the lesser-known work of a well-known figure and then on the important contributions of a forgotten figure. For example, we reexamine Katherine Mansfield's place within networks of modernist figures while also highlighting her work as an editor and a poet. Along with studying Mansfield's collected stories, students use the *MJP* to look at Mansfield's 1913 contributions to *The Blue Review*: they examine page images that include advertisements and reviews alongside the work of poets and other short fiction writers. Mansfield not only contributed stories to the magazine but was also its associate editor. One of very few women contributors, she appears alongside D. H. Lawrence, W. H. Davies, and the illustrator Max Beerbohm. The *Blue Mountain Project* has a full-text version of *The Signature*, the short-run magazine authored and edited by Mansfield, her husband John Middleton Murry, and Lawrence, though here Mansfield's works appear under the pseudonym "Matilda Berry." Because "Katherine Mansfield" is already a pseudonym for Kathleen Beauchamp, the author's choice at this moment in her career to publish under a different name could facilitate discussions of authorial personae and the role literary reputation played in the modernist period, particularly for women.[5] Mansfield was part of a long tradition of authors who published under pseudonyms or initials (or anonymously).

At *MAPP*, one can explore Mansfield's relationship with Woolf and the Hogarth Press in a material way. Handprinted in 1918, Mansfield's early story *Prelude* was one of the Hogarth Press's first publications. Students view images of the first edition, read related correspondence and production material, and trace who bought copies of that first edition by looking at sales of the title in the press's order books. The sales and distribution information furthers a discussion of literary reputation, illustrating that small sales to the right people is one way to accrue "symbolic capital" (in Pierre Bourdieu's sense of the term). Given the opportunity to view images of original documents—and noting the different covers for *Prelude* due to a disagreement over the artwork, or the less-than-perfect inking of some pages—students are reminded that there are many people involved in producing a book and that literature does not spring, fully formed, from an author's mind.

We also highlight the work of a lesser-known figure. As we saw with Hubback, researching and writing about a minor figure can be rewarding and is facilitated by proliferating DH resources. Students choose a figure—an author, a press worker, a translator, an illustrator—and write a biography and a synopsis of published work with a focus on this figure's connection to the history of modernism and publishing. We offer tips on how to do primary research in physical libraries and online, pointing students to archives and sites like *Orlando: Women's Writing in the British Isles from the Beginnings to the Present*, where they look for traces of these little-studied contributors to modernism. Students work in pairs or groups to share information, research strategies, and the joy of discovery; for many undergraduates coming from nonscience backgrounds, it is their first time doing collaborative research. In addition to writing a biography, students compile a list of the most useful resources on the person as an aid for others who might also be interested in their figure. This assignment allows students to see their research as useful to others, to imagine its impact on a larger scholarly project. They see the contributions of their figures, and they see their own contributions. Such work creates a sense of the individual historical figure, the obscure life that students have come to care about.

Part 4: Book Arts

In an attempt to further uncover the hidden labor involved in the production of a book, we turn next to book design, cover art, and illustration.

MAPP and *MJP* are excellent resources for exploring cover art of the modernist period, as is the Web in general. Female artists include Woolf's sister and the creator of the Hogarth Press's house style, Vanessa Bell; Dora Carrington; and the lesser-known Enid Marx and Pearl Binder.

We incorporate hands-on exercises including printing, paper-making, and bookbinding workshops that involve students in the process of handprinting. The Woolfs handprinted for the first few years of the Hogarth Press and often marbled paper and bound books and pamphlets themselves.[6] *MAPP* has a compilation of examples of the handprinting undertaken at Hogarth as well as multiple covers for individual works.

We learn from Woolf's diary that Leonard and Virginia Woolf visited Chelsea Polytechnic of Art in 1939, where Leonard talked about his work as a publisher and Virginia viewed illustrations that students had prepared for her 1928 pseudobiography and love letter to Vita Sackville-West, *Orlando*, none of which have survived, unfortunately (*Diary* 5: 206–07).[7] One assignment might require students to produce their own cover art and illustrations for the work (Woolf herself orchestrated the fascinatingly complex illustrations). In preparation, students use *MAPP* to review the extensive collection of book art at Hogarth in order to gain a sense of the aesthetics of the period and the experimentation at the press. Another assignment might ask students to compile a catalog of book covers for different editions of a modernist work using sites such as *eBay* and *AbeBooks*. (Jean Rhys might be an interesting subject in this regard.)

Part 5: Marketing, Consumption, Big Data

Woolf saw the potential of involving students in what we now call data collection, in crowdsourcing, and in the kind of "humanities lab" model advocated by Latham and Scholes in "The Rise of Periodical Studies." Woolf noted in 1929, "What one wants, I thought—and why does not some brilliant student at Newnham or Girton supply it?—is a mass of information. . . . All these facts lie somewhere, presumably, in parish registers and accounts books" (Room 41). In the penultimate part of the course we turn to the postpublication marketing and movement of books, looking at how modernist books were advertised, where and how they were sold, and who purchased them. This part allows for projects dealing with quantitative data and lends itself to various types of visualization. Students appreciate the opportunity to interface with a broader world outside of the classroom using such mechanisms as crowdsourcing online book dealers and collectors for ownership information, which enables a public humanities component. As Woolf also suggests when she advocates for collaboration in *A Room of One's Own*, many hands make lighter work of gathering information about the oftentimes imperceptible underpinnings of modernism.

For those students more at home in the digital realm, Alan Liu's *DH Toychest* provides an excellent tool kit. The resources available on Liu's site allow students to self-train at home and to take advantage of existing skill sets and digital proficiencies. These resources can also be used in an in-class lab setting with the instructor or other experts on campus. In our experience, this skill building can be accomplished in a week or two. Students have built graphs and pie charts using quantitative data from Woolmer's *Checklist of the Hogarth Press* and *MAPP*—for instance, graphs that display the number of women authors published at the press compared to men over time. Focusing on the work rather than the person, students have mapped distribution, consumption, and readership of Hogarth Press titles. We also introduce students to Robert Darnton's concept of a "communications circuit" (503), a description of the stages a book passes through and the many people involved in this process. Often unfamiliar with an approach from the field of book history, students express surprise and delight that they have never really considered books from this perspective. Students create a map of the trajectory of a book or a series of books using databases such as *WorldCat* for holdings within and outside the United States and *Library Hub Discover* for holdings in the United Kingdom, which allows them to track extant copies of first editions. The fact that there is sometimes only one edition of a certain text makes this task more manageable.

MAPP makes available full scans of archived order books from the University of Reading's Hogarth Press business archive. Undergraduate research assistants are engaged in transcription and in paleography, identifying and creating a catalog of the different hands of the business managers, many of whom were women. In this way, students gain a greater awareness of the hidden labor of the print trade (see Morgan).

Part 6: Modernist Spectacle

We close the class with a fun and creative exercise, a reconstruction of a modernist salon à la Stein and Alice B. Toklas's rue de Fleurus, Natalie Barney's Neuilly salon, or the Bloomsbury Group's Memoir Club. As

Joanne Winning argues, the modernist party functions as "a generative site in which intellectual and literary authority is defined and disseminated and in which cultural influence and intervention takes place" (128). Students are encouraged to engage individually or collaboratively in curatorial work. For instance, students might create and present an online exhibition showcasing various issues or editions of a particular text, from magazines to book publications. Students might also dress up as a specific modernist writer, artist, or character and create a performance that reflects that figure's contribution to modernism and embodies students' digital learning. While students might choose to write a more traditional essay for the final project, they are also encouraged to use tools such as WordPress, PowerPoint, and Prezi to create more dynamic projects. Omeka is one of a number of easy-to-learn types of open-source exhibition software that is perfect for a course such as this. By closing in this way, we celebrate the innovative work of women modernists and offer students another way to engage creatively with the writers they've studied. This class is fundamentally about collaborative making and participation, learning that is always in process.

Notes

1. See Foster in this volume for theorizing a feminist digital humanities in the classroom.

2. On pulps and middlebrow publications, see Earle; Hammill and Hussey.

3. On Fauset, see Scott.

4. Ridge also worked as an editor at *New Masses*; see Svoboda. All resources discussed here, along with others, may be found on the companion website to this volume (modwomen.mla.hcommons.org).

5. See Green for a discussion of anonymity, pseudonymity, and collaboration in terms of the woman writer and periodicals ("Recovering Feminist Criticism" 56).

6. For an example, see *A MYRIAD*, a student book arts project supervised by Claire Battershill at Simon Fraser University, the link to which is available on the companion website to this volume.

7. The draft of Leonard Woolf's talk is available in the University of Sussex archives.

Works Cited

Bourdieu, Pierre. "The Forms of Capital." *Handbook of Theory and Research for the Sociology of Education*, edited by J. Richardson, Greenwood, 1986, pp. 241–58.

Burdick, Anne, et al. *Digital_Humanities*. MIT Press, 2012.

Churchill, Suzanne. "Modernist Periodicals and Pedagogy: An Experiment in Collaboration." *Transatlantic Print Culture, 1880–1940: Emerging Media, Emerging Modernisms*, edited by Ann Ardis and Patrick Collier, Palgrave Macmillan, 2008, pp. 217–36.

———. "The Work of Scholarship in the Age of Digital Reproduction." *Mina Loy: Navigating the Avant-Garde*, minaloy2017.suzannechurchill.com/site-intro/1-the-work-of-scholarship-in-an-age-of-digital-reproduction/. Accessed 28 May 2020.

Collier, Patrick. "What Is Modern Periodical Studies?" *Journal of Modern Periodical Studies*, vol. 6, no. 2, 2015, pp. 92–111.

Cunard, Nancy. *These Were the Hours*. Southern Illinois UP, 1969.

Darnton, Robert. "What Is the History of Books (Revisited)?" *Modern Intellectual History*, vol. 4, 2007, pp. 495–508.

Earle, David M. *Re-covering Modernism: Pulps, Paperbacks, and the Prejudice of Form*. Routledge, 2009.

Green, Barbara. "The Feminist Periodical Press: Women, Periodical Studies and Modernity." *Literature Compass*, vol. 6, no. 1, 2009, pp. 191–205.

———. "Recovering Feminist Criticism: Modern Women Writers and Feminist Periodical Studies." *The Future of Women in Modernism*, special issue of *Literature Compass*, edited by Tory Young and Jeff Wallace, vol. 10, no. 1, 2013, pp. 53–60.

Hammill, Faye, and Mark Hussey. *Modernism's Print Cultures*. Bloomsbury Academic, 2016.

Latham, Sean, and Robert Scholes. "The Rise of Periodical Studies." *PMLA*, vol. 121, no. 2, Mar. 2006, pp. 517–31.

Liu, Alan, curator. *DH Toychest: Digital Humanities Resources for Project Building*. 2013–2017, dhresourcesforprojectbuilding.pbworks.com/w/page/69244243/FrontPage. Accessed 19 June 2019.

Mao, Douglas, and Rebecca L. Walkowitz. "The New Modernist Studies." *PMLA*, vol. 123, no. 3, May 2008, pp. 737–48.

Morgan, Peter. "Anatomizing Hands and Anonymous Labor." *Modernist Archives Publishing Project*, 15 Nov. 2017, www.modernistarchives.com/content/anatomizing-hands-and-anonymous-labor.

Ross, Stephen, and Jentery Sayers. "Modernism Meets Digital Humanities." *Literature Compass*, vol. 11, no. 9, 2014, pp. 625–33.

Scholes, Robert, and Clifford Wulfman. "How to Study a Modern Magazine." *Modernism in the Magazines: An Introduction*, Yale UP, 2010, pp. 143–67.

Scott, Bonnie Kime, editor. *The Gender of Modernism: A Critical Anthology*. Indiana UP, 1990.

Svoboda, Terese. *Anything That Burns You: A Portrait of Lola Ridge, Radical Poet*. Schaffner Press, 2016.

Wernimont, Jacqueline. "Whence Feminism? Assessing Feminist Interventions in Digital Literary Archives." *Digital Humanities Quarterly*, vol. 7, no. 1, 2013, pp. 1–23.

Winning, Joanne. "'Ezra through the Open Door': The Parties of Natalie Barney, Adrienne Monnier, and Sylvia Beach as Lesbian Modernist Cultural

Production." *The Modernist Party*, edited by Kate McLoughlin, Edinburgh UP, 2013, pp. 127–47.

Woolf, Virginia. *The Diary of Virginia Woolf.* Edited by Anne Olivier Bell, Harcourt Brace Jovanovich, 1977–85. 5 vols.

———. A Room of One's Own *and* Three Guineas. Penguin Books, 1993.

Woolmer, J. Howard. *A Checklist of the Hogarth Press, 1917–1946.* Woolmer, 1986.

Laura Heffernan, Aislinn Kelly, and Deanna McMichael

Digital Archives and Women's War Writing

The last fifteen years have seen a rise in the number of out-of-print books and locally held archival materials made available for public use in digital form. This digital revolution has opened up the nooks and crannies of literary history to new forms of reading as well as to new readerships. Optical character recognition (OCR) software allows scholars to use keywords to search vast bodies of printed material and to use machine reading to browse corpuses of noncanonical literature and ephemera. These new databases and archives also reward close reading. Indeed, as Peter Stallybrass argues, they have "changed our relation to the ownership of knowledge": "One of the most radical aspects of database is its power to separate knowledge from academic prestige and from its attendant regime of intellectual property" (1581). Materials previously accessible only by those with credentials and travel budgets now lend themselves to classroom use, transforming students into researchers charged with the exciting and daunting task of discovering and evaluating primary documents—and building new literary histories to accommodate them.

For students and scholars of First World War writing, and of modernist women's writing more broadly, digital archives and repositories promise to restore to view an entire body of war writing penned by women—writing that has, until now, been largely lost to posterity. Of the over two thousand poets who published war poems between 1914 and 1918, nearly a quarter were women. Active duty soldiers, by comparison, made up only a fifth (Buck 87). Though women's war poetry appeared nearly everywhere during the war—in collections by individual authors, in anthologies, in national and local newspapers, and in a range of periodicals—it would, in the years to come, be gradually effaced by the enormous poetic output of surviving soldiers in the 1920s, by chauvinist editors, and by critics who center their literary histories at the war front (Buck 87). Since the 1980s, feminist critics have worked to recover, historically contextualize, and anthologize war poetry by women, but in many cases this revaluation involved plucking these poems from the material contexts in which they were written and read.

Today students can count and encounter women's war poetry, as well as other forms of war writing, in their original print contexts. Students can read women's war poems published in newspapers—the Library of Congress has digitized the entire seventy-one-week print run of *The Stars and Stripes* newspaper published in France by the American Expeditionary Forces. Students can flip through the digital pages of journals with small print runs—the University of Oxford's *First World War Poetry Digital Archive* contains all extant copies of the Craiglockhart War Hospital's in-house publication, *The Hydra*.[1] Students can also read full-text volumes of poetry long out of print—an advanced search in *HathiTrust* for publications in the United Kingdom between 1914 and 1918 turns up entire volumes of war poetry such as *A Book of Poems for the Blue Cross Fund to Help Horses in Wartime*. In these and other publications, women's war poems retain their original place alongside poems by soldiers and male noncombatants, and amid news columns, board reports, and advertisements. In addition, digital archives such as Oxford's *Great War Archive* provide access to a broader spectrum of women's war writing: letters, nurses' notebooks, scrapbooks for preserving war news, and handkerchiefs featuring embroidered poems tell the story of how ordinary women used writing during the war to connect with others, to memorialize their journeys and their work, to lend meaning to what was at times unassimilable.

This chapter provides several points of entry into the vast array of digitized forms of war writing. We offer exercises built around *The First World War Poetry Digital Archive*'s copies of *The Hydra*, and around an autograph book kept by a nurse named Phyllis Haviland, which can be found in *The Great War Archive*. We also describe how digital tools enhance the teaching of a canonical work of women's war writing: Vera Brittain's memoir, *Testament of Youth*. These exercises were developed in an upper-level course, Literature of World War I, offered at the University of North Florida during the centenary of the First World War. However, each of these exercises would work well in a variety of courses. For instance, a week-long unit on *The Hydra* could form part of a survey of modernist or twentieth-century British literature, or part of a short unit on modernist little magazines. In a broader survey course or a course on modernist poetry, exercises centered on Haviland's autograph book would help students understand the everydayness of poetry in the early twentieth century; alternatively, exercises relating to the book could flesh out a unit on women's experiences of the Great War. Lastly, Brittain's *Testament of Youth* could and should be taught in courses on modernist literature; the memoir is important, for instance, in that it captures the war's effect on culture and language—the shift, as Paul Fussell describes it, from "innocence" to "irony" (3).

While we suggest concrete exercises to guide students' interactions with digital books, journals, and artifacts, we also recommend that instructors let students loose in these databases (in strategic ways), charging them with finding documents or artifacts to add to the syllabus, a textbook, or an anthology. In our course, students played a key role in selecting the primary course materials for our syllabus by exploring databases and choosing documents or artifacts for inclusion. (Indeed, this article is coauthored by two former students, Aislinn Kelly and Deanna McMichael, on whose primary research it draws.) Because the contents of these archives fall outside the literary-historical record, they offer students the opportunity to discover and learn the value of a text or artifact about which no one has written—an experience that our class found freeing. Students described their encounters with relatively unknown women war writers as completely different—"less English-y," as one student said—from purchasing and reading a new edition of Virginia Woolf's *To the Lighthouse*. Their new familiarity with an array of war writing—not all of which was good—also gave them a more expansive sense of who writes and why and for whom. Even as these archives allowed us to move well beyond Fussell's once groundbreaking, now orthodox cast of Great War writers, our work with these ephemeral and everyday materials ultimately confirmed Fussell's claim that this was the most literary of wars—a moment when one could not even sign an autograph book without including a short sentimental or parodic stanza.

Women and *The Hydra*

The First World War Poetry Digital Archive preserves all extant copies of *The Hydra*, the magazine published at Craiglockhart War Hospital between April 1917 and July 1918. Each issue of *The Hydra* features contributions by staff members; hospital patients, many of whom were recovering from shell shock; and those unaffiliated with the hospital. Wilfred Owen edited several issues of the journal, and some of his first published poems appeared in its pages, including the Keatsian "Song of Songs" and "The Next War," a sonnet personifying death. Students paging through these issues will also find several poems by "S. S.," or Siegfried Sassoon; *The Hydra* first published, for example, Sassoon's "Dreamers" ("Soldiers are dreamers; when the guns begin / They think of firelit homes, clean beds and wives") and "Base Details," a scathing portrait of the "scarlet Majors" who "speed glum heroes up the line to death." In the journal's pages, students will also discover notices of the clubs and pastimes in which the shell-shocked inmates were encouraged to participate; notices of the Field Club's outings to the local oil works or to the McVitie and Price biscuit factory in Edinburgh; the Poultry Club's reports on their breeding hens; and the Boys Training Club's accounts of visiting local schools to organize scouting clubs.

Students may also be surprised to find that many contributions to the magazine were penned by women, about women, or addressed to women. Many also recorded the fact of women's daily presence at the hospital as entertainers, arts-and-crafts instructors, and nurses. *The Hydra* contains, for example, a set of dreamy, bohemian poems by Iris Barry, who would become England's first female film critic after the war. (To our knowledge, this has gone unremarked by Barry scholars and biographers.) *The Hydra* also published several poems by Margie Callandar Rule, the daughter of a Scottish MP who lived alone in the countryside, including "Some Thoughts" ("Life is one huge interrogation mark. 'Why?' is ever on our lips") and "Supplication," which describes "[t]he blank to-morrows, and the future naught" the poet faces in the absence of her beloved. We also come across many anonymous poems likely submitted by women, such as "The V.A.D.'s Lament": "There was so much I might have said, / So much I wished to say, / So many tender loving things / Before you went away."

Other issues of *The Hydra* contain further unexpected content created by female celebrities and nurses. The July 1918 issue, for instance, contains a letter by Violet Loraine, the musical theater star who recorded the First World War hit "If You Were the Only Girl (in the World)," which debuted in the 1916 musical revue *The Bing Boys Are Here*. Loraine's letter voices her support of the war effort and suggests that all women, in their own way, must follow suit: "Britain's women must prove worthy of the valor of their men . . . we women cannot go to war and fight as you have done, but we *are* doing our best . . . we are comrades all, meeting the most diabolical foe that ever trod God's earth, as one, shoulder to shoulder, we stand for liberty." The July 1918 issue also contains a short story by A. Nichol Bruce and R. Scots titled "Sister Mary's Solace," which explores the uncharted territory of war trauma experienced by nurses. The story, which implies the tragic death of its eponymous hero, highlights nurses' vulnerability and decries the lack of "wound gratuity" available to them (Bruce and Scots 8).

In an exploratory first pass with *The Hydra*, students could look for contributions by or about women, and class presentations on individual findings could generate further discussion. For instance, a student who selects "Sister Mary's Solace" could ask the class to consider its depiction of war trauma as suffered by women as well as by men. A presentation on Barry's poems could consider whether and how we might define these poems as war writing, despite the fact that they contain no explicit mention of war. Presentations like these could serve as a foundation for a project that requires students to select writing for and organize an anthology that represents their new perspective on women's writing of the First World War.

A more focused approach could ask students to consider how contributions by women in *The Hydra* might speak back to those war poems written about women at the home front. For example, students could read Loraine's letter alongside Sassoon's "Blighters," which takes place in a "crammed" music hall full of cackling patrons and "prancing ranks / Of harlots." Students could compare other famous war poems about women—such as Owen's "Disabled" or Sassoon's "Glory of Women"—with women's writing in *The Hydra*. In this respect, students might be encouraged to discuss the date and place of each work's publication; students could also consider the content and form of each poem, and their own reactions to reading *The Hydra* alongside canonical texts.

A Nurse's Autograph Book

In addition to *The First World War Poetry Digital Archive*, Oxford has assembled *The Great War Archive*, a publicly available repository of over

6,500 digital items, each of which relates to an individual's experience of the First World War (ww1lit.nsms.ox.ac.uk/ww1lit/gwa). *The Great War Archive* gives students a chance to explore a much wider array of genres of war writing. For example, a search for items tagged "autograph book" results in a number of these artifacts—pocket-size blank books that people carried with them and invited others to write in. The pages of these books contain signatures, remembrances, photographs, private jokes, parodies of nursery rhymes and more serious verses, pencil sketches, and sometimes elaborate illuminated pages and full-color portraits or landscapes. For their original owners, these books served as personal souvenirs, records of shared experiences and parting rituals. For us, they provide a glimpse of the many short-term friendships and acquaintanceships created by the war; they remind us of the youthfulness of many of the nurses and soldiers; and they offer us an informal record of these men's and women's reactions to their war experiences in the moment rather than after the fact.

Using these resources, we suggest an exercise that uses an autograph book kept by Phyllis Haviland, a nurse who served at the Second London General Hospital, housed at St. Mark's College, which served mainly patients with eye injuries. (Haviland later moved to the County of Middlesex War Hospital in St. Alban's.) Haviland's book opens with a poem she wrote herself, a dedication of the album to her "wounded heroes"—the soldier patients who filled the pages of her book with notes, sketches, signatures, and countless poems. The book contains a poem about having a wisdom tooth removed, a parody of Rudyard Kipling's "If" about a war nurse slogging through her work, a poem comparing Voluntary Aid Detachments (VADs) to Queen Victoria, poems about saying farewell to Haviland, poems about war wounds, and poems about the guilt of being returned to the home front. These poems are not all good, but they help students shed light on an era in which poetry was a part of everyday life; considered as a whole, Haviland's autograph book gives students a window on women's roles in wartime and makes palpable the youthfulness of the men and women involved in the war.

We opened discussion of Haviland's book by considering its form. Many students drew comparisons between the autograph books and the social media platforms of the present day, each drawing or poem from the autograph book functioning like a tagged picture or a post written to mark a moment of friendship or a shared experience. We considered how the autograph book might be described as a social medium—were these signatures, drawings, and scraps of verses intended to be read by others? How public was the autograph book meant to be? After discussing the book's form, we moved to its contents, which seemed at once both relatable and enigmatic. A page containing pasted photographs of "Soldier's Orphans" immediately conveyed the war's generational loss while a sketch of a bulldog smoking in uniform with the caption "When You Are Ready. I Am" remained compellingly opaque. We discussed whether and how we might be able to track down some of the more obscure references using these same digital archives as well as Google and scholarly database searches.

For a more focused exercise, Haviland's book pairs well with Fussell's chapter "Oh What a Literary War." In it Fussell describes how soldiers drew on an English literary canon in their writing about the war; everyone from the officer Rupert Brooke to the jokesters writing in *The Wiper's Times* trench magazine could be expected to refer to Alexander Pope, for example (156). By reading John Keats's "Ode on a Grecian Urn" alongside Edmund Blunden's "Vlamertinghe: Passing the Chateau, July, 1917," which opens with the first line of Keats's poem, students can begin to analyze why and how war poets drew on a national canon. Students will then be prepared to return to Haviland's autograph book with an eye to whether and how the soldiers and friends who left poems in her book also drew on national literature—in the parody of Kipling's "If," for example. Students can also expand Fussell's analysis by considering how the autograph book draws on and makes references to popular and local cultural forms in addition to a national canon.

Vera Brittain's *Testament of Youth*

Brittain's memoir *Testament of Youth* anchored and paced our course. Every few weeks, we read a few chapters of Brittain's memoir, which stretches from the idyllic years before the war to her VAD postings in London, Malta, and finally France, to the years after the war in which she attempted to return to normal life as a student at Oxford, despite having lost her brother, her fiancé, and two close friends to the war. Reading Brittain's memoir in segments throughout the term, interspersed with materials that dealt with different phases of the war, gave us the feeling that we were moving through the war and its aftermath with Brittain.

Though *Testament* is already a staple of First World War courses in English and history departments, it would also work well as part of a modernism survey—particularly within a unit focused on the experimental modernist practices of collage and allusion. Brittain first began *Testament* in 1922—modernism's annus mirabilis—by typing up her old diary entries. As she worked on the memoir for the next decade, she drew not only on her diaries but also on letters, poems she exchanged with her fiancé, sheet music, official memoranda, recruiting posters, transcriptions of conversations she had with classmates at Oxford, and excerpts from *Time and Tide*. These source materials are reproduced in Brittain's memoir—at times in striking graphic arrangements designed to evoke their original contexts. In addition to its use of source documents, *Testament* offers a firsthand account of the development—and limits—of women's formal education in the early decades of the twentieth century. Accordingly, Brittain's memoir would pair well with Woolf's *A Room of One's Own* or any number of modernist novels set in schools, such as James Joyce's *A Portrait of the Artist as a Young Man*.

Testament also provides a thorough account of life before, during, and after the war in provincial Buxton, in London, and at Oxford; it works especially well as a window into the popular culture of the 1910s. Brittain includes so many references—to extension-school lecturers, theatrical productions, popular songs and poems, novels, silent films—that our class began to research and write footnotes for the memoir, working together in a collaborative-editing document. We reserved class time to begin the process: students divided up the first few chapters of the memoir, agreed on a house style for the formatting of the notes, and began searching online for information about any and all of Brittain's cultural references. As we searched, we listened to the parlor music, marching songs, and music hall ditties Brittain mentions, and we looked at stills from the 1913 silent film adaptation of *David Copperfield* that Brittain attended in the cinema with her fiancé, Roland (Bentley). Gradually, our communal Google Doc filled up with hyperlinks, embedded images, and sound files, emerging as a minimuseum of life in the war years.

The final chapters of *Testament of Youth* describe the aftermath of war, beginning with the "horrid year" of 1919 (467). In a chapter entitled "Survivors Not Wanted," Brittain describes her horror-filled dreams and listless days as she resumes student life at Oxford, absent all her close companions. At the same time, she describes the overarching feeling of apprehension the war leaves in its wake: "Only gradually did I realise that the War had condemned me to live to the end of my days in a world without confidence or security" (469). The issues raised in Brittain's final chapters were solidified using Woolf's "The Mark on the Wall" and selections from Paul K. Saint-Amour's *Tense Future* (1–25), the latter of which reveals the interwar years as a time marked not by peace but by the anticipation of further violence—a future-oriented, apprehensive trauma shared by men and women, combatants and civilians alike. Like our work with the digital records of everyday women's war writing, these final readings invited us to imagine a literary history of the First World War that recognizes women as its central actors.

Note

1. See this volume's companion website (modwomen.mla.hcommons.org) for all resources mentioned here.

Works Cited

Bentley, Thomas, director. *David Copperfield.* Hepworth Pictures, 1913.

Blunden, Edmund. "Vlamertinghe: Passing the Chateau, July, 1917." Silkin, p. 106.

Brittain, Vera. *Testament of Youth.* 1933. Penguin Books, 2005.

Bruce, A. Nichol, and R. Scots. "Sister Mary's Solace." *The Hydra*, no. 9, July 1918, pp. 8–9. *The First World War Poetry Digital Archive*, ww1lit.nsms.ox.ac.uk/ww1lit/collections/document/3141/2079.

Buck, Claire. "British Women's Writing of the Great War." *The Cambridge Companion to Literature of the First World War*, edited by Vincent Sherry, Cambridge UP, 2005, pp. 85–112.

Fussell, Paul. *The Great War and Modern Memory.* Oxford UP, 2000.

Haviland, Phyllis. "Phyllis Haviland Sketchbook." *The First World War Poetry Digital Archive*, ww1lit.nsms.ox.ac.uk/ww1lit/gwa/document/8816.

Keats, John. "Ode on a Grecian Urn." *Norton Anthology of Poetry*, 5th ed., edited by Jon Stallworthy et al., W. W. Norton, 2005, p. 938.

Loraine, Violet. "A Message from Miss Violet Loraine." *The Hydra*, no. 9, July 1918, p. 10. *The First World War Poetry Digital Archive*, ww1lit.nsms.ox.ac.uk/ww1lit/collections/document/3141/2081.

Owen, Wilfred. "Disabled." Silkin, p. 194.

Rule, Margie Callandar. "Some Thoughts." *The Hydra*, no. 9, July 1918, p. 15. *The First World War Poetry Digital Archive*, ww1lit.nsms.ox.ac.uk/ww1lit/collections/document/3141/2086.

———. "Supplication." *The Hydra*, no. 2, Dec. 1917, p. 12. *The First World War Poetry Digital Archive*, ww1lit.nsms.ox.ac.uk/ww1lit/collections/document/5627/5318.

Saint-Amour, Paul K. *Tense Future: Modernism, Total War, Encyclopedic Form.* Oxford UP, 2015.

Sassoon, Siegfried. "Base Details." *The Hydra*, no. 2, Dec. 1917, p. 9. *The First World War Poetry Digital Archive*, ww1lit.nsms.ox.ac.uk/ww1lit/collections/document/5627/5315.

———. "Blighters." *War Poems of Siegfried Sassoon.* W. Heinemann, 1919, p. 17.

———. "Dreamers." *The Hydra*, no. 10, Sept. 1917, p. 10. *The First World War Poetry Digital Archive*, ww1lit.nsms.ox.ac.uk/ww1lit/collections/document/3132/1889.

———. "Glory of Women." Silkin, p. 132.

Silkin, Jon, editor. *The Penguin Book of First World War Poetry.* Penguin Books, 1979.

Stallybrass, Peter. "Against Thinking." *PMLA*, vol. 122, no. 5, Oct. 2007, pp. 1580–87.

"The V.A.D.'s Lament." *The Hydra*, no. 3, May 1917, p. 13. *The First World War Poetry Digital Archive*, ww1lit.nsms.ox.ac.uk/ww1lit/collections/document/5123/4272.

Woolf, Virginia. "The Mark on the Wall." *The Complete Shorter Fiction of Virginia Woolf*, 2nd ed., edited by Susan Dick, Harcourt Brace Jovanovich, 1989, pp. 83–89.

Lisa Mendelman

Recounting the Literary History of Modern Women Writers: Teaching Quantitative Methods to Undergraduates

This essay focuses on teaching quantitative methods derived from digital humanities to address the challenges of teaching the literary history of modern women writers.[1] Using my undergraduate seminar Sex without Consequence: Modern Fiction and Femininity, I discuss how work with archival platforms and analytic programs facilitates student learning in two arenas: reading and the writing of literary history. I lay out the rationale, the methodology, and the learning outcomes of this pedagogical approach. I describe how learning developing archival protocols enhances students' understanding of what's at stake in the materials we select and the methods we employ. I consider how experimenting with these evolving practices encourages students to reexamine canonical authors, recuperate understudied writers, and reevaluate extant narratives about modernist-era art and culture. I elucidate how this approach helps students hone traditional skills of close reading and historically informed argumentation, involves them in thinking about the contingencies of aesthetic categorization and canon formation, familiarizes them with the tradition of recovery, and introduces them to the limitations and opportunities of constructing literary history through contemporary digital means.

Why Use Digital Methods?

I teach digital research practices as a way to grapple with the challenges of writing literary history. An orientation to these practices early on in the course explains this rationale, emphasizing literary history as an ongoing process of inquiry and identifying digital research as an extension of this dynamic. The orientation centers on two research protocols: the first uses archival platforms to uncover original reviews of our initial novel, Willa Cather's *The Song of the Lark*; the second focuses on the concept of keywords and the use of tools like the Google Books Ngram Viewer and Voyant Tools. I have taught this course as an upper-division English seminar and as a lower-division general education course; in each context, I assume that students have no familiarity with these tools and have not engaged in prior thinking about the uses and ramifications of digital research for literary scholarship.[2]

The orientation glosses how our digital work extends the tradition of recovery while intersecting with current concerns about research methods. As we endeavor to historically contextualize the explicit concerns of a single text, our methods evoke recent interests in the emergence of alternatives to symptomatic criticism (e.g., Eve Kosofsky Sedgwick's reparative reading, Stephen Best and Sharon Marcus's surface reading, Heather Love's descriptive reading, Timothy Bewes's "reading with the grain").[3] In addition to such current concerns, Margaret Cohen has argued for narratological approaches to the archive to "reconstruct the lost horizon of the poetics that have shaped different kinds of novels" and other literary objects (58). Our incursion into quantitative methods aligns with recent efforts to synthesize evolving interpretive approaches with more traditional scholarly modalities. Jeffrey Drouin, in another specific instance, calls for a "medium-data (as opposed to big-data) approach" that "skim[s] . . . the data soup in ways that enhance our close reading of the material and the context writ large" (16). Stephen Ramsay's "algorithmic criticism" similarly "channel[s] the heightened objectivity made possible by the machine into the cultivation of those heightened subjectivities necessary for [critical] work" (77). A special issue of *American Literary History* and forums and clusters in *PMLA*, *American Periodicals*, *Feminist Modernist Studies*, and *Social Text* have elaborated how digital research in literary studies works simultaneously toward historical and contemporary ends.[4]

My course model relies on externally developed applications, rather than those built by me or my students. I end the orientation by discussing how the types of applications we use inform our results. We meditate on the hidden mechanisms that underlie our search processes and consider how the resulting tabulations and visualizations influence the claims we can make. As Elizabeth Maddock Dillon ("By Design" and "*Translatio Studii*"), Britt Rusert, and Jacqueline Wernimont all point out, the opacity and perceived objectivity of digital methods sustains long-standing issues of archival curation and legibility.[5] We talk about the merits and drawbacks of digitized and special collections (e.g., ease of access, loss of textual materiality, potential for unexpected findings, availability of knowledgeable support). For students interested in more advanced macroanalytic approaches, I highlight additional online resources (e.g., the *Stanford Literary Lab*). These resources, and quantitative work in general, can be challenging for novices. Yet as Claire Battershill and Shawna Ross exhort, there are generative outcomes to confronting such challenges in the classroom. Along with the field-specific and broader educational outcomes I detail below, Wernimont proposes that "working to include students" in digital humanities practices supports both "their own [immediate] sense of agency" and a larger feminist project of "decentered," "transformative authority"—"a particularly urgent project now at a time when students too often fail to see the relevance of either academic or political feminisms to their lives" (20).[6] Teaching digital research to undergraduates can renew and remodel the missions, as well as the methods and materials, of recovery work.

How to Do Things with Digital Archives

On the second day of class, each student undertakes online archival and analytic work. To streamline this crash course in digital research, I maintain a personal website that features links to digital platforms, some of which require a paid subscription, but most of which are open access.[7] The orientation uses this website as a springboard.

We begin by experimenting with *ProQuest*'s *Periodicals Archive Online* and *ProQuest Historical Newspapers* to retrieve original reviews of Cather's *The Song of the Lark*. These platforms provide an opportunity to discuss credible resources, viable search terms, and productive search parameters. For example, we talk about searching for "Cather+'The Song of the Lark'" in order to avoid results about the 1884 Jules Breton painting from which the novel takes its name. Students work in groups to read and discuss different articles found using one of the *ProQuest* platforms. This exercise brings into focus textual concerns that students often do not recognize as hot-button topics, and draws attention to how expectations of women writers shape assessments of form and content. For example, students are often struck by the reviewers' insistence on *Lark*'s immediate relevance due to its professional woman protagonist and by the ways sentimentalism's gendered cultural inheritance inflects discussions of characterized feeling and textual affect—praise for Cather's "uncommon sincerity," Thea's "melancholy passion," and the "quickening sympathy" she inspires; criticism of Cather's turn to "wearisome objective detail" and "a sociological treatise" in the epilogue (Boynton 461; Peattie; Cooper; Bourne 153, 155). These findings, I point out, complicate *Lark*'s subsequent critical reputation as one of Cather's less modernist, more sentimental works.

This activity leads into a discussion about the challenges of using individual archival materials to theorize literary history. We discuss why it behooves us to read as much material as possible to get a sense of representative and idiosyncratic perspectives. We talk about the profiles of different periodicals (e.g., sources of funding, targeted readership, political allegiances); categories like middlebrow and little magazines; and the cultural status of certain reviewers (e.g., Randolph Bourne, H. L. Mencken). Students meditate on how these qualities might shape a given book review. A *ProQuest* search also returns advertisements for the novel, which allows us to think through the strategic angles of the literary marketplace. I provide an overview of other online repositories holding period materials, and we talk about how different media formats, including visual artifacts, provide information on attitudes toward working womanhood, sexual mores, and related topics.

We discuss turning a similar lens on authorial materials with *The Willa Cather Archive*. The archive's extensive digital holdings include a photo gallery; fully searchable transcriptions of eight of Cather's books, many of her interviews, speeches, public letters, and other nonfiction writings; and original periodical reproductions and transcriptions of much of her short fiction. The site also features born-digital scholarly content, such as a calendar of Cather's letters, a geographic chronology of her life, and a tool for textual analysis of her complete fiction. We talk about how these diverse media help us recover Cather's literary innovations, situating them within historical contexts and genealogies of American letters and women's writing. We also talk about the limitations of this information. As a frame, I raise Drouin's question about "whether the data output of the digital surrogate is fundamentally separate from the object from which it derives" (16).

The *Cather Archive* thus serves as a point of departure for the thornier component of the course orientation, the introduction to quantitative tools.

I present the challenges of this brief tutorial as such—a way to think about the possibilities and restrictions of evolving digital approaches to literary scholarship. I note that my interest, and that of the course, focuses on how to synthesize emerging quantitative tools with the traditional qualitative methods of close reading and historical contextualization.[8] To that end, we employ the Google Books Ngram Viewer to track the course's key term: *sex*. The Ngram Viewer is a search engine that charts the frequency of one or more terms, as the terms appear in a corpus of digitized books published in a given language, time frame, and national context. The Ngram Viewer's database currently includes sources printed from 1500 to 2008 and allows users to select from specialized corpora like American English, British English, and English fiction—each available in 2009 and 2012 versions. Entering "sex" into the search box, setting a time frame of 1800 to 1950, and selecting "American English" produces a graph that indicates a steep increase in the instances of *sex* in the database from 1906 to 1931.[9]

We talk about what kinds of claims can be made about this result. We look at the different search forms that the Ngram Viewer supports ("wildcard search," "inflection search," "case insensitive search," "part-of-speech tags," "ngram compositions"). While the site details these options, it provides little information about its database content or its search algorithms. We talk about the importance of making claims that acknowledge these interpretative limitations (e.g., "Google's American English 2012 database indicates"), rather than treating the ngrams as sources of knowledge about society or cultural discourse. We discuss engaging these ngrams as supplements to an argument primarily supported by close reading. I emphasize thinking *with* rather than *through*—the ngram as a gesture to scale, not a definitive metric. Thinking with graphic representation along these lines helps students develop critical distance from their close reading practices and encourages them to keep their eye on their analytical, argumentative framework.

Shifting to single-text analysis, we experiment with Voyant Tools. Voyant Tools is an open-source application that generates a host of text analytics such as word-frequency lists, word clouds, frequency-distribution plots, and KWIC (key word in context) displays. The night before the class in which I introduce Voyant Tools, I circulate a clean digital version of *Lark* for students to use during this portion of the orientation; we discuss why clean texts are necessary for generating legible results.[10] Students follow along on their individual computers as we run the document through Voyant's basic algorithm. This process generates an array of quantitative data, including adjustable visualizations, which appear on a dashboard. I hone in on findings that can be integrated into arguments driven by close reading. For example, Voyant tells us that *Lark* averages 14.4 words per sentence, while its most frequent words are *thea* (which appears 1,059 times), *like* (556 times), *mrs* (432), *little* (353), and *archie* (337); *sex*, meanwhile, appears only once. We talk about how recurrent terms and the incidence of related words illuminate lines of inquiry that can be developed through close reading. For example, *like* indicates Cather's widely recognized interest in analogy, *mrs* suggests *Lark*'s interest in marriage's centrality to female identity, and *archie* reflects the novel's rerouting of the primary male character's role from romantic suitor to professional mentor. (Archie is Thea's childhood doctor, subsequent friend, eventual financier, and perennial support.) While Archie's signal presence resonates with the attention of reviewers to the demands of contemporary professional femininity, the frequency of *mrs* would seem to work against that. We discuss how we might reconcile this information by analyzing the novel's renderings of marriage and gendered characterization.

In closing, we discuss the scholarly concerns outlined in the prior section. I highlight how our research protocols, tentative conclusions, and ensuing questions echo these concerns and, in so doing, constitute the challenges of writing literary history. We end by brainstorming how students might extend our findings and navigate these challenges in their individual research.

The Student Uses of Digital Archives

Students' digital research informs the course's two major assignments: a keyword-driven presentation and a final course paper focused on digital-archival research. For the presentation, students choose one or more organizing concepts that generate related terms for qualitative and quantitative assessment. The week following the orientation, for example, students in one class engaged one of *Lark*'s reviews as a starting point for interrogating distinctions between literary modes. In her 1915 review, Elia W. Peattie asserts, "Miss Cather's method of delineating her heroine is so deeply romantic that it goes past all mere sentimentality, down into the very roots of romance, where the waters of reality spring eternally." Intrigued by this hierarchical model, students selected *realism*, *romanticism*, and *sentimentalism* as keywords and explored these modes of representation in Cather's novel using associated affective terms (e.g., variants of *feel*) and passages devoted to detail. Subsequent presentations sought to complicate received understandings of modernist-era literary categorization by looking at characteristics and qualities commonly associated with this classification. One group, for example, explored the rhetoric of science and technology in Edith Wharton's satire *Twilight Sleep* in order to detail her interest in isolation and clinicism as imbricated crosscurrents of modernist sensibility. Another took up the entanglements of race and disability in Jessie Redmon Fauset's *Plum Bun* using variants of *ability* and words like *handicap*. The final presentation of the semester synthesized many of these prior lines of inquiry in its analysis of E. L. James's *Fifty Shades of Grey*. Selecting *sentimentalism* and *intertextuality* as their organizing concepts, students asked, "Is Ana a sentimental character? How do the intertextual references inform sentimentality in this text?" In response, they aggregated literary allusions and tropes (e.g., the juxtaposition of James's protagonist with that of Thomas Hardy's *Tess of the d'Urbervilles* [1891], tropes of visceral and emotional experience). These findings, they argued, suggested that *Fifty Shades* "reflects the stagnation in representations of female sexuality as submissive."

Students' final papers for the course synthesized digital resources to further assess the vexed expectations of interwar female authorship and to reconstruct historical contexts that laid the groundwork for the underappreciation of many of these literary innovations. One student, for example, detailed the internal contradictions articulated by Black and white reviewers of *Plum Bun* in African American and Canadian periodicals. Other students looked at the rhetoric of flapper feminism in and in response to Anita Loos's *Gentlemen Prefer Blondes*; discussions of divorce in and in response to *Twilight Sleep*; and the complexities of racialized corporeality indexed and appraised by *Plum Bun*. Students also engaged archival materials in order to interrogate received understandings of interwar literary categories. Contemporaneous reviews, students noted, frequently criticize these novels for qualities that we now recognize as modernist hallmarks, even as these novels have been subsequently understood as other than modernist or simply forgotten. In other words, these novels have lost on both counts: they were negatively evaluated for their modernist quality at the time of their original publication and negatively evaluated thereafter for not being adequately modernist, or simply not evaluated at all. For example, one student looked at classical allusion and hard-boiled sensibility in Frances Newman's neglected *The Hard-Boiled Virgin*, using reviewers' "dismissals of the intentionally provocative title" to frame an inquiry into Newman's avant-garde aesthetic. Another student researched the opinions of Wharton's contemporaries on the anesthetic procedure used in childbirth that is referred to in Wharton's title, *Twilight Sleep*, and generated an evocative keyword—*blue babies*—using regional newspaper articles. In short, students' research demonstrated and expanded on our ongoing discussions about the dynamism of literary history.

Quantitative research confronts students with iterations of the challenges of deriving meaningful data from cultural discourse. It is easy enough to track the usage of popular phrases like *sex expression*, *flapper*, and *hard-boiled* using the Ngram Viewer. But how, my students asked, might they link these trends to how a given novel engages them? Could they parse cultural change and continuity based on linguistic patterns? A more technologically ambitious group wondered if they might track the recurrence of euphemism from *The Hard-Boiled Virgin* to *Fifty Shades of Grey*. If they could figure out how to generate a clean corpus to run through Voyant, they wondered, could they develop arguments about the consistencies of cultural taboo while remaining attentive to historical specificities of gender, race, and sexuality? Even in a graduate-level introductory digital humanities course in which students learned to program and construct data sets, Andrew Goldstone ultimately observed "a very healthy caution about drawing conclusions from the data" as "my students did not have all the methodological tools they needed to draw the conclusions they wanted" (5). My own students encountered versions of the challenges Goldstone describes in his students' projects, which largely "involved spotting trends over time" (5). The challenges Goldstone itemizes include trend interpretation ("how do we know a trend is real, and not a random fluctuation?"), explanations for "contrasts among subsets of their data," and "more possibilities for choosing data to collect in the first place" (5). These challenges lead Goldstone to recommend "teaching the problems of quantitative methodology as problems" (13). At the undergraduate level, we can teach the problems of conducting digital research as an opportunity to hone critical skills in media access and analysis.

Teaching digital research methods thus works to both literary-historical and present-day critical ends. Students enrich their understandings of

American interwar literature as they write papers, give presentations, and complete other coursework that locates women writers firmly in this and other lineages of letters. They also read across diverse media, synthesize distinct analytical modes, recognize conceptual through lines, and generate original knowledge. Through it all, they rethink their own interpretive premises as well as their received understandings of modern women writers. Such self-reflexive reading and writing practices are the premise of academic recovery work as well as the basis of media literacy. As they participate in these evolving traditions, students help make new the literary history of modern women writers.

Notes

1. I use the term *modern* to signal a diversity of aesthetic commitments articulated by the women writers considered in my course and in this essay. I introduce these vexations of literary categorization and modernist identification on the first day of class; throughout the term, we discuss the implications of categories like avant-garde, middlebrow, ethnic writing, proletarian fiction, and New Negro or Harlem Renaissance art. My course focuses on novels published by American authors between 1915 and 1935, for which reason the class and this essay also describe the primary texts as interwar works.

2. This essay focuses on an undergraduate seminar devoted to American women writers, but the assignments and activities it details can be modified to include other anglophone literature; they can also be adapted for use in larger lecture classes and for graduate coursework. *ProQuest*'s repositories include many periodicals outside the United States and, as my students consider, many modernist works were reviewed in transatlantic publications. See the companion website to this volume for the variety of material and platforms available (modwomen.mla.hcommons.org). In larger classes, group size could be scaled up without jeopardizing the value of group work for each individual. Graduate students could engage more substantially with the questions of current research methods and could also undertake more thoroughgoing archival work. For more on teaching digital methodology at the graduate level, see Goldstone's engaging meditation "Teaching Quantitative Methods."

3. In 1993 John Thurston offered a definition of "symptomatic criticism" as a reading practice that "uncovers the buried problematic of a text," typically by decoding its underlying ideology. Each of the authors noted in parentheses above discuss this practice of bad faith critical analysis en route to developing an alternative; Flaherty also offers a helpful overview of this critical conversation.

4. See Augst; Cordell et al.; Brown et al. See also the feature on Franco Moretti's *Distant Reading* in the May 2017 issue of *PMLA* and the 2018 digital humanities cluster in *Feminist Modernist Studies* edited by Amanda Golden and Cassandra Laity. Hammond offers an accessible gloss of these evolving theoretical and interpretive concerns and proposes a synthetic model of "digital and traditional scholarship" (i).

5. Matthew Jockers also addresses some foundational concerns of digital approaches to literary scholarship.

6. For more on the feminist potential of digital scholarship, see Posner and Klein's special issue of *Feminist Media Histories* and the *Feminist Modernist Studies* digital humanities cluster mentioned above. See also Foster in this volume.

7. These sites and other suggested resources are listed on the companion website to this volume.

8. Goldstone highlights the pervasiveness of this synthetic impulse in digital literary studies. Because "present-day literary scholarship is fundamentally uncertain about how to make a convincing scholarly argument using quantitative evidence," Goldstone observes, "it has a habit of postponing or avoiding methodological debate in the name of open-ended exploration or disciplinary pluralism" (2). The "most typical" version of this move "is the appeal to the complementarity of 'close' and 'distant' readings" (2).

9. An image of this graph may be found on this volume's companion website.

10. Clean texts, also called plain texts, feature accurate spellings and punctuation, page numbers and headers distinct from text, no HTML, and so forth. Current text-cleaning freeware and software options include AntFileConverter (converts Word and PDF to plain text), Calibre (provides a variety of functions for e-books), and TextCleanr (removes HTML and other digital traces).

Works Cited

Augst, Thomas, editor. *Archives.* Special issue of *American Literary History*, vol. 29, no. 2, Summer 2017.

Battershill, Claire, and Shawna Ross. *Using Digital Humanities in the Classroom: A Practical Introduction for Teachers, Lecturers, and Students.* Bloomsbury Academic, 2017.

Best, Stephen, and Sharon Marcus. "Surface Reading: An Introduction." *Representations*, vol. 108, no. 1, 2009, pp. 1–21.

Bewes, Timothy. "Reading with the Grain: A New World in Literary Criticism." *Differences*, vol. 21, no. 3, 2010, pp. 1–33.

[Bourne, Randolph.] "Diminuendo." *New Republic*, 11 Dec. 1915, pp. 153–55. *The Unz Review*, www.unz.com/print/NewRepublic-1915dec11-00153/.

Boynton, H[enry] W[alcott]. "Varieties of Realism." *Nation*, 14 Oct. 1915, pp. 461–62. *The Unz Review*, www.unz.com/print/Nation-1915oct14-00461a02/.

Brown, Vincent, et al. "Roundtable: Cartographies of the Archive: Mapping and the Digital Humanities." *Social Text*, vol. 33, no. 4, 2015, pp. 131–51.

Cather, Willa. *The Song of the Lark.* 1915. Penguin Books, 1999.

Cohen, Margaret. "Narratology in the Archive of Literature." *Representations*, vol. 108, no. 1, 2009, pp. 51–75.

Cooper, Frederick Taber. "Some Novels of the Month." *Bookman*, Nov. 1915, p. 323. *ProQuest*, search.proquest.com/docview/124750562/9F60A7CAF9074C97PQ/1?accountid=14512.

Cordell, Ryan, et al. "Forum: Digital Approaches to Periodical Studies." *American Periodicals*, vol. 26, no. 1, 2016, pp. 1–24.

Dillon, Elizabeth Maddock. "By Design: Remapping the Colonial Archive." *Social Text*, vol. 33, no. 4, 2015, pp. 142–47.

———. "*Translatio Studii* and the Poetics of the Digital Archive: Early American Literature, Caribbean Assemblages, and Freedom Dreams." *American Literary History*, vol. 29, no. 2, 2017, pp. 248–66.

Drouin, Jeffrey. "Modernist Journals Project: From Garage to Data-*Potage*." *American Periodicals*, vol. 26, no. 1, 2016, pp. 16–22.

Fauset, Jessie Redmon. *Plum Bun*. 1928. Library of America, 2017.

Flaherty, Matthew. "Post-critical Reading and the New Hegelianism." *Arcade: Literature, the Humanities, and the World*, 2015, arcade.stanford.edu/content/post-critical-reading-and-new-hegelianism.

Goldstone, Andrew. "Teaching Quantitative Methods: What Makes It Hard (in Literary Studies)." *Debates in the Digital Humanities 2018*, edited by Matthew K. Gold and Lauren F. Klein, U of Minnesota P, 2018, pp. 1–15.

Hammond, Adam. *Literature in the Digital Age: An Introduction*. Cambridge UP, 2016.

James, E. L. *Fifty Shades of Grey*. Vintage Books, 2012.

Jockers, Matthew. *Macroanalysis: Digital Methods and Literary History*. U of Illinois P, 2013.

Love, Heather. "Close but Not Deep: Literary Ethics and the Descriptive Turn." *New Literary History*, vol. 41, no. 2, 2010, pp. 371–91.

Newman, Frances. *The Hard-Boiled Virgin*. 1926. U of Georgia P, 1993.

Peattie, Elia W. "Miss Willa Cather's 'The Song of the Lark.'" *Chicago Daily Tribune*, 9 Oct. 1915, p. 10. *ProQuest*, search.proquest.com/docview/173956756/60C2A9E69CAF4124PQ/1?accountid=14512.

Posner, Miriam, and Lauren F. Klein, editors. *Data*. Special issue of *Feminist Media Histories*, vol. 3, no. 3, 2017.

Ramsay, Stephen. *Reading Machines: Toward an Algorithmic Criticism*. U of Illinois P, 2011.

Rusert, Britt. "New World: The Impact of Digitization on the Study of Slavery." *American Literary History*, vol. 29, no. 2, 2017, pp. 267–86.

Sedgwick, Eve Kosofsky. *Touching Feeling: Affect, Pedagogy, Performativity*. Duke UP, 2003.

Thurston, John. "Symptomatic Criticism." *Encyclopedia of Contemporary Literary Theory: Approaches, Scholars, Terms*, edited by Irena R. Makaryk, U of Toronto P, 1993, p. 638.

Wernimont, Jacqueline. "Whence Feminism? Assessing Feminist Interventions in Digital Literary Archives." *Digital Humanities Quarterly*, vol. 7, no. 1, 2013, pp. 1–23.

Wharton, Edith. *Twilight Sleep*. 1927. Scribner, 1997.

Louise Kane

Theorizing and Teaching Women's Periodical Networks through Digital Humanities

In May 1933 Marianne Moore wrote to Bryher (the pen name of Annie Winifred Ellerman). After meeting in 1920, the pair had become close correspondents, and Moore's letter expressed gratitude for the "unmatched friendship" Bryher demonstrated in supporting Moore through a period of financial difficulty (Letter to Bryher [16 May]). Wanting to alleviate Moore's problems, but eager not to offend her by offering money outright, Bryher had asked Moore to contribute a piece to *Close Up*, the film magazine Bryher had founded with Kenneth Macpherson in 1927. Moore was "delighted to try an article . . . I doubt that there is anyone living who is more enthusiastic about movies than I am" (Letter to Bryher [16 May]). After accepting Moore's piece, Bryher "stunned" Moore by sending a check for fifteen dollars, an amount usually reserved for the magazine's long-term contributors (Letter to Bryher [14 June]). While Moore was touched by Bryher's kindness, it was the invitation to join the network of writers, artists, and filmmakers publishing in *Close Up* that impressed her most: "How struck I immediately was," she wrote, "by this whole group of yours" (Letter to Bryher [15 May]). Moore's participation in this network did not end there. When Bryher bought *Life and Letters* in April 1935 (she renamed it *Life and Letters To-Day* to reflect the magazine's new beginning), Moore was quickly signed up as a regular contributor.

This unique form of female networking and interaction in the early twentieth century is this essay's concern. As materialist criticism has highlighted, "Anglo-American modernism was unusual in the degree to which its principal protagonists interacted with one another through shared institutional structures" (Rainey 6). Several studies have explored how many of these interactions and institutions—from the groups of writers themselves to editors, publishers, printers, and distributors—were women-centered. Bryher and Moore's correspondence and their shared involvement with *Close Up* exemplify the network of modernist women writers that Gillian Hanscombe and Virginia L. Smyers describe: "They all seemed to write to each other, or about each other. They introduced one to the other. . . . They were all either writing, or publishing what the others were writing, because they believed in each other's work" (xvii). Susan Stanford Friedman has posited Bryher and H.D. as the key figures in this female network, explaining how, by the mid-1930s when *Life and Letters To-Day* first appeared, their initial "circle" of friends—all of whom were given affectionate noms de plume—had evolved into a "larger web of entanglements and negotiation" (xl).

But fewer scholars have examined Bryher's cultivation of these networks through her periodicals. Bonnie Kime Scott notes that Bryher and H.D. were part of "a hidden network of women for whom periodical and book publishing became a female profession" (xxxiv). Lucy Delap and Maria DiCenzo utilize the "concerns of feminist media history" as a framework for exploring the gendered networks of collaboration, dissent, and friendship that underpinned feminist periodicals like *The Freewoman* and *The Englishwoman* (58). Limited attention has been given to Bryher's periodicals. James Donald and colleagues note that "a strong contingent of female literary modernists" who "began to write on cinema" were able to emerge through *Close Up* (7). Renata Morresi has identified *Life and Letters To-Day* as a clear "example" of a modernist periodical that embodies "women's hidden cultural networks" (377).

This essay reasserts the importance of Bryher's magazine networks, arguing that periodicals are network-rich, dialogic primary texts that can also act as pedagogical aids for the teaching of modernist women writers. The little magazine is, after all, a form of media for which so many women writers wrote, but for which surprisingly few are remembered.

The simultaneous emergence of new modernist studies, together with digital humanities (especially its data-visualization component) and periodical studies, has placed new emphasis on periodicals and their networks.[1] Yet despite recent attempts to theorize the periodical, we still do not really know how to study and teach these networks, or the magazines they defined.[2] This essay details an easily adaptable assignment that draws on data visualization and network analysis to offer instructors and students at undergraduate and graduate levels a point of entry into the teaching and study of modernist periodicals.

The aim of the assignment is to expose literary and cultural networks of women writers and the periodicals in which they published. In doing so, the assignment revises the language of concealment implicit in oft repeated definitions of women modernist networks as hidden or obscured, offering students and instructors a methodology through which they can begin to excavate the writerly communities that lie buried within the complex, heterogeneous, and generically murky text that is the little magazine. As Robert Scholes and Clifford Wulfman have cautioned, no method for the study of periodicals constitutes "the only method or pattern," offering instead "a place to start" (144). The assignment below is proposed in the same spirit: it is offered as neither the best way to study periodical networks nor the most sophisticated, but it presents a way of introducing students to the periodical as an autonomous textual object. It could be used as a partial mode of assessment for any course exploring modernist texts, or an independent study option for a senior special topics course.

Interpreting and Teaching the Network

Before the assignment is outlined, it is important to explain the two key ideas that underpin it. The first is data visualization. The second is Sean Latham's identification of a magazine's table of contents as a means of sorting a magazine's "data" (32). Applying data visualization—the representation of data through visual aids such as maps, charts, and graphs—to periodicals is a relatively recent practice. Since Franco Moretti used "graphs, maps and trees" to study literary texts (67), several projects have applied data visualization to periodical studies. The *Modernist Journals Project Lab* is perhaps the best-known example: the site uses graphs and charts to visualize contributors, content, and other variables such as periodicity. Data visualization asks us to conceive of periodicals as databases, as Latham suggests. Outlining the editorial problems involved in digitizing magazines, he argues that "preparing a digital text means learning how to think about an object's discrete parts . . . and how those parts might then be assembled for end users. . . . The initial problem is thus how to identify the basic units of a magazine" (53). We can extend this argument to the teaching of magazines.[3] Identifying the "basic units" of a modernist magazine is the "initial problem" we encounter. Students' first impressions of periodicals are often defined by confusion: What is the magazine's format? Where are its main texts? Who are its contributors? How do the texts fit with the advertisements? How do the texts and their authors connect to each other? For Latham, viewing the magazine's table of contents as a program that allows readers to interpret the database of the little magazine is "one way to proceed" (53): "The table of contents . . . emphasizes this database-like quality of the magazine, acting essentially as a parser, or a paper-based program for sorting the data" (38).

The assignment below applies the above approaches. Four steps are involved: the selection of magazines for study (as noted above, there are many possibilities depending on one's objectives); the collection and recording of data from table of contents pages into an Excel file; the conversion of this raw data into a data visualization (in this case the "radar diagram" option found under Excel's "Insert Graph" function); and, finally, the interpretation and analysis of these visualizations and the periodical networks they map.

It is necessary to provide some contextual information about the two magazines—*Close Up* and *Life and Letters To-Day*—that this sample version of the assignment uses. Established to promote "the film for the film's sake" (Macpherson 6), *Close Up* was the first English-language magazine focused on film criticism. Backed financially by Bryher, the monthly publication first appeared in July 1927 and became renowned for its international contributors, including the Soviet filmmaker Sergei Eisenstein, the Japanese poet Yone Noguchi, and Andor Kraszna-Krausz, a Hungarian photographer and founder of the Focal Press, a leading photographic publishing company. Under its editor, Kenneth Macpherson, who was aided unofficially by Bryher, many women writers published in *Close Up*, including H.D., Moore, Dorothy Richardson, Gertrude Stein, and Mary Butts.

After *Close Up* folded in July 1933, Bryher bought the ailing monthly *Life and Letters* in April 1935, appointing Robert Herring and Dorothea "Petrie" Townshend as editor and assistant editor. Despite public assurances that they wanted "to preserve" existing contributors and readers (Herring, Editorial 1), Bryher and Herring agreed privately that they liked "the shape and format" of the magazine, "but not the contributors" (Herring, Letter to Bryher [15 Apr.]). Keen to feminize the magazine's contributory network, Bryher wrote to Herring demanding the inclusion of more women writers, prompting confusion on his part: "I wonder why you and H. D. try to make one 'sex-conscious.' I am not at all interested in who writes the stuff as long as it is what one thinks should be written" (Letter to Bryher [23 Apr.]). Bryher achieved her aims: when the first issue of *Life and Letters To-Day* appeared as a quarterly in September 1935, its newly experimental mix of prose, poetry, film, and music reviews, and its replacement of original contributors like Cecil Day Lewis and St. John Ervine with *Close Up* writers—H.D., Richardson, Moore, Lotte Reiniger, Barbara Low, and Alice Modern—set it apart as a distinctly modernist, women-influenced magazine. After incorporating several other periodicals, *Life and Letters To-Day* ceased publication in 1950.

The Assignment

Students begin by selecting a single magazine, or a set of magazines. This magazine selection can be made synchronically (e.g., all issues of *The Egoist* published in 1914) or diachronically (e.g., a selection of issues of *The Egoist* and linked magazines like *The New Freewoman*). Here, I have selected the first two issues of *Close Up* and *Life and Letters To-Day*, both of which can be found in *Internet Archives*'s fully searchable *Close Up* resource (archive.org/details/closeup02macp). As J. Stephen Murphy recognizes, the sheer amount of data available in magazines is both "the blessing and the curse of periodical studies," and while "the potential for revelation is great," students and instructors alike risk "getting completely lost in the archive or . . . being too intimidated to even enter" (vi). It is therefore important that students not overload themselves with material, so selection criteria are key.

The next stage requires students to record the data of the magazines' tables of contents as an Excel table. Table 1 records data from the table of contents pages of the first two issues of *Close Up*, with columns for contributor name and genre of publication (article or essay, poetry, short story, review, artwork or photography). In the columns indicating the genre of publication, the number of contributions for each genre are inserted.

At this stage students are able to conduct basic research on contributors. For example, cursory research will reveal that Macpherson and Bryher were in a marriage of convenience when *Close Up* began, and that the

Table 1. *Close Up*, July 1927 and August 1927, contributions by author and genre

Contributor	Article or Essay	Poetry	Short Story	Review	Artwork or Photography
Kenneth Macpherson	2	0	0	0	0
Bryher	2	0	0	0	0
H.D.	2	1	0	0	0
Dorothy Richardson	2	0	0	0	0
Robert Herring	0	0	0	1	0
Jean Prévost	2	0	0	0	0
E. L. Black	1	0	0	0	0
Oswell Blakeston	1	0	0	0	0
Gertrude Stein	0	0	1	0	0
Marianne Moore	0	0	0	1	0
E. Eliott	1	0	0	0	0
René Crevel	1	0	0	0	0
M. de L. Walch	0	1	0	0	0
Man Ray	0	0	0	0	1

pair lived with H.D. in an unusual "domestic *ménage à trois*" (Walton 230). A Google search shows that contributors like Richardson and Stein were long-term correspondents of both Bryher and H.D. Adding the second dataset from the first two issues of *Life and Letters To-Day* shows how many of *Close Up*'s contributors—both women and men—published in *Life and Letters To-Day.* We see how this act of reading "magazines as miscellany, as database, or as network" serves to "emphasize patterns of repetition, interlocking systems of mediation" (Hammill et al., "Introduction" iv), exposing the networks within and among periodicals in a way that other reading methods may not.

The third step is creating visualizations. While large-scale projects like the *Modernist Journals Project Lab* use data-visualization software like Gephi or Tableau to map the types of data seen above, the average student may feel more apprehensive than encouraged when it comes to using these complex tools. Excel's "Insert Graph" function offers an accessible alternative: with just one click, students can convert the data seen in table 1 into graphs. Here, the data is converted into radar diagrams (figs. 1 and 2), the genres of contributions represented by varying line styles.

The final part of the assignment involves the interpretation of this data. Students can (and need to) supplement the quantitative data of the

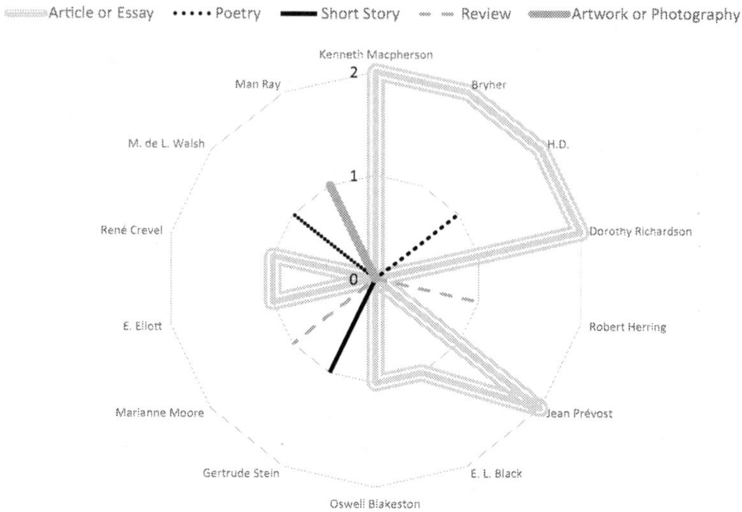

Figure 1. Radar diagram showing contributors to the first two issues of *Close Up* (July and Aug. 1927), by genre and number of contributions.

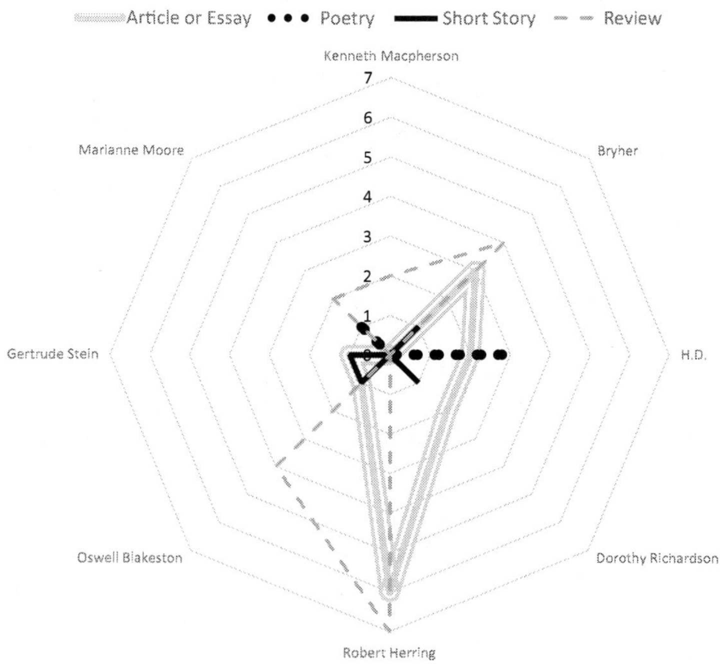

Figure 2. Radar diagram showing contributors to the first two issues of *Close Up* who also published in the first two issues of *Life and Letters To-Day* (Sept. and Dec. 1935), by genre and number of contributions.

diagrams with qualitative interpretations and analyses of their findings. For example, a student looking at the diagrams in figures 1 and 2 may want to point out that every woman contributor to *Close Up*'s first issues also published in the first two issues of *Life and Letters To-Day*. Students could also use the diagrams as a basis for more in-depth study and close readings of a specific writer's contributions. A fascinating potential reading suggested by the radar diagrams is a comparison of H.D.'s poetic contributions to both magazines. How, for instance, does H.D.'s "Projector," published in *Close Up*'s July 1927 issue, anticipate "The Dancer" and "The Poet," published in the September and December 1935 issues of *Life and Letters To-Day*? Students could combine two or more diagrams, or even progress to using Orange or Ucinet software for more extensive visualizations. They could develop approaches from different disciplinary angles: a semantic study of words repeated throughout women's contributions to both periodicals or a project expanding the initial dataset through the inclusion of another magazine. For instance, a student could add *The Egoist* to the original dataset to see how H.D.'s earlier imagist poetics evolves in later periodicals of the 1930s. Students could present their findings as a longer essay, or, alternatively, as an in-class presentation or a video submission.

Adapting the Assignment

While the assignment outlined above takes *Close Up* and *Life and Letters To-Day* as case studies, instructors could use any periodical(s). One possibility would be to adapt the assignment to a set of magazines whose gender network noticeably evolved. The most obvious example of this is the arc of Dora Marsden's *Freewoman* (1911–12) into *The New Freewoman* (1913) and later *The Egoist* (1914–19), a magazine effectively dominated by Ezra Pound. Students could use the assignment to examine whether the contributor network to Marsden's short-lived magazine (subtitled "The New Feminist Review") was, in fact, any more female, feminized, or feminist than that of *The Egoist*, especially in the light of the public letter in the latter's first issue, in which Pound, Allen Upward, Huntly Carter, Richard Aldington, and Reginald Wright Kaufmann declared themselves the "men of letters" behind the journal's new direction ("Views and Comments" 244).

Another adaptation would ask students to produce for their final assignment a character profile of a magazine complete with more extensive graphs generated from Excel data. (Excel offers a variety of different graph options, and students can drill down into certain variables.) These graphs could provide information on contributor demographics (gender, average age, geographic location) together with records of contributor frequency, average word length of contribution, and a list of two to three other magazines in which the contributor also appears. This data could be used to support or challenge key critical ideas about a given magazine—for example, the perceived internationalism of John Middleton Murry's *Athenaeum* or the question of Katherine Mansfield's editorship of *Rhythm* (to what degree Mansfield, rather than Murry, directed the magazine's increased engagements with and promotion of interdisciplinary modernisms). Students could then use the magazine character profile to produce a report summarizing key findings or a comparative essay that explores modernist tendencies in two different magazines, such as *Athenaeum* and *Rhythm*.

Expanding the Network

The above assignment and its various iterations offer ways of promoting engagement with networks of modernist women writers that were well represented but not immediately visible in modernist periodicals. Aside from its use in the classroom, the project has potential for wider scholarship. In The Future of Modernist Periodical Studies, the seminar I organized during the 2017 Modernist Studies Association Conference, Clifford Wulfman urged the necessity of a publicly accessible magazine database. Researchers, Wulfman argued, need to collaborate in the production of "a database of general 'descriptive metadata'" drawn from "tables of contents for issues in a format that can (relatively) easily be produced by scholars and students, but that is sophisticated enough for powerful machine use" (4). The assignment outlined above could form the start of a project like this, in which students and research assistants input basic metadata such as contributor name, contribution title, periodical title, and year of publication into a simple, Web-hosted, publicly visible form. The form would be optimized for CSV (comma-separated values), allowing website moderators to convert the data into large-scale visualizations charting the interconnected periodical contributions of a vast corpus of modernist writers. As the project develops, instructors, scholars, and independent researchers, together with historians and librarians, could make contributions, resulting in the continued alteration and expansion of these visualizations as they accrue new data.

This multiauthored repository would mimic the original collaborative mode of production of the modernist periodical, the contributions forming a networked online database. Researchers could use this database to conduct further study of largely invisible networks of modernist women writers. They could explore the publishing practices and contributions of a wide range of underrepresented or marginalized writers whose periodical contributions are hard to track down, a project that would illuminate some hitherto unseen connections among diverse and geographically disparate writers. An especially fruitful possibility would be a study comparing women's networks present in anglophone modernist periodicals with women's networks in magazines published in the Caribbean or Latin America.

For example, a quick scan of the table of contents pages of *Bim*[4]—the Barbados-based little magazine established by Frank Collymore in December 1942—highlights a network of forgotten Caribbean women writers who were prominent contributors to the magazine in its formative years, such as Joyce Gittens, Anna Sealy, and Margaret Saint. It would be intriguing to compare this female network as it emerged in the early 1940s to the one we have traced in *Life and Letters To-Day.* Eric Bulson has argued that in the 1930s and 1940s "all of the qualities associated with the littleness of modernist magazines in the West were getting modified to accommodate the development of modern Anglophone literature in the Caribbean" (196). However, the poetic experiments Gittens and Saint conducted in *Bim* show that it was not so much the case that Caribbean women writers were modifying qualities of little American or British magazines, but that they were producing in the pages of *Bim* their own anglophone Caribbean modernisms, especially in terms of poetic innovation, that were not dissimilar to the forms of modernist experimentation that women writers like H.D., Bryher, and Moore developed in *Life and Letters To-Day* in the later 1940s.

A magazine database has the potential to illuminate critically overlooked connections between geographically disparate networks of women writers, forcing us to reconsider how we periodize and geolocate modernism. Additionally, a more collaborative approach to the study of periodicals—whether in the form of a potential database or digital humanities-based student assignments like the one described here—brings opportunities to incorporate more undergraduate research into courses and classrooms. The collaborative nature of a magazine database naturally lends itself to group projects, where an assignment calling for use of the database, or contributions to it, could be integrated into introductory courses as a means of stimulating active, practice-based research skills. Even without the database, students could complete the exercise outlined above as part of introductory-level global literature or digital humanities courses, using online print runs of magazines to conduct primary research, which they could then incorporate into an extended annotated bibliography assignment, a group research essay, or a presentation.

The possibility of posing student assignments like the one outlined here evidences the vast and fluid evolution of modernist studies and its subdisciplines. The "temporal expansion" resulting from the new modernist studies has enabled modernist scholarship to encompass "artifacts from the middle of the nineteenth century and the years after the middle of the twentieth," resulting in an "extremely fruitful rethinking of relations among the key terms *modernism*, *modernization*, and *modernity*" (Mao and Walkowitz 738). This teaching strategy evinces this "temporal expansion": if we accept that women writers were still publishing modernist works in *Life and Letters To-Day*, which last appeared in 1950, we must reconsider our periodization of modernism. Along with posing periodization questions, periodicals offer possibilities for reconfiguring our understanding of the vast networks of women writers who constructed these modernisms. Letters like the one Moore wrote to Bryher offer representations of modernism's social networks, but magazines offer epistemological windows into the precise ways these social networks feed textual innovation. Looking through these windows allows us to see the densely linked, vastly productive, and defiantly woman-centered networks of modernist textual production and transmission that, like the magazines themselves, demand further attention.

Notes

1. Sean Latham and Robert Scholes's influential assertion that the simultaneous "cultural turn" and "development of digital archives" contributed to the rise of modern periodical studies builds on earlier work by Victorianists (517), who have long recognized the "special value of the periodical press" and the need to theorize periodicals (Beetham 20).

2. A special issue of the *Journal of Modern Periodical Studies* titled *Magazines and/as Media*, edited by Faye Hammill and colleagues, is an example of this theorization of periodicals, shaped in part by the "What Is a Journal? Toward a Theory of Periodicals Studies" roundtable held at the Modern Language Association's Annual Convention in Boston in 2013.

3. For more on the teaching of magazines, see the essay by Gordon and Southworth in this volume.

4. See the University of Florida's online *Index to Bim*, the link to which is available, along with other resources mentioned, on the companion website to this volume (modwomen.mla.hcommons.org).

Works Cited

Beetham, Margaret. "Towards a Theory of the Periodical as a Publishing Genre." *Investigating Victorian Journalism*, edited by Laurel Brake et al., Palgrave Macmillan, 1990, pp. 19–32.

Bulson, Eric. *Little Magazine, World Form*. Columbia UP, 2017.

Delap, Lucy, and Maria DiCenzo. *Feminist Media History: Suffrage, Periodicals, and the Public Sphere*. Palgrave Macmillan, 2011.

Donald, James, et al., editors. *Close Up, 1927–33: Cinema and Modernism*. Princeton UP, 1998.

Friedman, Susan Stanford. "Editorial Statement." *Analyzing Freud: Letters of H.D., Bryher, and Their Circle*, edited by Friedman, New Directions Publishing, 2002, pp. xxxix–xliv.

Hammill, Faye, et al. "Introduction: Magazines and/as Media: Periodical Studies and the Question of Disciplinarity." Hammill et al., *Magazines*, pp. iii–xiii.

Hammill, Faye, et al., editors. *Magazines and/as Media: Periodical Studies and the Question of Disciplinarity*. Special issue of *Journal of Modern Periodical Studies*, vol. 6, no. 2, 2015.

Hanscombe, Gillian, and Virginia L. Smyers. *Writing for Their Lives: The Modernist Women, 1910–1940*. Women's Press, 1987.

Herring, Robert. Editorial. *Life and Letters To-Day*, vol. 13, no. 1, 1935, pp. 1–2.

———. Letter to Bryher. 15 Apr. 1935. Bryher Papers, box 19, folder 712. General Collection, Beinecke Rare Book and Manuscript Library, Yale University.

———. Letter to Bryher. 23 Apr. 1935. Bryher Papers, box 19, folder 712. General Collection, Beinecke Rare Book and Manuscript Library, Yale University.

Latham, Sean. "Unpacking My Digital Library: Programs, Modernisms, Magazines." *Making Canada New: Editing, Modernism, and New Media*, edited by Dean Irvine et al., U of Toronto P, 2017, pp. 31–61.

Latham, Sean, and Robert Scholes. "The Rise of Periodical Studies." *PMLA*, vol. 121, no. 2, Mar. 2006, pp. 517–31.

Macpherson, Kenneth. "As Is." *Close Up*, vol. 1, no. 1, 1927, pp. 5–15.

Mao, Douglas, and Rebecca L. Walkowitz. "The New Modernist Studies." *PMLA*, vol. 123, no. 3, May 2008, pp. 737–48.

Moore, Marianne. Letter to Bryher. 15 May 1933. Bryher Papers, box 38, folder 1362. General Collection, Beinecke Rare Book and Manuscript Library, Yale University.

———. Letter to Bryher. 16 May 1933. Bryher Papers, box 38, folder 1362. General Collection, Beinecke Rare Book and Manuscript Library, Yale University.

———. Letter to Bryher. 14 June 1933. Bryher Papers, box 38, folder 1362. General Collection, Beinecke Rare Book and Manuscript Library, Yale University.

Moretti, Franco. "Graphs, Maps, Trees: Abstract Models for Literary History—1." *New Left Review*, vol. 24, Nov.-Dec. 2003, pp. 67–94.

Morresi, Renata. "Two Examples of Women's Hidden Cultural (Net)work: Nancy Cunard's Onion and *Life and Letters To-Day*." *Networking Women: Subjects, Places, Links: Europe-America: Towards a Rewriting of Cultural History, 1890–1939*, edited by Marina Camboni, Edizioni di Storia e Letteratura, 2004, pp. 377–86.

Murphy, J. Stephen. "Introduction: Visualizing Periodical Networks." *Journal of Modern Periodical Studies*, vol. 5, no. 1, 2014, pp. iii–xv.

Rainey, Lawrence S. *Institutions of Modernism: Literary Elites and Public Culture*. Yale UP, 1998.

Scholes, Robert, and Clifford Wulfman. *Modernism in the Magazines: An Introduction*. Yale UP, 2010.

Scott, Bonnie Kime. *The Women of 1928*. Indiana UP, 1995. Vol. 1 of *Refiguring Modernism*.

"Views and Comments." *The Egoist*, vol. 1, no. 13, 1914, pp. 244–46. *Modernist Journals Project*, modjourn.org/issue/bdr521013/.

Walton, Jean. *Fair Sex, Savage Dreams: Race, Psychoanalysis, Sexual Difference*. Duke UP, 2001.

Wulfman, Clifford. "The Rise and Fall of Modern Periodical Studies." Unpublished typescript.

J. Ashley Foster

Activism and Feminist Digital Pedagogy: Virginia Woolf, Muriel Rukeyser, and the Spanish Civil War

When Virginia Woolf calls for the destruction of universities and a reformation of the college system along the lines of "an experimental college, an adventurous college," theorizing "the new college, the poor college" (*Three Guineas* 43), she challenges those in classrooms everywhere to consider how the models of pedagogy we employ shape social and cultural practices and institutions.[1] For Woolf, war and peace are habits that are taught. Indeed, *Three Guineas* exposes how institutions of higher education are invested in reinforcing a capitalist, patriarchal system, one that the progressive women's college Woolf imagines would disrupt. One of the reasons to teach modernist women writers is to help students engage theories of peace, equality, and social justice, and to explore how these theories contribute to activist discourses seeking more sustainable, egalitarian models for society. The question that follows for a socially concerned teacher is how to share the vision of modernist women writers in a way that encourages students to critically and reflectively grapple with the revolutionary ideals these writers put forth.

This essay draws on my experiences teaching a first-year writing seminar, Peace Testimonies in Literature and Art, at a small liberal arts college, outlining in particular the creation of a digital humanities and special collections exhibition based on student work entitled *Testimonies in Art and Action: Igniting Pacifism in the Face of Total War.* I describe how feminist digital pedagogical techniques were employed and offer an approach that allows students to study the works of Woolf and Muriel Rukeyser in conversation with those by their contemporaries Langston Hughes and Pablo Picasso, all of whom can be read as part of an activist network surrounding the Spanish Civil War. I demonstrate that a feminist digital pedagogy is suited to teach students about modernism, women's writing, and the Spanish Civil War. I begin by showing how teaching Spanish Civil War materials as modernist texts is in itself a project of historical recovery that calls for a feminist digital pedagogical approach. I then describe the student work that led to the launch of the standing and digital exhibition *Testimonies in Art and Action*, and I conclude by considering how such work unleashes the radical potential of the classroom and contributes to the ongoing call in digital humanities for conceptualizing digital pedagogy as a form of scholarship.

Lost Voices of the Spanish Civil War

As Valentine Cunningham, Noël Valis, and Helen Graham have each discussed, the Spanish Civil War (1936–39) occupies a nostalgic, almost mythological space in the social imaginary of literary production and cultural discourses relating to the 1930s. Global public intellectuals saw the conflict in Spain as a fight of good against evil and as an opportunity to quash the Fascist movement. Thousands of foreign volunteers from around the world joined the International Brigades to fight Fascism in Spain. The American authors Hughes and Rukeyser traveled to Spain and wrote eyewitness journalistic and poetic accounts. Picasso created the iconic *Guernica*, marking the travesty of the bombing of the eponymous town, for display at the 1937 World's Fair in Paris, and Woolf responded with *Three Guineas.* Meanwhile, Quakers organized an extensive relief effort that fed, clothed, and housed a generation of Spaniards. Because passions ran so high and so many were polarized, the dominant historical narrative is that Europe militarized and a growing peace movement collapsed. However, teaching *Three Guineas*, *Guernica*, the relief work in Spain, and Hughes's and Rukeyser's journalism and poetry shows that many approached the ethical issues prompted by the slaughter of civilians in Spain in a variety of highly nuanced ways.

Though the Spanish Civil War became an international affair—with people all over the world responding with aid, support, money, food, and at times arms—it is widely forgotten in history classes taught in the United States today. Not only has it been written out of curricula, it has also been relegated to the periphery of modernist studies, though the work of scholars such as Gayle Rogers and Jessica Berman has rendered its significance more visible. To teach the Spanish Civil War as integral to modernist literature is to engage in a historical recovery project on several registers. If the work of those who participated in the public debates of the 1930s is politically neutralized or lost, then Spanish Civil War pacifism and humanitarian activism has been doubly lost—written not only out of the textbooks but also out of the specialist monographs and historical texts of Spanish Civil War studies.

To invite students to consider the multiplicity of discourses that flourished during the Spanish Civil War is to illuminate a moment in history where public intellectuals had genuine hope for a reformation of social structures and formulated revolutionary concepts around peace, equality, and freedom. For example, though Hughes and Rukeyser supported the Second Spanish Republic's military efforts against Fascism and therefore cannot be considered absolutist pacifists, their writings on Spain evoke visions of peace that rely on a social justice mission, complicating and adding to an understanding of pacifist activism. Drawing on the work of Jane Marcus in *Art and Anger*, Amanda Golden argues that if feminist pedagogy "means teaching students to engage the complexity of literary history," then "a feminist digital pedagogy prepares them to navigate the past and present, developing control over changing modes of communication while assessing and designing new resources" (42). It is this complexity and navigation of past and present that we must keep in mind as we develop methods and strategies for our classrooms.

Feminist digital pedagogy is the combination of feminist and digital pedagogical strategies. What distinguishes digital pedagogy from the use of technology in the classroom is embeddedness, critical reflexivity, and a transformation of the types of arguments and assignments one can design; in other words, digital pedagogy generates new epistemologies. Whereas one can use technology as a supplement in the classroom, digital pedagogy transforms the type of work, and therefore the type of research questions, one can pursue.[2] Digital pedagogy is ensconced in the digital humanities and activates digital humanities tools to open new channels for student thinking and research. A feminist digital pedagogy uses these tools to engage collaborative practices that decenter the authoritative structure of the classroom, distributing power throughout the learning community while moving away from the patriarchal hierarchy of the authoritative "I" that Woolf combats so vehemently in *A Room of One's Own*.[3]

As Jacqueline Wernimont points out, such democratizing considerations might be part of many liberatory pedagogical practices. Jesse Stommel argues along similar lines, contending that a deconstruction of authoritative hierarchy is inherent in digital pedagogy practices. Yet Wernimont cautions us against the "growing invisibility" of feminism, whose scholarship has been "systematically subsumed under some other—any other—banner. Not only does this make the work of scholarly feminism invisible . . . it also creates a vision of 21st-century feminism as what is left over" (1). A feminist digital pedagogy maintains its feminist roots and seeks to position women and gender noncomforming persons as active contributors to public, cultural, artistic, and literary discourses, and looks to recover voices relegated to the margins of society. This type of pedagogy provides one of many possible answers to Marcus's question, "How can feminist criticism construct the *other plot* by reading the fictions of history and history in fictions differently?" ("Asylums" 134). In what follows, I will show how students used digital humanities tools to illuminate that this "*other plot*"—a reference taken from Woolf's *Between the Acts*—is one of peace. Students' work on the *Testimonies in Art and Action* website and exhibition illuminates the relation between women and peace, modernism and peace, and women and their male contemporaries.[4]

Reading the Other Plot

The digital pedagogy enacted in the construction of *Testimonies in Art and Action* is feminist in several respects: the emphasis on collaborative work; the use of digital tools to situate women writers, in this case Woolf and Rukeyser, as key contributors to the public debate on Spain; the use of archival and special collections material to recover the often silenced voices of peace activists and humanitarian relief workers; and the blurring of boundaries between student and scholar.[5] This exhibition was an extensive undertaking that stood for two and a half months in Magill Library's Sharpless Gallery at Haverford College. It was the product of the collaborative efforts of many individuals, including myself, the students in four sections of the Peace Testimonies course, the coordinator of digital scholarship Laurie Allen, the curator of rare books and manuscripts and head of Quaker and special collections Sarah Horowitz, and library staff members and student workers. It featured three installations over nine months, including three pop-up exhibitions, student presentations of projects, and a roundtable panel discussion with modernists from the field. I collaborated with Allen to build a series of assignments on Neatline, a plug-in for the exhibition platform Omeka. Although Neatline was originally designed for mapping, one can use any image, including a page of a text, as a base layer. Students could then digitally annotate that base layer, creating essays in the form of pop-ups and embedding images as well as hyperlinks to the other student projects. Using this tool allowed students to read archival materials alongside the assigned texts. Students made connections among the units in the class, their own work, and that of their peers, hyperlinking recurrent themes within and between texts. The project eventually became an intricate scholarly web that traced and illuminated main themes of Spanish Civil War pacifist activity.

Students' digital annotations started with a base image of the primary text where they highlighted the portions of a very small section of what they wanted to analyze. They then annotated those sections with historical and archival context, drawing connections among the various ancillary materials and the finished product. For example, students studied the stages of the making of *Guernica* in order to trace the evolution of the painting; considered Woolf's Three Guineas *Reading Notebooks*, housed online, which contain newspaper clippings that Woolf implicitly or explicitly references in *Three Guineas*; and consulted the journalism and poetry written in Spain by Hughes and Rukeyser.[6] Students then wrote 250-word analyses on the highlighted portions of the base image and uploaded these to Neatline.

Reading the archival materials intertextually alongside the primary texts, students were able to highlight how pacifist critique intersects with other social justice movements, including feminism. For example, Alexandra Corcoran traced newspaper clippings in the reading notebooks to *Three Guineas*'s discussion of dress in order to highlight how patriarchal hierarchies and "stratification" lead to war:

> One article Woolf saved was entitled "City Pageantry in Sunshine"; the clipping details the swearing-in ceremony of a new, male mayor of London. Indeed, it is this "pageantry" that seems to vex Woolf. Drawing on the language of the article, she writes, "They [the Outsiders] will dispense with the . . . official pageantry in which only one sex takes an active part" (*Three* 134). Here, Woolf makes clear that pomp and dress

> are essential to the ascriptive *hierarchy* of pre-war Britain. . . . Hence, dress . . . helps to create this stratification, making it a real and legitimate cause of war.

Here, Corcoran brings together a reading of Woolf's archive and *Three Guineas* to illuminate that the "language of the article," which celebrates the type of practices that lead to militarism, appears in *Three Guineas* as a foundational foil for the imaginary "Outsiders' Society" (*Three Guineas* 126), women whose remit it is to create peace: they will "dispense" with the "official pageantry," a statement that marks how Woolf's pacifism is embedded in a feminism that rejects hierarchal traditions.

Another student, Teruha Stergios, continued the discussion of feminism and pacifism in her consideration of Woolf's argument that because women have been relegated to the outside of society, they have a special ability to help prevent war. Stergios writes:

> Throughout *Three Guineas*, Woolf shows that . . . lack of individuality exists in England's patriarchal and aggressively hierarchical society. She targets this exact consequence of war and argues that women, who have been denied entrance to this system, can infuse society with a new "intellectual liberty." She believes that the position women have been oppressed into can be used positively, because they are not part of the patriarchy, which promotes blind obedience.

This statement shows how students worked through women's contributions in their annotations, and how they explored the relation between patriarchal inequality and war.

Students engaged in the feminist recovery of pacifist voices through materials from special collections. Using primary documents, they also considered the refugee and civilian aid network that organized in response to the Spanish Civil War. For the physical exhibition, each student chose one item that would be exhibited and wrote the exhibition label for that item. This allowed students to focus on common tropes used by activist and artistic networks and within the literature produced by Woolf and Rukeyser. In so doing, students demonstrated their engagement in a larger public conversation. One student, Tomás Alejandro Manuel Ebro Matias, connected the iconic, threatening imagery of a bomber airplane in the special collections item *They Still Draw Pictures!*—a fundraising booklet produced by the American Friends Service Committee—to Rukeyser's "Mediterranean." In a caption explaining a child's terrifying drawing of a plane, Matias explained, "Rukeyser's poem and the drawing above demonstrate that civilians are at the mercy of the military plane, the choice whether to be bombed or not is not theirs to make. This paints a portrayal of contemporary war as the greatest atrocity, the need then, is to give people the right of choice back." When students develop a sense of the relations among the archival documents, ephemera, and the literature of the time, they realize that Rukeyser and Woolf were actively engaged in discourses of war and peace and that they were responding to their present moment, which helps students illuminate and create connections among politics, art, culture, literature, and history.

The hyperlinks joining the annotations on the *Testimonies in Art and Action* website facilitate conceptual connections among Hughes, Rukeyser, Picasso, and Woolf, and situate Rukeyser and Woolf as important nodes in modernist networks. A student-designed poster created a mind map of the annotations and connections among them, showing the ways the various philosophies of Hughes, Picasso, the Quakers, Rukeyser, and Woolf converge and diverge. Clusters of annotations under concept bubbles such as "racial equality," "freedom," "social justice activism," and "communism" displayed the ongoing relation of pacifism to a variety of progressive movements. Through these projects, students were able to trace how the art and activism of Hughes, Picasso, Rukeyser, and Woolf imagined the possibility of the other plot—peace.

As previously mentioned, the collaborative space created by the exhibition extended beyond digital platforms and into the community. A commitment to and application of feminist digital pedagogy facilitated co-writing and collaboration on multiple levels: students worked together in groups to write and hyperlink their *Three Guineas* annotations; they edited one another's work and peer-reviewed and fact-checked one another's research; as a group, we wrote the curatorial statements for the pop-up exhibitions and the exhibition catalog; and we cooperatively brainstormed details pertaining to the opening and launch of the exhibitions and the presentations of the projects. The pop-up components of the exhibition featured student voices and provided students with an opportunity to showcase their digital humanities projects, thereby facilitating students' entrance into academic discourse communities throughout and beyond the Haverford community. Students grappled with questions of gender and race in relation to war and peace, colonialism and oppression, and a rising Fascism in the 1930s. They also teased out how Woolf and Rukeyser treated these issues in dialogue with their male contemporaries. As my colleagues and I have argued, work on the exhibition facilitated students' growth into "producers of a critical discourse that challenges the status quo position that violence is perpetually necessary" (Foster, Horowitz, and Allen 3). Working on the exhibition expanded the walls of the classroom and the critical-discursive framework in order to turn students into scholars.

Feminist Digital Pedagogy and Breaking Down Borders

The field of digital humanities builds certain borders that feminist digital humanists ask us to call into question. One important border to be blurred is the hard-line distinction between digital pedagogy and digital scholarship. Margaret Konkol speaks to the necessity of getting past the premise that "the output of digital humanities is knowledge and the output of digital pedagogy is student learning." Instead, Konkol argues that "students can and do create new knowledge" and that "teaching is about give and take, active dialogue, making knowledge, and welcoming new thinkers into the world of ideas and problems." Indeed, the caution against the reproduction of hierarchies in the digital world, and the potential of the digital humanities—if used critically, reflectively, and deliberately—to subvert those hierarchies is a necessary topic to the socially concerned digital humanist. Employing Black feminism to analyze the "mediation between the universal and the particular" in the digital humanities, Roopika Risam warns that "the centers of digital humanities produce their own margins" (359, 363). How to expand, reframe, subvert, or undo these margins is part of the task of the feminist digital scholar. By trespassing on the ancient wisdom, by calling into question metanarratives—in Risam's example, by "rewrit[ing] the maps of the global digital humanities" (363), in the case of the *Testimonies* exhibition, by thinking the other plot—feminist digital humanities asks us to challenge the rigid borders of inclusion and exclusion that shape our world.

Testimonies in Art and Action asked students to think through a difficult central research question—what is an ethical response to total war?—and to examine how artists and activists of the 1930s negotiated this problematic in the face of the Spanish Civil War and the Second World War. Students came to recognize that Woolf and Rukeyser were great thinkers of peace, even though their pacifisms manifested very differently. Digital projects allowed students to discover links between art and activism and to see how modernist tropes, aesthetics, and concerns circulated on a transnational plane. Analyses of the individual lines and passages of key primary works, when read alongside paratexts and other supplementary material, revealed the depth, complexity, and polyphonic nature of these works. Connecting these passages to other texts and materials allowed students to analyze how concerns for peace circulated on a larger transnational scale. Students' projects attended to issues of gender and race in relation to war, peace, colonialism, and oppression. These projects examined how modernist women writers treated such issues in relation to their male contemporaries, and in the process, students truly grappled with the other plot—the alternative possibility—that resides within radical modernist women's writings.

Notes

The course Peace Testimonies in Literature and Art and the ensuing exhibition were based on my dissertation, *Modernism's Impossible Witness: Peace Testimonies from the Modernist Wars.* The central research questions of the exhibition were informed by this research and are currently being developed into a book. Versions of this chapter were presented at the 2018 Modernist Studies Association Conference held in Columbus, OH, 8–11 November; the 2017 Modern Language Association Annual Convention, held in Philadelphia, PA, 5–8 January; and the 2017 symposium Remembering Muted Voices: Conscience, Dissent, Resistance and Civil Liberties in World War I through Today, held in Kansas City, MI, 19–22 October. I would like to express my deep gratitude to Laurie Allen, Sarah Horowitz, and Terry Snyder for their vision, collaboration, and support. Profound thanks also go to all the students at Haverford College who worked on the exhibition, especially the Peace Testimonies course members. A very special thanks to students Christina Bowen, Adetomiwa Famodu, Ann-Victoria Isaac, Sophie McGlynn, Marcelo Jauregui-Volpe, and Ian Wheeler for dedicating their summer hours to help with this exhibition, and a big thank you to the support of the Haverford College libraries, the faculty and staff at Haverford College, and our distinguished visitors on opening night who helped make this undertaking possible. For the full acknowledgements, please see the *Testimonies in Art and Action* digital exhibition page (ds-omeka.haverford.edu/peacetestimonies).

1. In a like-minded gesture, *Communal Modernisms*, edited by Hinnov et al., opens with a consideration of Woolf and her commentary on university structures.

2. Jesse Stommel emphasizes the need for reflexivity and for a consideration of how digital spaces change learning and ascertains "that open and networked educational environments must not be merely repositories of content. They must be platforms for engaging students and teachers as full agents of their own learning." Ruben R. Puentedura's SAMR model shows how digital technologies are used to create new ways of learning, with recourse to four categories: Substitution, Augmentation, Modification, and Redefinition, the first two of which are classified as a type of "enhancement," the latter two as a type of "transformation."

3. For the feminist pedagogies and feminist digital pedagogies and theory that inform this assessment, see Marcus, "Afterword"; Golden; Konkol; Risam; and Wernimont.

4. See the exhibition website for all student work discussed here. The link to the website is also available on the companion website to this volume (modwomen.mla.hcommons.org).

5. For more about the work on and launch of the exhibition, with different examples of student work, see the essay by Foster, Horowitz, and Allen, which focuses on the use of archives and digital humanities platforms as a means of radicalizing student voices.

6. See all selections by Hughes; and Rukeyser, "Barcelona" and *Life*.

Works Cited

Berman, Jessica. *Modernist Commitments: Ethics, Politics, and Transnational Modernism.* Columbia UP, 2012.

Cunningham, Valentine. "Introduction." *Penguin Book of Spanish Civil War Verse*, edited by Cunningham, Penguin Books, 1983, pp. 25–94.

Foster, J. Ashley. *Modernism's Impossible Witness: Peace Testimonies from the Modernist Wars.* 2014. Graduate Center, City U of New York, PhD dissertation.

Foster, J. Ashley, Sarah M. Horowitz, and Laurie Allen. "Changing the Subject: Archives, Technology, and Radical Counter-narratives of Peace." *Radical Teacher*, no. 105, 2016, pp. 2–12.

Golden, Amanda. "Feminist Digital Pedagogy." *Jane Marcus Feminist University: The Documentary Record*, featured section of *Virginia Woolf Miscellany*, edited by Cori L. Gabbard and J. Ashley Foster, no. 93, Spring-Summer 2018, pp. 42–43.

Graham, Helen. "Transnational Lives: Spain and Europe's Wars of Social Change." *Crossing Borders: The Spanish Civil War and Transnational Mobilisation*, Birkbeck College and the Cañada Blanch Centre, London School of Economics and Political Science, 30 June–1 July 2016. Public lecture.

Hinnov, Emily M., et al., editors. *Communal Modernisms: Teaching Twentieth-Century Literature and Culture in the Twenty-First-Century Classroom.* Palgrave Macmillan, 2013.

Hughes, Langston. "Addressed to Alabama." *The Daily Worker*, 23 Jan. 1938, pp. 2+.

———. *The Collected Poems of Langston Hughes.* Edited by Arnold Rampersad, Alfred A. Knopf, 1995.

———. "Hughes Bombed in Spain." *Baltimore Afro-American*, 23 Oct. 1937, p. 1.

———. "Hughes Finds Moors Being Used as Pawns by Fascists in Spain." *Baltimore Afro-American*, 30 Oct. 1937, p. 1.

———. "Madrid Getting Used to Bombs: It's Food Shortage That Hurts." *Baltimore Afro-American*, 20 Nov. 1937, p. 3.

———. "Madrid's Flowers Hoist Blooms to Meet Raining Fascist Bombs." *Baltimore Afro-American*, 27 Nov. 1937, p. 3.

———. "Milt Herndon Died Trying to Rescue Wounded Pal." *Baltimore Afro-American*, 1 Jan. 1938, p. 2.

———. "'Organ Grinder's Swing' Heard above Gunfire in Spain." *Baltimore Afro-American*, 6 Nov. 1937, p. 1.

———. "Soldiers from Many Lands United in Spanish Fight." *Baltimore Afro-American*, 18 Dec. 1937, p. 13.

Konkol, Margaret. "Public Archives, New Knowledge, and Moving Beyond the Digital Humanities / Digital Pedagogy Distinction." *Hybrid Pedagogy*, 8 Sept. 2015, hybridpedagogy.org/public-archives-and-new-knowledge/.

Marcus, Jane. "Afterword: Some Notes on Radical Teaching." Hinnov et al., pp. 189–98.

———. *Art and Anger: Reading Like a Woman*. Ohio State UP, 1988.

———. "The Asylums of Antaeus: Women, War, and Madness—Is There a Feminist Fetishism?" *The New Historicism*, edited by H. Aram Veeser, Routledge, 1989, pp. 132–51.

Puentedura, Ruben R. "SAMR in the Classroom: Developing Sustainable Practice." *Ruben R. Puentedura's Blog*, 28 Nov. 2014, www.hippasus.com/rrpweblog/archives/2014/11/28/SAMRInTheClassroom_DevelopingSustainablePractice.pdf.

Risam, Roopika. "Navigating the Global Digital Humanities: Insights from Black Feminism." *Debates in the Digital Humanities 2016*, edited by Matthew K. Gold and Lauren F. Klein, U of Minnesota P, 2016, pp. 359–67.

Rogers, Gayle. *Modernism and the New Spain: Britain, Cosmopolitan Europe, and Literary History*. Oxford UP, 2012.

Rukeyser, Muriel. "Barcelona, 1936." *Life and Letters To-Day*, vol. 15, no. 5, 1936, pp. 26–33.

———. *Life of Poetry*. 1949. Paris Press, 1996.

———. "Mediterranean." *Out of Silence: Selected Poems*, edited by Kate Daniels, Triquarterly Books / Northwestern UP, 2000, pp. 44–49.

Stommel, Jesse. "Critical Digital Pedagogy: A Definition." *Hybrid Pedagogy*, 18 Nov. 2014, hybridpedagogy.org/critical-digital-pedagogy-definition/.

They Still Draw Pictures! American Friends Service Committee / The Spanish Child Welfare Association of America, 1938.

Valis, Noël. Introduction. *Teaching Representations of the Spanish Civil War*, edited by Valis, Modern Language Association, 2007, pp. 7–20.

Wernimont, Jacqueline. "Whence Feminism? Assessing Feminist Interventions in Digital Literary Archives." *Digital Humanities Quarterly*, vol. 7, no. 1, 2013, pp. 1–23.

Woolf, Virginia. *Between the Acts*. 1941. Annotated and introduced by Melba Cuddy-Keane, Harcourt, 2008.

———. *A Room of One's Own*. 1929. Annotated and introduced by Susan Gubar, Harcourt, 2005.

———. *Three Guineas*. 1938. Annotated and introduced by Jane Marcus, Harcourt, 2006.

———. Three Guineas *Reading Notebooks*. Monks House Papers/B.16f. (Sussex), Southern Connecticut State University, 2001, woolf-center.southernct.edu/bloommap.html.

Part VIII

Transformational Pedagogy

Julie Goodspeed-Chadwick

Modernist Women Writers, Feminist Pedagogy, and the New Modernist Studies Classroom

Despite the expansion of modernist studies into other critical methodologies and fields, Urmila Seshagiri notes that the current "process of canon-formation—and deformation, and reformation—constitutes the simplest and yet the most complex act in feminist scholarship about modernism. We can only speak about what we have read." It is in our classrooms and our scholarship that canon formation is addressed, redressed, or reaffirmed; in providing a counterpoint to T. S. Eliot, James Joyce, and Ezra Pound, by reading and centering women writers in relation to their canonical male counterparts, we allow students to engage in work that maps the contours of traditional modernist study while also exploring other possibilities in the landscape. As Seshagiri argues, "Feminist method should be as indispensable to the study of modernism as women were to the movement's multiple strands." Recent scholarship and feminist praxis in modernist studies encourage us to consider how we might bring both women writers and feminist approaches to our teaching of modernism.

In its various manifestations, new modernist studies foregrounds a contestation of boundaries, an engagement in recovery work, and a deployment of an interdisciplinary critical apparatus. Douglas Mao and Rebecca L. Walkowitz emphasize "expansion" (737): the expansion of time, geography, and definitions, as well as the "inclusion of a variety of alternative traditions" (739). As Helen Sword contends, equipping ourselves with various strategies and techniques for teaching modernism in current or innovative fashion aligns our research with our pedagogical responsibilities; it also makes our teaching reflective of the current landscape of modernist studies, requiring that students attend to issues of diversity, inclusivity, and identity politics as readers and citizens in a global world. By advocating diverse and inclusive approaches to women's studies, we demonstrate our commitment to uncovering timely, relevant, and significant issues in modernist studies. New modernist studies and feminist pedagogy not only reimagine important feminist concepts but also have the potential to revitalize interdisciplinary approaches and teaching strategies. Presented under the umbrella of new modernist studies, the feminist concepts of intersectionality, positionality, and feminist recovery will be highlighted in this essay.

Integrating Women's Studies in the New Modernist Studies Classroom

Theorizing new feminist directions in her exploration of crip theory—a "mode of pressing back against dominant pressure, [which allows us to analyze] the force of social norms as they impinge upon bodies, minds, and psyches, especially those which deviate from culturally constructed ideals"—Madelyn Detloff suggests that "it may be useful to think about our socially produced knowledge gaps as incidences of *inattention* or *failure to attend*." Detloff reminds us that we may not know what tools or methodology "will be best for dismantling oppressive structures," and that we may need additional strategies and practitioners at work at any given time on a "thorny or multifaceted issue." The concepts I outline here are meant to redirect attention to the issue of power and its manifestations in literary studies, with an eye toward teaching modernist women writers in a new modernist studies classroom using repurposed tools and strategies.

Developed by Kimberlé Crenshaw, *intersectionality* is the notion that the various aspects of an individual's identity (e.g., sex, gender, race, ethnicity, socioeconomic status, and sexual orientation) cannot be separated from one another because they form a unique constellation of subjectivity or subject positioning. In answer to the question, "What or how should we do (approach, study, re-present) women's literature for it to have a future in modernist studies?," Sonita Sarker proposes that a turn to women's studies and its concepts may be a viable option because women's literature was initially a category unto itself in both modernist studies and women's studies (10). Sarker likewise suggests that the concept of intersectionality belongs in new modernist studies (10). Similarly, Elisabeth Frost has commented that this term, though not new in women's studies, "need not be abandoned" because of its relevance. These discussions and the 2017 *Modernism/Modernity* Print Plus cluster on modernism and feminist praxis (see Detloff; Fernald; Kennedy-Epstein; Seshagiri; Sherrard-Johnson; Ziarek) indicate a concern for the future of literature by women and feminist methodologies, underscoring that while new modernist studies adopts women's studies terms and approaches theoretically, the field as a whole has been slower to follow in practice in the twenty-first century.

We can understand subject positioning in terms of intersectionality using the concept of positionality, which defines individuals "not in terms of fixed identities, but by their location within shifting networks of relationships, which can be analyzed and changed" (Maher and Tetreault 164). For example, as Audre Lorde points out, women are marginal in relation to men, but Black women are marginal compared with middle-class white women (633). And we can move beyond fixed identities in order to analyze how gender, and identity at large, is constructed while focusing on the contexts of authors and works (Maher and Tetreault 225). If we view "mastery, voice, and authority" as "relational and evolving" instead of "dependent on a fixed view of society and peoples' place in it," then a radical transformation of the classroom can take place both in terms of content and pedagogical methodologies (166). The concept of positionality has everything to do with identity and power and provides students with the vocabulary and conceptual framework with which to examine power dynamics in texts written by and about women, especially when such texts are compared with canonical texts written by men.

The scholarship of Anne E. Fernald, Rowena Kennedy-Epstein, Cherene Sherrard-Johnson, and Ewa Ziarek prompts us—through a variety of authors, genres, and texts—to think about how we might conceptualize positionality as critically and pedagogically integral to the new modernist studies classroom. We might, for instance, analyze literature and biography within the context of a precise historical moment in order to see how lives and texts respond to and are molded by often oppositional cultural forces (Fernald). We can also engage in feminist recovery efforts by highlighting positionality, as Kennedy-Epstein does in her overview of the fate of modernist women writers such as Mina Loy, Zora Neale Hurston, Josephine Herbst, and Muriel Rukeyser in relation to canonicity. According to Kennedy-Epstein, these women "saw their work fall out of print or struggled to get new work published. Their exclusion from the literary marketplace and cultural institutions, often carried out under the nominal charge of 'aesthetic failure' or political naïveté, in actuality reflected animus for being leftists, feminists, lesbians, single mothers and dissidents." We might also adopt an approach similar to that of Ziarek, who repositions Nella Larsen's short story "Sanctuary" as a piece that reveals and addresses a history of disenfranchisement: the disenfranchisement of Larsen herself, of Black bodies, and of Black stories in the United States. Sherrard-Johnson examines the power differentials and positionality inherent in the New Negro movement, the Harlem Renaissance, and new modernist studies, reclassifying Rose McClendon as an avant-garde performer who both wrote about and performed in plays that depicted and challenged intersectional oppression. Such arguments showcase the breadth and depth of new modernist studies as it functions in concert with women's studies; presenting such an overview in the classroom enables the agenda of a newly conceptualized feminist-modernist studies for the twenty-first century. As Jessica Berman asserts, feminist-modernist studies should "invite a variety of lived experiences, positionalities, and understandings of gender and sexual identity" ("Practicing" 10).

Feminist recovery work and challenges to traditional paradigms are integral in both new modernist studies and women's studies. As Jane Garrity reminds us, "The labor of seemingly old-fashioned feminist recovery work is still far from done" (21), and we can support and sustain past, present, and future feminist recovery efforts when we teach modernist women writers. Berman concludes that "[p]racticing feminist recovery today must mean not only searching out and valuing under-recognized writing by women around the world, but also engaging from a feminist perspective" ("Practicing" 18). She argues that feminist recovery informs the global, transnational, or planetary turn and always has because new modernist studies remains indebted to early modernist-feminist work in its "erasing [of] center-periphery distinctions" (9). Feminist recovery is critical in pursuing agendas, texts, authors, and themes that remain incomplete or unidentified, and it prompts a reconsideration of positionality and, consequently, of power, while also demanding greater inclusivity on our part as teachers and scholars.

One strategy in addressing recovery is to teach "the conflicts," as Gerald Graff describes it. This could involve highlighting modernist keywords or concepts or interrogating representations in texts by authors who occupy different positions in relation to the canon or whose work foregrounds underrepresented identities. We can pair recovered writers or texts with work more typically encountered on syllabi or in anthologies to show how such marginal writers and texts are important in the formation of our understanding of what modernism is and what it can encompass, as well as what the forces of modernity look like.[1] In so doing, we may well see that modernism can only be understood through the lenses of positionality and intersectionality.

While teaching the conflicts might thus entail pairing writers and interrogating their perceived similarities and differences, this approach involves more than simply comparing and contrasting: because the conflicts are contextual and intertextual, they are necessarily contingent on the texts we read, the authors we study, and the theoretical and pedagogical approaches we adopt. In other words, teaching the conflicts, as I invoke it here, would require us to identify and interpret how intersectionality, positionality, and feminist recovery manifest on the syllabus and in assigned readings. This pedagogical approach can show us how our field has been constructed (i.e., who is included in our survey textbook, how many pages are devoted to a given author, what work is featured) as well as how a feminist approach to new modernist studies dismantles our assumptions about texts and the teaching of them, while also giving us a lens with which to foreground certain authors, texts, and issues. For instance, I teach Kay Boyle alongside Ernest Hemingway to demonstrate that neither is apolitical and that both are in fact very invested in depictions of modernity.

Framed by concepts from women's studies, these pairings or groupings can serve to ignite conversations about modernist aesthetics and approaches to modernism and modernity in the undergraduate classroom. Some possible pairings of modernist writers include the following: Amy Lowell and Pound; Hurston and Langston Hughes; Boyle and Hemingway; and Loy and F. T. Marinetti. The following issues can be considered when studying the texts, artifacts, and lives of these authors: sex, gender, and sexuality; race and ethnicity; nationality; socioeconomic status; canonicity and aesthetics; and privilege, literary genre, and the avant-garde.

Depending on the curricular needs of one's department, it is possible, and perhaps desirable, to pair modern and modernist women writers, as I do in the course Women and Literature and Feminist Theory. Writers who treat a common theme; who work within similar or vastly different genres, styles, or aesthetics; or who simply compose or publish texts within the same year can benefit from examinations geared toward intersectionality and positionality and from examinations that are driven by feminist recovery impulses. A terrific place to start for generative purposes related to a course reading list is Maren Tova Linett's chronology of works by modernist women writers and historical events, featured in *The Cambridge Companion to Modernist Women Writers* (xi-xxiii). For those who wish to further feminist recovery efforts by teaching authors who are not, or not yet, anthologized, countless possibilities await. Although I teach from an anthology for the course described here, I also dedicate a class session to teaching texts that are related to the feminist recovery efforts of my own research; I teach poems by the Baroness Elsa von Freytag-Loringhoven, a feminist Dadaist. Other noncanonical modern and modernist interwar candidates might include those suggested by Kristin Bluemel and Phyllis Lassner, whose work aims to expand our concept of who and what texts are considered modern or modernist: Margery Allingham, Enid Bagnoll, Phyllis Bottome, Ann Bridge, Katherine Burdekin, Agatha Christie, Janet Flanner, Storm Jameson, Margaret Kennedy, Helen MacInnes, Daphne du Maurier, Betty Miller, Dorothy L. Sayers, and Stevie Smith. In particular, Bluemel and Lassner urge us, as feminist-modernist scholars and teachers, to consider teaching Holocaust writers, such as Charlotte Delbo, Karen Gershon, Lotte Kramer, and Erica Marx, because the Second World War defined the modern world and responses to that world; these authors and their texts have yet to be studied and plumbed in the important ways they might be. Berman encourages us to consider adding Swarnakumari Devi, Iqbalunnisa Hussain, Vernon Lee, Una Marson, Jean Rhys, Cornelia Sorabjee, women writers of color, and other writers who occupied intersecting and underrepresented identities to our reading lists ("Practicing" and *Modernist*). As we can see, there is no shortage of modern or modernist women writers whom we can feature in our courses.

Pairing Modernist Women Writers with Male Counterparts

If intersectionality, positionality, and feminist recovery are the concepts that undergird our discussions—and, indeed, our reading list—in our new modernist studies classrooms, then there is a need to enter into conversations about ideologies, values, aesthetics, and artistry, issues that have everything to do with modernist studies. What follows is an overview of literary groupings to be taught from a feminist, new modernist studies perspective, which other teachers may find generative in designing their own courses and structuring dialogues in their respective classrooms.

Amy Lowell and Ezra Pound

We begin with Amy Lowell. Lowell and her literary output were derided after she died: as a fat lesbian with money and status, she was threatening in many ways to a modern, heteronormative reading public. During her lifetime, she represented a threat to Pound in her development and support of imagism; her gendered aesthetics, which celebrated female bodies and identities, and her poetic voices and speakers, which occupied both feminine and masculine subject positions, were distasteful to Pound, who was envious of her wealth and publishing network. These conflicts are reflected in Lowell's "Venus Transiens" and "Madonna of the Evening Flowers" and in Pound's "A Pact" and "Canto XLV." "Venus Transiens" first appeared in the 1915 anthology *Some Imagist Poets*, which did not include Pound and which was a successor to the 1914 anthology edited by Pound, *Des Imagistes*. "Venus Transiens" and "Madonna of the Evening Flowers" foreground female bodies and identities. Both poems make women their primary subjects, rather than objects, and both speakers view their subjects with reverence. Lowell's poems offer imagery that pivots on associations with feminine beauty, splendor, and secular-sacred holiness. Respectful in tone, the poems feature a female gaze distinct from the male gaze of traditional lyric poetry. In contrast, Pound's "A Pact" and "Canto XLV" assume an aggressive tone in their treatment of traditionally masculine subjects: poetry and its aesthetics as the business of men and the effects of economics and business in the public sphere. Viewing their subjects as objects, both of Pound's speakers employ the traditional male gaze. In "A Pact," the speaker identifies Walt Whitman as a forefather whom he detests and to whom he is indebted; as a result, the speaker resolves to engage in sharpening the poetic aesthetics heralded by Whitman. "Canto XLV"—often referred to as the usura poem—centers men and their work; in Pound's view, women remain on the periphery and serve men as brides or "whores" (line 47). Pound's literary debt and lineage is entirely masculine, whereas Lowell's poetry characteristically centers women, in these two instances Venus and the beloved stand-in for the Madonna.

Zora Neale Hurston and Langston Hughes

With the pairing of Hurston and Hughes, we dedicate ourselves to the study of how gender and race intersect and how this intersection in the United States makes Hurston's position in American life and letters vastly different from that of Hughes. Hurston's and Hughes's literary work bears this out: although both authors strove to represent Black life and culture, especially the oral and improvisatory traditions, and although both are read as representative of the Harlem Renaissance, Hughes outshone Hurston in their respective lifetimes and continues to outshine her today. The historical dismissal of Hurston likely stems in part from Hurston's belief that she did not have to cast her lot with the men of the Harlem Renaissance. Her texts treat women's interpersonal lives, and while her work is very much about gender, race, and class, she was perceived by her contemporaries neither as racially motivated nor as an early advocate of civil rights. In contrast, Hughes and other Black intellectuals of the time endorsed rather militant racial politics that they believed would uplift African Americans. Having grown up in Eatonville, Florida, an incorporated Black town with a Black governing structure, Hurston came from a very different background and believed that she could and should invoke, portray, and celebrate ordinary Black lives because, in her view, Black people and their culture were already uplifted. If others had a problem with Blackness, then that was their problem, not hers, a personal world view detailed in Hurston's "How It Feels to Be Colored Me." Missing from this essay is a sense of tragedy, anger, resentment, or militant racial politics. Instead, Hurston argues that she sometimes feels she has no race or that her sense of self transcends race. By the end of the essay, Hurston creates a metaphor for diversity; as she sees it, people are simply bags of different colors that are filled with items both worthless and priceless. Her short story "The Gilded Six-Bits" traces the enduring love—as well as the relationship problems sparked by materialism—of Missie May and Joe, each of whom receives equal narrative attention. Reading Hughes is a very different experience: his "Mother to Son" and "I, Too" detail the hardships caused by structural inequalities and inequities and the subsequent deferral of advancement and empowerment for Black people in white society. Both poems advocate for resilience in terms of identity politics and agitate for a different kind of beauty. While we see how conflicts emerge when Hurston and Hughes are taught in tandem, the issue of beauty in its relation to Blackness is one that Hughes shares with Hurston.

Kay Boyle and Ernest Hemingway

Boyle and Hemingway make for an intriguing pairing in the classroom because of the parallels in their lives and work. Both were white, award-winning American authors. Both cared about and were knowledgeable about politics, especially when it came to matters of war and its devastating effects. Both were expatriates who witnessed war firsthand. Boyle and Hemingway even shared similar political views concerning the Second World War: both were staunchly against the Nazi regime, for instance. However, while Boyle and Hemingway both demonstrated extraordinary abilities as writers and enjoyed success during their lifetimes, Hemingway is a literary giant in the American canon while Boyle is a footnote (again). In 2007, a short story by Boyle was anthologized in *The Norton Anthology of American Literature*, suggesting Boyle's deserved but hard-won canonical status, but the story was removed in the subsequent 2011 edition of the anthology and was not replaced with any of Boyle's other work.[2]

Even though Boyle did not consider herself a feminist—she thought being a feminist meant one was a separatist—her work is a better reflection of the values associated with championing equality and analyzing power structures that we find in women's studies, as we see in her once-anthologized story "The White Horses of Vienna," than we find at face value in Hemingway's work, much of which promulgates veiled or open misogyny, as evidenced in his anthologized "The Snows of Kilimanjaro." Boyle's "The White Horses of Vienna" presents readers with an investigation of identity politics: it is a story that illustrates the ugliness and inhumanity of anti-Semitism in the face of goodness and humanity. Hemingway's "The Snows of Kilimanjaro" prompts us to recognize (our own) gendered values and to interrogate those values as we interpret the story's embedded gendered representations. We can analyze issues of power and positionality through characters who occupy different intersectional identities, namely the character of the entitled, white Harry, a writer struggling with writing and traumatic experiences, and his "rich bitch" of a wife (1987). This woman is referred to generically as a woman (rather than by a proper name) in most instances, though she is Harry's caretaker. Her lack of individuality suggests her positioning as a sexualized object: Harry says he would like to destroy her in bed after referring to her as a "bitch." I suspect that the ability of Hemingway's texts to discursively form our ideas about American masculinity continues to enthrall many. Teaching Boyle alone, or paired with Hemingway in order to uncover similarities in aesthetics and differences in attitude and values, would go a long way in advancing the feminist recovery work of new modernist studies in American literature.

Mina Loy and F. T. Marinetti

In another pairing I introduce Loy and Marinetti. Both authors are associated with futurism, and my students find them particularly difficult writers in terms of accessibility. Their proclivity to shock their readers is part of the futurist aesthetic; they are known for the aggressive and unsettling politics in their manifestos: Loy's "Feminist Manifesto" and Marinetti's "Manifesto of Futurism." Coming from a cosmopolitan background, Loy was an English national who lived in several countries before becoming an American. Unlike Marinetti, her work is unequivocally feminist. While Marinetti's "Manifesto of Futurism" operates within a masculine ideological system that glorifies war and opposes feminism, Loy's "Feminist Manifesto" glorifies a radical feminism that supports the demolition of patriarchal structures and relations. For Loy, feminism in its current form is inadequate. What is needed is a feminism that imagines a new reality, one populated with unmarried mothers and devoid of the concept of virginity. Loy argues that men and women are enemies and should only come together when it is mutually beneficial—for example, when both a man and a woman desire what Loy terms "the sexual embrace" (1503). With vastly different visions of the future and of gendered positionality, Marinetti's and Loy's manifestos, when read in parallel, reveal more conflicts than compromises. Students will be more likely to view futurism as versatile in form and approach if we include both Marinetti and Loy as part of our course reading lists; students will see that Marinetti's manifesto operates within a patriarchal system that prioritizes masculine identities, power, and authority while Loy's manifesto conceptualizes the demolition of such a system in her radical feminist revisioning.

Other pairings may present themselves to instructors as they think about their programs of study for majors and minors and cross-listed courses or elective courses for students in other disciplines. In choosing such pairings, instructors may also wish to consider their own teaching and research agendas as well as the necessary pedagogical configurations and approaches that materialize in their classrooms. For instance, instructors may decide to pair women writers, such as Hurston and Boyle, examining similarities and differences in terms of style, genre, content, and treatment of certain issues. When Hurston and Boyle are read together, we see in both authors a feminist acknowledgement that the personal is political. Should instructors wish to pair modernist men, such as Pound and Hughes, students could be invited to examine how race informs and transforms notions of American masculinity, which, like femininity, is a malleable construct. A pairing of Hurston and Hemingway—authors with decidedly original voices—would reveal significant differences along the axis of race, ethnicity, and socioeconomic status and their representations in American society.

This essay has endeavored to provide selected concepts and framing techniques from women's studies as a means of structuring a course that draws on the orientations of new modernist studies. In doing so, the essay suggests ways instructors might reapproach modernism and modernist writers, with equal emphasis given to modernist women writers. This approach might also be helpful for students who plan to take the GRE Literature in English Test or other forms of assessment that evaluate an understanding of canonical literature—and for the teachers of these students. Instructors can also use texts other than those suggested within these pages, setting up new pairings in order to reread modernist women writers alongside their oftentimes more famous modernist male counterparts. When we as instructors highlight the concepts of intersectionality, positionality, and feminist recovery in our presentation of modernist authors and in our discussions of their work, we position ourselves and our courses to embody new possibilities and to approach the best of what (feminist) new modernist studies has to offer.

Notes

1. This project is a long-ranging one: scholars such as Bonnie Kime Scott and Marianne DeKoven have addressed women writers and modernism in connection with feminist recovery work and canonicity.

2. The 2017 edition does not feature Boyle either.

Works Cited

Baym, Nina, et al., editors. *The Norton Anthology of American Literature.* 7th ed., vol. D (1914–45), W. W. Norton, 2011.

Berman, Jessica. *Modernist Commitments: Ethics, Politics, and Transnational Modernism.* Columbia UP, 2012.

———. "Practicing Transnational Feminist Recovery Today." *Feminist Modernist Studies*, vol. 1, no. 1, 2018, pp. 9–18.

Bluemel, Kristin, and Phyllis Lassner. "Feminist Inter/Modernist Studies." *Feminist Modernist Studies*, vol. 1, no. 1, 2018, pp. 22–35.

Boyle, Kay. "The White Horses of Vienna." 1935. Baym et al., pp. 2038–49.

Crenshaw, Kimberlé. *On Intersectionality: Essential Writings*. New Press, 2019.

DeKoven, Marianne. *Rich and Strange: Gender, History, Modernism*. Princeton UP, 1991.

Detloff, Madelyn. "Metics, Methods, and Modernism." *Mind the Gap! Modernism and Feminist Praxis*, cluster of *Modernism/Modernity* Print Plus, edited by Urmila Seshagiri, vol. 2, cycle 2, 7 Aug. 2017, doi.org/10.26597/mod.0023.

Fernald, Anne E. "Choice and Change: Modern Women, 1910–1950." *Mind the Gap! Modernism and Feminist Praxis*, cluster of *Modernism/Modernity* Print Plus, edited by Urmila Seshagiri, vol. 2, cycle 2, 7 Aug. 2017, doi.org/10.26597/mod.0024.

Frost, Elisabeth, participant. "Why Women's Poetry Now?" Roundtable. Modernist Studies Association Conference, Pittsburgh, PA, 8 Nov. 2014.

Garrity, Jane. "Modernist Women's Writing: Beyond the Threshold of Obsolescence." Young and Wallace, pp. 15–29.

Graff, Gerald. *Beyond the Culture Wars: How Teaching the Conflicts Can Revitalize American Education*. W. W. Norton, 1992.

Hemingway, Ernest. "The Snows of Kilimanjaro." 1936. Baym et al., pp. 1983–99.

Hughes, Langston. "I, Too." 1925. Levine et al., p. 836.

———. "Mother to Son." 1922. Levine et al., p. 835.

Hurston, Zora Neale. "The Gilded Six-Bits." 1933. Baym et al., pp. 1713–21.

———. "How It Feels to Be Colored Me." 1928. Levine et al., pp. 533–36.

Kennedy-Epstein, Rowena. "The Spirit of Revolt: Women Writers, Archives and the Cold War." *Mind the Gap! Modernism and Feminist Praxis*, cluster of *Modernism/Modernity* Print Plus, edited by Urmila Seshagiri, vol. 2, cycle 2, 7 Aug. 2017, doi.org/10.26597/mod.0025.

Levine, Robert S., et al., editors. *The Norton Anthology of American Literature*. 9th ed., vol. D (1914–45), W. W. Norton, 2017.

Linett, Maren Tova, editor. *The Cambridge Companion to Modernist Women Writers*. Cambridge UP, 2010.

Lorde, Audre. "Age, Race, Class, and Sex: Women Redefining Difference." *Literary Theory: An Anthology*, edited by Julie Rivkin and Michael Ryan, Blackwell Publishing, 1998, pp. 630–36.

Lowell, Amy. "Madonna of the Evening Flowers." 1919. Levine et al., pp. 181–82.

———. "Venus Transiens." 1915. Levine et al., pp. 180–81.

Loy, Mina. "Feminist Manifesto." 1914. Levine et al., pp. 1502–05.

Maher, Frances A., and Mary Kay Thompson Tetreault. *The Feminist Classroom: An Inside Look at How Professors and Students Are Transforming Higher Education for a Diverse Society*. Basic Books, 1994.

Mao, Douglas, and Rebecca L. Walkowitz. "The New Modernist Studies." *PMLA*, vol. 123, no. 3, May 2008, pp. 737–48.

Marinetti, F. T. "Manifesto of Futurism." 1909. Levine et al., pp. 316–18.

Pound, Ezra. "Canto XLV." 1937. Levine et al., p. 313.

———. "A Pact." 1913. Levine et al., p. 297.

Sarker, Sonita. "On Remaining Minor in Modernisms: The Future of Women's Literature." Young and Wallace, pp. 8–14.

Scott, Bonnie Kime, editor. *The Gender of Modernism: A Critical Anthology.* Indiana UP, 1990.

Seshagiri, Urmila. "Mind the Gap! Modernism and Feminist Praxis." *Mind the Gap! Modernism and Feminist Praxis*, cluster of *Modernism/Modernity* Print Plus, edited by Seshagiri, vol. 2, cycle 2, 7 Aug. 2017, doi.org/10.26597/mod.0022.

Sherrard-Johnson, Cherene. "Rose McClendon's Playbill: The Vagabond Modernism of New Negro Theater." *Mind the Gap! Modernism and Feminist Praxis*, cluster of *Modernism/Modernity* Print Plus, edited by Urmila Seshagiri, vol. 2, cycle 2, 7 Aug. 2017, doi.org/10.26597/mod.0026.

Sword, Helen. "Introduction: MSA Teaching Forum Cluster: Making It New: Innovative Approaches to Teaching Modernism." *Modernism/Modernity*, vol. 16, no. 3, Sept. 2009, pp. 471–73.

Young, Tory, and Jeff Wallace, editors. *The Future of Women in Modernism.* Special issue of *Literature Compass*, vol. 10, no. 1, 2013.

Ziarek, Ewa. "Towards a Transformative Feminist Aesthetics: Antagonism, Commodification, and the 'Racial Contract' in Larsen's 'Sanctuary.'" *Mind the Gap! Modernism and Feminist Praxis*, cluster of *Modernism/Modernity* Print Plus, edited by Urmila Seshagiri, vol. 2, cycle 2, 7 Aug. 2017, doi.org/10.26597/mod.0027.

Julia Bloch

Teaching Gwendolyn Brooks's Pedagogical Activism

In "Gay Chaps at the Bar," first published in the 1945 collection *A Street in Bronzeville*, Gwendolyn Brooks uses the keywords of pedagogy to stage a critique of the complex set of racial barriers faced by African American soldiers returning home from the Second World War. In a cascade of slant rhymes and assonance, shaped by a meter that tends toward the iambic but skids with dense and compressed rhythms, the servicemen speak as a collective "we" whose return to the United States oscillates between jubilance and despair, and whose remembered and fresh experiences back home merge with the traumas of the war zone. The soldiers begin by easing back into the familiar speech of ordering drinks at the bar, conflating the qualities of vocal tones with the flavors of mixed drinks: "Whether the raillery should be slightly iced / And given green, or served up hot and lush" ("Gay Chaps" 64). As the soldiers then play on the vernacular of flirtation, their barroom talk slides into a discourse on when to deploy "white speech" and when or whether to speak at all about the horrors of war:

> And smart, athletic language for this hour
> Was not in the curriculum. No stout
> Lesson showed how to chat with death. We brought
> No brass fortissimo, among our talents,
> To holler down the lions in this air. (64)

The servicemen link their unpreparedness for war—they received no "curriculum" or "lessons" in "how to chat with death"—with the crushing norms of racial segregation in the United States. They lack the "smart, athletic language" that might have emboldened them in the isolating experience of combat, and they lack the volume of a marching band, the "brass fortissimo," that might "holler down" the wild creatures of war abroad as well as the menacing ones back home.

In addition to illustrating Brooks's long-standing reflexive approach to form—the soldiers' "iron feet" in a later section of "Gay Chaps at the Bar" refer both to shackles and to the confines of poetic meter (75)—the sonnet reveals a poetics attentive to its pedagogical imperatives. Brooks's poem, when read alongside the pedagogical activism that undergirded her career as a mid-century modernist and as a member of the radical, community-oriented aesthetics of the Black Arts movement, offers a key set of terms and practices for addressing a number of issues in poetics pedagogy, including how to formalize relations of power both in and outside the university. Brooks offers a paradigmatic example of a poet whose work helps us think critically about how institutional boundaries inflect innovation in the field of poetry as well as in the field of pedagogy. It is instructive that "Gay Chaps at the Bar," a poem largely about the limits of speech, uses the terms "curriculum" and "lesson," terms that point toward language's many structures of power. The pedagogical arguments embedded in Brooks's poem invite a number of different concrete approaches to teaching her work in the classroom, approaches that center diverse sources of knowledge and that allow classrooms to become spaces that reflect on their own institutional boundaries and histories—and on their social relevance.

Brooks and the University

The pedagogical activism of Brooks is palpable in her mid-century modernist poetry, the period of her work that begins in 1945 with *A Street in Bronzeville* and ends, or at least shifts, with her break with European and Anglo modernist forms in 1967, when she aligned her aesthetics with the revolutionary poetics of the Black Arts movement.[1] Her poems of the 1940s—with their compressed sonnet and ballad forms, their recurrent abstractions and conceptual imagery, and their tendency to navigate tensions between received and modernist forms—engage with poetic form itself as a matter of pedagogy. Her 1949 long poem *Annie Allen*, for example, indicts a curriculum that has failed the African American subject—but in this case, what is indicted is not just the "smart, athletic language" that appears in "Gay Chaps" but also the institution that administers it.

In the third section of *Annie Allen*, Brooks's reflexive approach to form manifests as a critique of both motherhood and pedagogy. After asking, "What shall I give my children? who are poor" (116), the poem's speaker deliberates over what it means to parent children who are destined to enter oppressive social institutions:

> The little crooked questionings inbound,
> Concede themselves on most familiar ground,
> Cold an old predicament of the breath:
> Adroit, the shapely prefaces complete,
> Accept the university of death. (119)

The children are described in a series of abstractions, as mere "questionings" and "shapely prefaces" rather than embodied human selves, and the "predicament" they face is an "old" one: their "acceptance" of "the university of death" seems inevitable. The word *university*—derived from a number of Anglo-Norman and Old French terms that include *corporation*, *community*, *totality*, and *universality*—indicates both the materiality of knowledge and its creation and mediation. Brooks's lines not only use the university as a metaphor for oppressive poverty but also expose the totalizing capacities of higher education: the "children of the poor" resign themselves to being destroyed by an institution that otherwise promises enlightenment and social mobility. The poem lays out an early poetic blueprint for the pedagogical activism Brooks pursued when she began teaching thirteen years later—not long before her poetry became radicalized by her exposure to the Black Arts movement, a radicalization that manifested, coincidentally, at a conference in an academic setting: the Black Writers' Conference at Fisk University.[2]

Brooks's pedagogy did more than transfer skills and knowledge. It confronted power and legitimacy. Her pedagogical practices emerged from an unconventional teaching career that spanned a number of schools and community settings: her first teaching experience came in 1962, when she taught a three-and-a-half-week course on American literature at the University of Chicago (she had previously been recommended for a position at Roosevelt University, but was told she lacked the necessary degree).[3] In 1963, she taught her first poetry workshop at Chicago's Columbia College. Appointments followed at Elmhurst College; Northeastern Illinois State College; the University of Wisconsin, Madison; and the City College of New York, where she commuted for two years to teach poetry as a distinguished visiting professor of the arts (Brooks, "Report" 78–79). In a 1972 autobiographical essay, "Report from Part One," Brooks suggests she was keenly aware of how the specific traditions, texts, and learning objectives leveraged in her classroom conveyed a certain attitude toward the university as an institution with its own set of ideologies and power dynamics. Brooks writes that her poetry workshop focused both on the instruction of received form—"the sonnet (Shakespearean and Petrarchan, with Spenserian optional), the ballad, blank verse, free verse, the Japanese forms haiku and tanka, the verse play, the 'Beat' poem, the heroic couplet" (80)—and on discussion and debate techniques—"panel discussions, debates, round-robin response" (81)—that engaged with historical and political texts by Black thinkers such as A. B. Spellman, Larry Neal, Alain Robbe-Grillet, and Lerone Bennett (81). She writes that she rejected white-only curricula, filling her syllabi with "black literature and Jewish literature, rarely touched upon by standard texts" and paying out of pocket to bring African American writers to her classroom (82).

Brooks's descriptions of how she opened up her classroom resonate with the aims of critical literacy. One passage from her essay reads as an especially lively articulation of critical literacy's privileging of students' own voices over what Paulo Freire famously describes as the "banking model": a classroom in which the teacher simply "deposits" knowledge into the student with no other direction of exchange (72). Brooks's essay details how she instead foregrounds the knowledge fundamental to her own students' speech:

> Today's young people want IN, want to express themselves, to say what is on their minds.
>
> They do not so much want "answers," for who, they stress, can solve for them?—they do not so much wish to discuss as to *speak*, simply. They want to be free to make, to create. If they are not allowed to create, they break. In a vacuum, breaking seems to them a form of creation.
>
> More fervently now than ever before they want assurance that what they are doing in a school situation will strengthen or embroider their lot IMMEDIATELY. They want to feel that they are achieving or changing something on the spot. ("Report" 82)

Brooks aimed to meet her students' demands for an education relevant to their social particularity, and to cultivate a learning community committed to social transformation: enlightenment inside and outside the classroom. Her description recalls Ira Shor's articulation of critical pedagogy as a mode in which students can think beyond the curriculum to "examine their learning in school, their everyday experience, and the conditions in society" (12).

If the "university of death" in *Annie Allen* was meant to condemn the university as an oppressive power structure, then Brooks's own pedagogy sought to rewrite the university as a site of self-empowerment, and to move beyond the bounds of the university altogether. It is also possible that Brooks sought to refurbish the specific role the university played as a symbol of the white gatekeeping of knowledge in her own neighborhood, the South Side of Chicago. In an essay first published in *Negro Digest* in June 1951, Brooks recalls a moment that startlingly exposes the University of Chicago, where she herself would later teach, as a site of racial violence. One evening, as Brooks and her young son walked through the campus, a group of young white men hurled rocks and racist epithets at them; they never took that path again. As Brooks puts it in "How I Told My Child about Race":

> Formerly I had felt that if any place at all was safe, the university district, mecca of basic enlightenment and progressive education would be safe. The buildings, with their delicate and inspiring spires, seemed now to leer, to crowd us with mutterings—"Oh no, you black bodies!—no sanctuary here. You have found no sanctuary, you will find no sanctuary anywhere. This beauty is not for you, the architects, the builders, did not have the elongations of your filthy shadows in mind as they worked, as they shaped." (qtd. in Flynn 490)

Figuring the university's very architecture as segregationist, Brooks anticipates what the education-studies scholar Maisha Fisher refers to as Brooks's "pedagogy of possibility" (11). Members of the Black Arts movement committed to taking education beyond the traditional classroom setting: rather than approaching literacy as a tool for assimilation, these artists approached literacy as central to the discourse of Black pride. Brooks and other members of the Black Arts movement rejected the centrality of the university, seeking instead to instill communal values in literacy work by bringing poetry to nonacademic venues, including bars and taverns, prisons, and neighborhood gathering spots. As Brooks proposed in a 1967 interview, "Let us *take* art to those who are not going to get it otherwise" ("Summer, 1967" 142). As such, she led a writing workshop with "some of the very able members of South Side teen gangs" (142); she mentored Etheridge Knight while he was incarcerated in Indiana State Prison; and when she was appointed poet laureate of the United States in 1985, she launched community workshops, visited community centers, and funded readings by young poets around Washington, DC, extending her pedagogical reach beyond the walls of the classroom.

Locating the seeds of Brooks's pedagogical activism in her mid-century modernist poetry invites comparisons with the pedagogical work of other modernist and mid-century women poets, including those who worked in nonacademic settings or who did not hold graduate degrees. We might consider Brooks's poetic pedagogy alongside, for example, Gertrude Stein's theories of composition or Lorine Niedecker's naturalist and historiographic poetics. We might also consider what the feminization of teaching as a profession reveals about gendered dynamics in poetry of the United States. The pedagogies of modernist women poets resonate with more recent calls for an open classroom from feminist, postcolonial, and ethnic studies, such as bell hooks's call for a multilingual classroom environment, Gayatri Chakravorty Spivak's work on translation and close reading as tools of cultural critique, and Joan Retallack and Juliana Spahr's work on making students cocreators of meaning in the classroom. "I . . . am qualified to enter at least the kindergarten of new consciousness now," Brooks writes of her political awakening, thereby asserting a new pedagogical model for social transformation that she had imagined decades earlier ("Report" 86).

Poetry in and beyond the Classroom

"In the time of detachment, in the time of cold, in this time / tutor our difficult sunlight," Brooks writes in her poem "The Good Man" (511).[4] Brooks's demands for a student-centered, inductive, historically relevant learning space can be met using various concrete teaching practices. These practices include writing-based activities, creative thinking, and assignments that draw on disparate forms of knowledge.

Any discussion of Brooks and pedagogy should acknowledge the relevance of Brooks's poem "We Real Cool," first published in 1959 in *Poetry* magazine and later in the 1960 collection *The Bean Eaters*. A classroom set piece, "We Real Cool" remains Brooks's most frequently anthologized poem. It is also, of course, a parable of the failure of education in four tight couplets that have been widely analyzed for their intricate investigation of nonconformity and rhetorical defiance.

Typically taught as a master lesson in form—in terms of line breaks, enjambment, staccato rhythm, Black vernacular, and rhyme—"We Real Cool" can also help students explore the limits of disciplinary knowledge. In my own classroom, I use writing-based strategies in which students draw on disparate forms of knowledge to enter the poem.[5] With "We Real Cool," I play a recording of Brooks reading the poem and ask students as they listen to circle or underline one or two words that strike them in some way as memorable, beautiful, puzzling, or otherwise important. After we hear the recording, rather than laboring to identify features such as alliteration or rhyme, we begin associatively. I ask students to take one of the words they circled or underlined and to begin a new piece of writing in response to that word: to write associatively, in any form, critically or creatively. This exercise can then be taken in a number of different directions: we might simply read our pieces aloud, creating an aural map of the poem; we might repeat the exercise with a different word, and then share the writings verbally or display them on a chalkboard or a projector to create a wildly associative set of annotations; or we might identify similarities and differences among students' writings before commencing with an analysis of the poem's formal structures, including its use of repetition and sound. Students inevitably draw on prior knowledge from a range of disciplines: a student writing on the word *strike* might think of labor unions; a student writing on *jazz* might turn to music or reflect on the sound of Brooks's voice; a student writing on *we* might wax philosophical about the collective subject.

Even the most idiosyncratic writing—which may veer away from the poem itself because it is anachronistic or intensely personal—widens the field of inquiry by giving students an opportunity to reflect on what they themselves have written—its syntactical patterns, its conceptual leaps—before they go on to master the form of Brooks's poem. By locating students' own vocabularies or habits of thinking at the heart of literary analysis, associative writing followed by synthesis and analysis allows students to reflect on the process of close reading, and consequently on the disciplinary norms at work in their own classrooms.[6] As Emily Rainey and Elizabeth Birr Moje have argued, making those norms transparent helps remind us of a core theory of activist pedagogy—that disciplinary norms are never neutral.

The exercise described above encourages reflective thinking and context-based close reading. A related activity puts disparate texts in dialogue and fosters links between creative and analytical thinking. I might ask students to read Brooks's 1960 poem "The Last Quatrain of the Ballad of Emmett Till" alongside a short paragraph from a nonfiction or theoretical text, such as Hannah Arendt's 1958 work on political freedom, *The Human Condition* (a text that includes the line "This revelatory quality of speech and action comes to the fore where people are *with* others and neither for nor against them—that is, in sheer human togetherness" [180]). Students discover unexpected connections and insights across these texts when they complete a series of short, in-class writing prompts that encourage divergent approaches: I might ask students to tell a story about X; to take a position on Y; to respond associatively to a given word or phrase; or to write a found poem of fourteen lines using only the language in Brooks, Arendt, and students' own freewritings. We then put the texts in direct dialogue using writing prompts such as the following: rewrite your story using the language from one of your other prompts; rewrite your story using the language from a partner's writing; rewrite your response to a creative prompt from the point of view of Mamie Till; imitate the ballad rhythms of Brooks's poem by rewriting the Arendt quotation as a poem. Such exercises allow students to use the language they themselves have generated to dive back into discussions of the texts at hand with greater attention to the formal and stylistic qualities of literary language.

An approach that focuses on students' own language is key: while discussion-based strategies may privilege the staking of positions over the generation of ideas, writing-based practices, including compositional constraints encountered in creative exercises, keep students rooted in the page and lead them to formal insights. For example, some students might identify how Arendt's claim that "to be isolated is to be deprived of the capacity to act" (188) illuminates both the pensive portrayal of Till's mother (i.e., the point of view) and the pared-down imagery (i.e., the use of poetic economy to enact absence) in Brooks's poem. Other students might dwell on what the ethical implications of Arendt's statement reveal about Brooks's portrait of Mamie Till: why does Brooks describe her as "sorry"? Whose imagination powers this poem—Brooks's? Till's? our own? How do the constraints of ballad meter create an uneasy tension with an out-of-control civil landscape? And, further: how does a poem such as Brooks's convey something about civil rights history that a historical or theoretical text such as Arendt's—laboring under a different set of vocabularies, forms, and disciplinary norms—cannot?

Brooks was a poet attuned to the limits and possibilities of language. She was also a teacher who responded to the urgent pressures of her moment, who sought to remake the classroom, both on and off campus, as a space of social inquiry and even of radical change. Pedagogical techniques that reflect Brooks's vision help students reflect critically on the space of the classroom in ways that intersect with the pedagogical activism of the Black Arts movement as well as with the critical possibilities of poetry more broadly. If we are to understand modernism in terms of its engagement with various cultural forms rather than as a set of discrete literary acts, then a teaching practice attentive to Brooks's pedagogical activism also invites inquiry into modernist culture itself—and into modernism's relevance for understanding broader structures of language, power, and meaning.[7]

Notes

1. Questions surrounding Brooks's place in modernism in the United States often circle around her relation to literary authority, including the assumptions related to race and literacy that shaped her pedagogical practice; her use of European and Anglo modernist forms, as well as her use of nonstandard English, links her with writers such as Paul Laurence Dunbar and Melvin Tolson, whose work negotiates the culturally burdened spaces of literary heritage and authority. I argue elsewhere that while Brooks's mid-century modernist work is frequently read as less politically urgent than her later poetry, it is this work in particular that dramatizes competing narratives of experimentalism and politics for African American poetics, for modernism, and, in a broader sense, for an understanding of what it means to write poetry as social critique; see Bloch. On Brooks, see also the essays by Slankard and Sorensen in this volume.

2. Brooks describes meeting Amiri Baraka and other members of the Black Arts movement at Fisk University in 1967 as a pivotal moment for her poetic practice: "An almost hysterical Gwendolyn B. walked about in amazement, listening, looking, learning. . . . *I* had never been, before, in the general presence of such insouciance, such live firmness, such confident vigor, such determination to mold or carve something DEFINITE" ("Report" 84–85).

3. In a 1967 interview, Brooks acknowledged the way her teaching career ran up against normative standards for legitimacy: "I don't consider myself a teacher. I don't have teacher's training or certificates, and I'm sure that I've been accepted in schools because my Pulitzer Prize represents a diploma of some sort" (qtd. in Gayles 33). Brooks won the Pulitzer Prize for her 1949 poem *Annie Allen*; she was the first African American to be awarded the prize in any category.

4. "The Good Man" first appeared in the 1986 collection *"The Near-Johannesburg Boy" and Other Poems*. The poem is dedicated to Haki R. Madhubuti, the founder of Third World Press, which became Brooks's publisher when she left mainstream publishing houses for the independent African American press.

5. I learned writing-based strategies at Bard's Institute for Writing and Thinking, which uses a set of principles drawing on a range of writing-centered pedago-

gies from Peter Elbow, Ken Macrorie, Janet Emig, Ann Berthoff, and others; see Vilardi and Chang.

6. See also Tate in this volume for a pedagogical practice informed by creative writing strategies, and the essays by Reginio and Berke in this volume for approaches to teaching poetry.

7. In identifying Brooks as a modernist, instructors invite important inquiry into the relation between disciplinary narratives of Anglo and white European modernism and the movements with which Brooks is typically identified: the Harlem Renaissance, the Black Arts movement, and the Chicago Renaissance. See especially work on this topic by Shockley; Schultz; and Nielsen.

Works Cited

Arendt, Hannah. *The Human Condition.* U of Chicago P, 1998.

Bloch, Julia. "'Shut Your Rhetorics in a Box': Gwendolyn Brooks and Lyric Dilemma." *Tulsa Studies in Women's Literature*, vol. 35, no. 2, 2016, pp. 439–62.

Brooks, Gwendolyn. *Annie Allen*, Brooks, *Blacks*, pp. 77–140.

———. *Blacks.* Third World Press, 1987.

———. "Gay Chaps at the Bar." Brooks, *Blacks*, pp. 64–75.

———. "The Good Man." Brooks, *Blacks*, pp. 510–11.

———. "The Last Quatrain of the Ballad of Emmett Till." Brooks, *Blacks*, p. 340.

———. "Report from Part One." Brooks, *Report*, pp. 37–86.

———. *Report from Part One.* Broadside Press, 1972.

———. "Summer, 1967." Interview conducted by Paul M. Angle. Brooks, *Report*, pp. 131–46.

———. "We Real Cool." Brooks, *Blacks*, p. 331.

Fisher, Maisha. *Black Literate Lives: Historical and Contemporary Perspectives.* Routledge, 2009.

Flynn, Richard. "'The Kindergarten of New Consciousness': Gwendolyn Brooks and the Social Construction of Childhood." *African American Review*, vol. 34, no. 3, 2000, pp. 483–99.

Freire, Paulo. *Pedagogy of the Oppressed.* Translated by Myra Bergman Ramos, Continuum Books, 2006.

Gayles, Gloria Wade, editor. *Conversations with Gwendolyn Brooks.* U of Mississippi P, 2003.

hooks, bell. *Teaching to Transgress: Education as the Practice of Freedom.* Routledge, 1994.

Nielsen, Aldon. *Black Chant: Languages of African-American Postmodernism.* Cambridge UP, 1997.

Rainey, Emily, and Elizabeth Birr Moje. "Building Insider Knowledge: Teaching Students to Read, Write, and Think within ELA and across the Disciplines." *English Education*, vol. 45, no. 1, 2012, pp. 71–90.

Retallack, Joan, and Juliana Spahr. "Introduction: Why Teach Contemporary Poetries?" *Poetry and Pedagogy: The Challenge of the Contemporary*, edited by Retallack and Spahr, Palgrave Macmillan, 2006, pp. 1–10.

Schultz, Kathy Lou. *The Afro-Modernist Epic and Literary History: Tolson, Hughes, Baraka*. Palgrave Macmillan, 2013.

Shockley, Evie. *Renegade Poetics: Black Aesthetics and Formal Innovation in African American Poetry*. U of Iowa P, 2011.

Shor, Ira. *Empowering Education: Critical Teaching for Social Change*. U of Chicago P, 1992.

Spivak, Gayatri Chakravorty. *An Aesthetic Education in the Era of Globalization*. Harvard UP, 2012.

Vilardi, Teresa, and Mary Chang, editors. *Writing-Based Teaching: Essential Practices and Enduring Questions*. State U of New York P, 2009.

Megan Hicks, Emma Slotterback, Katie Starliper, and Julie Vandivere

The Positive Power of Ignorance: Organizing an International Conference on Modernist Women Writers with Undergraduates

We are four individuals—one professor and three students—who cohosted the twenty-fifth Annual International Conference on Virginia Woolf in 2015 at Bloomsburg University, a midsize, rural, public university that had never before hosted an international conference. Since that conference we've shared many conversations about the benefits of such an undertaking, and here we've tried to consolidate that dialogue. After some deliberation we decided to write this essay as a collective *we* and to present our impressions from the students' perspectives. Although our professor, Julie Vandivere, aided us as we wrote this essay—posing questions, synthesizing arguments, editing—we ultimately found that her voice merged with ours, a development that illustrates the power of this sort of experience. In writing this essay, we found ourselves inspired by Jacques Rancière's *The Ignorant Schoolmaster*, which argues that the cycle of master leading student must be broken lest one stunt the student's intellectual growth. Organizing a conference is a fundamentally different experience than that of the classroom, where formulaic assignments often inhibit intellectual curiosity and subsequently intellectual growth. Our work on the conference turned us into intellectual leaders: in keeping with Rancière's vision, we were not led by our professor; rather, responsibility was required of us, which forced us to discern the creativity, originality, and precision of our own minds. After two years of working as equals and an intense week of conversing with scholars, our strongest conviction is that undergraduates need to be given responsibility and to be trusted with that responsibility. They need to engage with scholars in contexts that extend beyond the registration table. They need to be the face that helps when computers don't work, but they should also be the face that asks intelligent questions in panel discussions. They need to be the face that sits next to you at the banquet and has read all of Woolf's work and wants passionately to discuss the connection they saw between your paper and another's.

Preparing for the Conference

The conference showed us the value of an intensive undergraduate experience that deepened our knowledge such that we understood, appreciated, and could participate in academic and theoretical discourse. In 2014, the year before our conference, our university offered to pay the expenses of any student whose paper was accepted to the twenty-fourth Annual International Conference on Virginia Woolf at Loyola University, Chicago. Ten students worked throughout the academic year to prepare and send abstracts; we were accepted. This conference would give us an idea of what lay ahead.

Even though some of us spoke to nearly empty rooms and none of us had our papers chosen as selected papers, the experience inspired us, overwhelmed us, and set our imaginations alight. The conference presented a stark juxtaposition to the classrooms we occupied as English majors, classrooms in which we studied a long line of male writers. The conference gave us the opportunity to learn about women writers who were previously unknown to us and to see them set in relief against other women writers, rather than couched among male writers, which allowed us to recognize new aspects of their work.

The chance to see scholars discuss a range of women writers was, more than anything, what made our experience in Chicago so meaningful; there we saw a seemingly marginalized subject we had spent months studying with a single professor become a passion for women writers shared by a thriving community of scholars. We came to view ourselves as part of a large, smart, engaged group studying the literary products of women. We learned that loving books, words, and ideas can create a community that transcends age, experience, and place. We learned that scholars with doctorates can fangirl—that we too can fangirl—and still be serious and intellectual. We felt we were standing on new ground, a ground not bogged down by tradition and male voices. Discussions became more meaningful. We felt that we were helping shape something that was still coming into being.

The task of organizing our own Woolf conference together with other undergraduates succeeded in large part because of this first conference experience, but women-centered learning played an equally important role. Studying the modernist period in depth allowed us to understand an important period in the history of feminism as we became versed in the women writers fighting for suffrage and against the rising tide of war. When one studies how modernist women writers shifted focus from a feminist to a pacifist discourse, one is able to explore tensions between feminism and other social priorities, both within modernism and in the present day. Modernism's innovative and destabilizing features allow for radical forms of thinking often expressed by the writers we studied. This inspired us to create a conference that embraced modernist women writers and the revolutionary ideas their works give voice to. We went home charged with excitement, imagining papers we could present, sessions we could chair, and the logistics of creating a conference that would live up to the one we envisioned in our minds.

Back in Bloomsburg, we asked ourselves how we could instill in the community the same excitement we had experienced at Loyola; we began writing grants, creating reading groups, and approaching high schools about the opportunity for students to read and write about modernist women's texts in their English classes. Our efforts to reach out to local schools and businesses triggered interest from charitable foundations committed to revitalizing rural towns, promoting public education, and creating opportunities for high school students to attend college. We connected with our university's charitable foundation and created an account for tax-deductible donations. We wrote grant applications to a local foundation, requesting funds to place copies of Woolf's *Mrs. Dalloway* and *A Room of One's Own* in high school classrooms across the region and to research, develop, and provide to area high schools lesson plans on Woolf. We worked with high school faculty members and students to develop papers for a special session of the Woolf conference meant for young scholars.

The opportunity to organize this miniconference for high school students provided us with the experience we needed as we worked as interns on the larger conference. We taught Woolf's essays in high school classes, wrote grant applications, and created a call for papers. We selected papers for sessions, reserved classrooms, managed finances, and distributed scholarship money. This work—and the skills we gained from it—guaranteed our involvement in the decision-making processes of the international conference.

The Conference Approaches

In the process of organizing the conference, we discovered that a model less invested in hierarchy created a sense of interdependence and good will. Some students were involved in late-stage logistics. These students drove shuttles, hung banners, moved trash cans, and helmed the registration table. This work was integral to the conference as a whole. We felt a tangible sense of accomplishment in seeing that our work, however insignificant it might have seemed while we were doing it, was necessary to make the conference run smoothly. The students who worked on the conference saw themselves as a part of a community, one that shared a passion for the work of modernist women writers.

Every student worker was seen as valuable to the team, whether they were hanging flyers downtown or helping choose the menu for the reception banquet. No rigid hierarchy was imposed on the student team; everyone was important, and we bonded as a group. It was important to us that no one felt as though they were a replaceable hired hand. By and large, our involvement was predicated on our desire to be a part of the experience. The opportunity to manage the details of the conference was both overwhelming at times and excellent preparation for future work. We had to correspond with conference attendees in and outside the United States and with other offices on campus; to manage spreadsheets used to keep track of the number of meals we needed to order, rooms we needed to book, and seats we needed on the shuttle buses; and to attend to a thousand other minute but critical details. This work provided us with experience hard to obtain as undergraduates. Our work experiences up to that point in our lives had been as peripheral entities in the professional world, in much the same way as undergraduate students are often peripheral entities in the world of academic conferences. Our deep involvement in planning the conference served as an intellectually enriching voyage into the world of scholars and as an introduction to the practical aspects of adult responsibility.

A scholarly conference that involves undergraduate students creates communities that also involve students in overlapping networks. Before the conference, we had only ever seen our professors in the English department as classroom fixtures. The conference showed us a different side of them, one that was profoundly generous and always willing to help. We remember sitting in a room with a handful of English professors and a group of students as we discussed conference preparations and logistics, joking to relieve any unbidden stress. Those professors not only helped us edit our papers and taught us how to present but also drove shuttles, donated money, led local reading groups, and sometimes, at the end of a long day, paid for our dinner and ice cream. We became allies in the monumental task of organizing a conference, and those relationships continued beyond the final panel. Collaborations extended beyond the English department as we worked with other departments to create theater performances and art exhibitions. Perhaps even more important, we became involved in the processes of grant writing and grant fulfillment, learning to trust those who invest money in community building and those who benefit from it. The experience also taught us that community members and high school students can be excited by the important and timeless questions posed by literature. We watched as more and more people began to share in our love of Woolf as we built a community from the ground up.

The Conference Arrives

This section of the essay, like the conference itself, occupies the least amount of space, for we worked on the conference for close to two years and it was over in a few short days. More than two years later we still carry with us the lessons of that experience. There are, however, a few points that should be stressed.

The conference not only gave students practice presenting arguments but also forced students to consider the different needs of a listening audience versus a reading audience. Undergraduates often experience the community of academic discourse from its margins. However, conference presentation allowed us to participate in that community as insiders rather than as outsiders looking in. Before our presentations we imagined our audiences: our fellow undergraduates coming to support us, graduate students who might be finding their own footing in the academic world, and expert scholars with years of experience. We knew that these were real people who would give us feedback. This knowledge provided us with a greater sense of discursive immediacy, especially when compared with the more routine academic experience of writing a paper for a course. We knew that our audience had chosen to attend our panel specifically—they had had several other choices and had felt perhaps most attracted to our work. The knowledge that we had an engaged audience—some of us for the first time in our academic careers—made our presentations more meaningful. It was even more exciting to see the high school students with whom we had worked experience similar feelings and emotions: they were proud, nervous, and excited, and, to our delight, they had become Woolf fangirls and fanboys. In that moment, we saw the ripple effect of our work and felt oddly like seasoned professors who had helped their students discover a new passion.

This experience was so powerful because of the diversity of conference participants. At first, it felt like we were spreading the word to those people one might expect to find at a Woolf conference. Once we began receiving registration e-mails, however, we quickly realized that this one conference in a remote, little-known town in Pennsylvania was bringing together people from over fifteen different countries on five continents. The conference created a sense of community, a space for writers, readers, learners, and thinkers from around the world to collaborate, to share ideas, and to enjoy each other's company and thoughts. We saw the deepest truth of reading realized before our eyes: you're never alone when you read. It was as though these people, who otherwise rarely if ever saw each other, came to the conference and became the best of friends. We had never before realized the power of reading the same books, discussing varied ideas, and collaborating with people from all over the world. It was an inspiring and empowering experience to see ourselves as part of this phenomenon, where scholars from around the world were eager to share and discuss their ideas with us. We saw what was so often hidden from us in the classroom—a rich and welcoming academic community in which ideas developed and thrived.

Along with our call for papers, we had sent out an international art call for works on paper that interpreted the legacy of modernist women writers. The response was overwhelming. Some art embraced feminism, while others focused on Woolf's interest in the sensations. Even though we sent out a call for works on paper, we received a tremendous diversity of media, from fiber art to photography. We were floored by the number of artists who wrote to us about Woolf herself, about how much they loved her, about how she had inspired or saved them. We realized Woolf was everywhere, influencing people from a variety of disciplines. Our community expanded once more, and we loved seeing the literature we held so dearly cross over into the visual. The conference's emphasis on visual art was especially important because of our focus on Woolf's female contemporaries—the community of women who responded to the world through art and literature. The opening reception included an exhibit in the university gallery and the announcement of the judges' awards for best in show. The artists who traveled to the opening reception to see the work in the art exhibit and hear the awards announced mingled with scholars who studied Woolf and her contemporaries. The conference was abuzz with academics and artists standing side by side, responding to their world and to Woolf's, discussing the object of their fascination. And beside them were the students and professors who had worked so hard to bring them together. In this moment, intellectual appreciation and emotional experience came together, epitomizing what the conference had come to mean to us.

"The Ignorant Schoolmaster" and the Ignorant Student

The conference ultimately provided us with an educational experience that was more flexible, more individual, and more powerful than that which is typical of the classroom. When presenting at a conference, the student finds something they want to learn about as well as something they want to teach another person about—that something being how the student experiences Woolf.

According to Rancière, an "ignorant schoolmaster" refrains from asking leading questions that force the student onto an unnatural path. Instead, the ignorant schoolmaster asks only ignorant questions—those questions that ensure understanding and that help the student discover the information that interests *the student*. Conferences have the potential to ask the ignorant questions. Apart from a vague theme, the conference has no investment in what ideas we might explore or present; it allows us space for free play in which we can create our own scholarship. Our professor was able to fill the gaps left by Rancière's ignorant schoolmaster, the conference. The written and unwritten rules of the academic world are often difficult to understand, especially for those who are inexperienced with that world. Before the conference, we approached scholarship as outsiders. A book or journal article about Woolf or other women modernists was an object for consumption, one created by a distant, unseen entity operating within an academic world that did not include us. To read these texts in a traditional classroom setting can often feel like a means to an end—a means of finding support for an argument or of gaining enough knowledge to participate in a classroom discussion. Conference participation provided an entryway into the academic world and allowed our professor and mentor to teach us about scholarship not as outsiders but as newcomers.

As undergraduates, we were somewhat worried that we might be perceived as inadequate to the task of conference organization and participation by those masters who allow both their will and their intelligence to guide that of the student, thus stunting the student's intellectual growth. Being taught the rules of scholarship by a mentor and being given the freedom to choose our own presentation topics gave us the confidence to enter the academic world as new scholars. Rancière's ignorant schoolmaster and ignorant student are perhaps not ideals that can be achieved in the real world because the attainment of some forms of knowledge require the assistance of an insider. Having two teachers—the conference, on the one hand, and our actual teacher and mentor, on the other—helped bridge this gap: the former allowed us to discover what we wanted to learn while the latter guided us in what we needed to learn in order to be admitted to certain kinds of academic spaces.

Those scholars who focus on modernist women writers provide a particularly fertile community for this kind of learning because their work tends to value both inclusivity and destabilization. Our conference focused on networks of influence, collaboration, and friendship among modernist women writers, a fact best embodied by a project that we created for display in the conference's lounge, a project that replicated Bonnie Kime Scott's famous graphic on the networks of modernism (xxiii). On several poster boards, we wrote the names of the women writers whose work was being discussed at the conference. Participants were then invited to use markers to draw lines between names while noting the connections between the women—for example, some chose to connect Woolf to Vita Sackville-West, Woolf's inspiration for the novel *Orlando*. At the end of the conference, we had a visual representation of not only the community of female modernists we were talking and writing about but also the kinds of connections that we wanted the conference itself to foster.

The conference provided an authentic learning experience that is difficult to emulate in a classroom. The typical teacher-student relationship wasn't as pronounced because we all took on the role of both teacher and student at different times throughout the planning and execution of the conference. The opportunity to learn about Woolf and her female contemporaries—and to then organize a conference around them—fostered intellectual discovery and community building. Our work on the conference helped us develop our leadership skills, our professionalism, and our connection to our university; the conference itself welcomed us into the community of academic discourse. For these reasons, conference planning was the most powerful experience of our undergraduate careers. It helped mold us not just as scholars or as professionals but also as human beings.

Works Cited

Rancière, Jacques. *The Ignorant Schoolmaster: Five Lessons in Intellectual Emancipation.* Translated by Kristin Ross, Stanford UP, 1991.

Scott, Bonnie Kime. *The Women of 1928.* Indiana UP, 1995. Vol. 1 of *Refiguring Modernism.*

Part IX

Resources

Companion Website

For resources in addition to those listed below, including digital resources and suggested course readings, see the companion website to this volume at modwomen.mla.hcommons.org.

Guides to Modernism and Modernist Studies

Baldick, Chris. *The Modern Movement. The Oxford English Literary History*, vol. 10 (1910–40), Oxford UP, 2004.

Brooker, Peter, et al., editors. *The Oxford Handbook of Modernisms.* Oxford UP, 2010.

Latham, Sean, and Gayle Rogers. *Modernism: Evolution of an Idea.* Bloomsbury Academic, 2015.

Levenson, Michael, editor. *The Cambridge Companion to Modernism.* Cambridge UP, 1999.

Marshik, Celia, editor. *The Cambridge Companion to Modernist Culture.* Cambridge UP, 2014.

Maude, Ulrika, and Mark Nixon, editors. *The Bloomsbury Companion to Modernist Literature.* Bloomsbury Academic, 2018.

Rabaté, Jean-Michel, editor. *A Handbook of Modernism Studies.* Wiley-Blackwell, 2013.

Ross, Stephen, editor. *The Routledge Encyclopedia of Modernism.* Routledge, 2016–, www.rem.routledge.com/.

Sherry, Vincent, editor. *The Cambridge History of Modernism.* Cambridge UP, 2017.

Wollaeger, Mark, and Matt Eatough, editors. *The Oxford Handbook of Global Modernisms.* Oxford UP, 2012.

Teaching Modernist Studies and Modernist Women Writers

Barrett, Eileen, and Ruth O. Saxton, editors. *Approaches to Teaching Woolf's* Mrs. Dalloway. Modern Language Association, 2009.

Daugherty, Beth Rigel, and Mary Beth Pringle, editors. *Approaches to Teaching Woolf's* To the Lighthouse. Modern Language Association, 2001.

Debo, Annette, and Lara Vetter, editors. *Approaches to Teaching H.D.'s Poetry and Prose.* Modern Language Association, 2011.

Enszer, Julie R. "'She Who Shouts Gets Heard!': Counting and Accounting for Women Writers in Literary Grants and Norton Anthologies." *Feminist Studies*, vol. 42, no. 3, 2016, pp. 720–37.

Esdale, Logan, and Deborah M. Mix, editors. *Approaches to Teaching the Works of Gertrude Stein.* Modern Language Association, 2018.

Hinnov, Emily M., et al., editors. *Communal Modernisms: Teaching Twentieth-Century Literature and Culture in the Twenty-First-Century Classroom.* Palgrave Macmillan, 2013.

hooks, bell. "Toward a Revolutionary Feminist Pedagogy." *Talking Back: Thinking Feminist, Thinking Black*, South End Press, 1989, pp. 49–54.

Marsh, Nicky, and Peter Middleton, editors. *Teaching Modernist Poetry.* Palgrave Macmillan, 2010.

McLendon, Jacquelyn Y., editor. *Approaches to Teaching the Novels of Nella Larsen.* Modern Language Association, 2016.

Penner, Erin K. "Making No Apologies for Difficulty: Putting Modernist Form at the Center of Classroom Discussions." *Journal of Modern Literature*, vol. 37, no. 2, 2014, pp. 1–19.

Rosowski, Susan J., editor. *Approaches to Teaching Cather's* My Ántonia. Modern Language Association, 1989.

Sedgwick, Eve Kosofsky. *Touching Feeling: Affect, Pedagogy, Performativity.* Duke UP, 2003.

Soto, Michael, editor. *Teaching the Harlem Renaissance: Course Design and Classroom Strategies.* Peter Lang, 2008.

Sword, Helen. "Introduction: MSA Teaching Forum Cluster: Making It New: Innovative Approaches to Teaching Modernism." *Modernism/Modernity*, vol. 16, no. 3, Sept. 2009, pp. 471–73.

Feminist-Modernist Studies

Fernald, Anne E., editor. *Women's Fiction, New Modernist Studies, and Feminism.* Special issue of *Modern Fiction Studies*, vol. 59, no. 2, 2013.

Garrity, Jane. "Found and Lost: The Politics of Modernist Recovery." *Modernism /Modernity*, vol. 15, no. 4, 2008, pp. 803–12.

Laity, Cassandra. "Introduction: Toward Feminist Modernisms." *Feminist Modernist Studies*, vol. 1, nos. 1–2, 2018, pp. 1–7.

Seshagiri, Urmila. "Mind the Gap! Modernism and Feminist Praxis." *Mind the Gap! Modernism and Feminist Praxis*, cluster of *Modernism/Modernity* Print Plus, edited by Seshagiri, vol. 2, cycle 2, 7 Aug. 2017, doi.org/10.26597/mod.0022.

Young, Tory, and Jeff Wallace, editors. *The Future of Women in Modernism.* Special issue of *Literature Compass*, vol. 10, no. 1, 2013.

Gender and Sexuality

Abraham, Julie. *Are Girls Necessary? Lesbian Writing and Modern Histories.* U of Minnesota P, 2008.

Ardis, Ann L., and Leslie W. Lewis, editors. *Women's Experience of Modernity, 1875–1945*. Johns Hopkins UP, 2003.

Benstock, Shari. *Women of the Left Bank: Paris, 1900–1940*. U of Texas P, 1987.

Carlston, Erin G. *Thinking Fascism: Sapphic Modernism and Fascist Modernity*. Stanford UP, 1998.

Conor, Liz. *The Spectacular Modern Woman: Feminine Visibility in the 1920s*. Indiana UP, 2004.

DeKoven, Marianne. *Rich and Strange: Gender, History, Modernism*. Princeton UP, 1991.

Doan, Laura, and Jane Garrity, editors. *Sapphic Modernities: Sexuality, Women and National Culture*. Palgrave Macmillan, 2006.

English, Elizabeth. *Lesbian Modernism: Censorship, Sexuality and Genre Fiction*. Edinburgh UP, 2015.

Felski, Rita. *The Gender of Modernity*. Harvard UP, 1995.

Frost, Elisabeth. *The Feminist Avant-Garde in American Poetry*. U of Iowa P, 2003.

Garrity, Jane. *Step-daughters of England: British Women Modernists and the National Imaginary*. Manchester UP, 2003.

Hackett, Robin. *Sapphic Primitivism: Productions of Race, Class, and Sexuality in Key Works of Modern Fiction*. Rutgers UP, 2004.

Joannou, Maroula, editor. *Women Writers of the 1930s: Gender, Politics and History*. Edinburgh UP, 1999.

Lassner, Phyllis. *British Women Writers of World War Two: Battlegrounds of Their Own*. Palgrave Macmillan, 1998.

Light, Alison. *Forever England: Femininity, Literature and Conservatism between the Wars*. Routledge, 1991.

Linett, Maren Tova, editor. *The Cambridge Companion to Modernist Women Writers*. Cambridge UP, 2010.

Love, Heather. *Feeling Backward: Loss and the Politics of Queer History*. Harvard UP, 2007.

Marshik, Celia, and Allison Pease. *Modernism, Sex and Gender*. Bloomsbury Academic, 2018.

Medd, Jodie. *Lesbian Scandal and the Culture of Modernism*. Cambridge UP, 2012.

Miller, Jane Eldridge. *Rebel Women: Feminism, Modernism and the Edwardian Novel*. U Chicago P, 1994.

Parsons, Deborah L. *Streetwalking the Metropolis: Women, the City, and Modernity*. Oxford UP, 2003.

Pease, Allison. *Modernism, Feminism, and the Culture of Boredom*. Cambridge UP, 2012.

Scott, Bonnie Kime, editor. *Gender in Modernism: New Geographies, Complex Intersections.* U of Illinois P, 2007.

Ziarek, Ewa Płonowska. *Feminist Aesthetics and the Politics of Modernism.* Columbia UP, 2012.

Black Modernisms

Baker, Houston A., Jr. *Modernism and the Harlem Renaissance.* U of Chicago P, 1987.

Cheng, Anne Anlin. *Second Skin: Josephine Baker and the Modern Surface.* Oxford UP, 2011.

Etherington, Ben. *Literary Primitivism.* Stanford UP, 2017.

Gilroy, Paul. *The Black Atlantic: Modernism and the Harlem Renaissance.* Cambridge UP, 1993.

Hardison, Ayesha K. *Writing through Jane Crow: Race and Gender Politics in African American Literature.* U of Virginia P, 2014.

Hutchinson, George, editor. *The Cambridge Companion to the Harlem Renaissance.* Cambridge UP, 2007.

———. *The Harlem Renaissance in Black and White.* Harvard UP, 1995.

Kramer, Victor A., editor. *The Harlem Renaissance Re-examined.* AMS Press, 1987.

Lemke, Sieglinde. *Primitivist Modernism: Black Culture and the Origins of Transatlantic Modernism.* Oxford UP, 1998.

Schwarz, A. B. Christa. *Gay Voices of the Harlem Renaissance.* Indiana UP, 2003.

Sherrard-Johnson, Cherene. *Portraits of the New Negro Woman: Visual and Literary Culture in the Harlem Renaissance.* Rutgers UP, 2007.

Shockley, Evie. *Renegade Poetics: Black Aesthetics and Formal Innovation in African American Poetry.* U of Iowa P, 2011.

West, M. Genevieve. *Zora Neale Hurston and American Literary Culture.* UP of Florida, 2005.

Global Modernisms

Berman, Jessica. *Modernist Commitments: Ethics, Politics, and Transnational Modernism.* Columbia UP, 2012.

———. "Practicing Transnational Feminist Recovery Today." *Feminist Modernist Studies,* vol. 1, no. 1, 2018, pp. 9–18.

Doyle, Laura, and Laura Winkiel, editors. *Geomodernisms: Race, Modernism, Modernity.* Indiana UP, 2005.

Emery, Mary Lou. *Modernism, the Visual, and Caribbean Literature.* Cambridge UP, 2007.

Evans, Elizabeth F. *Threshold Modernism: New Public Women and the Literary Spaces of Imperial London.* Cambridge UP, 2019.

Friedman, Susan Stanford. *Planetary Modernisms: Provocations on Modernity across Time.* Columbia UP, 2015.

Gikandi, Simon. *Writing in Limbo: Modernism and Caribbean Literature.* Cornell UP, 1992.

Hayot, Eric, and Rebecca L. Walkowitz, editors. *A New Vocabulary for Global Modernism.* Columbia UP, 2016.

Kalliney, Peter. *Modernism in a Global Context.* Bloomsbury Academic, 2016.

Marcus, Jane. *Hearts of Darkness: White Women Write Race.* Rutgers UP, 2004.

Seshagiri, Urmila. *Race and the Modernist Imagination.* Cornell UP, 2010.

Snaith, Anna. *Modernist Voyages: Colonial Women Writers in London, 1890–1945.* Cambridge UP, 2014.

Walkowitz, Rebecca L. *Cosmopolitan Style: Modernism beyond the Nation.* Columbia UP, 2006.

Winkiel, Laura. *Modernism, Race and Manifestos.* Cambridge UP, 2008.

Modernist Difficulty

Diepeveen, Leonard. *The Difficulties of Modernism.* Routledge, 2002.

Frost, Laura. *The Problem with Pleasure: Modernism and Its Discontents.* Columbia UP, 2013.

Lyon, Janet. *Manifestoes: Provocations of the Modern.* Cornell UP, 1999.

Mahaffey, Vicki. *Modernist Literature: Challenging Fictions.* Blackwell Publishing, 2007.

The Middlebrow

Beauman, Nicola. *A Very Great Profession: The Women's Novel, 1914–39.* Virago, 1983.

Botshon, Lisa, and Meredith Goldsmith, editors. *Middlebrow Moderns: Popular American Women Writers of the 1920s.* Northeastern UP, 2003.

Clark, Suzanne. *Sentimental Modernism: Women Writers and the Revolution of the Word.* Indiana UP, 1991.

Hammill, Faye. *Women, Celebrity, and Literary Culture between the Wars.* U of Texas P, 2007.

Harker, Jamie. *America the Middlebrow: Women's Novels, Progressivism, and Middlebrow Authorship between the Wars.* U of Massachusetts P, 2007.

Humble, Nicola. *The Feminine Middlebrow Novel, 1920s to 1950s: Class, Domesticity, and Bohemianism.* Oxford UP, 2004.

Rubin, Joan Shelley. *The Making of Middlebrow Culture.* U of North Carolina P, 1992.

The Women's Suffrage Movement

Chapman, Mary. *Making Noise, Making News: Suffrage Print Culture and U.S. Modernism.* Oxford UP, 2014.

Green, Barbara. *Spectacular Confessions: Autobiography, Performative Activism, and the Sites of Suffrage, 1905–1938.* St. Martin's, 1997.

Rosen, Andrew. *Rise Up, Women! The Militant Campaign of the Women's Social and Political Union, 1903–1914.* Routledge and Kegan Paul, 1974.

Stowell, Sheila. *A Stage of Their Own: Feminist Playwrights of the Suffrage Era.* U of Michigan P, 1992.

Tickner, Lisa. *The Spectacle of Women: Imagery of the Suffrage Campaign, 1907–14.* U Chicago P, 1988.

Modernist Periodical Studies and Print Culture

Ardis, Ann, and Patrick Collier, editors. *Transatlantic Print Culture, 1880–1940: Emerging Media, Emerging Modernisms.* Palgrave Macmillan, 2008.

Binckes, Faith, and Carey Snyder, editors. *Women, Periodicals and Print Culture in Britain, 1890s–1920s: The Modernist Period.* Edinburgh UP, 2019.

Brooker, Peter, and Andrew Thacker, editors. *The Oxford Critical and Cultural History of Modernist Magazines.* Oxford UP, 2009.

Churchill, Suzanne W., and Adam McKible, editors. *Little Magazines and Modernism: New Approaches.* Routledge, 2016.

Clay, Catherine, et al., editors. *Women's Periodicals and Print Culture in Britain, 1918–1939: The Interwar Period.* Edinburgh UP, 2017.

Green, Barbara. "Feminist Periodical Culture." *Literature Compass*, vol. 6, no. 1, 2009, pp. 191–205.

———. *Feminist Periodicals and Daily Life: Women and Modernity in British Culture.* Palgrave Macmillan, 2017.

Hammill, Faye, and Mark Hussey. *Modernism's Print Cultures.* Bloomsbury Academic, 2016.

Jaillant, Lise. *Cheap Modernism: Expanding Markets, Publisher's Series and the Avant Garde.* Edinburgh UP, 2017.

———, editor. *Publishing Modernist Fiction and Poetry.* Edinburgh UP, 2019.

Keyser, Catherine. *Playing Smart: New York Women Writers and Modern Magazine Culture.* Rutgers UP, 2010.

Marek, Jayne E. *Women Editing Modernism: "Little Magazines" and Literary History*. UP of Kentucky, 1995.

Marks, Patricia. *Bicycles, Bangs, and Bloomers: The New Woman in the Popular Press*. UP of Kentucky, 1990.

Scholes, Robert, and Clifford Wulfman. *Modernism in the Magazines: An Introduction*. Yale UP, 2010.

Film and Radio

Cohen, Debra Rae, et al., editors. *Broadcasting Modernism*. UP of Florida, 2009.

Marcus, Laura. *The Tenth Muse: Writing about Cinema in the Modernist Period*. Oxford UP, 2007.

Trotter, David. *Cinema and Modernism*. Blackwell Publishing, 2007.

Digital Humanities

Battershill, Claire, and Shawna Ross. *Using Digital Humanities in the Classroom: A Practical Introduction for Teachers, Lecturers, and Students*. Bloomsbury Academic, 2017.

Battershill, Claire, et al. *Scholarly Adventures in Digital Humanities: Making the Modernist Archives Publishing Project*. Palgrave Macmillan, 2017.

Churchill, Suzanne W., et al. "Feminist Designs: Modernist Digital Humanities and *Mina Loy: Navigating the Avant-Garde*." *Feminist Modernist Digital Humanities*, special cluster of *Feminist Modernist Studies*, edited by Amanda Golden and Cassandra Laity, vol. 1, no. 3, 2018, pp. 243–56.

Gold, Matthew K., and Lauren F. Klein, editors. *Debates in the Digital Humanities*. U of Minnesota P, 2019, dhdebates.gc.cuny.edu/projects/debates-in-the-digital-humanities-2019.

Miller, Cristanne. "The *Marianne Moore Archive* and Feminist Modernist Digital Humanities." *Feminist Modernist Digital Humanities*, special cluster of *Feminist Modernist Studies*, edited by Amanda Golden and Cassandra Laity, vol. 1, no. 3, 2018, pp. 257–68.

Pressman, Jessica. *Digital Modernism: Making It New in New Media*. Oxford UP, 2014.

Ross, Shawna. "Toward a Feminist Modernist Digital Humanities." *Feminist Modernist Digital Humanities*, special cluster of *Feminist Modernist Studies*, edited by Amanda Golden and Cassandra Laity, vol. 1, no. 3, 2018, pp. 211–29.

Ross, Stephen, and Jentery Sayers. "Modernism Meets Digital Humanities." *Literature Compass*, vol. 11, no. 9, 2014, pp. 625–33.

Singh, Amardeep. "Visualizing the Uplift: Digitizing Poetry by African American Women, 1900–1922." *Feminist Modernist Digital Humanities*, special cluster of *Feminist Modernist Studies*, edited by Amanda Golden and Cassandra Laity, vol. 1, no. 3, 2018, pp. 269–81.

Wernimont, Jacqueline. "Whence Feminism? Assessing Feminist Interventions in Digital Literary Archives." *Digital Humanities Quarterly*, vol. 7, no. 1, 2013, www.digitalhumanities.org/dhq/vol/7/1/000156/000156.html.

Notes on Contributors

Steven Ambrose is an affiliated faculty member in Emerson College's Department of Writing, Literature, and Publishing. His research interests include twentieth-century queer literature—particularly the lesbian novel—feminist and queer theory, and pedagogies that center the needs of queer students.

Nancy Berke is the author of *Women Poets on the Left: Lola Ridge, Genevieve Taggard, Margaret Walker* (2001). Her articles have appeared in *Legacy*, *The Times Higher Education Supplement*, *American Studies*, and elsewhere. She has contributed to the feminist anthologies *Gender in Modernism* (2007) and *A History of Twentieth Century American Women's Poetry* (2016). A former Fulbright Scholar in Belgium, she is professor of English at LaGuardia Community College, City University of New York.

Julia Bloch is director of the creative writing program at the University of Pennsylvania, an associate in the Bard College Institute of Writing and Thinking, an editor of *Jacket2*, a Pew Fellow in the Arts, and the author of three books of poetry and of essays on twentieth-century poetry and poetics.

Geneviève Brassard is associate professor of English and gender and women's studies at the University of Portland, where she offers courses in British, Irish, European, and women's literatures.

Bridget Chalk is associate professor of English at Manhattan College, where she teaches modernism and contemporary British and anglophone literature. She is the author of *Modernism and Mobility: The Passport and Cosmopolitan Experience* (2014) as well as articles in *Twentieth-Century Literature*, *Modernism/Modernity*, and elsewhere.

Matthew Cheney is assistant professor and director of the Interdisciplinary Studies Program at Plymouth State University. His work has been published in *Woolf Studies Annual*, the *Los Angeles Review of Books*, *Electric Literature*, *Conjunctions*, *One Story*, and elsewhere. His collection *Blood: Stories* won the Black Lawrence Press's Hudson Prize.

Sarah E. Cornish is associate professor of English and director of graduate studies at the University of Northern Colorado, where she teaches courses in transatlantic modernism, modern women writers, twentieth-century British literature, and film studies. She has published her work in *Feminist Modernist Studies*, *Twentieth-Century Literature*, and *Virginia Woolf Miscellany*. She is cofounder of the Feminist Inter/Modernist Association.

Lois Cucullu, associate professor of English at the University of Minnesota, is the author of *Expert Modernists, Matricide, and Modern Culture* (2004). Her essays have appeared in *Signs*, *Differences*, *Modernism/Modernity*, and *Modernist Cultures*. Among her recent awards is the Christopher Isherwood Foundation Fellowship for her book project, "A Queer Progress: The 'Naturalization' of Christopher Isherwood."

Melissa Dinsman is assistant professor of English at York College, City University of New York, and the author of *Modernism at the Microphone* (2015). Her research focuses on the intersections of late modernism and media aesthetics, specifically during the Second World War. Dinsman's work can be found in *The Space Between*, *Modernism/Modernity*, and *International Yeats Studies*.

Sarah Fedirka is associate professor in the Department of English at the University of Findlay, where she teaches modernist and postcolonial literatures. Her work focuses on modernist little magazines of the British colonies.

J. Ashley Foster is assistant professor of twentieth- and twenty-first-century British literature with emphasis in digital humanities at California State University, Fresno. She is lead curator of the student special collections and digital humanities exhibitions *Testimonies in Art and Action* and *Surveying Utopias: A Critical Exploration* and the author of numerous articles.

Amanda Golden is associate professor of English at New York Institute of Technology. She is the author of *Annotating Modernism: Marginalia and Pedagogy from Virginia Woolf to the Confessional Poets* (2020) and the editor of *This Business of Words: Reassessing Anne Sexton* (2016). She has published her work in *Modernism/Modernity*, *Woolf Studies Annual*, and *The Space Between: Literature and Culture, 1914–1945*.

Julie Goodspeed-Chadwick is Chancellor's Professor of English; an affiliated faculty member in women's, gender, and sexuality studies; and director of the office of student research at Indiana University–Purdue University, Columbus. She is the author of *Modernist Women Writers and War: Trauma and the Female Body in Djuna Barnes, H.D., and Gertrude Stein* (2011) and *Reclaiming Assia Wevill: Sylvia Plath, Ted Hughes, and the Literary Imagination* (2019). She is editing, with Peter K. Steinberg, *The Collected Writings of Assia Wevill*.

Elizabeth Willson Gordon is Canada Research Chair in Modern Literature and Print Culture and associate professor of English at King's University. She has written about publishing history, women's writing, digital humanities, and feminist collaboration. She cofounded the *Modernist Archives Publishing Project* (*MAPP*) and is coauthor of *Scholarly Adventures in Digital Humanities*.

Laura Heffernan is associate professor of English and director of the Digital Humanities Institute at the University of North Florida. Her work on twentieth-century histories of literary criticism and literary pedagogy has appeared in *Modernism/Modernity*, *PMLA*, *Victorian Studies*, and *The Chronicle of Higher Education*.

Megan Hicks completed a BA at Bloomsburg University and an MA at Bucknell University. Her current scholarship explores the manifestations and permutations of imperial ideology in Victorian and neo-Victorian children's literature.

Emily M. Hinnov is professor of English at Great Bay Community College, where she teaches writing, literary modernism, British literature, and interdisciplinary humanities. She is the author of *Encountering Choran Community: Literary Modernism, Visual Culture and Political Aesthetics in the Interwar Years* (2009). She is also a coeditor of *Communal Modernisms: Teaching Twentieth-Century Literature and Culture in the Twenty-First-Century Classroom* (2013).

Louise Kane is assistant professor of global modernisms at the University of Central Florida. She has published widely on periodicals and modernist cultures, including articles and chapters on magazines and female experience, gendered periodical networks, and digital humanities methods for the study of periodicals.

Aislinn Kelly earned a degree in English from the University of North Florida in 2017 and is pursuing an MA in English at the University of Sussex.

Emily Kopley is a research affiliate in the Department of English at Concordia University in Montreal. She has taught at Stanford University, McGill University, and Université de Montréal. Her work has appeared in *The Review of English Studies*, *English Literature in Transition*, *Mémoires du Livre*, *The Times Literary Supplement*, and elsewhere.

Celia Marshik is professor of English and affiliate professor of women's, gender, and sexuality studies at Stony Brook University. She is the author of *British Modernism and Censorship* and *At the Mercy of Their Clothes: Modernism, the Middlebrow, and British Garment Culture* and coauthor of *Modernism, Sex, and Gender*.

Ann Mattis is associate professor in the English department at University of Wisconsin, Green Bay. Her book *Dirty Work: Domestic Service in Progressive-Era Women's Fiction* was published in 2019 as part of the University of Michigan's Class: Culture series. Her research and teaching interests focus on women's labor, intimacy, and, most recently, popular feminism and comedy.

Deanna McMichael earned a degree in English from the University of North Florida in 2016 and works as a marketer in Jacksonville, Florida.

Lisa Mendelman is assistant professor of English and digital humanities at Menlo College. She works in the medical and digital humanities, with a focus on gender, race, and affect in twentieth-century America. She is the author of *Modern Sentimentalism: Affect, Irony, and Female Authorship in Interwar America* (2020).

Naomi Milthorpe is senior lecturer in English at the University of Tasmania, where her research focuses on modernism, satire, and twentieth-century literary culture. Milthorpe is the author of *Evelyn Waugh's Satire: Texts and Contexts* (2016) and the volume editor of Waugh's *Black Mischief*, to be published in the *Complete Works of Evelyn Waugh* (Oxford UP).

Robbie Moore is lecturer in English at the University of Tasmania. His research focuses on space and place in late Victorian and modernist literature and culture, and he is currently completing a monograph on the modernist hotel, which will be published by Edinburgh UP.

Jennifer P. Nesbitt is associate professor of English at Penn State University, York. She writes about interwar women writers, anglophone Caribbean literature and material culture, and media depictions of feminism. Nesbitt is the author of *Narrative Settlements: Genre and Geography in British Women's Fiction, 1918–1939* (2005).

Kristina Quynn is assistant professor with a joint appointment in the Graduate School and English department at Colorado State University, Fort Collins. She coedited *Reading and Writing Experimental Texts: Critical Innovations* (2017). Her current book project explores sustainable writing practices for faculty members, postdocs, and graduate students who teach, research, write, and build careers in higher education today.

Robert Reginio is professor of English in the College of Liberal Arts and Sciences at Alfred University, where he teaches drama, modernist poetry, and the novels of Virginia Woolf and James Joyce. He is the editor of the collection *Samuel Beckett and Contemporary Art.*

Beth C. Rosenberg is associate professor at the University of Nevada, Las Vegas. She has published two books on Virginia Woolf, *Virginia Woolf and Samuel Johnson: Common Readers* and the coedited collection *Virginia Woolf and the Essay.* Her work has also appeared in *Modernism/Modernity*, *Woolf Studies Annual*, *Synthesis*, and *Modern Language Notes.*

Tamara Slankard is associate professor of English and assistant dean for general education at Baker University, where she teaches American literature and gender studies. Her articles have been published in *The Faulkner*

Journal, *Journal of American Culture*, and *Journal of the Midwest Modern Language Association*.

Emma Slotterback is a seventh grade English teacher in the Central Bucks School District in Pennsylvania. She is currently working on completing her master's degree in instructional technology at Wilkes University.

Carey Snyder is associate professor of English at Ohio University. Her recent work includes editing the Broadview edition of H. G. Wells's *Ann Veronica* (2015) and coediting *Women, Periodicals, and Print Culture in Britain, 1890s–1920s*. Her articles have appeared in *Modern Fiction Studies*, *Woolf Studies Annual*, *Journal of Modern Periodical Studies*, and elsewhere.

Jennifer Sorensen is associate professor of English and a co-coordinator of the women's, gender, and sexuality studies program at Texas A&M University, Corpus Christi. Her book, *Modernist Experiments in Genre, Media, and Transatlantic Print Culture*, was published in 2017 by Routledge in the Ashgate Studies in Publishing History series.

Helen Southworth is professor of English at the University of Oregon. She has published broadly on modernism, Virginia Woolf, print culture, and digital humanities. She is the author of *Fresca: A Life in the Making*, a coauthor of *Scholarly Adventures in Digital Humanities: Making the Modernist Archives Publishing Project*, and the editor of *Leonard and Virginia Woolf: The Hogarth Press and the Networks of Modernism*. She is a cofounder of the *Modernist Archives Publishing Project* (*MAPP*).

Katie Starliper completed a BA in English and studio art at Bloomsburg University and is presently working on an MA in English at Mississippi State University.

Bronwen Tate is assistant professor of teaching in the Creative Writing Program at the University of British Columbia, Vancouver. Her debut poetry collection, *The Silk the Moths Ignore*, national winner of the 2019 Hillary Gravendyk Prize, is forthcoming from Inlandia Institute. Her poems and essays have appeared in *Journal of Modern Literature*, *Bennington Review*, *The Rumpus*, *Denver Quarterly*, *LIT*, *TYPO*, and elsewhere.

Vicki Tromanhauser is associate professor and chair of English at the State University of New York, New Paltz. Her articles have appeared in *Journal of Modern Literature*, *Twentieth-Century Literature*, *Woolf Studies Annual*, and *Virginia Woolf Miscellany* as well as in various essay collections, including *Handbook to the Bloomsbury Group* (2018) and *Literature and Meat since 1900* (2019). She received the Andrew J. Kappel Prize in Literary Criticism for 2012 and serves on the editorial board of *Twentieth-Century Literature*.

Janine Utell is Homer C. Nearing, Jr., Distinguished Professor in English at Widener University. She is the author of *James Joyce and the Revolt of Love* (2010), *Engagements with Narrative* (2015), and *Literary Couples and Twentieth-Century Life Writing* (2019) and the editor of *The Comics of Alison Bechdel* (2020). She is working on a monograph about modernist women's writing and anger.

Julie Vandivere is director of the Honors College and professor of English at Bloomsburg University of Pennsylvania. She has published articles, editions, and collected essays on many modernist women writers, including H.D., Bryher, Virginia Woolf, Peggy Guggenheim, Emily Coleman, Emilia Pardo Bazán, and Rosa Chacel.

Beth Wynstra is assistant professor of English at Babson College, where she also serves as artistic director of The Empty Space Theater Company. She holds a PhD in theater studies from the University of California, Santa Barbara, and a certificate in directing from the School of Drama at Yale University.